Auvillar © Alexia Adamski

LightFoot Guide to the Via Podiensis

Edition 3
Pilgrimage Route to Santiago de Compostela

Le Puy-en-Velay to Ronceveaux
by
Angelynn Meya

www.pilgrimagepublications.com
Copyright © 2024 Pilgrimage Publications All rights reserved.
ISBN: 978-2-917183-37-3

The contributors have done their best to ensure the accuracy and currency of the information in this Lightfoot Guide, however they can accept no responsibility for any loss, injury or inconvenience sustained by any traveller as a result of information contained in the guide. Changes will inevitably occur within the life-span of this edition and the contributors welcome notification of such changes and any other feedback that will enable them to enhance the quality of the guide.

LightFoot Guide to the Via Podiensis: Pilgrimage Route to Santiago de Compostela in France, From Le Puy-en-Velay to Roncevaux/*Roncesvalles*

3rd edition, August 2024
Photographs:
By Alexandra Huddleston, Alexia Admaski and Angelynn Meya.
Cover photo: Le Puy-en-Velay, rue des Tables © Alexandra Huddleston
Maps: Paul Chinn

Editor: Paul Chinn

Map data based on openstreetmap.org © OpensStreetMap contributors.

The GR® hiking routes described in this guide have been reproduced with the permission of the FFRP.

Pilgrimage Publications welcomes any comments or corrections that could improve this guidebook. Please write to us at mail@pilgrimagepublications.com

Pilgrimage Publications has 4 very basic aims:
To enable those who share our 'wanderlust' to follow pilgrim routes all over the world.
To ensure Lightfoot Guides are as current and accurate as possible, using pilgrim feedback as a major source of information.
To use eco-friendly materials and methods for the publication of Lightfoot Guides and travel books.
To promote eco-friendly travel.

Also by Lightfoot Guides:
Lightfoot Guide to the via Francigena:
Canterbury to The Great Saint Bernard Pass
he Grand Saint Bernard Pass to Saint Peter's Square
Lightfoot Guide to the Three Saints Way:
Winchester to Mont St Michel
Mont St Michel to St Jean d'Angely
Lightfoot Guide to the via Domitia:
Arles to Vercelli
Lightfoot Companion:
to the via Francigena–Canterbury to The Grand Saint Bernard Pass
to the via Francigena–The Grand Saint Bernard Pass to Saint Peter's Square
to the via Domitia
Lightfoot Guide to Foraging–Wild Foods by the Wayside
A guide to over 130 of the most common edible and medicinal plants in Western Europe
Your Camino
A guide to assist in preparation for a pilgrimage to Santiago de Compostela
Slackpacking the Camino Frances
Taking (some of) the pain out of you pilgrimage to Santiago de Compostela
Camino Lingo
A cheats' guide to speaking Spanish on the Camino English/Spanish and Dutch/Spanish

Contents

Your Lightfoot Guide to The Via Podiensis		7
Planning Your Trip		8
With Whom To Go?		9
Where To Stay?		10
Finding Your Way		13
What To Take?		15
On Your Way		17
Practical Information		18
History of the Way of Saint James		19

VELAY
22

1	Le Puy-en-Velay to Saint-Privat d'Allier	23.6 km	23
	Historic Route via Bains	*9.7 km*	29

MARGERIDE
33

2	Saint-Privat-d'Allier to Saugues	19.9 km	34
3	Saugues to Le Sauvage	19.6 km	40
4	Le Sauvage to Les Estrets	21.1 km	45

AUBRAC
51

5	Les Estrets to Finieyrols	24.0 km	52
6	Finieyrols to Aubrac	18.9 km	58
7	Aubrac to Saint-Côme-d'Olt	24.1 km	64
	Route via Bonneval Abbey	*35.3 km*	69

LOT RIVER VALLEY
72

8	Saint-Côme-d'Olt to Estaing	20.6 km	73
9	Estaing to Espayrac	23.1 km	79
10	Espayrac to Conques	12.4 km	83
11	Conques to Livinhac-le-Haut	23.7 km	88
	GR®6 to Livinhac-le-Haut	*11.5 km*	91

QUERCY
93

12	Livinhac-le-Haut to Figeac	23.6 km	94
13	Figeac to Gréalou	20.2 km	99
	Route via Rocamadour	*129.7 km*	103
	Célé Valley	*72.8 km*	117
	Saint-Cirq-Lapopie	*7.7 km*	123
14	Gréalou to Limogne-en-Quercy	29.9 km	126
15	Limogne-en-Quercy to Mas-de-Vers	22.1 km	132
16	Mas-de-Vers to Cahors	18.3 km	136
17	Cahors to Lascabanes	23.3 km	142
18	Lascabanes to Lauzerte	25.8 km	146
19	Lauzerte to Moissac	27.9 km	150

GASCONY
154

20	Moissac to Auvillar	22.3 km	155
21	Auvillar to Castet-Arrouy	21.9 km	161
22	Castet-Arrouy to Lectoure	11.0 km	165
23	Lectoure to La Romieu	18.6 km	169
24	La Romieu to Larressingle	19.9 km	172
25	Larressingle to Éauze	29.8 km	177
26	Éauze to Lanne-Soubiran	29.3 km	183
27	Lanne-Soubiran to Aire-sur-l'Adour	19.5 km	188
28	Aire-sur-l'Adour to Arzacq-Arraziguet	34.2 km	192
29	Arzacq-Arraziguet to Arthez-de-Béarn	30.3 km	197
30	Arthez-de-Béarn to Navarrenx	32.0 km	201

BASQUE COUNTRY
206

31	Navarrenx to Aroue	19.2 km	207
32	Aroue to Ostabat	23.9 km	211
33	Ostabat to Saint-Jean-Pied-de-Port	22.7 km	215
34	Saint-Jean-Pied-de-Port to Roncevaux	24.7 km	221
	Wet Weather Descent	*4.8 km*	226

Preface

In the Middle Ages, pilgrims from across Europe converged upon the Spanish sanctuary of Santiago de Compostela, where James, one of Jesus' 12 apostles, was believed to be entombed. To reach the Iberian peninsula, they often had to first cross France. And the via Podiensis, the oldest of the French pilgrimage routes, was one of the main trails that they used.

The via Podiensis starts in the city of Le Puy-en-Velay, in south central France and ends almost 800 kilometres later at the foot of the Pyrenees near the Spanish border. From there, it joins the *Camino Francés*, the famous main pilgrimage route that runs across northern Spain to the Cathedral of Santiago de Compostela.

Because of its dramatic landscapes, cultural and culinary richness, historical heritage and well developed infrastructure, today, the via Podiensis remains not only an important pilgrimage route but is also one of the most popular hiking trails in France.

This guidebook is intended to provide modern pilgrims with all of the information they need to successfully complete this journey and to meet their personal goals. Regardless of your motivation to walk the via Podiensis, or "*Le Chemin*" (in pilgrim-speak), it promises to be an enriching human, spiritual, cultural and linguistic adventure.

In preparing this guidebook, I would like to thank the many pilgrims whom I met along the Chemin, and who shared their stories, comments and recommendations. I would also like to thank my friends Alice Mignon, Rick Sherfey, Matthieu Warnier, Rime Sabbah, Diane Jalles and Rosanna Decicco for their help in verifying much of the information herein, as well as Alexandra Huddleston and Alexia Adamski for their moving photographs and the Mignon family for their kind support.

Changes will inevitably occur within the life-span of this edition. If you have comments or corrections to improve this guidebook for future users, we would be grateful to hear from you. Please write to us at:

mail@pilgrimagepublications.com.

Bon Chemin!

Angelynn Meya

Your Lightfoot Guide to The Via Podiensis

Stages. This book divides the 781 kilometre route from Le Puy-en-Velay to Roncevaux into 34 stages that average 23 kilometres in length (or about 5 3/4 hours of walking per day at a moderate pace of 4 km/hr). Each stage includes a route summary, detailed instructions, map, elevation profile, historical and cultural overviews and information about accommodation. Generally, stages end in larger villages or towns that have basic amenities, commerce and cultural sites. But this is not always the case. Some stages end in villages with limited resources or accommodation. In these cases, plan in advance to secure accommodation and food. The stages in this guide are suggestions. You should feel free to create your own stages based on your own rhythm and needs. Accommodation is available all along a stage and has been listed in this guide. But if you are just starting your pilgrimage, we recommend that you walk not more than 25 km per day.

Instructions and Map. While the route is very well marked, each stage in this guide includes a map and detailed route instructions. Each instruction corresponds to a GPS waypoint and is numbered with the distance (in kilometres) from the start of the stage and is accompanied with a description and a visual verification. To reduce clutter on the maps, waypoints are shown with a minimum separation of 1 km but all are listed in the text. GPS waypoint data can be downloaded without charge at www.pilgrimagepublications.com.

In addition to the path, the maps indicate the location of accommodation options, tourist information points and amenities including water points 💧, toilets 🚻, grocery stores 🛒, cafe/bars 🍺, restaurants 🍴 and ATMs 💵

Shells before Saint-Jean-de-Laur

Planning Your Trip

When to go? The Le Puy route is practicable from April until the end of October, with the most popular months being May, June and September. May is an ideal month to cross the Aubrac plateau, when wild orchids are in blossom. Those seeking a more solitary experience often set off in October.

Leaving in July and August will generally be hot. In August, the French go on holiday, meaning that there are more tourists and vacationers along the route and accommodation may be harder to come by. For those planning to go all the way to Santiago de Compostela in one go, leaving from Le Puy in April or May is best, as this means crossing Spain in June or July, before the August heat.

When not to go? Best to avoid the route in winter, from November through March, as there may be significant snow cover and the route will not be easy to follow. Crossing the Margeride, the Aubrac Plateau or the Pyrenees could be dangerous. Moreover, much accommodation will be closed, the days are shorter, and with colder temperatures you would need to carry more materials and more weight.

Our Lady of Le Puy © Alexia Adamski

How long will it take? The length of your trip depends on how much time you have as well as your physical stamina. The trip from Le Puy-en-Velay to Ronceveuax described in this guide takes 34 days, excluding rest days. Continuing on to Santiago de Compostela from Roncevaux would take an additional four weeks, which means more than two months of walking.

However, few are those that have the luxury of so much time. Those that do, tend to be students, retirees or people in between jobs. Most pilgrims tend to make the journey in segments thus completing the pilgrimage over several years. Each year they walk for a week or more starting in the place at which they ended the previous year. Others choose to do only certain sections for cultural or spiritual reasons. For example, the most popular section of the route is the 10 day walk from Le Puy-en-Velay to Conques, after which the number of pilgrims diminishes significantly.

When planning your trip, try to remain flexible and to not over plan. You may regret being tied down to a fixed schedule, when you find that you want to linger a bit longer in a certain place.

With Whom To Go?

Solo. Walking the route alone is a safe and enriching journey. It is also easy to make friends. Solitude after all is a choice. Going solo will also mean that it is much easier to find accommodation and tailor your trip to suit your own tastes.

Groups. Travelling in groups of three or more will require some forward planning to secure accommodation.

Children. Travelling with children is generally not recommended, unless they are sufficiently independent and old enough to walk and carry their own backpacks. Some families travelling with smaller children use donkeys to transport children and equipment.

Bicycles. Many of the stages of the via Podiensis are not practicable by mountain bike, or require a high level of expertise, this is particularly the case in the stages that cross the Massif Central, from Le Puy-en-Velay to Cahors which are steep and rocky both on the descent and ascent. If you do wish to do the via Podiensis by bike, there are alternative routes that follow roads. These routes are described in other guide books and further information is available on the Internet.

Dogs. It is not recommended to take your dog. This is because dogs, particularly larger breeds, have a hard time handling day-after-day long distance walking. Moreover, not all accommodation is dog friendly. If you nevertheless wish to take your dog, you will need to adapt your journey to suit the dog's needs, including walking shorter distances, taking rest days, avoiding heat and certain sections of the route (e.g. those that pass through open cow pastures), and organizing logistics (booking dog-friendly accommodation, transporting food, etc.). You should also consult your veterinarian before heading off and purchase specialized equipment, if needed (such as dog shoes or paw cream).

Horses and donkeys. Some pilgrims make the journey by horse or donkey. Forward and logistical planning will be needed, particularly for accommodation. There are a number of companies that provide horse and donkey rentals, including fully equipped animals. There are certain portions of the path that are not practicable by horse, but alternative routes are available.

Donkey in Sant-Côme-d'Olt

Where To Stay?

The via Podiensis' infrastructure is well developed and varied, with the furthest distance between accommodation being about a two hour walk (or 8 km). The choice of accommodation depends on budget, preference and location. The accommodation listed in this guidebook has been carefully selected based on personal experience and recommendation. Accommodation for each stage as well as a short distance beyond the stage end and is of the following types:

Pilgrim Hostels and Religious Hostels. Pilgrim Hostels represent a minority of hostels on the *Chemin*. They are considered special places that embody the "spirit" of the route and are often either owned by families or Christian organisations and operated by volunteers, many of whom are former pilgrims. A number of these ask no more than a donation of whatever the pilgrim can afford and are sometimes called *donativos*. Religious hostels are often housed in operating convents or monasteries and offer the possibility to take part in religious services.

The principle behind *donativos* is that they offer lodging and meals to pilgrims, who in turn donate a sum that they think appropriate or which they can afford. The money left by pilgrims one day covers the costs of pilgrims staying the next day, and so on. *Donativos* also permit those with financial difficulty to accomplish the *Chemin*, and thus they embody a kind of solidarity. They are not for profit organisations and do not receive public subsidies. The general rule is to pay an amount of money that reflects both your means and the market rate. In other words, if possible pay what you would have paid for equivalent services at a commercial hostel. For example, half board at a commercial hostel would cost around €40-50; an equivalent amount should be left at a *donativo* for the same services, if possible.

Commercial and Municipal Hostels (*Gîte d'étapes*): These represent typical pilgrim accommodation. Accommodation is basic, and includes a dormitory or shared bedrooms, bathrooms and kitchen and often a washing machine, which can be used for an additional charge (around €3). The majority of *gîtes* are clean and well maintained. Sheets are not generally provided, though blankets usually are. The average price varies from €15 to €25, per night. Reservations can usually be made between 24 and 48 hours in advance, unless you are travelling in a group, which will require greater notice. Most *gîtes* do not open

Where To Stay?

before the afternoon (around 2p.m.), so there is no need to rush to arrive early. They often offer an option of half-board (called "*demi-pension*"), which will include dinner and breakfast. Dinners are usually communal and a good opportunity to meet other pilgrims.

Hotels and Bed & Breakfasts (*chambre d'hôtes*): Bed & breakfasts are a step up in the accommodation ladder. Here you will stay in someone's house and have your own room (usually a double or family sized room), clean sheets and private bathroom. Breakfast is normally included in the price. Bed & breakfasts generally require advance reservations. Hotels are not the usual places that pilgrims stay; but now and again you may want to splurge.

Camping: In addition to spaces for tents, many camp sites offer mobile home or cabin rentals. Hot showers, toilets, groceries and restaurant facilities are often available during the summer season. Campsites are, however, usually located off the main route. A few people opt for *camping sauvage*, or camping discretely off the route in unauthorised areas. While this can be a beautiful experience, it is important to follow the Leave No Trace Principles developed by the Centre for Outdoor Ethics (www.lnt.org).

Tourist Offices (*Offices de Tourisme*). Most towns and large villages have Tourist Offices with staff that speak English and can assist with finding and booking accommodation. This is a great resource for anglophones. In smaller villages the mayor's office–*Mairie*–will assist, although they are only open for limited hours each week.

Some establishments try and cater for multiple needs e.g. both the pilgrim and standard tourist business and offer both hostel and more upmarket options. We have indicated this by using multiple icons.

Reservations: It is best to reserve in advance if you are more than one person. Reservations can usually be made 24 to 48 hours in advance. Reservations are particularly recommended between Le Puy-en-Velay and Figeac, one of the most frequented sections of the route.

Pricing: Inflation naturally leads to price increases for accommodation but the increases will generally be lower in hostels than in the tourist sector. We have banded the prices to suggest relative expense and have separated into bed alone, bed and breakfast and half-board. For current exact pricing check at the time of booking or using the web links. The table below shows the banding at the time of writing. There will be seasonal effects in the tourist sector - the table assumes mid-season - but the pricing in hostels is generally fixed within a year. Hostels will generally charge per person whereas tourist accommodation is charged per room/couple.

Where To Stay?

	Band	Bed	Bed & Breakfast	Half-Board
(per person)	A	>30€	>35€	>50€
	B	21-30€	26-35€	41-50€
	C	<21€	<26€	<41€
	D	Donation	Donation	Donation
(per couple)	A	>70€	>85€	>100€
	B	51-70€	71-85€	86-100€
	C	<51€	<71€	<86€
		Pitch		
(per person)	A	>15€	-	-
	B	9-15€	-	-
	C	<9€	-	-
	D	Donation	-	-

E.g. ....Price:-,C,B indicates a commercial hostel with bed alone not available or not quoted (-), Bed & Breakfast costing less than 26€ (C) and half-board (dinner, bed and breakfast) costing 41-50€ (B) for one person.

Budget: Budgets depend on your financial situation, needs and preferences. The two main costs to consider are accommodation and food. At the time of writing, the average daily cost of a comfortable pilgrimage on the Via Podiensis, staying in pilgrim hostels is around €40-€50/person/day. It is possible to lower overall costs, by preparing your own meals, in which case budgeting €12/day for food, should be sufficient. Costs can be further reduced by camping.

Finding Your Way

This guide includes not only the main pilgrimage route, the via Podiensis, from Le Puy-en-Velay to Roncevaux, but also a number of alternative routes, that may be particularly attractive to certain pilgrims. The via Podiensis route and the main alternative routes are described below.

Via Podiensis. The modern via Podiensis is the main route that is taken by pilgrims. It is clearly way marked with the white and red bands of the French long distance hiking routes known as the *Grande Randonées*. This book follows the hiking route numbered GR®65, which is oriented nearly constantly in a south-westerly direction. The route starts in the volcanic mountains of Velay, crosses the solitary Aubrac Plateau, passes through the Lot river valley and the brandy vineyards of Armagnac to end in the Basque region of the Pyrenees. It passes through several medieval villages that have been selected for inclusion in the association of the Most Beautiful Villages of France (*Les Plus Beaux Villages de France*). Like the *Camino Francés* in Spain, several sections of the *Chemin* are identified on the UNESCO world heritage list, which recognizes its "key role in religious and cultural exchange and development in the later Middle Ages." The most challenging section of the route is the first 10 days, where the climbs and descents are the steepest.

Abbey of Bonneval Alternative Route. After Aubrac, there is an alternative route that leads to the remarkable Bonneval Abbey, a Cistercian abbey founded in 1147, and then re-joins the GR®65 in Espalion. It adds no extra time to the hike, unless you wish to spend an extra day at the abbey (recommended). The route, which is not well frequented, is challenging, with some steep descents. It is marked by light blue way markings and crosses spectacular plateaus and forests before arriving at the abbey, which is hidden in a forest valley. The abbey is self-sufficient and today houses a Cistercian convent and a small chocolate factory. The sisters also offer board to pilgrims. For the more adventurous, spiritually oriented or nature loving, this detour is recommended.

Rocamadour. The alternative route through Rocamadour takes six days (as opposed to four on the main GR®65) and uses the red and white way markings typical of the GR®. Rocamadour, revered for its miraculous black Madonna, has been an important Christian pilgrimage destination since the Middle Ages. Today, this stunning village built into the cliffs is the second most visited site in France. This route, which is less popular than the via Podiensis, is well marked. From Figeac it follows the GR®6 north through the villages of Cardaillac, with its lovely medieval centre, and Gramat. The approach to Rocamadour through the valley of Alzou is particularly stunning. From Rocamdour, the path then heads south on the GR®46 through the Causses of Quercy Nature Reserve, before re-joining the Lot River in the village of Vers. There, the route takes the GR®36, which runs alongside the Lot River to the city of Cahors, where it reconnects with the main *Chemin* (GR®65).

Célé Valley. From Figeac, the alternative route through the Célé Valley, which also uses red and white way markings takes five days (as opposed to four days on the GR®65), despite being about 10 kilometres shorter than the main route. It is generally considered more

Finding Your Way

beautiful than the main route, as it crosses the limestone hills typical of the Causses region, passes beautiful villages built into the cliffs and follows the refreshing Célé river. The route, known as the GR®651, begins at Mas-de-la-Croix (after Figeac), where it descends into the Célé Valley to the lovely medieval village of Espagnac. From there, it climbs and descends along the limestone cliffs, in dry and often difficult and rocky terrain, passing through several historic villages on the Célé River, before re-joining the Lot near the village of Bouziès. There, the route takes the GR®36, which runs alongside the Lot river to the city of Cahors, to reconnect with the main *Chemin* (GR®65). In Bouziès it is also possible to make a day trip (recommended) to Saint-Cirq-Lapopie, considered one of the most beautiful villages in France, and which is a lovely four kilometres walk south along the Lot river.

Way markings. With the exception of the blue way markings of the Bonneval Abbey alternative route, all of the routes described in this guide are very clearly way marked with the white and red bands of the French long distance hiking routes known as the *Grande Randonées*. These markings appear regularly on trees, rocks, walls and posts, and particularly at forks or crossroads. There are four marks to look for:

In addition, the *Chemin* is often way marked by a stylized scallop shell of Saint James, where the lines represent the roads of Europe leading to Santiago de Compostela. Frequently, there are signposts indicating the number of kilometres to the next village.

The *Chemin* sometimes crosses other routes, which are often way marked with other colours, such as yellow bands. These can be ignored. Stay focused on the red and white markings of the GR®s.

Keep straight on

Turn right

Turn left

Wrong Way

What To Take?

Traditional wisdom is that your backpack should weigh no more than 10% of your body weight. For example, if you way 75 kilos (165 pounds), your backpack should not weigh more than 7.5 kilos (16.5 pounds). Bear in mind that you will also have to add the weight of water (about 2 litres or 2 kilos.)

Mental preparation for your trip begins when reflecting on what is truly essential to take. The more weight the tougher the walk.

PACKING CHECKLIST

Backpack (35-40 litres): Your backpack should be suited to your morphology and have a rain cover.

Sleeping bag liner or super thin sleeping bag: Many hostels provide blankets so that a liner is generally sufficient.

Foot wear: (1) Light-weight hiking shoes that are water resistant, but breathable. No need to take hiking boots, which are too heavy and ill-suited for long distance walking and (2) flip flops or sandals, for the evening

Walking poles (optional)

Water bottles (at least 2 litres) or Camel-Bak (optional)

Documents: Identity Card/Passport, Insurance Card, credit cards, Pilgrim Passport, and ziploc bag to put them in.

Miscellaneous: Safety pins (to hang clothes to dry), knife, headlamp, basic sowing kit, adapter/converter, cell phone and charger, camera (optional)

Clothing: Invest in clothes that are specifically adapted to hiking or sport, and are breathable, lightweight and quick-dry:
- 2 quick dry T-shirts
- 1 long sleeved shirt
- 1 fleece or sweater for cool evenings
- 1-2 pairs shorts (quick-dry)
- 1 hiking pants
- 1 rain paints
- 1 ultra-light rain coat
- 3 underwear
- 3 pairs of hiking or running socks, which allow for ventilation and reduce friction
- Swim wear
- Pyjamas

Accessories and toiletries:
- Sun: hat, sunglasses, sun screen
- Toiletries: Quick-dry towel, shower gel/shampoo, toothbrush and tooth paste, moisturizer, nail clippers, comb/brush
- Earplugs (snoring protection)
- Soap/detergent for washing clothes.
- Health: First aid kit, blister prevention foot cream (applied before walking to reduce friction), 2nd skin blister patches, such as Compeed®, which is available in French pharmacies.
- Other medicines, as needed

Walking in autumn or early spring will require taking additional warmer, but breathable clothes, as well as a hat, gloves and scarf. This will add weight to your backpack.

What To Take?

Pilgrim Passport (*Carnet du Pèlerin* **or** *Crédential***).** The pilgrim's passport serves as proof that a pilgrim has undertaken a pilgrimage on the Way of Saint James. All along the *Chemin*, pilgrims collect passport stamps (*tampons*) from the places they spend the night, churches, museums, cafes, etc. The passport is then presented at the Pilgrim's Office in Santiago de Compostela as proof of their journey in order to receive a Compostela, or a certificate attesting to the successful completion of the pilgrimage.

While in Spain it is mandatory to have a Pilgrim Passport in order to stay in public hostels, this is not the case in France. In France, the passport is primarily required for *donativos* and Christian hostels. A Pilgrim Passport can be obtained from numerous pilgrims associations ahead of your trip, in Paris (from La Société Française des Amis de Saint Jacques de Compostelle, www.amis-de-compostelle.fr), from the Confraternity of Saint James www.csj.org.uk or at the Cathedral in Le Puy-en-Velay gift shop. To standardize the various passport models and to ensure that prices are affordable, the passport must be of a type approved by the Pilgrim's Office in Santiago.

Physical Fitness. No special training is required to do the *Chemin* if you are in generally good health and routinely exercise. Nevertheless, it is recommended that you start doing long distance hikes at least a couple of months before you set off. This will help you to develop endurance and strength, as well as to test your equipment (shoes and backpack). It will make the first days of your hike easier. Your capacities will quickly improve after a few days of walking the *Chemin*.

Boots © Alexia Adamski

On Your Way

Fountain © Alexandra Huddleston

Water. There are watering points all along the route. Take advantage of these to fill up your water bottles and avoid dehydration and related injuries, such as tendinitis. Cemeteries also generally have water spouts with drinkable water.

Eating. For an additional charge (around €5-7), many hostels propose breakfast starting at 7 a.m. Breakfast usually consists of coffee/tea and baguette with marmalade. To supplement this light start of the day, consider carrying snacks (fruits, nuts, etc.). Some hostels will offer to provide a picnic lunch for a further charge, Lunch is served in cafes and restaurants from 12:30 to 2 p.m. Most will offer a *plat du jour,* which is an inexpensive way to enjoy a hearty meal. Alternatively, it is easy to put together your own picnic by buying goods at a local market (*marché*) or grocery store (*épicerie*). Dinner is generally served from 7:30 p.m and consists of three courses and wine. Many hostels serve dinner, as part of half-board. Another option is to use the communal kitchen to cook your own meals. This may be the best choice if you have dietary restrictions or are on a limited budget. An increasing number of lodgings offer vegetarian meals. Ask in advance (i.e., when making your reservation) if this option is available.
The *Chemin* also represents a gastronomic journey. The cuisine changes regularly as the route passes through various regions–from Le Puy to the Basque country. In descriptions of the regions, this guide notes culinary highlights, which we encourage you to explore.

Business Hours. Business hours are generally from 9:30-12:00 and 14:00-18:00. Most private and public establishments close for two hours at midday. In small towns, shops are often closed on Sunday and Monday, though larger supermarkets may be open.

Baggage transport. Several companies offer services to transport backpacks from one stage to the next. In the morning, pilgrims leave their backpacks at the hostel, indicating where they plan to be that evening. A van picks up the baggage in the morning and drops it off at the destination. The hostels work with different transport companies and are generally happy to organise this service. Many people transport their bags daily while others use this service when they need a break. Transport costs between €5 and €10 per bag.

Practical Information

Arrival and Departure.
Plane. Le Puy-en-Velay is accessible by flying into Paris, Geneva or Lyons, and thereafter continuing by train or car.
Train. There is regular train service between Paris and Le Puy-en-Velay, via Lyon, Clermont-Ferrand or St-Etienne. The journey takes about 4.5 hours. Trains also run from Charles de Gaulle airport in Paris to Le Puy-en-Velay (about 5.5 hours). If travelling from the UK, in summer, Eurostar trains run from London to Lyon. There are also regular train connections between Geneva and Le Puy. From Saint-Jean-Pied-de-Port, return trains to Paris pass through Bayonne and Bordeaux. Return trains to Geneva are difficult. If in France, trains can be booked at www.sncf-connect.com. If outside of France, we recommend using the following website: www.thetrainline.com.

Car-share. An affordable and fun alternative is to travel by car, using the car sharing site www.blablacar.fr, which connects drivers and passengers willing to travel together between cities and to share the cost of the journey. You can register and create a profile on the website (in French).
Telephone. It is best to have a cell phone in France, mostly to be able to make reservations and in case of emergency. If you have an unblocked cell phone, you can purchase a SIM card for your phone once in France, such as at stores run by Orange or SFR (telecommunications companies). The phone store can register the SIM card (take your passport) and get your phone working. This can be done for example in Le Puy-en-Velay. Additional phone credits can be bought at *Tabacs* (tobacconists) along the route.
Medical Insurance and Assistance. EU citizens should have a European Health Insurance Card, a free card that simplifies access to medically necessary, state-provided healthcare during temporary stays in any of the 27 EU Member States. Contact information for doctors can usually be obtained from pharmacies, town halls or tourist offices. In France, patients generally pay for doctors' visits and medication out-of-pocket. These expenses may thereafter by partially reimbursed by insurance companies once proof is provided.
Banking and Cash. Along the route, and certainly in the larger towns, there are ATMs where you can withdraw cash. You should carry sufficient cash to pay for accommodation, as often these do not accept credit cards. Standard banking hours are Monday-Friday: 9:30-12:00 and 14:00-16:00, Saturday 9:30-12:00.
Internet. Wifi or wireless internet is available in many commercial hostels, but not always. Wifi is often available in cities (such as Le Puy-en-Velay, Figeac, Moissac or Cahors), while in rural areas, chances are slim.
Emergency numbers. The Europe-wide emergency number is 112 (fire, police, ambulance, coastguard, search and rescue). In France: police: 17; fire: 18, or 15: ambulance.

History of the Way of Saint James

Pilgrimage in the Middle Ages

Pilgrimage to holy places is common to all major religions. In Christianity, if life is a physical journey towards an eventual union with God in the afterlife, pilgrimage becomes a metaphor for that journey. In other words, by physically journeying towards a holy place, pilgrims make a spiritual journey towards God. In medieval Christendom, pilgrimage was also a redemptive act, whereby pilgrims' sins were forgiven. For example, making a pilgrimage to Santiago de Compostela during a Holy Year–when Saint James' feast day (25 July) fell on a Sunday, would mean release from purgatory in the afterlife.

During the Middle Ages, there were three major pilgrimage destinations: Jerusalem, Rome and Santiago de Compostela. The foremost of these was Jerusalem, which was linked to Christ's life and scenes from the Bible. However, when Jerusalem fell to the Arabs in 637 AD, pilgrimage to the Holy Land became less accessible, resulting in the growth of alternative pilgrimage sites, such as local shrines, relics brought from the Holy Land and the tombs of saints. Rome was a second important pilgrimage destination, as it housed the tombs of Saints Peter and Paul and the seat of the Catholic church.

The third destination was Santiago de Compostela, located in a remote corner of north western Spain, where it was believed that Saint James, one of Jesus' 12 Apostles, and brother of Saint John, was entombed.

According to the New Testament of the Bible, James the Greater, son of Zebedee, left being a fisherman on the sea of Galilee to follow Christ, and witnessed, amongst others, Christ's Transfiguration on Mount Tabor. He was also believed to have evangelized in Spain. Upon returning to Jerusalem from Spain, he was beheaded by Herod Agrippa I around 44AD. According to legend, James' followers placed his decapitated body in a rudderless boat that, guided by providence, made its way through the Mediterranean sea up the Atlantic coast to the coastal village of Iria Flavia (now known as Padron), on the northwest corner of Spain. In an account from the 12th century, the body was taken by oxcart for burial at a site known as Compostela. During the reign of the Bishop Theodomir of Iria Flavia (circa. 820-830), a hermit was led by a star to the field where the relics were rediscovered. The name "Compostela" could refer to the field of a star (*campus stellae*) although it is more likely a reference to the Latin word, burial (*compositum*).

Thereafter, the relics were placed in a reliquary and churches were successively built on the site. Santiago de Compostela's transformation from a local to an international pilgrimage destination is suggested by evidence of pilgrims coming from other countries, including Bishop Goldescalc, the bishop of Le Puy-en-Velay, who arrived in Compostela in 951. By the 12th century, pilgrims from abroad were regularly journeying to Santiago, with the pilgrimage being promoted by the Bishop of Santiago, who recognised the political and religious importance of the shrine.

One of the most important texts to emerge from this period was the 12th century Codex Calixtus, attributed to Pope Calixtus II. It was a spiritual and physical guide to pilgrimage to Santiago de Compostela. The Codex contained five

St James–Le Puy cathedral

History of the Way of Saint James

sections: (1) sermons, prayers, songs and hymns for the Saint's feast, (2) a narration of the 22 miracles performed by Saint James, (3) stories of the Saint's life and legends about the transport of his body from Jerusalem to Spain and the discovery of his tomb; (4) a history of Charlemagne's campaigns against the Moors in the 8th century, and (5) the Liber Santi Jacobi, a guide to the pilgrimage routes to Compostela through France and Spain.

The creation of the Codex and a magnificent church in Santiago de Compostela testified to the importance of Saint James by the 12th century. While the lack of records limits knowing how many pilgrims travelled there each year, annual visitors likely numbered in the thousands. Other evidence of the cult's importance were the images of Saint James in artwork along the pilgrimage routes.

Some churches were also dedicated to other saints and were pilgrimage destinations in their own right. These churches often contained a saint's tomb or relics, as in the case of Conques. The Codex encouraged "visiting" these Saints.

During this period, societal customs promoted religious pilgrimage. Laws were enacted to protect pilgrims and an infrastructure of hostels or hospices, bridges and other support services, including financial ones, developed to meet pilgrim's needs.

Pilgrimage to Santiago declined after the Renaissance. However, by the 21st Century it would experience an incredible resurgence, with more than 440,000 pilgrims arriving at the Cathedral of Santiago de Compostela in 2023.

The Via Podiensis and modern pilgrimage

Like the Camino Frances, the Via Podiensis traces its historical heritage to medieval texts. The earliest recorded pilgrim to Santiago from beyond the Pyrenees was Bishop Godescalc

Shells © Alexandra Huddleston

History of the Way of Saint James

of Le Puy-en-Velay who travelled in 950-951AD. According to a prayer included in a 10th century manuscript that tells of his pilgrimage, Godescalc was born on and was ordained a bishop on Saint James' feast day, suggesting that he personally identified with the Saint.

The second text that described the Le Puy route was the fifth book of the Codex Calixtus, which was the earliest guide to the pilgrimage routes to Compostela. The guide was written in Latin around 1140 by a Frenchman, and described four main pilgrimage routes in France, including one starting in Le Puy. According to the Codex, pilgrims from Burgundy and Germany would take the Le Puy route, along Roman roads, passing through Le Puy, Conques and Moissac.

However, during the Middle Ages, Le Puy was foremost a pilgrimage destination in its own right, rather than the starting point of the route to Santiago. Over the centuries, thousands of pilgrims flocked to the sanctuary to pay devotion to the Black Madonna, which was brought to Le Puy by Saint Louis, on his return from the crusades. To accommodate the multitudes, a new hospital (*Hotel-Dieu*) was built in the 15th century.

Indeed, the fact that Godescalc had travelled to Santiago was only rediscovered in 1866 when the 10th century manuscript described above was found in the National Library in Paris. Equally, historians question the lack of evidence for the supposed hundreds of thousands of medieval pilgrims that purportedly followed in Godescalc's footsteps to Santiago.

That Le Puy is the starting point for pilgrims bound for Santiago, was largely a 20th century phenomena, underpinned by the creation in the 1970s of a long distance hiking route, the GR®65, that recreated the pilgrim route from Le Puy to the Spanish border.

Thereafter, in 1987 the Council of Europe launched its Cultural Routes Programme and declared the Santiago de Compostela Pilgrimage Routes the first such cultural routes. The Council considered these routes "highly symbolic in the process of European unification," and appealed to public authorities, institutions and individuals to revitalize them. It concluded with the aspiration that travel along these routes could help to "build a society founded on tolerance, respect for others, freedom and solidarity." Significant efforts to revive the French pilgrimage routes, notably the via Podiensis, were made in the 1990s, led by the French Hiking Federation (*Fédération Française de la Randonnée Pédestre*). By 1998, seven sections of the via Podiensis as well as numerous monuments along the way were registered on UNESCO's World Heritage List. Consequently, since the 1990s the route has been very well developed.

The 21st Century has witnessed the true upsurge of pilgrimage. Never before have so many pilgrims walked to Santiago de Compostela, including on the via Podiensis. Each year tens of thousands set off from Le Puy, which has also become an important point of convergence for pilgrims coming from the east, such as from Switzerland, Austria and Germany. And these numbers are only likely to increase.

VELAY

The region of Velay makes up the south-eastern part of the Massif Central, the mountainous area in south-central France that comprises about 15 percent of the country. It is a volcanic region that was formed some 14 million years ago and is dotted with numerous small volcanoes and spires that rise above a wide basalt (volcanic stone) plateau. It is bounded in the west by the Allier river (crossed in Stage 2), which has etched deep gorges that separate Velay from the granite massif of Margeride to the west. The region's capital is Le Puy-en-Velay, the starting point of the Via Podiensis, and a city famous for being a Catholic sanctuary, for its lentils and other local products (such as, bobbin lace and the digestive liquor, Verveine, which is made from 32 different herbs).

Le Puy-en-Velay to Saint-Privat d'Allier

stage 1

Length:	23.6km
Ascent:	829m
Descent:	621m
Le-Puy:	0km
Roncevaux:	781km

Le Puy-en-Velay, rue des Tables © Alexandra Huddleston

Route–The path is well-marked with the red and white way markings of the GR°65, as well as wooden signposts and the shell of Saint James. The route gradually climbs along country roads, farm tracks and hiking trails across fields and villages. After Montbonnet there is a steep climb into the woods of the volcanic Mount Déves, followed by a steep descent into Saint-Privat-d'Allier, which can be slippery when wet. Note the lovely views of Le Puy, when leaving the city, the chapel of Saint Roch before Montbonnet and the views while descending to Saint-Privat-d'Allier.

Pointers–From Place du Plot, pay attention to correctly follow the way marking for the GR°65, as Le Puy is the starting point for several GR° routes. Pilgrim's Passport (La Crédential): You can obtain a pilgrim's passport and stamp from the Cathedral gift shop (after the pilgrims mass and blessing at 7a.m. or during opening hours). Reservations: Most people set off from Le Puy on the weekends, often resulting in accommodation being fully booked during the summer months. It is best to reserve accommodation in Le Puy in advance or set out on a weekday. Choice of routes: After Tallode, you have the choice to take the main GR°65, or take a historic variant passing through Bains and Fay, which will add approximately 2km to your walk. Both routes are equivalent in terms of difficulty, however, the variant is less frequented. Advance planning: If you don't plan on stopping for lunch in Montbonnet, you should shop for lunch the evening before as there are limited facilities on the route and shops won't be open early in the morning when you leave. Fill up on water before you set out and as you pass watering points. Market: There is a lively and colourful market at Place du Plot each Saturday morning, featuring local and regional produce and goods.

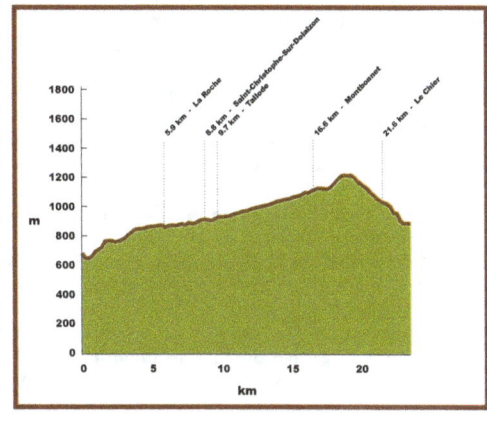

23

stage 1 — Le Puy-en-Velay to Saint-Privat d'Allier

Cultural Discoveries

Le Puy-en-Velay

The city of Le Puy-en-Velay (popl. 18,600, alt. 630m) (or Le Puy, from the Latin word podium, or elevated structure) sits in a four million year old volcanic basin, from which several volcanic spires emerge; these are the remains of volcanic necks that once ejected lava. In Le Puy, several of these spires are capped by Catholic monuments, such as the Cathedral of Le Puy, the Chapel of Saint Michael of Aiguilhe or the 84 metre rose-coloured statue of Our Lady of France.

Cathedral of Our Lady of Puy
(Cathédrale Notre-Dame-du-Puy)

Le Puy en Velay cathedral ©Alexandra Huddleston

The Cathedral of Our Lady of Puy is an UNESCO world heritage site. It traces its origins to a 5th century sanctuary, though the present structure was built in the 11th century, and was thereafter renovated on several occasions. It is an impressive Romanesque monument that has rich oriental influences, including a façade of alternating dark and light brick work and an inscription on the wooden door frame at the entrance to the cathedral in pseudo-Arabic script, which states: "There is no other God but Allah." Historians attribute these oriental features to influence from Moorish-Spain, including through pilgrimage, as well as from the crusades.

The church is accessible through an imposing staircase that rises into a series of three porches and gradually narrows into what is called the womb staircase, which emerges into the central nave of the cathedral directly opposite a 17th century black Madonna. An original Madonna was brought to Le Puy in 1254 by St Louis upon his return from the crusades and was highly venerated in the Middle Ages; it was, however, burned in 1794 during the French Revolution. The black Madonna's wardrobe includes 25 dresses, the oldest of which is from the 14th century and is on display in the cloister museum. The cathedral also has a several million year old flat volcanic rectangular stone called the Pierre des fieves, or apparition stone, which is believed to have healing powers and which relates to a legend from the 3rd century about the apparition of Mary.

Except for the winter months, mass is held daily at 7:00 a.m., followed by a pilgrim blessing that takes place in front of the 16th century polychrome stone statue of Saint James. The blessing ends with the singing of the Salve Regina, a Latin hymn dedicated to Mary which some believe was written in Le Puy in the 11th century.

Cloister and Treasury

Built in the 11th and 12th century, the cloister is an excellent example of Romanesque architecture, and is notable for its columns and polychrome decoration. It also has one of the oldest examples of ironwork in France–a 12th century wrought iron gate with patterns that resemble Arabic latticework. The cloister museum has an exceptional collection of liturgical embroidery from the 14th to 20th century.

Our Lady of France
(Notre-Dame de France)

Standing on the highest volcanic peak, called Corneille Peak, Our Lady of France is an imposing 16 metre rose-coloured statute of the Madonna and child, which was completed in 1860, following the Crimean War (1853-1856). The war posited France, Britain and the Ottoman Empire against Tsarist Russia, and concerned the rights of Christian minorities in the Holy Land as well as power over the waning Ottoman Empire. The monument was made from 213 canons taken during the battle of Sebastopol (1854-1855), a final siege in the war which ended when the Tsar sued for peace in 1856. This is one of the most visited monuments in the region.

Le Puy-en-Velay to Saint-Privat d'Allier — stage 1

Chapel of Saint Michael of Aiguilhe
(Chapelle Saint-Michel d'Aiguilhe)

Saint-Michel d'Aiguilhe

The Chapel of Saint Michael sits on an 82 metre volcanic spire that can be reached by 220 steps. The views alone are worth the climb. Built in 961, following Bishop Goldescalc's return from pilgrimage to Santiago de Compostela and dedicated to Saint Michael, the chapel was itself a pilgrimage destination. There are three oratories placed on the stairway leading to the chapel. In its vaulted interior are beautiful 10th/11th century frescoes, including of Christ in Majesty (seated as a ruler on a throne, as described in the Book of Revelation) and an original altar.

Place du Plot/Saturday Market

Place du Plot is the traditional starting point of the Via Podiensis. In 1548, local consuls set up a pillory here, where drunkards were put on display and endured public shaming. The Bidoire fountain dates from the 13th century and is the oldest in Le Puy. Today, Place du Plot holds a lively farmers' market on Saturday mornings. Of note is the local farmers' cheese *(fromage fermier de Velay)* and the famous green lentils of Le Puy.

Saint-Christophe-sur-Dolaison

Saint-Christophe-sur-Dolaison (popl. 1,000, alt. 900m) has a small 11th century Romanesque church that was built from the reddish volcanic stone of the region with a four-arched bell tower and a wooden altar depicting Saint Christopher, patron saint of travellers. Near the church are the remains of a communal oven, which was once a mainstay of village life. Families would take turns heating the oven with wood and baking bread. Along the route, several villages have communal ovens, some of which are still in use.

Saint Roch Chapel
(Chapelle Saint-Roch de Montbonnet)

Chapel of Saint-Roch

Built in the 11th century by the powerful Montlaur Family (their coat of arms is on the vaulted ceiling), this Romanesque chapel was first dedicated to Saint Bonnet and later to Saint Roch. According to legend, Saint Roch was born in the 14th century into a wealthy French family. But he gave up his possessions and went on pilgrimage to Rome where he tended to victims of the plague. After performing several miraculous cures, he succumb to illness and withdrew to the forest. There, he was cured by an angel and was supplied with water by a spring and with food by a local dog. In art, he is often depicted as a pilgrim showing a left leg infected by the plague and accompanied by a dog.

Saint-Privat-d'Allier

Saint-Privat-d'Allier © Alexandra Huddleston

The village of Saint-Privat-d'Allier (popl. 400, alt. 875m) is built on a rocky spur overlooking the Allier valley. Its 13th century castle (privately owned) played a strategic role in controlling the road to Gévaudan (the historic territory of the Gabali, a Celtic people, and which is today part of Margeride). The village's Romanesque church dates from the late 12th century and the priory (a religious house for clerics) is mentioned in a 12th century papal bull (letter from the Pope).

Le Puy-en-Velay to Saint-Privat d'Allier

stage 1

GR®65

(0.0) Descend Cathedral staircase and continue straight on rue des Tables**(0.1)**Turn left onto rue Raphaël[Pass the 15th Century Fountain des Tables before turning left]**(0.3)**Turn right onto rue Chénebouterie**(0.4)**Continue straight crossing Place du Plot[Pass fountain de la Bidoire to the left]**(0.4)** From Place du Plot turn right onto rue Saint-Jacques[Coloured ceramic relief of Saint James to the left] **(0.5)**Cross boulevard Saint Louis/N102 and continue straight on rue des Capucins**(0.7)**Continue straight on rue des Capucins climbing hill[Pass under bridge]**(1.0)**At the end of rue des Capucins turn right onto rue de Compostelle[Small park with statute of St. James to the left] **(1.0)**Keep left on rue de Compostelle[Continue climbing hill]**(1.3)**Turn right off rue de Compostelle onto foot path[Pass sports complex on the right]**(1.4)**Turn right rejoining rue de Compostelle[Follow row of hedges lining road to the right]**(1.8)**Leave main road and turn left onto track called the Ancienne route de Sauges[Signpost]**(1.9)**Continue straight on track[Pass stone wall on the right] **(2.6)**Continue straight on Ancienne route de Saugues[Cross of Jalasset (1621) on the left and picnic area to the right]**(3.5)** Continue straight on Ancienne route de Saugues and climb hill[Pass farm on right] **(4.6)**Cross the D589 and continue straight on track**(5.4)**At crossroads turn left in the direction of La Roche[Signposts indicate GR®65] **(5.8)**Cross the D589 and continue straight through village of La Roche[Village of La Roche visible ahead]**(5.9)**Take a sharp right in the hamlet of **La Roche** and descend on foot path**(6.0)** Continue straight on the road[Pass communal oven on the left]
(6.3) Turn left onto footpath heading towards valley[Picnic bench and information point to the left] **(7.0)**Leave foot path turning left onto track[Head towards farm]**(7.3)**Turn right onto track[After passing cross on the left with valley views. Yellow sign post] **(8.3)**Continue on tree-lined footpath**(8.6)** Pass mobile snack bar on the right**(8.7)**Enter village of Saint-Christophe-sur-Dolaison**(8.8)**Turn right at Place de l'eglise and cross **Saint-Christophe-sur-Dolaizon**[Church of Saint-Christophe and Auberge du Grand Chemin on the right]
(8.8) Turn right onto rue du Château[Head away from the town hall (la Mairie)]**(9.0)**After leaving village centre, turn right onto small road towards Tallode[Pass castle on the right]**(9.2)**Pass under the D906 and stay to the left towards Tallode[Underpass] **(9.7)**Enter hamlet of **Tallode**[Brown stone farmhouset to the right]
(9.9) Continue straight on road leaving Tallode[Pass cross on the right]**(10.2)**Continue straight on main road. The alternative route to Bains departs on the right (signpost)[Pass cross on left and follow signs towards hamlet of Liac] **(10.7)**Enter the hamlet of Liac and keep left on the main road[Pass stone cross on right]**(10.9)**Turn right onto footpath in village centre[Signposts]**(10.9)**Leave village of Liac. Continue straight on foot path**(11.1)**Continue straight on footpath[Stone walls and pastures]

Leaving Le Puy-en-Velay

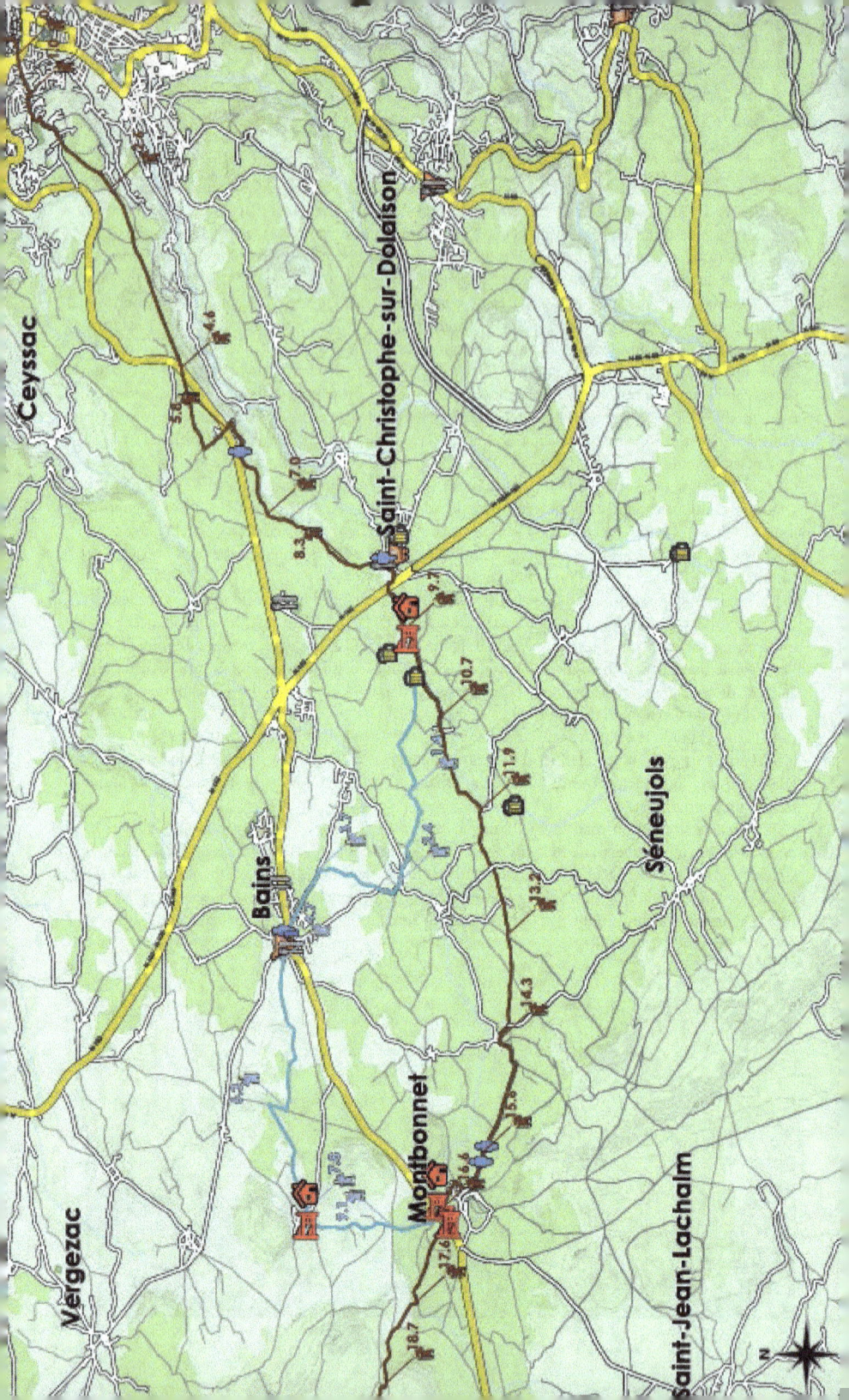

Le Puy-en-Velay to Saint-Privat d'Allier stage 1

(11.7) Continue straight towards the hamlet of Lic[Pass picnic area on the left] **(11.9)**After leaving Lic, turn right on footpath[Farm and signpost]**(12.2)**Stay to the left on track[Signpost]**(12.5)**Cross asphalt road and continue straight towards village of Montbonnet[Asphalt road]**(12.8)**At intersection continue straight on footpath following stone wall[Stone wall] **(13.2)**At intersection continue straight[Hills visible straight ahead]**(13.7)**Continue straight on foot path[Farm visible straight ahead] **(14.0)**Turn right onto the D621 towards centre of Ramourouscle[Hamlet visible to the right] **(14.3)** In hamlet centre at fork and fountain, turn left towards Montbonnet[Cross of Ramourouscle (1631) on left, fountain and signpost]**(14.6)**Stay right on asphalt road[Pass farm on left] **(15.6)**Continue straight on asphalt road[Pass picnic area on the left]**(15.8)**Stay to right on asphalt road[Village of Montbonnet visible ahead] **(16.6)**Turn left onto route de Saugues/D589 towards centre of **Montbonnet**. The alternative route from Le Bains meets the D589 here and rejoins the GR®65. [Welcome sign ahead]

(16.7) Turn right onto track before Gîte La Grange[Signpost]**(16.8)**Leave village of Montbonnet and continue straight on track[Pine hills visible ahead]**(17.1)**Continue straight on track towards hills[Pass between two barns]**(17.2)**Continue straight on tracks towards pine hills[Pass under power lines] **(17.6)**Turn right and cross over brook[Brook]**(18.1)**Continue straight on rocky trail ascending hill[Pine forest ahead]**(18.5)**Stay to the left at fork and continue ascent[Fork] **(18.7)**Turn right into pine forest[Pine forest]**(18.8)**Turn left in pine forest on track towards Lac d'Œuf**(19.0)**Continue straight on track[To the right is Lac de l'Œuf, a peat bog with a rich biodiversity]**(19.3)**Turn left onto asphalt road[Signpost]**(19.4)**Turn right descending onto track[Signpost] **(20.7)**Continue descent on road[Village of Le Chier visible below]**(21.2)**Cross road D589 and stay to the right towards village of Le Chier[Village of Le Chier visible to the right. Sign post "Le Chier" ahead]**(21.4)**Enter village of Le Chier[Stone farmhouse to the right]**(21.6)**Continue straight passing through village of **Le Chier**[Cross on right and town hall (la Mairie) on the left]

(22.0) At fork stay to the right. Steep descent[Sign post]**(22.2)**Continue steep descent on foot path[Saint-Privat-d'Allier visible to the left in valley]**(22.6)**Turn left onto narrow foot path. Steep and rocky descent into ravine. Slippery when wet; recommend alternative route[Sign post]**(23.0)**Continue straight on path crossing stream (Ruisseau Rouchoux) on wooden foot bridge[Pass mill on right as well as Cross of Piquermeule (16th century)] **(23.4)**Merge left onto D589 and continue straight into Saint-Privat-d'Allier[Sign post]**(23.6)**Arrive at Saint-Privat-d'Allier[Village centre (Le Kompost'l cafe ahead)]

Historic Route via Bains

Route—the historic alternative route through Bains, which uses the same white-red way markings as the main GR®65, adds approximately 2.5 kilometres to Stage 1. The route is relatively flat, but is less-frequented and not as well way-marked as the main route. Particular attention should be paid when entering and exiting villages. The route is shrouded in history. Notably, the village of Fay was closely associated in the 13th century with the Knights Templar (a powerful medieval Christian military order that played a decisive role in the crusades). The Romanesque church of Saint Foy in Bains was placed under the domain of the powerful Conques Abbey, of which it bears certain artistic traits.

Length:	9.7km
Ascent:	249m
Descent:	67m

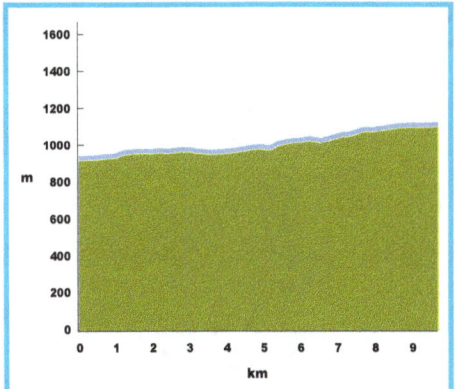

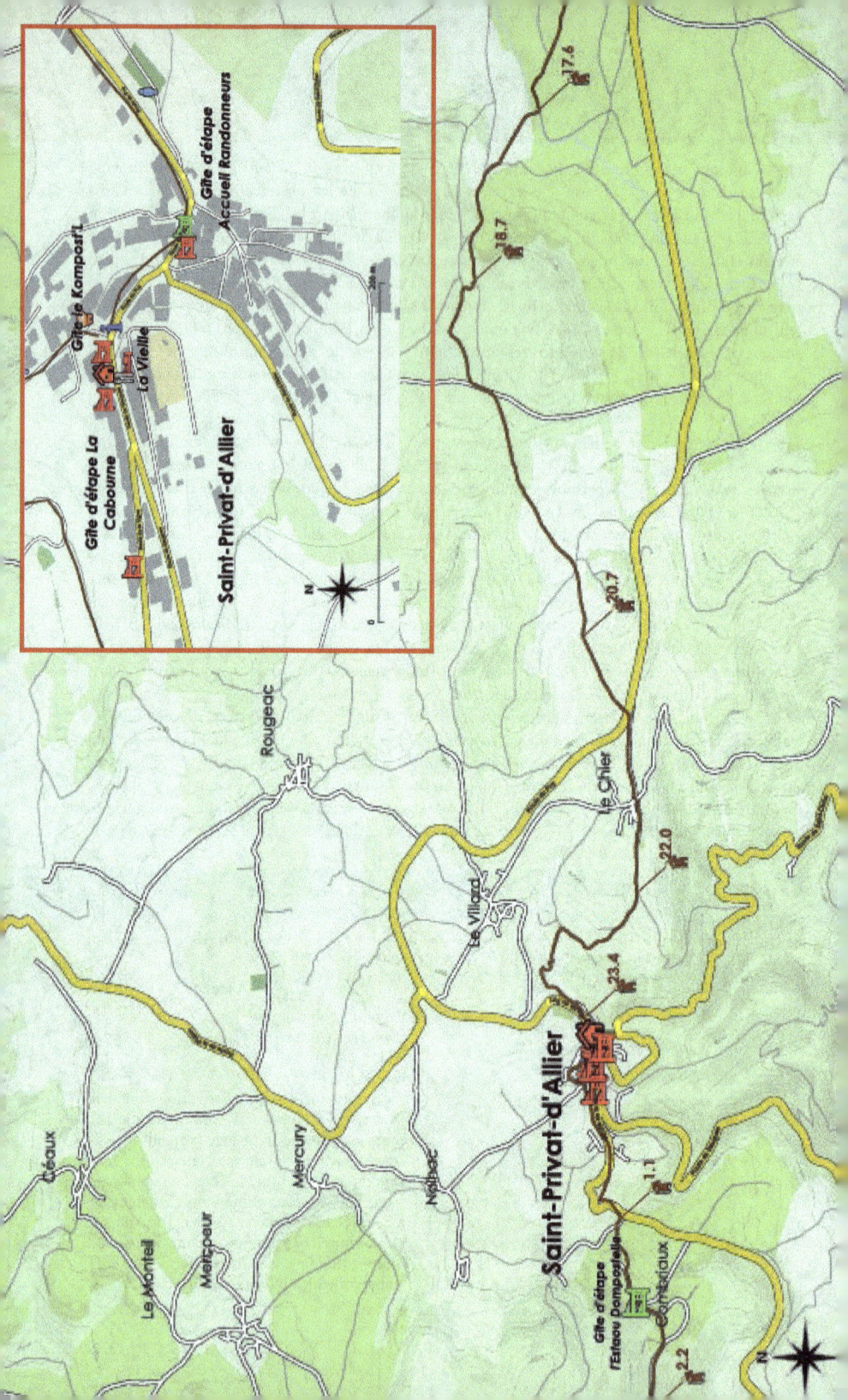

Le Puy-en-Velay to Saint-Privat d'Allier — stage 1

Cultural Discoveries

Bains

The 12th century Romanesque Church of Saint Faith (*Eglise Sainte-Foy*) in the village of Bains (popl. 1,400, alt. 975m) is classified as a historic monument. In 1105, the church fell under the authority of the Conques Abbey, whose patron saint is also Saint Faith. It is remarkable for its ornate Romanesque façade, including vaulted arched entrance and a stone baptismal font depicting the Virgin and the Baptism of Christ.

Historic Route

(0.0) To take variant towards Bains, leave main road and turn right on track[Sign posts] (0.1) Stay on track which veers to the left (0.5) Continue straight on track[Ignore track to the left which heads to Liac. Power lines to the right] (1.4) Turn right (2.0) At fork turn left towards village[Village of Augeac to the left] (2.1) Take first right on asphalt road towards village centre[Red house] (2.3) At end of street, turn left[Augeac village centre] (2.4) After crossing village turn right[Pass lavoir to the right] (2.5) Turn right onto main road, toward Bains[Pass former school house on the left] (2.8) Leave main Champ Richard road, and keep right on the small country road. Continue straight (3.7) Turn left onto route de Jales[Village of Bains visible to the left] (4.4) Continue straight and cross route de Saugues/D589[Church straight ahead] (4.6) In **Bains** pass church on left and take second left onto chemin de la Garde de Moutet[Signpost] (4.7) Continue straight on chemin de la Garde de Moutet, which becomes track[Pass cemetery on the right] (5.6) Continue straight on track[Pass red barn on the right and pine tree grove to the left] (6.3) At end of road turn right[Pine grove directly behind] (6.6) Take sharp left towards hamlet of Fay[Pine grove visible again] (7.2) Continue straight on track[Leave pastures behind] (7.8) Turn right onto asphalt road[Hamlet of **Fay** to the right] (7.8) At fork stay to the left[Leave village of Fay to the right. Pass Gîte du Velay on the right] (8.0) Turn left in the direction of Montbonnet (south) (8.6) Continue straight on road until reaching the village of Montbonnet[Fay should be behind you and village of Montbonnet visible ahead] (9.1) At intersection continue straight towards village of Montbonnet (9.7) Turn right on route de Saugues/D589 to rejoin GR°65

Accommodation and Tourist Information

Bains

Gîte d'étape privé l'Escole [Fanny and Mehdi], 39, impasse de l'Escole–Montbonnet, 43370 Bains, France; Tel:+33(0)471575103; +33(0)622719009; Email:gite@lescole.com; lescole.com; Price:-,-,C|-,-,A; *15 places in 4 rooms of 3 or 6 pers also private double rooms. Kitchen donkeys welcome*

Gîte d'étape–du Velay [Sylvette and Laurent], 93, rue des Pres de la Fontaine–Fay, 43370 Bains, France; Tel:+33(0)471027160; +33(0)759769438; Email:contact-gdv@grand-gite.fr; grand-gite.fr; Price:C,C,C|C,C,-; *In the charming hamlet of Fay, 6 private rooms and dormitory (10 places). Very welcoming hosts. Horses welcome.*

Gîte d'étape–la Grange [Christian and Françoise Gentes], 690, route de la Margeride–Montbonnet, 43370 Bains, France; Tel:+33(0)471575444; +33(0)620744743; Email:christiangentes@orange.fr; gitelagrangegr65.fr; Price:C,C,C; *15 places in 4 rooms of 3 to 4 pers. in modern and entirely renovated farmhouse.*

Auberge La Barbelotte [Géraldine Felce and Grégory Gourgon], 608, route de la Margeride–Montbonnet, 43370 Bains, France; Tel:+33(0)471004175; +33(0)650935407; Email:labarbelotte@gmail.com; labarbelotte.com; Price:A,-,-; *3 double and triple rooms. Horses welcome. English spoken restaurant*

stage 1 — Le Puy-en-Velay to Saint-Privat d'Allier

ℹ **Mairie de Bains**,Place de la Mairie, 43370 Bains, France; Tel:+33(0)471575082; Email:mairie-bains@wanadoo.fr; bains43.fr

Le Puy-en-Velay

🛏 **Relais du Pèlerin de Saint Jacques**,28, rue Cardinal de Polignac, 43000 Le Puy-en-Velay, France; Tel:+33(0)471094392; +33(0)637086583; podiensis.com; Price:D,D,-; *There are 27 places in dormitories and offers a jump straight into the pilgrim experience;* **PR**

🛏 **Grand Seminaire St-George**,4, rue Saint George, 43000 Le Puy-en-Velay, France; Tel:+33(0)471099310; Email:grandseminaire43@live.fr; recorriendomundos.com; Price:-,C,-; *208 places in dormitories and private rooms*

🛏 **Gîte-la Découverte**,18, rue Grangevieille, 43000 Le Puy-en-Velay, France; Tel:+33(0)638566056; Email:giteladecouverte@gmail.com; giteladecouverte.fr; Price:B,-,-; *Well equipped, 14 beds in a dormitory*

🛏 **Auberge de Jeunesse–Pierre Cardinal**[Centre Pierre Cardinal],9, Rue Jules Vallés, 43000 Le Puy-en-Velay, France; Tel:+33(0)471055240; Email:auberge.jeunesse@lepuyenvelay.fr; lepuyenvelay.fr; Price:C,C,-; *Located below the Cathedral, 50 places in various sized rooms*

🛏 **Maison Saint François**,6, rue Saint Mayol, 43000 Le Puy-en-Velay, France; Tel:+33(0)471059886; Email:reserva@giteasf43.fr; accueilsaintfrancoislepuy.jimdo.com; Price:-,C,C; *Single double and dormitory rooms in 16th century building between the Cathedral and Notre Dame de France run by Franciscan nuns*

🛏 **Appart Hôtel des Capucins**[Paul-Emilie and Klaus],29, rue des Capucins, 43000 Le Puy-en-Velay, France; Tel:+33(0)471042874; Email:contact@lescapucins.net; lescapucins.net; Price:A,-,-|B,-,-; *Commercial establishment with 19 places in hostel and 31 rooms. English spoken.*

ℹ **Office de Tourisme**,2, place du Clauzel, 43000 Le Puy-en-Velay, France; Tel:+33(0)471093841; Email:contact-tourisme@lepuyenvelay.fr; lepuyenvelay-tourisme.fr

ℹ **Le Camino** ,2, rue de la Manecanterie, 43000 Le Puy-en-Velay, France; Tel:+33(0)471090600; lecamino.org; *Museum café and information point credentials for sale*

Saint-Christophe-Sur-Dolaison

🛏 🏠 **Gîte d'étape-Chambre d'hôtes–la Maison Vieille**[Nicole and Michel Allègre],Tallode, 43370 Saint-Christophe-Sur-Dolaison, France; Tel:+33(0)749901349; +33(0)618113806; Email:michel.allegre38@sfr.fr; maison-vieille.fr; Price:B,B,B|-,B,B; *4 shared rooms for 17 people and 2 B&B rooms on a working farm*

Saint-Privat-d'Allier

🛏 **Gîte d'étape–l'Estaou Dompostelle**[Dom],56, route de la Besseyre–Combriaux, 43580 Saint-Privat-d'Allier, France; Tel:+33(0)471095891; +33(0)666406031; Email:estaou7@gmail.com; lestaoudompostelle.com; Price:C,C,C; *Charming house with 14 places in dormitory dinner made with local produce*

🛏 **l'Abri du Jacquet**,le Bourg, 43580 Saint-Privat-d'Allier, France; Tel:+33(0)471077553; Email:labridujacquet@gmail.com; labridujacquet.fr; Price:C,C,-; *15 beds in 3 dormitories*

🛏 🏠 **Un Escargot dans sa Coquille**,le Bourg, 43580 Saint-Privat-d'Allier, France; Tel:+33(0)611343149; Email:unescargotdanssacoquille@gmail.com; unescargotdanssacoquille.com; Price:C,B,-|B,A,-; *21 places in dorms also 3 B&B rooms* 🛏 **Gîte d'étape–Accueil Randonneurs**[Sandrine],le Bourg, 43580 Saint-Privat-d'Allier, France; Tel:+33(0)788507656; +33(0)663904134; Email:accueil.randonneurs@gmail.com; accueil-randonneurs.fr; Price:C,C,C; *Central location, 5 shared bedrooms for 2-4 people*

🛏 **Gîte d'étape–La Cabourne**[Hélène and Christophe],le Bourg, 43580 Saint-Privat-d'Allier, France; Tel:+33(0)471572550; +33(0)471572550; Email:lacabourne43@gmail.com; gite-lacabourne.fr; Price:-,-,B; *49 places in rooms of 2 to 6 people regional foods served in restaurant*

🛏 **Gîte le Kompost'L**,le Bourg, 43580 Saint-Privat-d'Allier, France; Tel:+33(0)471572478; lekompostl.fr; Price:C,C,C; *12 places in 5 dormitories kitchen available*

🛏 **La Vieille Auberge**,le Bourg, 43580 Saint-Privat-d'Allier, France; Tel:+33(0)471572056; Email:lavieilleauberge43@orange.fr; la-vieille-auberge.eu; Price:B,A,-; *Small hotel with restaurant private rooms*

ℹ **Mairie de St Privat d'Allier**,Le Bourg, 43580 Saint-Privat-d'Allier, France; Tel:+33(0)471572213; Email:info@mairie-saintprivatdallier.fr; mairie-saintprivatdallier.fr

MARGERIDE

Saugues © Alexia Adamski

Margeride is a 60km mountain chain in the south-eastern part of the Massif Central. The deep gorges of the Allier river act as its natural boundary with the volcanic region of Velay to the east.

Like the Alps, Margeride is only 10 million years old, yet the granite rock from which it was formed is Hercynian, dating to the collision of the African and North-American-North European continents some 350 million years ago. Today, its landscape includes granite highlands with meadows, slopes with recent pine growth and lowland peat bogs.

The generally high elevation of Margeride (1000m) renders the climate cool, and the mountains are covered with snow during the winter months. In mid-May, the highland meadows blossom with wild white narcissus which is used in French perfumes.

The Margeride highlands, specifically Mont Mouchet (1497m), were an important centre of French resistance during the Second World War. In 1944, French resistance fighters, known as the Maquis du Mont Mouchet, fought to forestall Nazi troops in the south from converging with those in Normandy, to the north, in aid of the Allied invasion of France. Today the Mont Mouchet Resistance Museum pays tribute to this period.

stage 2 — Saint-Privat-d'Allier to Saugues

Length:	19.9km
Ascent:	1126m
Descent:	1040m
Le-Puy:	24km
Roncevaux:	758km

Escluzels Madonna © Alexandra Huddleston

Route–The route is well marked and consists of asphalt roads, tracks and footpaths. Nevertheless this is one of the most challenging stages. The descent by footpath and road to the Allier river is steep, as is the long climb, mostly on roads, into the Margeride chain and the village of Saugues. Villages such as Roziers, Vernet and Rognac, before Saugues are typical of the region, reflecting the emphasis on agriculture and the use of porphyroid granite (granite with white felspar).

Pointers–Use caution when descending the steep footpath from Rochegude to Pratclaux, which can be muddy and slippery when wet.. In case of rain, consider taking the longer (but safer) track that descends to the D301 from the village of Rochegude.

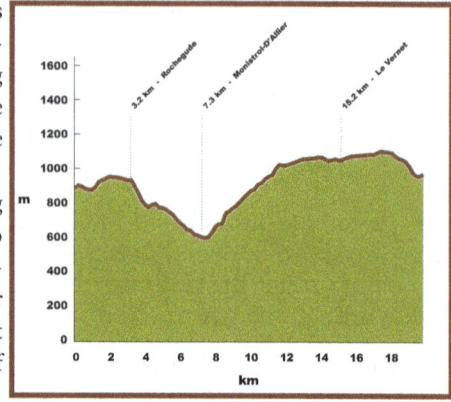

Views: There are lovely views of the Allier river valley from Rochegude (Chapel of Saint Jacques) and when climbing to Montaure from Monistrol-d'Allier.

Advance planning: After Monistrol-d'Allier, there are no cafés/restaurants/grocers until Saugues; consider buying lunch in Monistrol or ensuring provisions in Saint-Privat.

Festival: Each August, Saugues hosts a large Celtic festival, featuring Celtic music, crafts and foods - www.festivalengevaudan.com.

Saint-Privat-d'Allier to Saugues

stage 2

Cultural Discoveries

Rochegude

Rochegude, Chapel of Saint James

Perched on the volcanic Déves mountains opposite Margeride, Rochegude, meaning sharp rock, dominates the Allier valley. The fortress of Rochegude, today in ruins but for an impressive 6 metre tower, was once used as a watchtower to control the trade routes that passed through the valley. Next to the fortress is the **Chapel of Saint James** (*Chapelle de Saint-Jacques*), which was built into the rock. Note also the beautiful views of the river valley and the Margeride mountain chain.

Eiffel Bridge
(*Pont Eiffel*)

The Eiffel bridge is named after engineer Gustave Eiffel whose company designed and built the bridge in the late 19th century. At the time, Monistrol was growing rapidly thanks to the railway that was being built through the Allier gorge, and which is still in operation. The bridge was completed one year before the 1889 World's Fair at which the Eiffel Tower in Paris was unveiled.

Magdalene Chapel
(*Chapelle de la Madeleine*)

Built in the 17th century in a grotto below the village of Escluzels, the chapel was dedicated to Mary Magdalene, a follower of Jesus. In 1872, the tombs of several children and adults were discovered nearby. Of note is the wooden 18th century statue of Mary Magdalene and two wooden statues of Jesus and Mary Magdalene in niches built into the rock.

Saugues

Saugues (popl. 2000, alt. 960m) was an important stronghold in the historic Gévaudan, a territory of the Gabali, a Celtic people. In the 12th century, the village grew wealthy under the rule of the bishops of the city of Mende. However, all that remains of the village's medieval fortifications is the English Tower (*Tour des Anglais*), which was part of a 13th century fortress. The name "English Tower" dates to the Hundred Years' War, when in 1362 English mercenaries captured Saugues. A fire in 1788 destroyed most of the town's historic centre. The town, which was once known for its wooden carved clogs, holds a popular Celtic festival in the second week of August. A market is held on Monday and Friday mornings.

From 1764 to 1767, the famous **Beast of Gévaudan** (*Bête du Gévaudan*) terrorized the region. It was responsible for the deaths of over 100 people, mostly women and children. According to witnesses, it resembled a wolf and had enormous teeth and a sweeping tail. With public hysteria mounting, nobles, the army, civilians and even King Louis XV's huntsmen tried to hunt the animal down. But it was only after three years of terror that the beast was finally killed by Jean Chastel, a local. An animated museum, *Le Musée Fantastique de la Bête du Gévaudan*, recounts the story (in French only).

The 13th century Romanesque **Church of Saint Médard** (*Eglise Saint-Médard*) is registered as a historic monument. Of note are two wooden polychrome statues–an early 13th century statute of the Christ Child seated in the Virgin's lap, a position known as the Throne of Wisdom (*sedes sapientie*), and a 16th century pieta (a representation of Mary mourning over the dead body of Christ) in polychrome wood. There is also a shrine and statue of the patron saint of Saugues, Saint Bénilde, who dedicated his life to education and who is prayed to for healing cancer. See also the magnificent alter depicting Mary's Ascension by sculptor Pierre Vaneau (1653-1694) in the **White Penitents Chapel** (*Chapelle des Pénitents blancs*).

stage 2
Saint-Privat-d'Allier to Saugues
GR®65

(0.0) From village centre, turn right off the road D589, with Cafe/Gîte Kompost'l to the left and continue uphill towards Garage Jobert[Le Kompost'l and Garage Jobert]**(0.1)** Stay to the left around corner[Sign post]**(0.3)** Turn left onto Le Marchat trail[The village of Saint-Privat is below on the left] **(0.6)** Turn right onto D301 road, leaving village of Saint-Privat behind**(0.7)** Turn left onto foot path. Descend into the valley and cross the stream (Ruisseau de la Planchette)[After crossing under power lines. Sign posts]**(1.0)** Emerge from valley and cross road D301 road, continue straight[Sign post] **(1.1)** Turn right onto asphalt road[Head towards a brown stone house]**(1.1)** Turn left and continue straight on cobblestone road[Pass house with terrace on left]**(1.4)** Turn left onto asphalt road and cross through the hamlet of Combriaux**(1.6)** Leave road and turn right onto track through woods[Sign post] **(1.8)** Cross road and continue straight on track **(2.2)** Turn left onto road**(2.3)** Turn right onto footpath[Track runs parallel to road]**(2.5)** Turn right onto road[Pass under power lines]**(2.7)** For a little relief from the road, turn left onto the track**(3.1)** Merge left onto road[Village of Rochegude visible ahead] **(3.2)** In **Rochegude** centre, at château ruins and chapel, turn left[Sign post]
(3.2) Continue straight on footpath. Very steep and rocky descent**(4.1)** Turn left onto D301 road **(4.2)** Turn left ont onto track towards hamlet of Pratclaux[Hamlet visible]**(4.3)** Turn left onto asphalt road and then immediately right and cross hamlet**(4.7)** Leave asphalt road turning right onto track[Pratclaux directly behind]**(4.8)** Cross D301 road and continue straight on track**(5.0)** Turn right onto road**(5.1)** After passing brown stone house turn left onto track[Stone house to the left] **(5.3)** Turn right at fork[Head towards the valley]**(5.7)** Turn left onto road and descend into Monistrol-d'Allier[Monistrol visible in valley] **(6.9)** Take sharp right onto rue des Jacquets[Pass town hall (la Mairie) on the left]**(7.1)** Cross bridge built by the Eiffel Company (1888) spanning the Allier river towards village centre**(7.3)** In the centre of **Monistrol-d'Allier** turn left onto and stay on rue des Lombards[Immediately after cafe, Le Repos du Pèlerin, on the left]
(7.4) Turn left onto rue des Jacquets[River on right side]**(7.5)** Turn right onto Montée de la Madeleine which descends towards mill. From here the main climb to the Margeride plateau begins[Mill and stream (L'Ance)]**(7.8)** Leave road and turn right onto track, continue straight[Pass shed on the left. Beautiful river views of Monistrol to the right] **(8.3)** Turn right rejoining asphalt road**(8.5)** Turn left onto track and climb staircase[After passing iron cross with beautiful figure of Mary on the left and the Chapel of Madeleine on the right]**(8.7)** Turn right into village of Escluzels, followed by another immediate right**(9.0)** Continue ascent on road **(9.4)** Turn sharp left off the asphalt road,**(9.6)** cross the asphalt road, and climb towards the main road**(9.7)** Turn right onto the serpentine trail that climbs[Pine forest] **(11.5)** Enter hamlet of Montaure and continue straight on road[Village cluster to the right] **(12.0)** Turn left onto track leading to Roziers **(13.1)** Continue straight on track[Pass under power lines]**(13.4)** In Roziers village turn right on road and continue straight[Pass fountain]**(14.0)** Turn right at fork in the direction of Le Vernet[Sign post] **(15.2)** Turn left in the village of **Le Vernet** and continue straight through village[Fountain]
(15.4) After the last houses, turn left onto track that becomes a trail passing under power lines[Sign post] **(16.9)** Turn right onto road and continue straight through village of Rognac. Continue on road[Rognac visible to the right]**(17.9)** At fork stay to the left on trail and continue straight to departmental road D589[Farm to the left and sign post] **(19.0)** Cross D589 and continue straight on rue des Cimes to descend into Saugues[Wooden sculptures to the left]**(19.5)** Stay to the left on rue des Cimes followed by immediate right onto route du Puy to enter village of Saugues[Sign Post]**(19.9)** Arrive at Saugues centre[Office of Tourism]

stage 2 — Saint-Privat-d'Allier to Saugues

Accommodation and Tourist Information

Monistrol-d'Allier

L'Oustal du Blagaire[Patrick Viala],654, Route de La Molle, 43580 Monistrol-d'Allier, France; Tel:+33(0)620060489; Email:vialapatrick@icloud.com; loustaldublagaire.com; Price:-,B,-; *6 beds in 2 rooms 2 km from the trail*

Gîte - du Pont Eiffel,313, rue des Jacquets, 43580 Monistrol-d'Allier, France; Tel:+33(0)644728195; giteduponteiffel.fr; Price:-,-,C; *7 places in 3 rooms. Located beside the river, kitchen, horses welcome*

Le Repos du Pèlerin[Benjamin and Gaëlle],365, rue des Jacquets, 43580 Monistrol-d'Allier, France; Tel:+33(0)471572357; Email:reposdupelerin@gmail.com; lereposdupelerin.fr; Price:-,B,-; *Dormitory and private rooms*

Gîte d'étape - au Ricochet,route du Gévaudan, 43580 Monistrol-d'Allier, France; Tel:+33(0)659077066; Email:auricochet@gmail.com; gitelericochet.fr; Price:-,B,C; *Pilgrim only price 15 places in 5 shared bedrooms*

Gîte d'étape - la Tsabone[Patrick and Myriam Fourquet],Montée des deux chiens, 43580 Monistrol-d'Allier, France; Tel:+33(0)471061723; +33(0)615153839; Email:latsabone@yahoo.fr; latsabone.fr; Price:-,-,C; *12 beds. Very welcoming. Pasture for horses. Dinner is prepared using organic and local produce. Near the church*

Camping - le Vivier,Rue du Pain de sucre - le Vivier, 43580 Monistrol-d'Allier, France; Tel:+33(0)471572414; Email:contact@camping-le-vivier.fr; camping-le-vivier.fr; Price:C,-,-; *Dormitory tent, kitchen, tent spaces also available*

Mairie de Monistrol-d'Allier,187, rue des Jacquets, 43580 Monistrol-d'Allier, France; Tel:+33(0)471572121; monistroldallier.fr

Saint-Privat-d'Allier

Gîte - de Rochegude[Franck and Sophie Pascal],Lieu-dit Rochegude, 43580 Saint-Privat-d'Allier, France; Tel:+33(0)471027879; +33(0)633704810; Email: contact@giterochegude.f; giterochegude.fr; Price:C,C,-; *14 places in 3 and 4 person rooms.*

Gîte d'étape - de La Ribeyre[Christelle and Stéphane Robert],Lieu-dit Pratclaux, 43580 Saint-Privat-d'Allier, France; Tel:+33(0)663463709; Email: contact@gitedelaribeyre.com; gitedelaribeyre.com; Price:-,-,C; *A former barn with modern facilities. 12 beds in 3 rooms. Kitchen.*

Sauges

Le Chalet du Pèlerin,70, rue des Cimes, 43170 Sauges, France; Tel:+33(0)609600965; Email:lechaletdupelerin@yahoo.fr; lechaletdupelerin.com; Price:B,C,-; *Dormitory for 6 people, dinner available at extra charge*

Centre d'hébergement et d'Activities - La Margeride,8, rue des Tours Neuves, 43170 Sauges, France; Tel:+33(0)71776097; Email:accueil@lamargeride.com; lamargeride.com; Price:C,C,C; *Activity Centre 40 places in rooms of 2 or 5 beds private rooms available*

Gîte d'étape - d'Ici et d'Ailleurs[François and Clarisse],46, Rue de la Margeride, 43170 Sauges, France; Tel:+33(0)633605302; Email:contact@gitedida.fr; gitedida.fr; Price:B,-,B; *12 beds in small dorms. Closed Sundays in July & August,*

Gîte - à la ferme Itier-Martins,65, Rue des Noisetiers, 43170 Sauges, France; Tel:+33(0)672754648; Email:jesusvidal163@gmail.com; gite-itier-martins.fr; Price:-,-,B; *26 places in 8 rooms. Beautiful views of the countryside family atmosphere and meals made from farm products. Horses and donkey pasture.*

Gîte d'étape - Communal de Sauges,8, Rue de la Margeride, 43170 Sauges, France; Tel:+33(0)471778062; +33(0)665150432; Email:camping@saugues.fr; saugues.fr; Price:C,-,-; *Breakfast available at the campsite 15 places in small dorms*

Chambre d'hôtes - l'Arc en Ciel[Boris Pantel],1, rue du Mont Mouchet, 43170 Sauges, France; Tel:+33(0)471776860; +33(0)619192945; +33(0)7.68.28.13.60; chambredhotearcenciel.jimdo.com; Price:C,C,C; *3 rooms Dinner prepared using local products. Horses welcome.*

Chambre d'hôtes- l'Arche de Gabriel,Lieu-dit Roziers, 43170 Sauges, France; Tel:+33(0)471778578; +33(0)745172260; Email:larchedegabriel@gmail.com; larchedegabriel.fr; Price:B,B,-; *Dinner available at extra charge, camp in the garden for a small charge*

Chambre d'hôtes - les Gabales[Patricia and Maurice Gonneaud],70, avenue Lucien Gires, 43170 Sauges, France; Tel:+33(0)471778692; Email:info@lesgabales.com; lesgabales.com; Price:-,A,A; *A charming B&B in a 1930s manor house. Dinner recommended.*

Camping - de la Seuge,895 Avenue du Gévaudan , 43170 Sauges, France; Tel:+33(0)471778062; +33(0)665150432; Email:camping@saugues.fr; campingdelaseuge.fr; Price:C,-,-; *Chalets and tsabones (cabins on wheels) also available*

Mairie de Saugues,8, rue de l'Hôtel de Ville, 43170 Sauges, France; Tel:+33(0)471777130; Email:secretariat@saugues.fr; saugues.fr

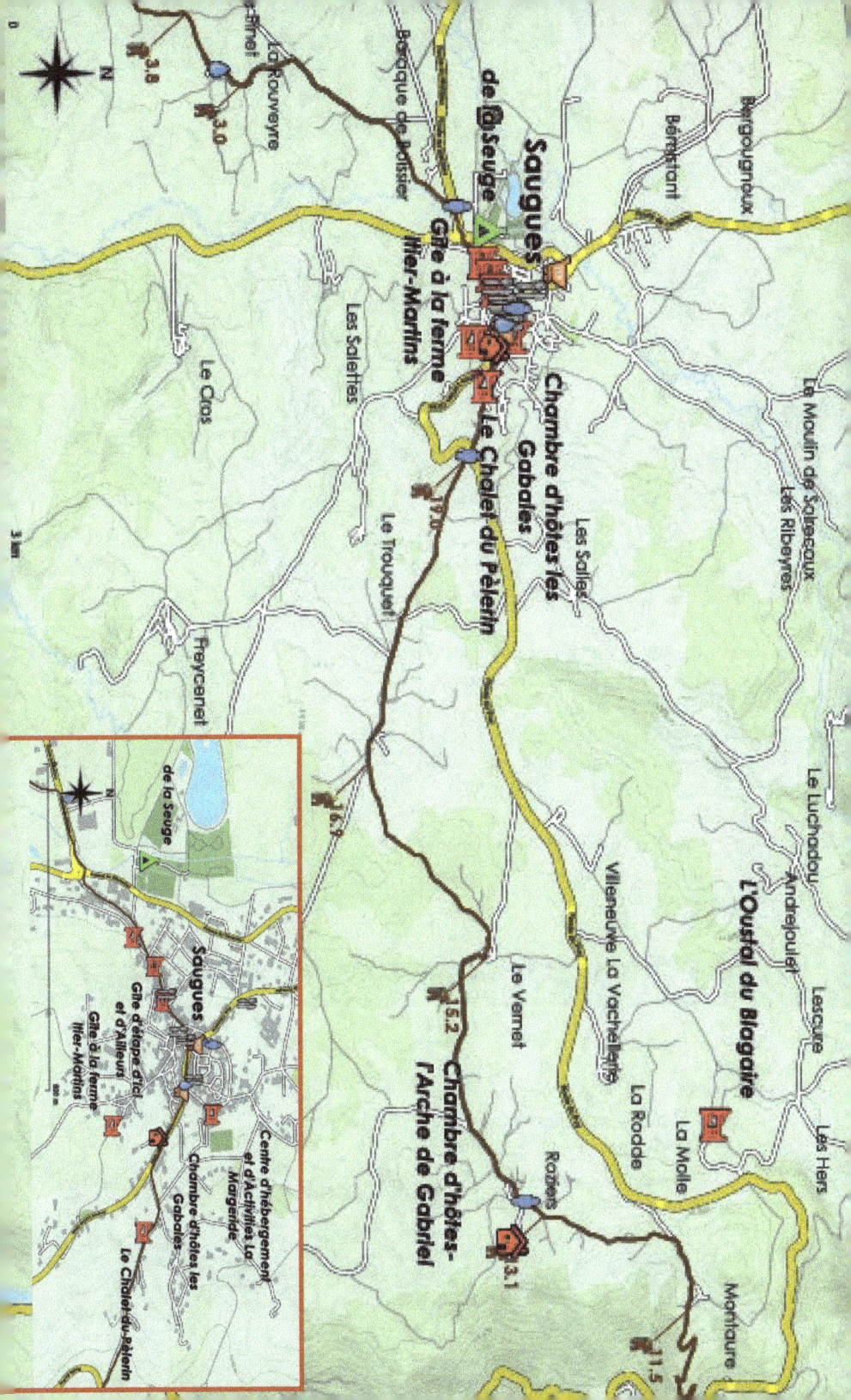

stage 3 — Saugues to Le Sauvage

Length:	19.6km
Ascent:	795m
Descent:	471m
Le-Puy:	44km
Roncevaux:	738km

Saugues © Alexandra Huddleston

Route- The route, which is well marked, consists mostly of rocky tracks and asphalt roads that climb and descend the largely barren landscape of the Margeride, crossing cattle pastures and pine forests until arriving at the monumental farm of Le Sauvage.

Pointers-Reservations: Accommodation at Domaine du Sauvage should be booked in advance, as space is limited.

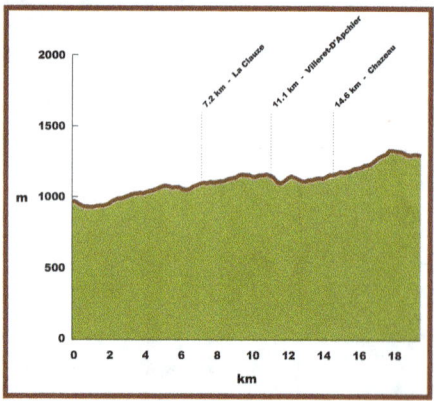

Cultural Discoveries

La Clauze

The tower of La Clauze, which is registered as a historical monument, is a rare octagonal tower perched on a granite block (without foundation). It is the remains of a fortress from the 14th century and an excellent example of regional medieval military architecture.

Saugues to Le Sauvage

stage 3

Villeret-d'Apchier

In the lower village is a natural spring (Source Saint-Pierre) dedicated to Saint Peter (one of Jesus' 12 disciples and the leader of the early Christian church), which was famous for its miraculous ability to heal eyes.

Domaine du Sauvage

The Domaine du Sauvage, with its imposing granite buildings, was used as a farm throughout the Middle Ages. Today, the Domaine is owned by the Department of Haute-Loire and operates as a farm, hostel and store/restaurant run by a cooperative of 40 farmers from the Margeride.

Forest before Le Sauvage © Alexandra Huddleston

GR®65

(0.0) With the Office of Tourism to the right continue straight on departmental road D589[Fountain and Office of Tourism on the right]**(0.1)** Stay to left on D589 through village**(0.4)** At fork stay to right on D589[Carved wooden mushroom sculptures on the left]**(0.7)** At round about continue straight on D589[Round about]**(0.8)** Cross bridge over La Seuge river and continue straight[Bridge]**(0.9)** Take first left on chemin de Saint Jacques also known as chemin du Pinet[Opposite large wooden pilgrim statue] **(1.2)** Continue straight on track[Leave houses on the right behind you]**(1.7)** At the end of the track turn left onto asphalt road leading towards hamlet of Pinet**(2.6)** At fork with iron cross bear left towards Le Pinet[Sign post and cross] **(3.0)** Enter Le Pinet**(3.4)** Stay to the right, leaving village behind, and continue straight on track[Village behind] **(3.8)** Follow road to the left heading towards pine grove[Pine grove]**(6.5)** Leave main track and turn right on footpath climbing hill **(6.6)** Rejoin track and continue straight**(7.2)** Enter village of **La Clauze** and continue straight on the road towards the tower of La Clauze[Sign post]
 (7.4) Merge onto main road D335 and continue straight to leave village[Tower of La Clauze visible on the left] **(9.4)** At fork stay right on left on the smaller road, direction Le Falzet[Sign post]**(9.9)** Enter village of Le Falzet, continuing straight on road**(10.2)** Continue straight on road leaving behind Le Falzet**(10.3)** At road's end turn left onto departmental road D335[Sign post] **(10.4)** After a short climb, take first right onto track and continue straight**(11.1)** Enter village of **Villeret-d'Apchier** and continue straight on road
(11.3) At end of road in village centre turn right and immediately left crossing the D587 and continue straight through village[Sign post. Pass Auberge des 2 Pèlerins on the right] **(11.4)** At bottom of steep hill and end of road turn left**(11.4)** Turn right, staying on road and continue straight[Sign post]**(12.2)** After steep climb reach intersection of roads and turn right[Sign post] **(12.9)** At end of track turn left and continue straight, climbing[Road passes between 2 houses. Hamlet of La Virlange] **(13.8)** At end of track turn right[Pass farm]**(14.0)** Leave road, staying to the left on track[Power lines to the right] **(14.6)** Enter hamlet of **Chazeau**

stage 3 — Saugues to Le Sauvage

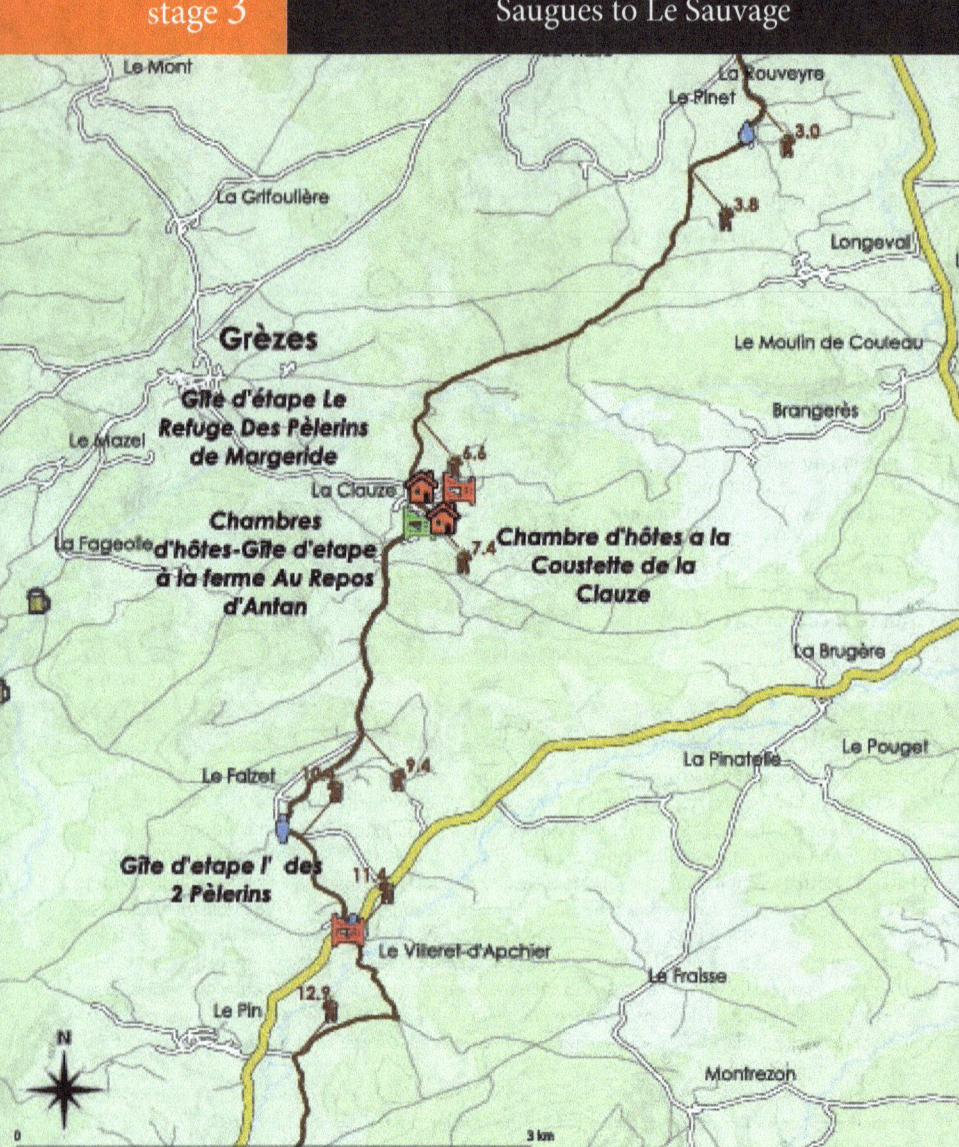

(14.7)Turn left in village centre and continue straight (climb)[Pass Chez Jerome] (14.8)Stay right leaving village behind(15.2)Cross department road D34 and continue straight on track[Sign post] (15.7)Leave larger track and turn left to ascend hill (17.5)Pass through cattle gate turn left and continue ascent[Cattle gate](17.7)Turn right on track through pine grove (18.3)Pass through the second gate and continue on the track. Turn right towards Le Sauvage[Monumental farm of Le Sauvage visible](19.5)Enter grounds of Farm Le Sauvage(19.6)Arrive at Le Sauvage

Saugues to Le Sauvage — stage 3

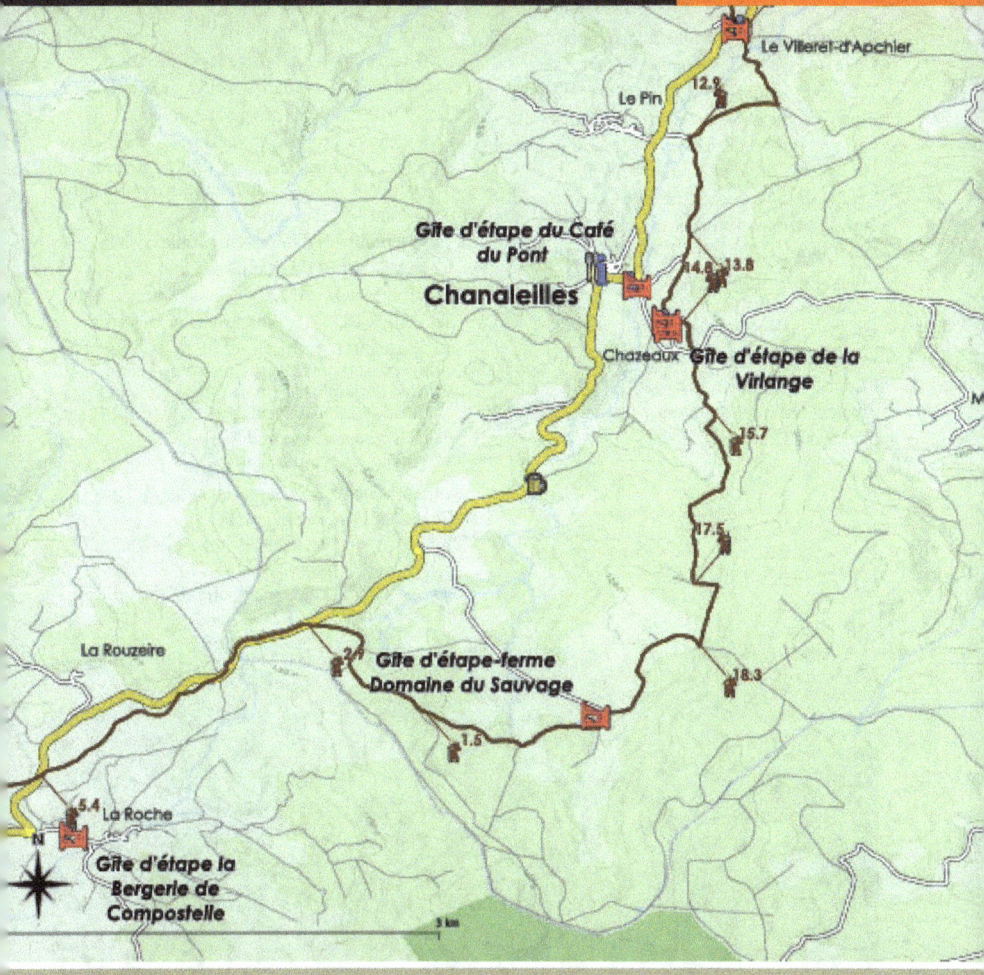

Accommodation and Tourist Information

Chanaleilles

Gîte d'étape - de la Virlange, Lieu-dit Chazeau, 43170 Chanaleilles, France; Tel:+33(0)632676354; Email:virlange@outlook.fr; gitedelavirlange.fr; Price:-,B,-; *12 places in dormitories also mini pods at additional cost*

Gîte d'étape - du Café du Pont [Mme Nicole Richard or Evelyne],Le Bourg, 43170 Chanaleilles, France; Tel:+33(0)651226429; +33(0)788356466; Email:evelynelomonaco@orange.fr; Price:C,B,-; *20 places in 2 rooms. Horses and donkeys welcome*

Gîte d'etape - l'Auberge des 2 Pèlerins[Steph and René],Le Villeret-d'Apchier, 43170 Chanaleilles, France; Tel:+33(0)471744723; +33(0)630668845; Email:contact@aubergedes2pelerins.com; aubergedes2pelerins.com; Price:C,C,C; *A welcoming hostel run by two former pilgrims who are members of a choral group and love singing. Kitchen. Accommodation for horses.*

stage 3 — Saugues to Le Sauvage

Gîte d'étape - les Noisetiers[Jerome],Lieu-dit Chazeau, 43170 Chanaleilles, France; Tel:+33(0)664638706; +33(0)637047713; Email:jeromelahondes8@gmail.com; les-noisetiers.webnode.fr; Price:-,-,B; *12 places in 4 rooms ina separate building on a working farm*

Gîte d'étape-ferme Auberge - Domaine du Sauvage,Domaine du Sauvage, 43170 Chanaleilles, France; Tel:+33471744030; Email:domainedusauvage@orange.fr; sauvage-en-gevaudan.fr; Price:C,B,B; *41 places in 2 gîtes kitchen and groceries available*

Mairie de Chanaleilles,Le Bourg, 43170 Chanaleilles, France; Tel:+33(0)471744107; Email:chanaleilles@wanadoo.fr; chanaleilles-hautgevaudan.fr

Grèzes

Gîte d'étape - Le Refuge Des Pèlerins de Margeride,122, la Clauze, 43170 Grèzes, France; Tel:+33(0)681206608; myhauteloire.fr/hebergement-groupe/gite-detape-le-refuge-des-pelerins-de-margeride; Price:-,-,C; *4 places in dormitory in a lovely old stone house typical of the Margeride*

Chambres d'hôtes-Gîte d'etape - à la ferme Au Repos d'Antan[Sonia and Michel Vidal],La Clauze, 43170 Grèzes, France; Tel:33(0)666476718; Email:sonia.vidal@orange.fr; aureposdantan.fr; Price:-,-,A|-,-,C; *A former farm with 4 guest rooms and a Finish pine hut for 2. Relaxed atmosphere. Dinner prepared with farm products which may include truffade (a local dish made with potatoes and cheese).*

Chambre d'hôtes - a la Coustette de la Clauze[Brigitte and Bernard Guinand],La Clauze, 43170 Grèzes, France; Tel:+33(0)982574588; coustette-de-la-clauze.fr; Price:-,A,A; *5 B&B rooms in a restored 15th century building next to the ruins of the Château de La Clauze.*

Breakfast Domaine du Sauvage © Alexandra Huddleston

Le Sauvage to Les Estrets — stage 4

Length:	21.1km
Ascent:	513m
Descent:	860m
Le-Puy:	63km
Roncevaux:	718km

Leaving Le Sauvage © Alexandra Huddleston

Route–The route, which is well marked, consists mostly of asphalt roads and tracks, as it continues to cross the Margeride. Shortly after the farm of Le Sauvage, the route reaches one of its highest altitudes, the Hospitalet ridge (1,304 metres). The Chapel of Saint Roch, with its magnificent views, marks the boundary between the Haute-Loire and Lozère departments.

Pointers–Between Le Sauvage and Le Rouget, be careful to stay on the GR®65, as opposed to the GR®4 (Tour of Margeride), which uses the same red/white way markings and which intersects twice with the GR®65. Caution: There are two steep descents: into Le Rouget, which can be slippery when wet, and in the forest before Estrets. Use caution.

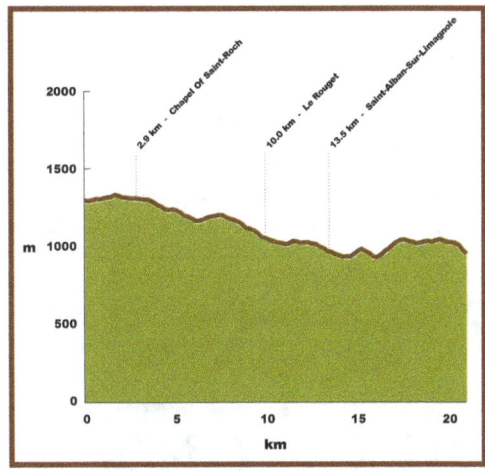

Advance planning: Do any necessary food shopping in Saint-Alban-sur-Limagnole, as the next grocers are in Aumont-Aubrac. Accordingly, there are no grocers or restaurants in Les Estrets, though meals can be reserved with accommodation.

stage 4 — Le Sauvage to Les Estrets

Cultural Discoveries

Col de l'Hospitalet & Saint Roch Chapel
(Chapelle de Saint-Roch)

Saint Roch Chapel © Alexandra Huddleston

In 1198, a hospital for pilgrims and travellers crossing the barren highlands was founded on the hill, Col de l'Hospitalet. The hospital and chapel, dedicated to Saint James, were under the protection of the Knights Templar (a Christian military order that came to prominence in the Middle Ages). While there is no vestige of the hospital, both a natural spring, purported to have healing properties, and a chapel that was constructed at the end of the 19th century, are dedicated to Saint Roch and bear remembrance to the former hospital. The current chapel was reconstructed in 1901.

Le Rouget

The name "Rouget" is derived from *rouge*, or red in French, which is the colour of the sandstone that was used to build the houses, walls and crosses of the village. In this region, including in St-Alban-sur-Limagnole, it is the most commonly used stone.

Church of Saint Alban
(Eglise paroissiale Saint-Alban)

Saint-Alban-sur-Limagnole (popl. 1450, alt. 950m) was the site of a medieval fortress in the Middle Ages and was one of eight fiefdoms of the Gévaudan. The village's 12th century red sandstone and granite church, which was likely part of a former monastery, is dedicated to Saint Alban, the first English Christian martyr. The oldest part of the church is the choir, which has lovely Romanesque sculpted capitals.

Les Estrets

During the Middle Ages, Les Estrets was a command post for the Knights of Malta (a medieval Christian military order), whose presence in the village is mentioned as early as 1266. The command post was strategically located on the Truyère river at the edge of the Aubrac plateau. The current church, which was built in the second half of the 19th century, is made out of granite and incorporated certain elements of the original medieval priory of the Knights of Malta.

Saint Roch Fountain © Alexandra Huddleston

Le Sauvage to Les Estrets — stage 4

GR®65

(0.0) From the entrance of Le Sauvage turn right and regain the track to leave the Domaine **(0.1)** At fork turn right and continue straight on track[Turn into forest grove] **(0.7)** Stay to the right on principal road and continue straight[Forest grove will be to your left] **(1.5)** Merge left onto track and continue straight through forest[Cross hill Col de l'Hospitalet (1304m)] **(2.9)** Turn left onto the D587 and continue straight until the **Chapel of Saint-Roch**

(3.5) Enter department of Lozere[Sign post] **(3.7)** Keep on the D587/D987 and continue straight in the direction of Lajo[Sign post] **(3.8)** At bend in the road, turn left off the D987 onto a track that descends[Track runs largely parallel to the D987 which is to the right] **(5.4)** Cross the D987 and continue straight on track[Sign post] **(6.1)** At intersection of tracks continue straight[Head towards pine forest and cross stream (Ruisseau de Gazamas)] **(6.9)** At intersection of tracks continue straight **(7.5)** Keep left/straight as dirt track merges with another track **(8.0)** At fork keep right[Pass through pine forest] **(9.1)** At end of track turn right[Sign post] **(9.8)** Enter village of Le Rouget **(9.8)** Turn left to cross the D987 and then keep right[Watering point on the right] **(10.0)** At end of road in **Le Rouget** turn left[Sign post]

(10.3) Turn right onto asphalt road[Pass wooden barn and pass under power lines ahead] **(10.8)** At fork keep right towards road D987[Pass stone cross] **(11.6)** Turn left onto D987[Head towards village of Saint-Alban-sur-Limagnole] **(11.7)** At fork turn left off D987 onto smaller road - rue des Quatre Vents[Sign post "Hôpital" and pass stone cross on the right] **(12.5)** Turn right[Signposts for village centre and Office of Tourism] **(12.6)** Turn left on rue Beau Soleil[Cross through hospital complex, Centre Hospitalier François-Tosquelles] **(12.8)** Turn right onto rue de l'Hôpital and descend to village centre[End of hospital complex] **(13.4)** At end of the road turn left onto main street - Grand Rue[Café de la Paix on right] **(13.4)** Continue straight on Grand Rue[Towards village centre] **(13.5)** In **Saint-Alban-sur-Limagnole** turn right off Grand Rue into square in front of the church[Place de l'Eglise]

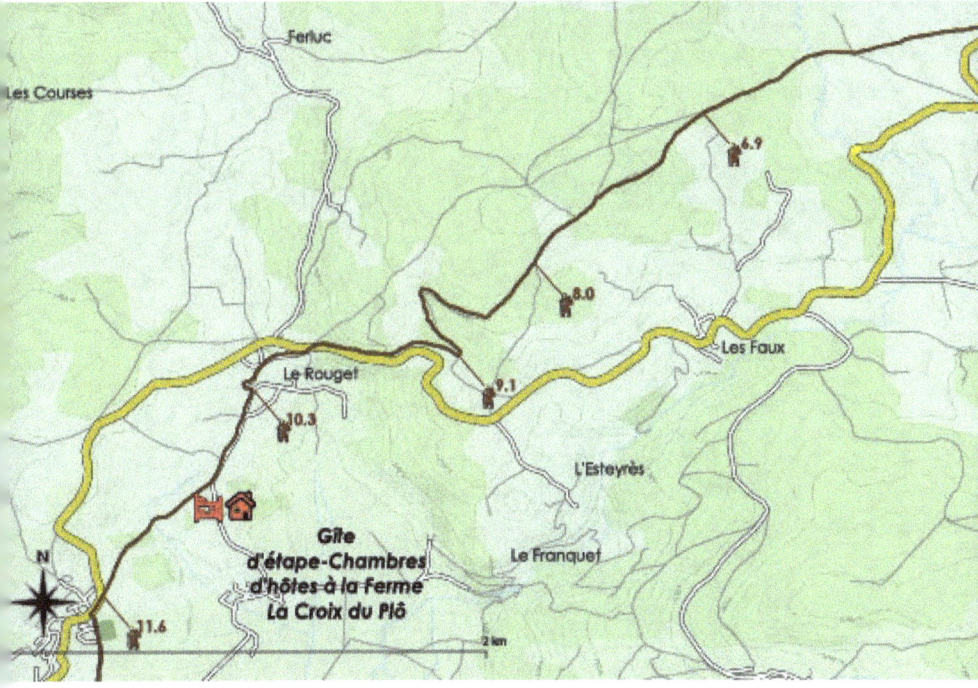

stage 4 Le Sauvage to Les Estrets

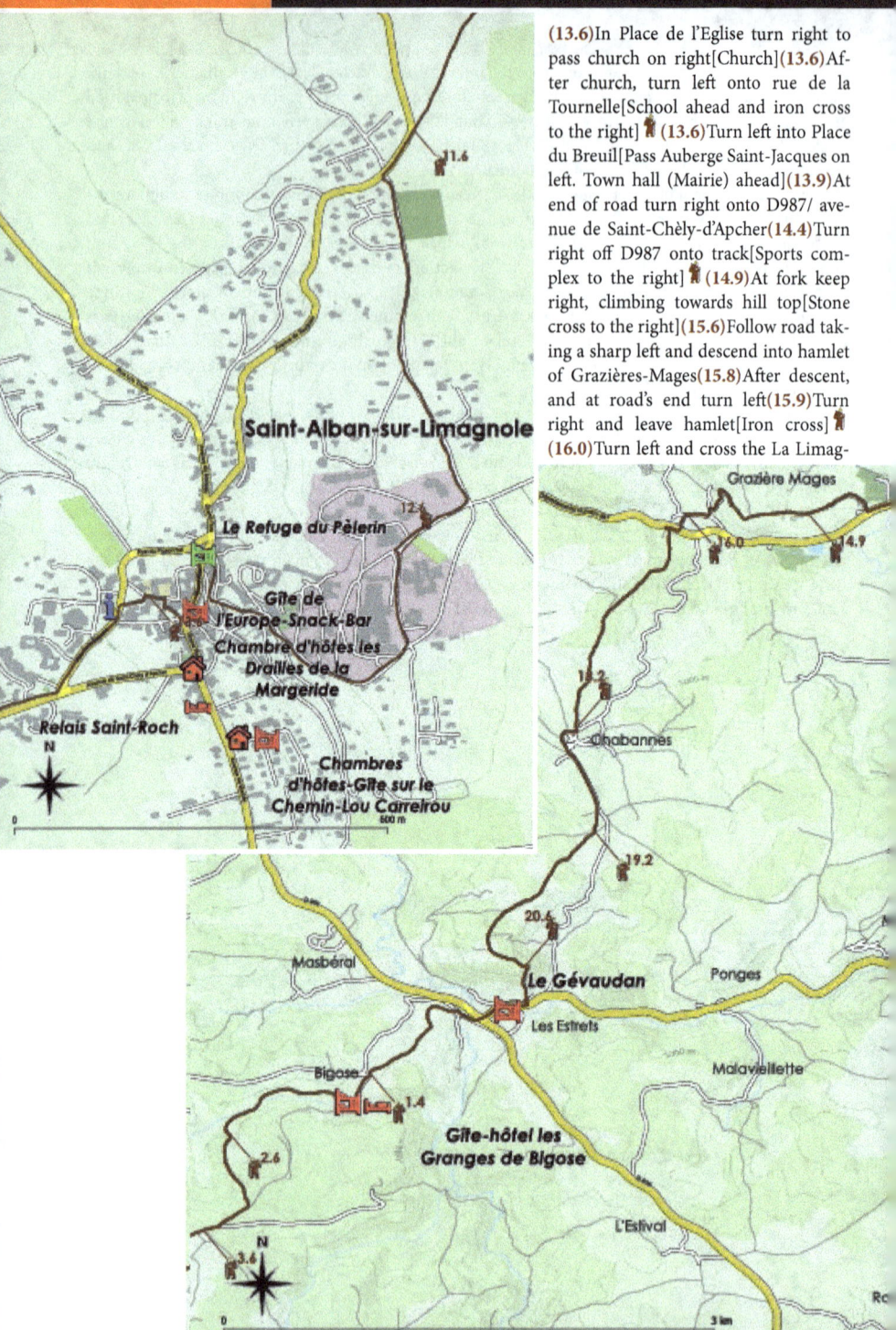

(13.6) In Place de l'Eglise turn right to pass church on right[Church]**(13.6)** After church, turn left onto rue de la Tournelle[School ahead and iron cross to the right] **(13.6)** Turn left into Place du Breuil[Pass Auberge Saint-Jacques on left. Town hall (Mairie) ahead]**(13.9)** At end of road turn right onto D987/ avenue de Saint-Chély-d'Apcher**(14.4)** Turn right off D987 onto track[Sports complex to the right] **(14.9)** At fork keep right, climbing towards hill top[Stone cross to the right]**(15.6)** Follow road taking a sharp left and descend into hamlet of Grazières-Mages**(15.8)** After descent, and at road's end turn left**(15.9)** Turn right and leave hamlet[Iron cross] **(16.0)** Turn left and cross the La Limag-

Le Sauvage to Les Estrets — stage 4

nole stream[Stream]**(16.2)**Cross the D987 and continue straight on trail (steep climb)[Sign post]**(16.2)** Stay on trail which veers right direction Les Estrets[Signposts] **(18.2)**Enter hamlet of Chabanes-Planes**(18.2)**Turn right onto road[Head in direction of village centre]**(18.2)**Continue straight on road which goes around the village[Picnic area and watering point on left]**(18.5)**Leave hamlet of Chabanes Planes and continue straight on road[Cross on right]**(19.0)**Turn right off road onto track[Sign post] **(19.2)**Turn right onto second track and continue straight **(20.6)**Keep to left on forest path and use caution in steep and rocky descent into Les Estrets**(20.9)**At end of trail, turn right into the village of Les Estrets, and then turn left[Church]**(21.0)**Turn right onto D7 road and continue straight to village centre[Head in direction of Church]**(21.1)**Arrive at Les Estrets village centre[Church]

Accommodation and Tourist Information

Fontans(Les Estrets)

Le Gévaudan[Pascal Rousset],Les Estrets, 48700 Fontans, France; Tel:+33(0)688909789; Email:pas.rousset@orange.fr; legevaudan-gite-chambre.com; Price:-,-,B; *30 places in dormitory and 6 private rooms in a restored farmhouse bordering pastures and a river. English spoken. Horses welcome. Aligot a typical potato and cheese dish is served at dinner*

Lajo

Gîte d'étape - la Bergerie de Compostelle[François Astruc],La Roche, 48120 Lajo, France; Tel:+33(0)0679698511; Email:francoiseastruc@yahoo.fr; Price:B,B,C; *12 places in 4 rooms renovated shepherds house on family farm close to chapelle Saint-Roch*

Rimeize

Gîte-hôtel - les Granges de Bigose[Valérie and Thierry Monniez],Lieu-dit Bigose, 48200 Rimeize, France; Tel:33(0)466471265; Email:contact@grangesbigose.com; grangesbigose.com; Price:-,-,B|A,A,A; *10 places in 2 dormatories. hôtel 9 rooms. Horses welcome.*

Saint-Alban-sur-Limagnole

Le Refuge du Pèlerin[Fabienne and Stéphane],37, Grand Rue, 48120 Saint-Alban-sur-Limagnole, France; Tel:+33(0)607471261; Email:ileane@orange.fr; lerefugedupelerin.com; Price:C,B,C; *12 places in 3 rooms additional places in a shepherd's tent. Camping also possible.*

Gîte de l'Europe-Snack-Bar,30, Grand-Rue, 48120 Saint-Alban-sur-Limagnole, France; Tel:+33(0)466311582; Email:bardeleurope@gmail.com; Price:C,C,C; *20 places central location*

Gîte d'étape-Chambres d'hôtes - à la Ferme La Croix du Plô[Valérie and Maurice Pic],Le Rouget, 48120 Saint-Alban-sur-Limagnole, France; Tel+33(0)466315351; +33(0)633556103; Email:lacroixduplo@orange.fr; chemindecompostelle.com; Price:C,C,C|A,A,A; *Gîte d'étape has 12 places in 3 rooms Also 3 rooms in chambres d'hôtes and space for camping. The welcome is warm on this working dairy farm. Accommodation on the first floor of a converted barn with beautiful views of the wooded landscape. Local produce is on the menu. Accommodation for horses. English spoken*

Chambres d'hôtes-Gîte - sur le Chemin-Lou Carreirou[Marie-Hélène Soubiran],Avenue de Mende, 48120 Saint-Alban-sur-Limagnole, France; Tel:+33(0)466315303; marie-helene-soubiran.business.site; Price:C,-,-|C,-,-; *A spacious and comfortable B&B with a welcoming host willing to share her local knowledge of the region. 5 rooms. English spoken. Horses welcome.*

Chambre d'hôtes - les Drailles de la Margeride[Véronique and Alain Trauchessec],10, Grand-Rue, 48120 Saint-Alban-sur-Limagnole, France; Tel:+33(0)681587791; Email:drailles.margeride@gmail.com; lesdraillesdemargeride.com; Price:-,B,A; *Dinner consists of regional specialities. 5 bedrooms accommodating 13 people an excellent B&B with a peaceful garden.*

Hôtel Relais Saint-Roch,Rue du Carreirou, 48120 Saint-Alban-sur-Limagnole, France; Tel:+33(0)466315548; Email:rsr@relais-saint-roch.fr; relais-saint-roch.fr; Price:A,-,-; *9 rooms in a 19th Century pink granite castle with gardens and heated swimming pool. A three-star hotel which welcomes guests with a glass of champagne. English spoken. Horses possible.*

Mairie de Saint-Alban-sur-Limagnole,Place de Breuil, 48120 Saint-Alban-sur-Limagnole, France; Tel:+33(0)466315029; Email:mairie.stalban48@orange.fr; stalbansurlimagnole.fr

stage 4

Le Sauvage to Les Estrets

Buron © Alexandra Huddleston

AUBRAC

Aubrac landscapes © Alexandra Huddleston

Aubrac is a sparsely populated high volcanic and granite plateau (average elevation 1200 metres) that is about 40km long and 20km wide, extending from the Truyère river in the north to the Lot river in the south. Like the Margeride, its rock base is granite, however, it was covered by fluid volcanic lava several metres deep some 6 to 9 million years ago.

This high plateau, which is covered with pastures, leads into thick beech and oak forests as it descends into the Lot river valley. The plateau boasts some 50,000 head of cattle. The beige long-horned Aubrac is the most common breed, and its sure-footedness makes it well-adapted to the terrain. While today the Aubrac breed is considered foremost for its highly prized meat, it was originally bred for dairy, which was traditionally prepared into cheese in *burons,* the shale and basalt huts that can be seen in some pastures. Certain cheeses are still produced in Aubrac, the most famous being *Laguiole.* The region is also known for its knife industry, notably the *Forge de Laguiole* (the main factory was designed by Philippe Starck) where local craftsmen use traditional techniques to make knives. The climate in Aubrac is mountainous, with snow covering the plateau in winter, and Spring bringing an explosion of native flowers, including wild narcissus and orchids.

On 25 May, the feast day of Saint Urbain, cattle are driven from the valleys onto the plateau, where they stay through the feast day of Saint Géraud on 13 October. The spring cattle drive, known as the *transhumance,* is the occasion of a popular and colourful celebration, in which cattle are decorated with flowers.

Aubrac landscapes © Alexandra Huddleston

The Via Podiensis crosses Aubrac for approximately 45 kilometres; the section between Nasbinals and Saint-Chély-d'Aubrac is listed as a UNESCO world heritage site.

stage 5 — Les Estrets to Finieyrols

Length:	24.0km
Ascent:	709m
Descent:	445m
Le-Puy:	84km
Roncevaux:	697km

Cross in Aubrac © Alexandra Huddleston

Route–The route, which is well marked, consists mostly of tracks and asphalt roads and footpaths. After Aumont-Aubrac, the route climbs and descends pastures and pine forests before entering the solitary and exposed Aubrac plateau, after Les Quatre Chemins.

Pointers–**Advance planning:** Do any necessary food shopping in Aumont-Aubrac, as there are no grocers until Nasbinals. Accordingly, there are also no grocers or restaurants in Finieyrols, though meals can be reserved with accommodation.

Caution: Ensure that you stay on the GR®65, as the GR®, Tour of the Aubrac Hills, which uses the red/yellow way markings intersects with the GR®65 in Aumont-Aubrac.

Reservations: The Fête de la Transhumance, the celebration that marks the driving of cattle from the valleys to the Aubrac plateau for the summer, occurs each year at the end of May and attracts almost 15,000 visitors a year. During this long weekend, accommodation between Aumont-Aubrac and Saint-Chely-d'Aubrac may be scarce. Best to reserve in advance.

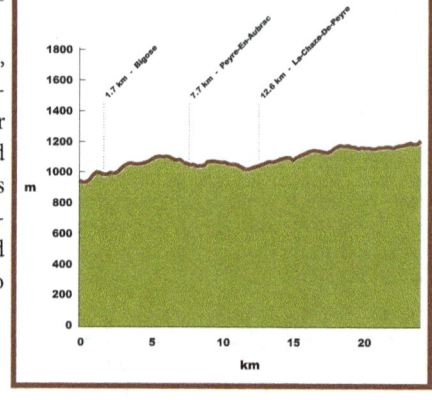

Les Estrets to Finieyrols — stage 5

Cultural Discoveries

Aumont-Aubrac

Aumont-Aubrac church

The village of Aumont-Aubrac (popl. 1100, alt. 1000m) developed around a fortified priory founded by the Barons of Peyre (one of eight fiefdoms in Gévaudan). The Church of Saint Stephen (Eglise Saint-Étienne) was built around the 12th century, and was thereafter extensively renovated. Certain Romanesque elements can be seen on the eastern side of the church. The village holds a market every Friday morning (Place du Foirail).

La Chaze-de-Peyre

La Chaze-de-Peyre (popl. 300, alt. 1040), which means house of stone, has a church dating from the 12th century with an impressive granite bell tower. One kilometre after the village, is the lovely Bastide Chapel (Chapelle de Bastide), named after the Bastide de Grandvialia family who contributed to the chapel's renovation in the 18th century. The original structure, built in 1522, was remodelled over the centuries and is now dedicated to the Our Lady of La Salette (commemorating Mary's apparition to two children at La Salette-Fallavaux, France in 1846).

Bastide Chapel © Alexandra Huddleston

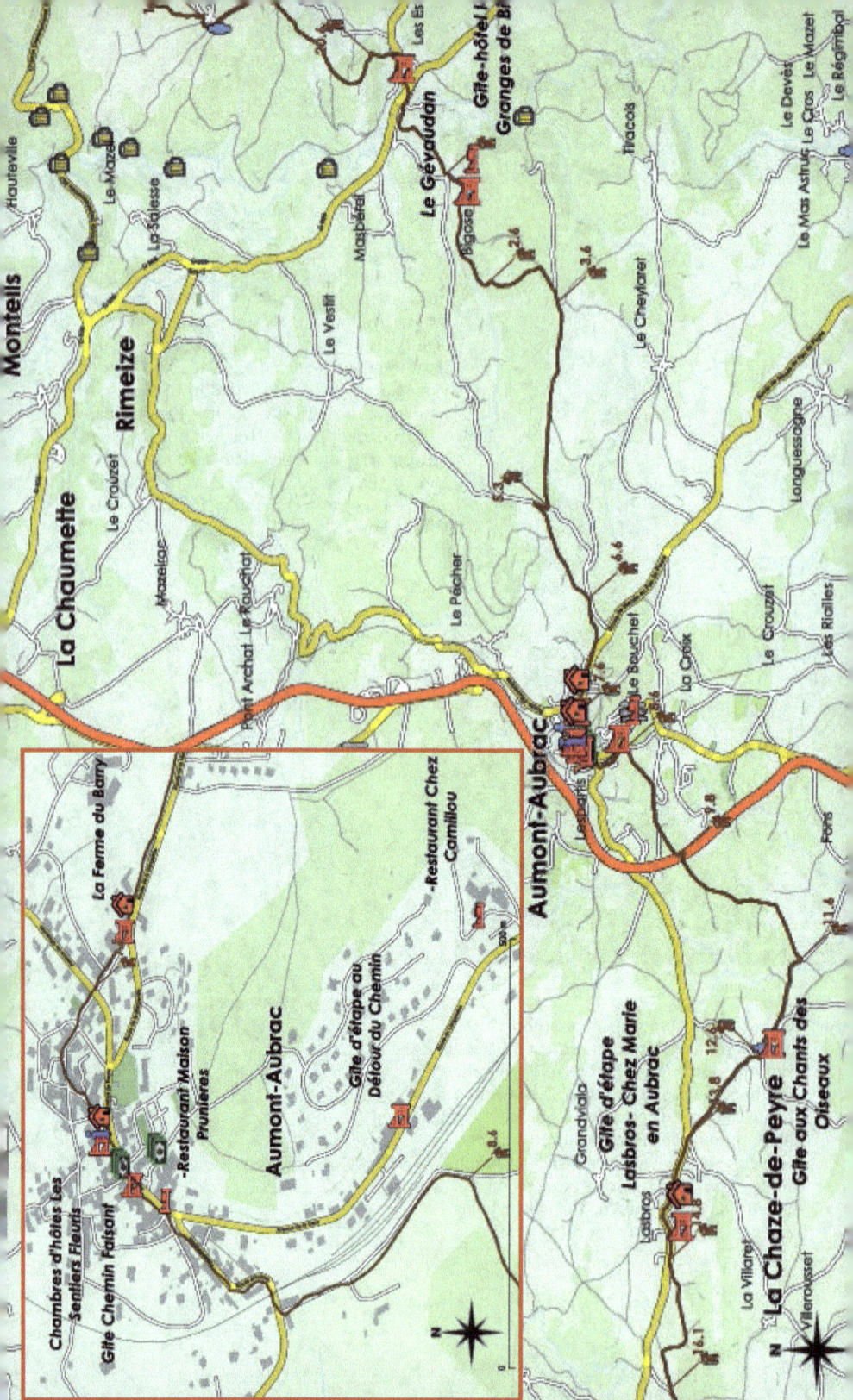

Les Estrets to Finieyrols — stage 5

GR®65

(0.0) With the church on the right, continue straight on D7 road[Church on the right and iron cross on the left]**(0.3)** Cross the D806 road and turn right at end of the road[Signpost]**(0.4)** Continue straight and cross bridge over the La Truyère river[Bridge and signpost]**(0.5)** Turn left onto track, the historic road to Aubrac, and climb[Pass between two large stone buildings] **(1.4)** Turn left onto the road towards the village of Bigose[Iron cross]**(1.6)** Enter village of Bigose and keep right on the road**(1.7)** Before Grange de **Bigose**, turn right onto track[Café]
(2.6) Continue straight, climbing, on trail passing along pine grove **(3.6)** Leave pine forest and continue straight on track[Track runs alongside forest to the right] **(5.5)** At end of track turn right onto D7 road[Signpost]**(5.5)** Turn left onto track direction Peyre-en-Aubrac[Signpost] **(6.6)** Keep right on track[D7 road to the left]**(7.1)** Turn right onto main road (D7) in the direction of the village centre**(7.5)** Turn right and descend small flight of stairs. Walk down rue du Barry Haut[Pass B&B] **(7.6)** Cross D809 (avenue du Gévaudan) and continue straight[Iron cross on left]**(7.7)** At fork in the centre of **Peyre-en-Aubrac** stay left on rue du Prieuré, climb. Reach the central square (Place du Portail) and turn right onto D809 road[Church to the right. Pass office of tourism on the right]
(8.0) Turn right onto D987 road[Pass fountain on the right. War monument to the left]**(8.2)** Pass under railway tracks and turn left onto chemin de la Gazelle[Railway tracks to the left] **(8.6)** Turn right onto the track that ascends hill[Signpost]**(9.1)** Turn right onto road chemin de Beauregard[New housing development "Beauregard" on the left]**(9.4)** Leave Peyre-en-Aubrac and turn left onto track[Signpost and pass beige wall] **(9.8)** Turn right and go through underpass beneath highway A75[Underpass]**(9.8)** Turn right after underpass, and then take first left and continue straight on track **(11.6)** Leave track and turn right onto asphalt road direction La Chaze-de-Peyre[Signpost]**(12.2)** At fork keep right to enter village of La Chaze-de-Peyre[Cemetery to the right] **(12.6)** In **La Chaze-de-Peyre** keep right on D69 road[Church on right and War Memorial]
(12.7) At fork keep left in the direction of Lasbros[Iron cross]**(12.9)** Leave village of La Chaze-de-Peyre. Continue straight on road[Signpost] **(13.8)** Turn left onto D987 and continue straight[Pass Chapel of Bastide to the right]**(14.4)** Enter village of Lasbros and continue straight on D987[Signpost] **(14.8)** After leaving village of Lasbros, turn left onto road that descends[Small stone cross (right)]**(15.8)** At end of road turn left and climb hill **(16.1)** Turn left onto asphalt road direction Quatre-Chemins and continue straight[Signpost. Thereafter cross the stream (Riou Frech)] **(18.5)** Cross D53 road and continue straight past small iron cross to merge left onto the D987 road[Iron cross. Pass Chez Regine on Left]**(18.8)** Turn left onto trail that passes through pine forest[Wooden gates] **(20.3)** Continue straight on track**(20.7)** Pass through gate and continue straight on trail[Gate]**(20.9)** Pass through second gate and continue straight on trail[Gate]**(21.0)** Cross road (La Bouge del Prat) and continue straight on trail through cow pastures[Stone Mill "Moulin de la Folle" to the right] **(23.3)** Continue straight on the road**(23.5)** Cross D73/Vierge de Fineyrols and continue straight on road**(24.0)** Arrive at Finieyrols[La Rose de l'Aubrac on the left]

Les Estrets to Finieyrols — stage 5

Accommodation and Tourist Information

La Chaze-de-Peyre

Gîte aux Chants des Oiseaux,Le Bourg, 48130 La Chaze-de-Peyre, France; Tel:+33(0)632844362; Email:colettegr@yahoo.fr; chemindecompostelle.com; Price:C,C,C; *7 places in 3 rooms no dogs*

Gîte d'étape Lasbros- Chez Marie en Aubrac,Lieu-dit Lasbros, 48130 La Chaze de Peyre, France; Tel:+33(0)466470894; +33(0)660677427; aubrac-gite-gr65.com; Price:-,-,B|-,-,A; *Reservations by telephone only. 14 places in small dormitories and 1 private bedroom. Very small village with no shops*

Gîte Café Les Quatre Chemins en Aubrac,Lieu-dit Les-Quatre-Chemins, 48130 La Chaze de Peyre, France; Tel:+33(0)975471634; +33(0)670115539; Email:les4chemins1@orange.fr; les4cheminsaubrac.fr; Price:-,-,B|-,-,B; *14 places*

Gîte aux Quatre Vents[Jean-Marc Granier and Marie Salvan],Lieu-dit Les-Quatre-Chemins, 48130 La Chaze de Peyre, France; Tel:+33(0)664193403; +33(0)652775180; Email:granier-jean.marc@orange.fr; chemindecompostelle.com/voie-puy-gr65-via-podiensis/hebergements/gite-etape-aux-quatre-vents-chaze-peyre; Price:C,-,C|C,-,-; *13 places in 5 rooms no dogs*

Peyre-en-Aubrac

La Ferme du Barry[Charles and Marie],9 Rue du Barry Haut, 48130 Peyre-en-Aubrac, France; Tel:+33(0)466429025; +33(0)671831746; Email:fermedubarry@yahoo.fr; gite-fermedubarry.fr; Price:B,-,B|-,B,A; *A restored farm famous for the aligot prepared by your host. Hostel has 24 places in rooms of 2 to 5 persons.*

Chambres d'hôtes - Les Sentiers Fleuris[Christianne Gibelin],7, place du Portail, 48130 Peyre-en-Aubrac, France; Tel:+33(0)466429470; Email:sentiersfleuris48@yahoo.fr; sentiers-fleuris.com; Price:B,B,B|-,A,A; *Centrally located well known for its homemade aligot. 20 places located in rooms of 2 to 3.*

Gîte d'étape - au Détour du Chemin,4, Route du Languedoc, 48130 Peyre-en-Aubrac, France; Tel:+33(0)786933500; Email:audetourduchemin48@gmail.com; audetourduchemin.fr; Price:-,C,C; *11 places in 4 rooms dinner available on some days*

Gîte - Chemin Faisant[Annie Lautard],15 Avenu de Peyre, 48130 Peyre-en-Aubrac, France; Tel:+33(0)624831936; +33686525747; Email:annie.lautard@live.fr; podiensis.com/hebergement/40-gite-detape-chemin-faisant; Price:C,C,-; *Breakfast extra 14 places central location*

Hotel-Restaurant Maison Prunieres,4, Place du Relais, 48130 Peyre-en-Aubrac, France; Tel:+33(0)466428552; Email:hotelprunieres@gmail.com; hotelprunieres.free.fr; Price:A,A,A; *Centrally located on the GR®65 with a welcoming staff. 40 rooms*

Hotel-Restaurant - Chez Camillou,319, route du Languedoc,, 48130 Peyre-en-Aubrac, France; Tel:+33(0)466428022; Email:chezcamillou@wanadoo.fr; camillou.com ; Price:A,A,A; *Lovely 3-star hotel located a walk from the city centre is renowned for its comfortable rooms attentive staff and Michelin starred restaurant (reservations required)*

Mairie d'Aumont-Aubrac,Place du Portail, 48130 Peyre-en-Aubrac, France; Tel:+33(0)466428002; +33(0)466428470; Email:mairie@peyreenaubrac.fr; peyreenaubrac.fr

Prinsuéjols-Malbouzon

Chambres d'hôte - La Rose de l'Aubrac[Caroline],Lieu-dit Finieyrols, 48100 Prinsuéjols-Malbouzon, France; Tel:+33(0)466457855; +33(0)608315561; Email:larosedelaubrac@gmail.com; larosedelaubrac.wixsite.com; Price:B,-,B|B,-,B; *14 places in 3 private rooms and a dormitory menu largely vegetarian*

Gîte d'étape - Domaine du Barena,Lieu-dit Ferluc, 48100 Prinsuéjols-Malbouzon, France; Tel:+33(0)671776756; Email:contact@domainedubarena.com; domainedubarena.com; Price:-,-,A; *20 places in 8 rooms well equipped including a spa*

Chambres d'hôtes Les Gentianes de l'Aubrac[Sylvie],Lieu-die Les Gentianes, 48100 Prinsuéjols-Malbouzon, France; Tel:+33(0)787112307; Email:lesgentianesdelaubrac@orange.fr; chemindecompostelle.com/voie-puy-gr65-via-podiensis/hebergements/gentianes-de-l-aubrac-prinsuejols/; Price:-,-,B; *5 rooms*

stage 6 — Finieyrols to Aubrac

Length:	18.9km
Ascent:	581m
Descent:	485m
Le-Puy:	108km
Roncevaux:	673km

Hiker after Rieutort © Alexandra Huddleston

Route– The route, which is well marked, consists mostly of tracks and footpaths, as it continues to cross the sun and wind-exposed Aubrac plateau, in what is one of the loveliest stages of the GR®65. After Nasbinals, there are climbs through cattle fields, including opening various gates.

Pointers–Culture: The 17km section of the GR®65 from Nasbinals to Saint-Chély-d'Aubrac has been recognized as a UNESCO world heritage site.

Cows: When crossing a field of cows, walk calmly at a normal pace and avoid getting between a cow and its calf.

Advance planning: Best to do any food shopping in Aumont-Aubrac, as there are no grocers until Saint-Chély-d'Aubrac. However, Maison d'Aubrac does sell regional delicacies. Meals in Aubrac can be reserved with accommodation.

Reservations: The Aubrac cross country race, which begins in Nasbinals takes place each June, during which time it is difficult to find accommodation in Nasbinals. Best to reserve in advance, if this overlaps with your trip.

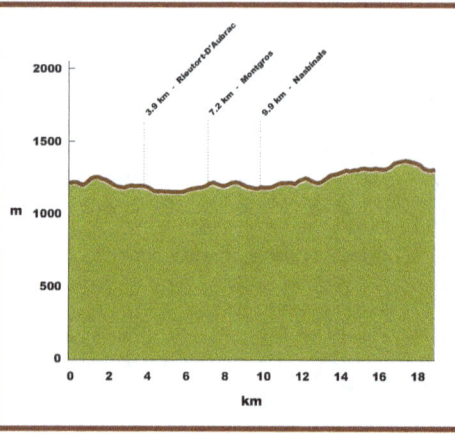

Finieyrols to Aubrac — stage 6

Cultural Discoveries

Rieutort-d'Aubrac

Note the communal oven and two impressive granite watering troughs.

Nasbinals

The economic centre of Aubrac, Nasbinals (popl. 500, alt. 1100) offers skiing in winter and hiking in summer. The 13th century church of Saint Mary (*Eglise Sainte-Marie*) is an example of regional Romanesque architecture and is built from brown basalt with a schist roof and a unique octagonal bell tower. The double vaulted entrance faces south and includes a remarkable sculpted capital showing a fight between Sagittarius (an archer that is half human and half horse) and a lancer.

Aubrac

Aubrac village © Alexandra Huddleston

The village of Aubrac (alt. 1300m) houses the remains of a medieval monastery and hospital (*dômerie*) that was founded in the 12th century by the powerful Conques Abbey upon the initiative of Adalard, a Flemish noble. The village, which offered pilgrims and travellers medical care and respite from the elements, became a regional political and economic power in the Middle Ages. However, the monastery was abandoned during the French Revolution and left to ruin. Today what remains is the church and tower with its "bell for the lost" that once rang out to guide travellers crossing the Aubrac plateau.

Church of Nasbinals © Alexandra Huddleston

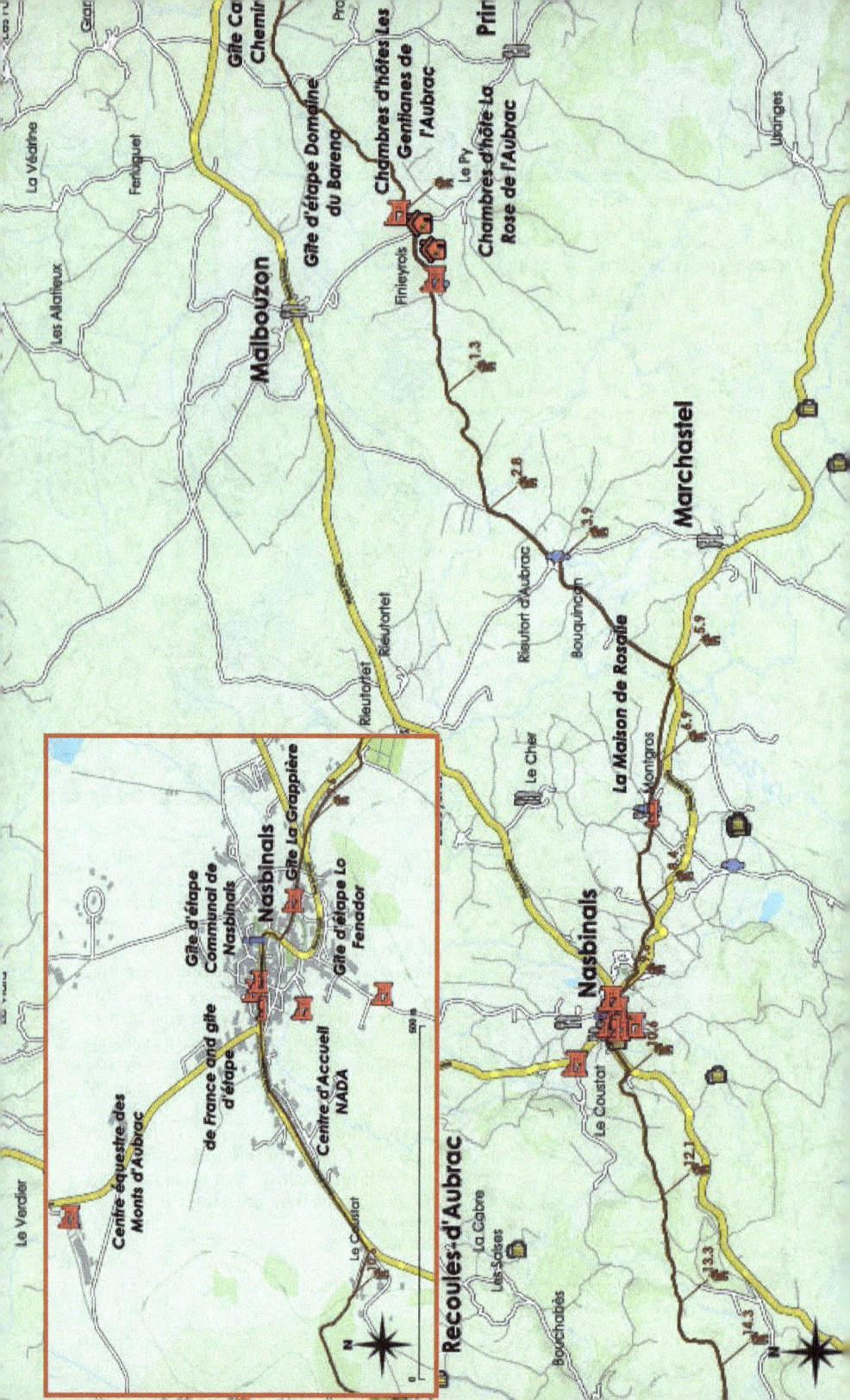

Finieyrols to Aubrac — stage 6

GR®65

(0.0) Follow road through Finieyrols[La Rose de l'Aubrac to the left]**(0.1)** At fork keep right and climb hill. Continue straight on road 🚶 **(1.3)** Continue straight on trail climbing hill[Rock formation called Roc des Loups (wolves) to the left]**(2.2)** Turn right and continue descent[Signpost] 🚶 **(2.8)** Turn left onto road and cross bridge/stream. Continue straight climbing hill[Stream (La Peyrade)]**(3.7)** Enter village of Rieutort d'Aubrac[Signpost] 🚶 **(3.9)** Turn right to leave **Rieutort-d'Aubrac** (curved road to right)[Communal oven and two historical granite watering troughs] **(4.1)** Leave village continuing straight on road[Stone wall borders road. Lovely views of plateau] 🚶 **(5.9)** Turn right onto D900 road and cross bridge over Le Bès river[Pass iron cross on the left side of the bridge]**(6.1)** Take first right on gravel road up hill and continue straight [Pass white and yellow road marker on the right] 🚶 **(6.9)** Turn right onto the road Le Carrouquet**(7.2)** Enter village of **Montgros** and continue straight towards village centre[Signpost]
(7.4) Continue straight on road to leave Montgros[Pass cross on right]**(7.6)** Continue straight on track[Stay to right of white iron cross] 🚶 **(8.4)** Cross road and continue straight on gravel track (climb)**(8.7)** Continue straight through intersection towards village[Nasbinals visible]**(9.3)** Turn right onto D900 and continue straight towards village centre[Tractor and farm equipment garage to the right]**(9.4)** After passing cemetery on the left turn left and then right to follow path running parallel to D900 road[Cemetery on left] 🚶 **(9.6)** Merge left onto D900 and continue straight**(9.7)** Continue straight on rue de la Pharmacie[Pass pharmacy on right]**(9.9)** In the centre of **Nasbinals** turn right in front of the church (place de l'Eglise) and continue straight on rue Principale[Church. Pass town hall on the right]
(10.1) Continue straight on rue Principale to leave village**(10.5)** Turn right at Le Coustat onto rue La Coustette[Turn right after house with pine hedges] 🚶 **(10.6)** Continue straight climbing into wood grove[Wood grove]**(11.0)** Keep right[Pass memorial to Pilgrim Patrick Coudert] 🚶 **(12.1)** Keep left at fork and head towards forest**(12.9)** Keep right[Cross stream (Ruisseau de la Cabre ou Pascalet)] 🚶 **(13.3)** Keep right and pass through gate (climb)[Gate and farm ahead]**(13.5)** After climbing hill pass through 2nd gate on left and continue straight following fence[Gate]**(13.8)** Pass through 3rd gate climb right through field[Gate] 🚶 **(14.3)** Pass through 4th gate and continue straight along fence[Gate and fence]**(14.7)** Pass through 5th gate and continue straight following fence[Gate] 🚶 **(15.4)** Pass through wood grove and then keep right[Follow stone wall]**(16.3)** Cross stream and pass through additional gate. Climb hill ahead[Gate] 🚶 **(17.2)** Pass through gate and continue straight toward wooden shed on hilltop[Gate]**(17.3)** Continue straight following stone wall[Pass shed on right]**(18.1)** Descend towards village of Aubrac[Follow stone wall. The enormous and austere Royal Aubrac, a former sanatorium, visible on hilltop to the right] 🚶 **(18.4)** Cross the D987 road and continue straight on track towards village of Aubrac[Village visible and signposts]**(18.7)** Continue straight on trail, passing around the back of the Church**(19.0)** Turn right onto asphalt road and arrive at Aubrac village centre[Place des Fêtes]

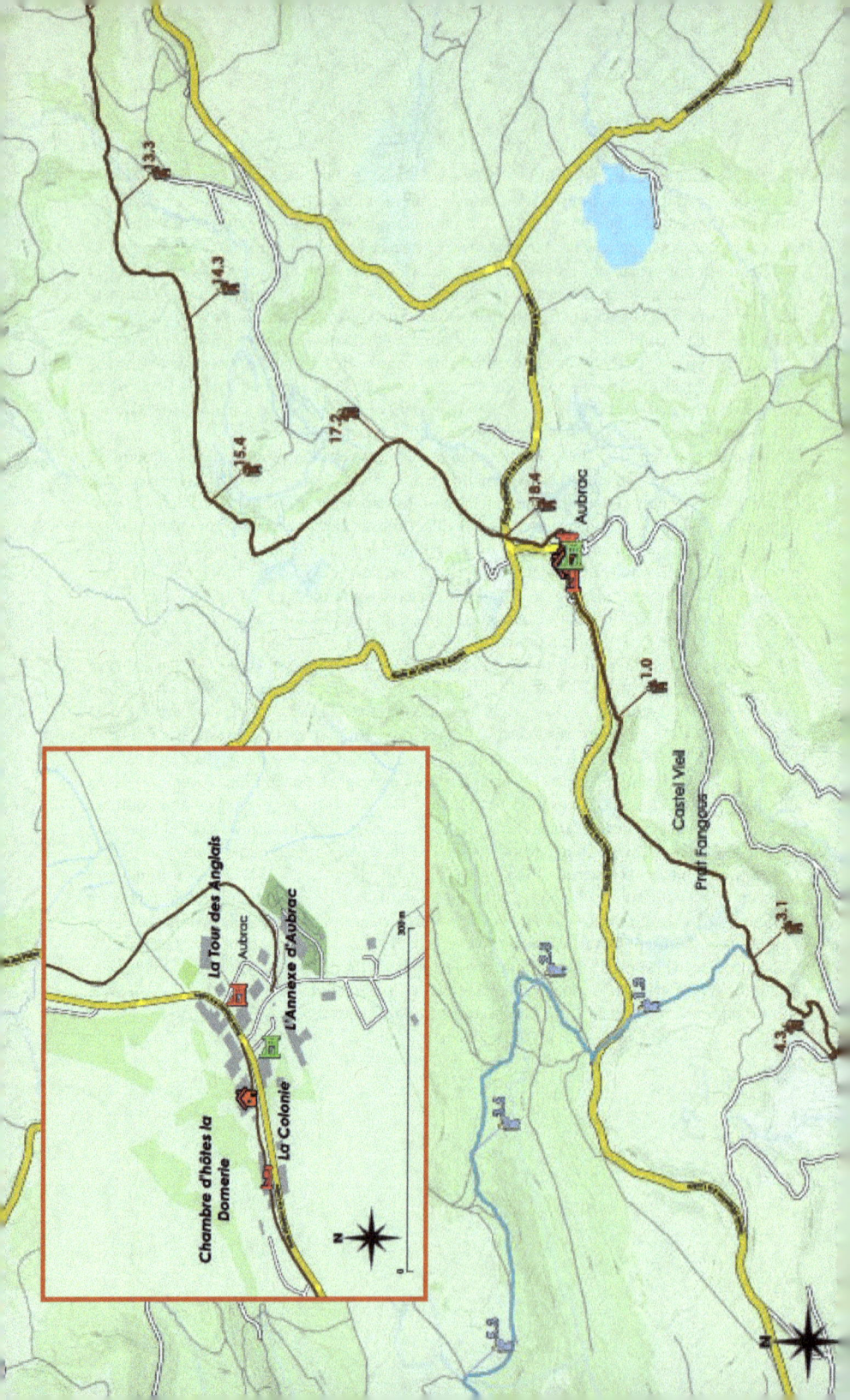

Finieyrols to Aubrac stage 6

Accommodation and Tourist Information

Nasbinals

Centre d'Accueil NADA[Village],Village, 48260 Nasbinals, France; Tel:+33(0)632184353; +33(0)466325042; Email:contact@nada-aubrac.com; nada-aubrac.com; Price:C,-,-; *38 places including 2 dormitories of 6 to 8 beds 13 rooms of 2 to 3 beds 2 bathrooms. Kitchen.*

Centre équestre des Monts d'Aubrac[Naëlle Hiron and Cédrick Moisset],Route de Saint-Urcize, 48260 Nasbinals, France; Tel:+33(0)466325065; Email:lafermedesmontsdaubrac48@orange.fr; equitation-aubrac-lozere.fr; Price:-,-,B; *Equestrian centre also offering accommodation to hikers. 22 places in rooms of 2 to 4*

Gîte d'étape - Communal de Nasbinals,Rue Principale, 48260 Nasbinals, France; Tel:+33(0)466325947; +33(0)466325017; Email:commune@nasbinals.fr; nasbinals.fr; Price:C,-,-; *19 places. Kitchen. Rudimentary.*

Gîte d'étape Lo Fenador[Anne and Patrick],Chemin de la Grange du Four, 48260 Nasbinals, France; Tel:+33(0)695083668; Email:accueil@lofenador.fr; lofenador.fr; Price:C,-,-; *10 places in 2 dormitories equipped kitchen*

Gîte La Grappière[Marjori Buffière],Rue de la Pharmacie, 48260 Nasbinals, France; Tel:+33(0)466321560; Email:marjori.lagrappiere@laposte.net; Price:-,C,-; *Hostel in a house with 15 places in a dormitory next to pharmacy and close walk to church. Kitchen.*

Hôtel de France and gite d'étape[Mr. Hervé Rey],Rue Principale, 48260 Nasbinals, France; Tel:+33(0)466325019; Email:hotel-derocrey@orange.fr; hotel-gite-rey-nasbinals.fr; Price:B,B,-|C,C,-; *5 rooms in simple centrally located hotel 19 places in gite d'étape. Welcoming staff.*

La Maison de Rosalie[Karine and Philippe],Lieu-dit Montgros, 48260 Nasbinals, France; Tel:+33(0)466325514; +33(0)670610961; +33(0)637106454; Email:maisonderosalie@orange.fr; hotel-aubrac.com; Price:B,B,A; *The house has been welcoming pilgrims since the end of the 19th century. Today there is a 2 star hotel with 9 bedrooms and a gîte offering 14 places in 4 rooms*

Mairie de Nasbinals,Rue Principale, 48260 Nasbinals, France; Tel:+33(0)4.66.32.50.17; Email:commune@nasbinals.fr; nasbinals.fr

St-Chély-d'Aubrac

L'Annexe d'Aubrac[Virginie and Darwin],Place des Fêtes - Aubrac, 12470 St-Chély-d'Aubrac, France; Tel:+33(0)675884119; +33(0)565487884; Email:contact@lannexe-daubrac.com; lannexedaubrac.com; Price:-,A,A; *Upscale elegant B&B with 5 rooms located in village centre with private garden. English spoken.*

La Tour des Anglais,76 chemin de la Dômerie - Aubrac, 12470 St-Chély-d'Aubrac, France; Tel:+33(0)565446863; +33(0)565442708; Email:mairie-st-chely-daubrac@wanadoo.fr; tourisme-en-aubrac.com/en/hebergement-collectif/gite-detape-communal-la-tour-des-anglais; Price:C,-,-; *Communal gîte d'étape in 14th century tower 16 beds in 2 dormitories kitchen available*

Chambre d'hôtes - la Domerie,D987 - Aubrac, 12470 St-Chély-d'Aubrac, France; Tel:+33(0)565442842; +33(0)756804466; Email:contacts@la-domerie.com; la-domerie.com; Price:-,A,A; *21 rooms and apartments with bar and restaurant. English spoken*

La Colonie[Cyril Lérisse],D987 - Aubrac, 12470 St-Chély-d'Aubrac, France; Tel:+33(0)565516479; Email:contact@la-colonie.com; la-colonie.com; Price:-,A,A; *Opulent accommodation located near the village centre on the GR°65. English spoken.*

stage 7 — Aubrac to Saint-Côme-d'Olt

Leaving Aubrac

Length:	24.1m
Ascent:	826m
Descent:	1762m
Le-Puy:	127km
Roncevaux:	654km

Route–The route is overall well-marked. From Aubrac, it descends on rocky tracks and footpaths through fields and forests to Saint-Chély-d'Aubrac. Thereafter it descends mostly on asphalt roads and tracks to the Lot River valley and Saint-Côme-d'Olt.

Pointers–Advance planning: Ensure sufficient provisions in Saint-Chély, as there are no grocers or restaurants until Saint-Côme-d'Olt. Caution: When leaving Saint-Chély-d'Aubrac, be careful not to follow the GR®6; it also uses the same red and white way markings.

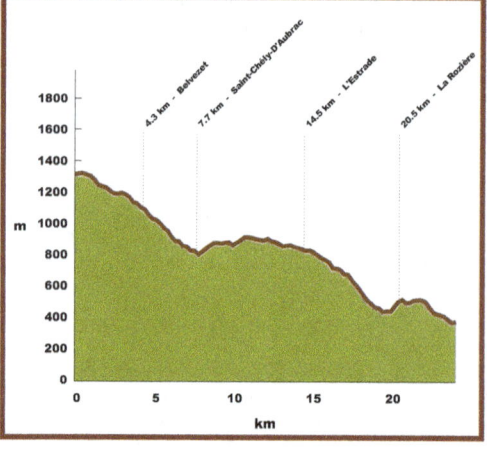

Aubrac to Saint-Côme-d'Olt — stage 7

Cultural Discoveries

Saint-Chély-d'Aubrac

In Saint-Chély-d'Aubrac (popl. 540, alt. 650m), there is the church of Our Lady of the Poor (*Notre-Dame-des-Pauvres*), which has a lovely sundial and a 15th century bell tower that was once a defence tower. When leaving the village, note the small bridge across the *boralde* (mountain stream), with its 16th century stone cross and a stylized depiction of a pilgrim holding a stick in one hand and a rosary in the other.

Saint-Côme-d'Olt

With many well preserved medieval buildings, the village of Saint-Côme-d'Olt (popl. 1,330, alt. 450m), which sits on the Lot River, is classified as one of the most beautiful villages in France. The village church (*Eglise Saint-Côme*) was built between 1522-1532 in a flamboyant Gothic style and has a rare twisted spire, which the French describe as "flaming" (*flammé*). Also of note are the 30 beautifully carved oak panels on the main doors.

stage 7

Aubrac to Saint-Côme-d'Olt

GR®65

(0.0) From Place des Fêtes, turn left onto road D987, direction Espalion [Pass Hôtel Restaurant de la Dômerie on right] **(0.3)** Continue straight on D987 road **(0.7)** Turn left onto track and descend [Signpost] **(1.0)** Continue straight [Pass cross on right] **(3.1)** Continue straight, passing cross on the right. To the right is also the turn off for the Alternative Route to Bonneval Abbey **(3.2)** Continue straight on track [Information panel to the right] **(3.7)** At fork keep left **(4.0)** Continue straight on trail [On left pass volcanic neck of Belvezet with the ruins of a fortress] **(4.3)** Turn left onto asphalt road (Vierge de Belvezet) and pass through farm houses of the hamlet of **Belvezet (4.4)** Take first right [Pass picnic area on the left] **(4.5)** Continue straight on road which curves right at farm **(4.7)** Turn right [Signpost] **(5.0)** Cross stream (Ruisseau de l'Aude) and descend on trail [Stream (Ruisseau de l'Aude)] **(5.6)** Continue straight and pass through two gates [Gates] **(6.0)** Continue straight [Pass abandoned farm house on left] **(6.1)** Turn left onto footpath, direction Saint-Chély-d'Aubrac, followed by a steep descent into ravine [Signpost] **(6.6)** Turn left onto asphalt road, which leads to Saint-Chély-d'Aubrac [Village visible] **(7.2)** Enter Saint-Chély-d'Aubrac [Cross and signpost] **(7.4)** Turn right onto D19/Route d'Aubrac and continue straight towards village centre **(7.6)** Turn left onto rue de la Marie [Public toilets to the right] **(7.7)** In the centre of **Saint-Chély-d'Aubrac** cross Place de la Marie [Pass war monument] **(7.7)** Turn left and descend on rue du Pont des Pèlerins [Descent towards river (Boralde de Saint-Chély) and historic bridge] **(7.9)** Cross Pont des Pèlerins [Note cross on bridge with depiction of pilgrim] **(8.0)** Turn right off asphalt road onto track that abuts cemetery [Signpost. Pass along cemetery wall on the right] **(8.4)** Turn left onto D19 road and take immediate right onto track [Signpost] **(8.6)** Continue straight on track which runs parallel to D19 road [Pass cross on the left. D19 to the right] **(8.9)** Merge onto the D19 road and take first right into the hamlet of Le Recours [Signpost] **(9.4)** After passing through hamlet turn right onto footpath that passes through forest [Signpost] **(10.7)** Turn right onto asphalt road and continue straight towards hamlet of Les Cambrassats [toilet to the right] **(11.0)** At fork keep right [Head towards the farm house and hamlet of Les Cambrassats (signpost)] **(11.1)** Take immediate left onto footpath [After first barn] **(11.6)** In the hamlet of Foyt, turn left onto trail [Farmhouse] **(11.8)** Turn right [Path cuts between pastures] **(12.1)** Turn right onto asphalt road, which was a former Roman road - Via Agrippa - in the direction of L'Estrade [Signpost] **(13.3)** Turn right onto dirt path [Signpost] **(14.5)** Continue straight and enter hamlet of L'Estrade [Pass farm on right] **(14.5)** At end of trail in hamlet centre turn right and continue straight to leave **L'Estrade** **(15.7)** Continue straight on path through forest (chestnut trees) on descent towards river valley **(18.0)** At intersection continue straight on trail, descending **(19.0)** Cross stream (Ruisseau de Cancels) and continue straight on trail **(19.0)** Turn right onto asphalt road **(19.2)** At fork follow footpath to the left of a picnic area **(19.5)** Turn left onto road D557 and cross bridge. Continue straight **(19.9)** Turn right off road. Steep climb on trail in the direction of La Rozière [Signpost] **(20.0)** Turn right onto track and continue climb straight **(20.5)** Arrive in hamlet of **La Rozière (20.5)** Continue straight through hamlet [Pass shrine to Mary on the left] **(20.9)** Turn right off track and descend [Signpost] **(21.6)** Turn left onto track and continue straight [Towards power lines] **(22.5)** Turn left onto asphalt road to enter hamlet of Cinqpeyres **(22.7)** Turn left onto foot path [Pass behind barn] **(22.9)** Turn right onto the road **(23.0)** Take first left onto rue de la Draille [Pass cross to the left] **(23.6)** Turn right onto gravel road D557 **(23.6)** Cross the D987 road and continue straight towards Saint-Côme-d'Olt centre [Signpost] **(23.7)** At end of road turn right [Pass vegetable gardens] **(23.9)** Turn left through underpass, then immediate right on rue Mathat to reach village centre **(24.1)** Continue straight crossing Place de la Porte Neuve. Pass through gate (porte) and turn left onto rue du Greffe **(24.1)** Arrive at Saint-Côme-d'Olt in Place Château de Castelnau [Church and Office of Tourism]

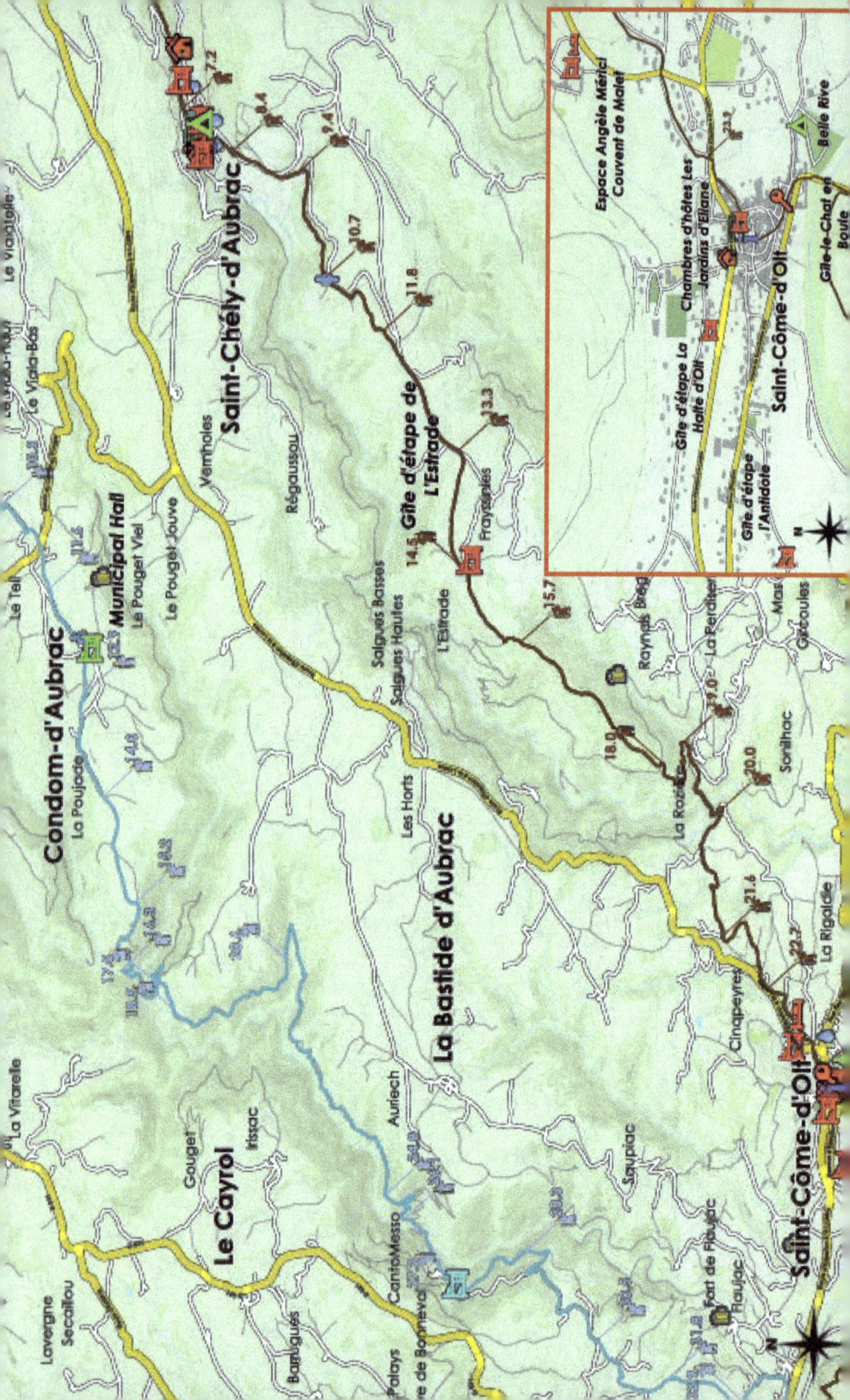

Aubrac to Saint-Côme-d'Olt

stage 7

Route via Bonneval Abbey

Route–From Aubrac it is possible to take a shorter alternative route to the Bonneval Abbey, a Cistercian abbey founded in 1147, and to re-join the GR°65 in Espalion, without adding extra time to the hike. The route, which is not very frequented, can be challenging, with some steep descents. It is marked by light blue way markings and crosses spectacular plateaus and forests before arriving at the abbey, which is hidden in a forest valley. The abbey is self-sufficient and today houses a Cistercian Convent and its craft chocolate factory. For the more adventurous, spiritually oriented or nature loving, this detour is recommended.

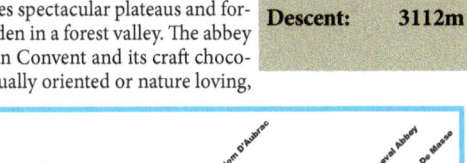

Length:	35.3km
Ascent:	2256m
Descent:	3112m

Pointers–The way markings can be unclear. Best to print out the detailed map of the route from the Abbey website before leaving or at the Maison d'Aubrac information point, in Aubrac www.abbaye-bonneval.com/fr/hotellerie/saint_jacques.php

Advance planning: Ensure to have sufficient provisions/water before setting off from Aubrac.

Reservations: Make reservations at the Abbey for the night/meals in advance. If you intend to spend the night in Condom d'Aubrac, call in advance. With advance notice, meals in Condom can also be organised at the local café.

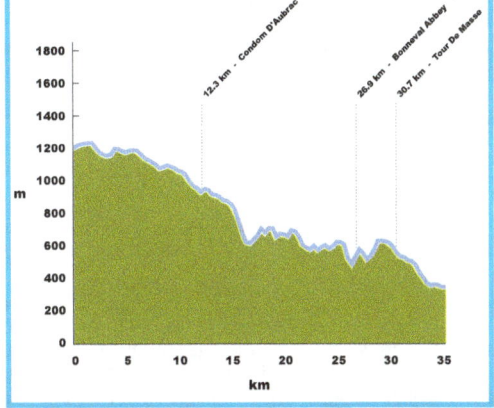

Cultural Discoveries

Abbey of Bonneval

The impressive Abbey of Bonneval was founded in 1147 on the edge of the Aubrac plateau. By the 12th-13th century, it was rich from donations and one of the most important monasteries in the region with significant lands and several granaries. The abbey nevertheless suffered both during the Hundred Years' War (the intermittent struggle between England and France in the 14th-15th centuries), during which it fell under English control, and the Wars of Religion (16th century conflicts between French Protestants and Catholics), when it was pillaged. The abbey was abandoned during the French Revolution, and its lands were sold and its buildings left to ruin. It wasn't until 1875, that a small community of Cistercian nuns, seeking a place to settle, began restoration works. This same religious community today numbers approximately 35 nuns. The congregation is largely self-sufficient and operates a chocolate factory (delicious chocolate for sale in the gift-store) as well as provides accommodation for pilgrims and guests. Historical sources suggest that the abbey was a stop for pilgrims in the Middle Ages. Guests are invited to take part in religious services, including the beautiful Gregorian chants for which the congregation is renown. Above the entrance to the abbey is a lovely 12th century Virgin and Child relief.

stage 7 — Aubrac to Saint-Côme-d'Olt

Route via Bonneval Abbey

(0.0)Turn right at cross and follow signpost for Tour des Monts d'Aubrac Route[Note that way markings are light blue for the Bonneval Route] (1.5)Turn left onto D987 road(1.5)Turn right into picnic area[Picnic area and cross](1.6)Immediately after passing through gate, keep left and head towards information board(1.6)Follow trail behind information board[Information board](2.2)Cross gravel road and continue straight descending (2.5)Cross stream using footbridge(2.6)Rejoin main path on left(3.1)Cross stream and continue on path(3.1)Enter Forêt Domaniale d'Aubrac[Signpost] (3.6)Cross stream and continue straight[Climb hill](3.8)Continue straight. Steep climb(4.5)Continue straight on track along forest[Forest to the left] (5.3)At end of road turn left, cross stream and take immediate left in the direction of Le Puech du Serre[Signpost] (7.3)Turn right and continue straight passing farm houses on the left(7.7)Turn right onto road(8.0)Turn right onto track[Pass farm house (left)] (8.8)Turn left onto track direction Pratmals[Signpost](8.9)Take immediate right onto track followed by immediate left[Trail passes between narrow stone walls](9.2)Cross track and continue straight(9.4)Merge straight onto track (descent) and take immediate left[Wooden cross on right] (10.5)Turn right onto asphalt road[Descend in direction of farm house](10.9)Turn left off asphalt road onto trail[After first sharp corner](11.2)Turn right onto the D900 road and then take immediate left (descend)[Turn before farmhouse](11.3)Turn right onto asphalt road and continue straight[Farm buildings] (11.6)Continue on narrow trail between stone walls/fields[Pass farmhouse to the left] (11.7)Turn left onto asphalt road and head towards village of Condom d'Aubrac(12.3)Enter village of **Condom d'Aubrac**[Signpost]
(12.3)Turn right in village centre[Pass church to the right](12.4)At end of street turn right[Cow statue to the right](12.5)Take immediate left and follow track between stone walls[Turn after school] (12.9)At end of track turn right and continue straight[Farm house](13.1)At end of path turn right onto asphalt road[Farm] (14.0)At fork keep right[Steel gate to the left] (15.2)Enter forest staying to the right on dirt path. Steep descent(15.5)Keep right and proceed with caution down steep incline towards valley (16.3)Before bridge take sharp left following path along river (Boralde Flaujaguèse) [Do not cross this bridge. River to the right](16.6)Cross river using concrete bridge(16.7)Follow path uphill along river (17.5)Follow path switch-backing up the hillside(17.8)Turn sharp right and continue switch-backing up hillside(18.0)Continue straight on track (18.5)Follow road along ridge[River valley to the right] (20.6)Continue straight on track[Trail chemin de Raymond on the left](21.0)Cross mountain brook and continue straight on track(21.5)Pass Roc de la Vache (cow rock) on right, with beautiful valley views (24.8)Continue straight on track[Pass Roc del Cayre on right] (25.0)Continue straight on track[Abbey visible across valley](25.2)Turn right onto narrow trail and switchback towards valley bottom. Steep[Signpost for Bonneval] (26.1)Continue down steep trail towards river[Pass ruins of farm house to the right](26.4)Reach valley bottom and cross bridge over river[Hydroelectric plant to the left](26.4)Turn left after crossing bridge and climb hill towards Abbey[Pass hydroelectric plant on the left](26.8)Continue straight on main path towards paved road and Abbey[Follow stone wall on right](26.9)Cross over gate (on the left side) and continue climb towards main road(26.9)To leave Bonneval Abbey, from the entrance continue straight on the asphalt road. Then, turn left onto the track[Cross. Trail eventually follows the stations of the cross (Chemin de la croix)](26.9)Turn right onto a asphalt road and arrive beside the **Bonneval Abbey**[Entrance of Bonneval Abbey]
(27.1)Pass through gate and cross pasture (27.2)Pass through gate and continue on trail[Path follows the Stations of the Cross (chemin de la croix)](27.4)Pass through gate and cross pasture[Gate] (27.6)Pass through gate and continue straight through forest[Gate] (28.7)At fork keep left climbing hill(29.0)

After switchback turn left onto road D661 and continue straight (30.5)Turn left off road onto track in direction of La Grange (granary)[Signpost](30.7)Turn left onto road[Pass granary on left **Tour de Masse**)]
(30.8)Turn right onto narrow track between stone walls and fields[Pass entrance to Granary and cross on left](31.5)Keep left on track[Pass ruins of house on left] (31.8) At fork keep right[Pass cross on right] (32.9)Continue on track (descent)[Pass between private houses, garden and pool](33.0)Descend left onto gravel road(33.1)Turn right onto asphalt road and continue descent(33.3)At end of road turn right(33.6)Turn right direction Espalion[Cross](33.9)Turn right onto the D987 road towards Espalion centre[Signpost and Lot River to the left] (35.0)Turn left onto rue du Dr Tremolières and continue straight towards city centre. [Before curve](35.3)After crossing bridge, turn right to regain the GR*65[Le pont Vieux bridge]

70

Aubrac to Saint-Côme-d'Olt   stage 7

Accommodation and Tourist Information

Castelnau-de-Mandailles
Gîte d'étape de L'Estrade[Betty and Hervé Brouzes],Lestrade, 12500 Castelnau-de-Mandailles, France; Tel:+33 (0)6 75 59 00 91; Email:gitelestrade@orange.f; gite-lestrade.fr; Price:-,-,B; *Modern recently renovated farmhouse/barn designed for pilgrims. 17 places in 5 rooms. Fully equipped kitchen. Welcoming local farming family. Accommodation for horses.*

Condom d'Aubrac
Municipal Hall[Mairie de Condom d'Aubrac],Le Bourg, 12470 Condom d'Aubrac, France; Tel:+33(0)5 65 44 27 11; Email:mairie@condomdaubrac.fr; Price:D,-,-; *In case of need this tiny welcoming village makes its municipal hall available to hikers. No beds (but mats are available) and no shower. Breakfast/dinner can be arranged in advance at the friendly Café Poujouly (+33 (0) 5 65 44 27 74). Call in advance.*

Le Cayrol
Abbaye Cistercienne Notre-Dame de Bonneval,Route de l'abbaye de Bonneval, 12500 Le Cayrol, France; Tel:+33(0)5 65 14 08 92; +33(0)7 89 05 02 42; Email:infos@le-quatorze.pelerins.bonneval@gmail.com; abbaye-bonneval.com; Price:D,D,D; *Beautiful working convent from the 12th Century with chocolate factory. Simple comfortable single rooms in convent complex or dormitory with 6 places in the Tour St-Jacques. Possibility to participate in vespers. Reservations required. English spoken.*
Mairie de Saint-Chély-d'Aubrac,Place de la Mairie, 12470 Saint-Chély-d'Aubrac, France; Tel:+33(0)565442708; +33(0)5.65.44.20.01; Email:mairie-st-chely-daubrac@wanadoo.fr

Saint-Chély-d'Aubrac
Gîte Saint André[Roland and Sylvie Nicoli],Chemin de la Vallée Libre, 12470 Saint-Chély-d'Aubrac, France; Tel:+33 (0)565 44 26 87; +33 (0)7 67 17 54 43; Email:info@gitestandre.fr; gitestandre.odoo.com; Price:B,B,B|B,B,B; *20 places in rooms of 2 3 or 4 persons. Lovely terrace with view.*
Gîte d'étape Chez Fanny et Jérémy[Fanny and Jérémy],Rue d'Espalion, 12470 Saint-Chély-d'Aubrac, France; Tel:+33 (0) 6 29 83 58 82; Email:fannyligniercocq@gmail.com; chezfannyetjeremy.fr; Price:-,C,-|C,-,-; *26 places in 7 rooms access to municipal camping fenced space for animals available*
Brasserie Le Relais Saint-Jacques-Chambres d'hôtes[Karine Vidal],Avenue de l'Aubrac, 12470 Saint-Chély-d'Aubrac, France; Tel:+33 (0) 6 47 32 04 08; Email:contact@le-relais-saint-jacques.fr; chambre-hote-saint-chely.fr; Price:-,-,B|-,-,B; *A father daughter duo welcome guests. 5 double rooms and 1 dormitory for 6 people. Centrally located near office of tourism. English spoken.*
Chambres d'hôtes La Tour des Chapelains,Rue de la Tour, 12470 Saint-Chély-d'Aubrac, France; Tel:+33 (0) 5 65 51 64 80; +33(0)669143338; Email:latour.j.c@gmail.com; tour-chapelains.fr; Price:-,B,A; *Unique accommodations in charming medieval tower. In city centre next to office of tourism. 3 B&B rooms.*

Hotel-Restaurant de La Vallée Les Coudercous,Avenue d'Aubrac, 12470 Saint-Chély-d'Aubrac, France; Tel:+33(0)5 65 44 27 40; Email:contact@lescoudercous.fr; lescoudercous.fr; Price:A,-,A; *21 rooms of 1 to 4 persons. English spoken.*
Mairie de Saint-Chély-d'Aubrac,Place de la Mairie, 12470 Saint-Chély-d'Aubrac, France; Tel:+33(0)565442708; +33(0)5.65.44.20.01; Email:mairie-st-chely-daubrac@wanadoo.fr

Saint-Côme-d'Olt
Espace Angèle Mérici - Couvent de Malet,250, Route de l'Estive, 12500 Saint-Côme-d'Olt, France; Tel:+33(0)5 65 51 03 20; Email:contact@hotel-malet-aveyron.fr; hotel-malet-aveyron.fr; Price:B,B,B|A,A,A; *An iconic stop of the GR°65. Beautiful and historic convent with 27 places in rooms of 3 to 6. English spoken. Free accommodation for horses and free wifi. Possibility to take part in religious services.*
Gîte d'étape del Romiou[Sabien and Sylvain],12, rue Crémade, 12500 Saint-Côme-d'Olt, France; Tel:+33 (0)6 35 59 16 05; Email:gitesaintcome@gmail.com; gite-delroumiou.jimdo.com; Price:C,-,B; *Space is a bit tight with 18 places (bunk beds) in 3 dormitories. English spoken. Accommodation for horses. Kitchen.*
Gîte d'étape La Halte d'Olt,15, route de Boraldette, 12500 Saint-Côme-d'Olt, France; Tel:+33(0)6 76 26 69 89; +33(0)6 70 08 38 72; Email:lahaltedolt@gmail.com; Price:C,-,-; *8 places in 2 dormitories*
Gîte d'étape l'Antidote,22, Chemin des Plantiers, 12500 Saint-Côme-d'Olt, France; Tel:+33(0) 641 906 289; Email:laurent.auz@gmail.com; giteantidote.jimdo.com; Price:-,C,C; *500m from the centre donkeys welcome no kitchen access*
Chambres d'hôtes Les Jardins d'Eliane[Jean-Raymond Lacan],3, Avenue. d'Aubrac, 12500 Saint-Côme-d'Olt, France; Tel:+33 (0) 5 65 48 28 06; +33(0)6 82 64 04 49; Email:les.jardins.d.eliane@wanadoo.fr; lesjardinsdeliane.com; Price:-,B,A; *In an old house centrally located operated by a baker and his wife. 5 B&B rooms. Pool and garden.*
Gîte le Chat en Boule[Danièle Barré],19, avenue de Saint-Geniez, 12500 Saint-Côme-d'Olt, France; Tel:+33(0)6 87 04 49 51; Email:danielebarre@orange.fr; gitesaintcomedolt.jimdo.com; Price:C,-,-; *2 independent apartments each sleeping 2 or 3 people*
Camping Belle Rive[David and Stéphanie Simbor],40, rue du Terral, 12500 Saint-Côme-d'Olt, France; Tel:+33(0)6 98 22 91 59; Email:contact@camping-bellerive-aveyron.com; camping-bellerive-aveyron.com; Price:B,-,-; *Reduced price for a camping place for pilgrims. Caravan chalet and pre-erected tent available for a minimum stay of 3 nights*
Mairie de Saint-Côme-d'Olt, 12500 Saint-Côme-d'Olt, France; Tel:+33(0) 5 65 44 07 09; Email:mairie@saint-come-olt.com; saint-come-olt.com

LOT RIVER VALLEY

A verdant and forested valley is created by the Lot River, which starts at an elevation of 1,241 metres in the Cévénnes mountains and flows 480 km west before joining the Garonne river, after Cahors.

The Lot River is an important presence on the Via Podiensis–it flows through the mining basin of Decazeville, it separates Aubrac from the *Causses* (limestone plateaus), loops around the city of Cahors (the historic capital of Quercy), and widens with the waters of many tributaries like the Célé river (followed on the alternative route through the Célé Valley) and the Dourdou river (crossed in Conques).

The stage between Saint-Côme-d'Olt and Estaing, largely follows the Lot, and is known as the *Pays d'Olt* (*Olt* being the Lot's name in Occitan). This stage is considered a world heritage site.

Saint-Côme-d'Olt to Estaing

stage 8

Length: 20.6m

Ascent: 937m
Descent: 997m

Le-Puy: 151km
Roncevaux: 630km

Lot River Valley landscape

Route- The route is well-marked, even in the city of Espalion, as it follows footpaths, tracks and asphalt roads through the lush Lot River valley. After crossing the Lot River in Saint-Côme d'Olt there is a steep and rocky climb to the statue of Notre-Dame-de-Vermus, with panoramic views of Espalion and the river valley. Apart from a short but steep climb out of Saint-Pierre-de-Bessuéjols, the route is thereafter mostly flat as it follows the southern bank of the Lot river to Estaing.

Pointers–**Culture:** The 20km section of the GR°65 from Saint-Côme-d'Olt to Estaing has been recognized on the UNESCO world heritage list.

Choice of routes: There is an unmarked variant to Espalion after Saint-Côme-d'Olt, which is flat and borders the Lot River, thus avoiding the steep climb to the statue of Notre-Dame-de-Vermus.

Note: The GR°65 does not enter Estaing, but rather continues along the Lot River. To visit Estaing, turn right off the GR°65 and cross the bridge into Estaing. To rejoin the GR°65, backtrack and pick up where you left off, continuing west along the river.

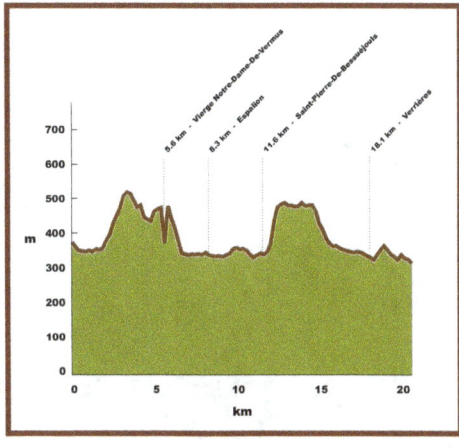

73

stage 8

Saint-Côme-d'Olt to Estaing

Cultural Discoveries

Espalion

Espalion (popl. 4,400, alt. 380m) is a dynamic and picturesque town on the Lot River, with a welcome bustle of shops, cafes and restaurants, as well as a lively market on Friday and Sunday mornings.

The town is dominated by the **Castle of Calmont-d'Olt** (*Château de Calmont d'Olt*), which in the Middle Ages served as a military fortress for the Barons of Calmont (the noble family that ruled the region until 1300), and which today houses an interactive museum dedicated to medieval warfare and offers spectacular valley views. The town also boasts the lovely **Old Bridge** (*Pont-vieux*), which was mentioned as early as the 11th century, and was once a toll bridge that had several towers and shops. The present red sand-stone bridge, dating from the 14th century, is a designated world heritage site and offers views of the historic river-side tanneries. Finally, the red-sandstone **Church of Saint Hilary of Persia** (*Eglise Saint-Hilarian-de-Perse*), built around the 12th century, was once part of a monastery complex that did not survive the 16th century Wars of Religion. The southern portal has an extraordinary tympanum depicting the Last Judgment, which bears some resemblance to the tympanum of the Church of Saint Faith in Conques. Inside, the church's vaults are covered with lovely 15th-16th century frescoes.

Except for its bell tower, the Church of Saint Peter (*Eglise Saint-Pierre*) was entirely rebuilt in the 16th century. However, the upper floor of the 11th century bell tower has an impressive chapel dedicated to Saint Michael with a carved alter, capitals and panels. To access the chapel, climb a steep staircase at the back of the church.

Estaing

Estaing (popl. 607, alt. 300m) is considered one of the most beautiful villages in France. The village is dominated by Estaing castle, a 15th century Gothic castle that was built on the site of a previous castle from 850. The Estaing family was one of the oldest noble families in France and had produced several famous knights and crusaders. Nevertheless, the name expired when the last male heir was guillotined in 1794, after which the castle passed to the order of Saint Joseph. In the early 20th century, the Giscard family took the d'Estaing name (e.g., Valery Giscard d'Estaing (former president of France)). The castle was purchased from the commune in 2005 by the Giscard d'Estaing family with the aim of renovating it and opening certain parts to the public. The 15th century Gothic bridge over the Lot is considered a world heritage site. In July and August, a market is held each Friday morning.

Saint-Pierre de Bessuéjouls

Saint-Pierre de Bessuéjouls © Alexandra Huddleston

Estaing © Alexandra Huddleston

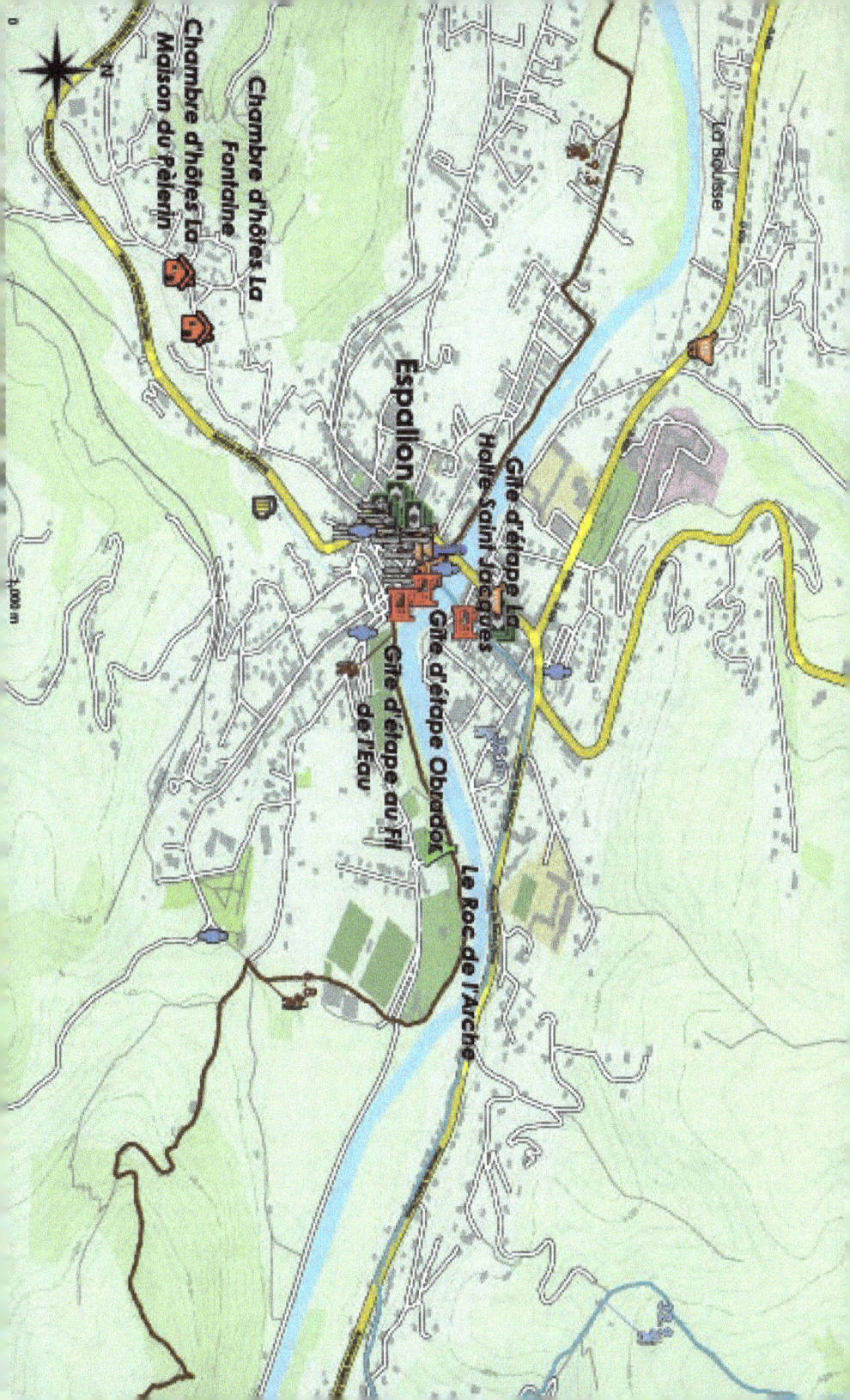

stage 8
Saint-Côme-d'Olt to Estaing
GR®65

(0.0) From Place de l'Eglise head south[Church will be to the left]**(0.0)** Take a right at Place Malimane and pass through former gate (porte)**(0.1)** Cross place de la Barrieyre and continue straight on rue du Terral**(0.2)** Turn right onto the D6 road and cross bridge over Lot River[Cross and river]**(0.4)** After crossing the river bridge, turn sharp rright onto the gravel road[towards the river] 🚶 **(1.1)** join the asphalt road and bear right**(1.9)** After crossing bridge turn left onto footpath, which climbs steeply[An umarked alternative route is to continue straight on the flat road to Espalion, thus avoiding the climb to the Notre-Dame statue] 🚶 **(3.1)** Keep left and continue climb[Signpost]**(3.4)** Turn right on track[Top of climb]**(4.0)** Turn right onto road 🚶 **(4.8)** Turn right in the direction of the Vierge Notre-Dame-de-Vermus[Signpost]**(4.9)** Turn left and continue straight on track[Cross through gravel pit]**(5.6)** Arrive beside **Vierge Notre-Dame-de-Vermus**. Continue on trail to left, steep descent[Statue and panoramic views of Lot River valley]

🚶 **(6.8)** Turn right[Follow stream (Ruisseau de Perse) on the right. church of Perse ahead]**(7.0)** Continue straight through sports complex and cross street (avenue Pierre Monteil)**(7.2)** Continue straight and follow trail next to the Lot River 🚶 **(8.0)** Turn right onto rue Saint-Joseph[Sculpture (bust) on the right]**(8.1)** Turn right at Place du Plo onto rue Arthur Canel[Pass Office of Tourism on the right]**(8.2)** Turn right onto rue Droite towards the old bridge (Le pont Vieux), and then immediate left on Quai Henri Affre. Here, the alternative route from the Abbey of Bonneval crosses the Le pont Vieux to rejoin the GR®65[Keep river to the right]**(8.3)** In the centre of **Espalion** cross D920/Boulevard Joseph Poulenc and follow Quai du 19 mars 1962 along the Lot River[Pont Neuf and Lot River to the right]

(8.8) Turn left, away from river, onto rue Dr Jean Capoulade[Cross]**(8.9)** Turn right onto rue Eugène Salettes 🚶 **(9.3)** Continue straight on gravel road**(9.6)** After short climb continue straight on asphalt road (Lotissement de la Crouzette)[Pass through residential area Les Hauts de Reversac]**(9.9)** At end of road turn right onto avenue de Saint-Pierre/D556[Cross on right] 🚶 **(11.1)** Turn left onto small road[Cross and signpost for "Eglise Romaine" (Romanesque church)]**(11.6)** Continue straight and enter hamlet of **Saint-Pierre-de-Bessuéjouls**[Church on right]

(11.8) After crossing bridge turn left on the road[Town hall (Mairie) and gardens to the right at the junction]**(11.8)** Bear right on the slip road**(11.9)** Turn right onto footpath, and climb to the plateau[pass barn on your left] 🚶 **(12.8)** Turn left onto asphalt road to reach hamlet of Briffoul[Signpost] 🚶 **(13.8)** Turn left[Leave behind hamlet of Le Briffoul]**(13.9)** Turn right onto trail through fields[Pass farm hanger on left] 🚶 **(15.0)** Continue descent on footpath[Pass through forest. Village of Beauregard becomes visible]**(15.4)** Enter village of Beauregard. Keep right on asphalt road[Pass castle on right]**(15.5)** Keep left and continue descent straight[Towards church of Sainte-Madeleine (Trédou)]**(15.6)** Turn left and continue straight descending hill[Cemetery] 🚶 **(16.1)** Turn right after crossing hamlet of Les Camps and continue straight[Head in direction of power lines]**(16.6)** At intersection continue straight on track[Away from power lines]**(16.9)** At end of road turn left. Direction Verrières[Signpost] 🚶 **(17.3)** At end of road turn right onto D100 (Route d'Estaing) and continue straight[Pass through hamlets of Les Acacias and Les Lilas]**(17.9)** Enter village of Verrières. Continue straight through intersection and old village centre[Signpost]**(18.1)** In the centre of **Verrières** turn left at end of road[Iron cross on the left]
🚶 **(18.3)** Keep right[Pass stone cross and Chapelle de Verrières on left]**(18.4)** Turn right onto the D556 road after crossing the bridge (pont des Pèlerins)[Bridge and stream (Ruisseau de Magrane)]**(18.6)** Turn left onto the D100 road[Signpost]**(19.1)** Turn left off the D100 road and follow footpath. Climb[Trail follows the D100 to the right] 🚶 **(19.8)** Rejoin the D100 road turning left in the direction of Estaing**(20.6)** From bridge head south, and take first right on rue Le Pont d'Estaing[Keep right of chapel. River to your right. Follow signpost for GR®65 and La Rouquette. Lot River to the right]**(20.6)** From bridge head south, and take first right on rue Le Pont d'Estaing[Keep right of chapel. River to your right. Follow signpost for GR®65 and La Rouquette. Lot River to the right]**(20.6)** Arrive at Estaing[Note: The GR®65 does not enter Estaing. After crossing the bridge to visit the village, backtrack to rejoin the GR®65]**(20.6)** Arrive at Estaing[Note: The GR®65 does not enter Estaing. After crossing the bridge to visit the village, backtrack to rejoin the GR®65]

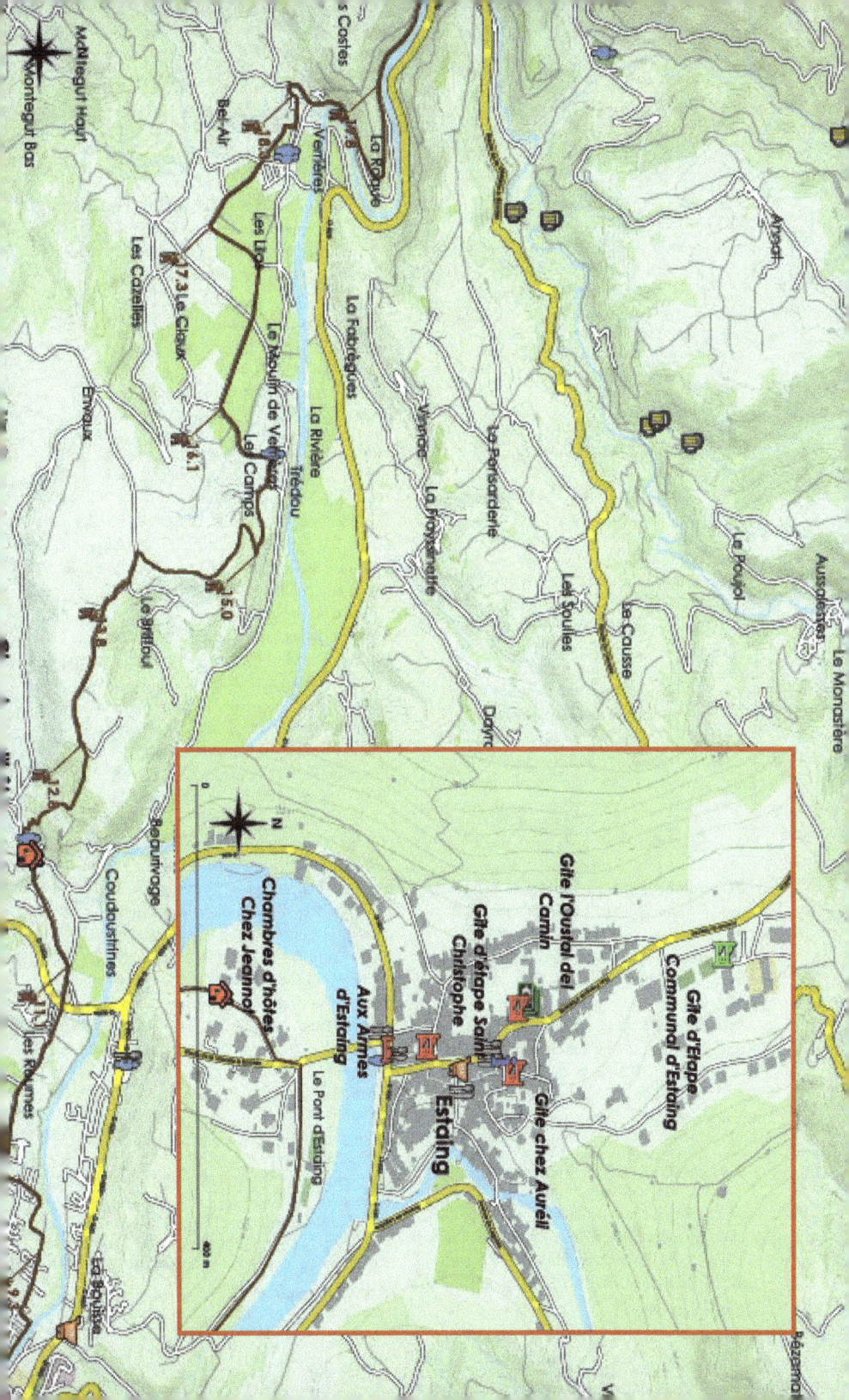

stage 8 — Saint-Côme-d'Olt to Estaing

Accommodation and Tourist Information

Bessuéjouls

🏠 **Chambres d'hôtes Domaine d'Armagnac**,Saint-Pierre, 12500 Bessuéjouls, France; Tel:+33 (0) 6 03 25 63 47; Email:domainedarmagnac@gmail.com; domaine-armagnac.com; Price:-,A,-; *A beautiful estate in a lovely village just after Espalion. 4 rooms in upscale B&B. Accommodation for horses. Kitchen.*

Espalion

Gîte d'étape La Halte Saint Jacques[Florian],8, rue du Docteur Trémolières, 12500 Espalion, France; Tel:+33 (0)628 303 830; +33 (0)565 663 561; Email:lahaltesaintjacques@hotmail.fr; gite-etape-espalion.fr; Price:C,C,B; *18 places in 4 rooms located in the historic centre close to the Pont Vieux*

Gîte d'étape Obrador,7, rue Arthur Canel, 12500 Espalion, France; Tel:+33 (0)565487152; Email:gite.obrador@orange.fr; gite.obrador.free.fr; Price:C,C,-; *Located in the city centre in an entirely renovated building on the Lot river.12 places in 3 rooms each with bathroom.*

Gîte d'étape au Fil de l'Eau[Stéphanie and Sophia],5, rue Saint Joseph, 12500 Espalion, France; Tel:+33 (0)677 585 308; Email:aufildeleau12500@gmail.com; gite-espalion-aufildeleau.fr; Price:B,B,-; *Close to the Vieux Palais (old palace) and on the banks of the Lot river. 15 places in 5 rooms. Kitchen. English spoken.*

🏠 **Chambre d'hôtes La Maison du Pèlerin**,3, rue de Bouquiès, 12500 Espalion, France; Tel:+33(0)651867530; +33(0)565442677; Email:nicolemonnaye@orange.fr; tourisme-aveyron.com; Price:-,B,-; *2 rooms each for 1 or 2 people*

🏠 **Chambre d'hôtes La Fontaine**[Mr. and Mrs. Regis],15, Chemin de Calmont, 12500 Espalion, France; Tel:+33 (0)5 65 48 45 91; +33(0)647867806; Email:christian.regis3@wanadoo.fr; tourisme-aveyron.com; Price:-,B,-; *4 rooms for 8 persons. A few minutes' walk from the city centre. Beautiful views of the Chateau de Calmont d'Olt. Terrace with garden and pool. Possible accommodation for donkeys*

⛺ **Camping Le Roc de l'Arche**,Rue du Foirail, 12500 Espalion, France; Tel:+33 (0)7 56 27 96 82; +33 (0)5 65 44 06 72 ; Email:info@rocdelarche.com; rocdelarche.com; Price:B,-,-; *Large shaded pitches beside the Lot*

ℹ️ **Office de Tourisme - Terres d'Aveyron**,2, boulevard Joseph Poulenc, 12500 Espalion, France; Tel:+33(0)5 65 44 10 63; Email:accueil@terresdaveyron.fr; terresdaveyron.fr

Estaing

Gîte d'Etape Communal d'Estaing,Place du Foirail, 12190 Estaing, France; Tel:+33 (0) 644 955 214; +33(0) 565 441 454; Email:gitecommunalestaing@gmail.com; estaing12.fr; Price:C,-,-; *Recently renovated clean and well equipped hostel housed in the former chapel of Saint Fleuret. Garden terrace and kitchen. 22 places in 5 rooms. English spoken.*

Gîte chez Auréli[Philippe],3, rue du Collège, 12190 Estaing, France; Tel:+33(0)6 95 82 15 95; Email:ChezAurelie12@outlook.fr; chezaurelie12.fr; Price:C,C,C; *8 places in 3 rooms in the medieval heart of the village*

Gîte d'étape Saint Christophe[Marie and Rémi],5, rue de Saint-Fleuret, 12190 Estaing, France; Tel:+33 (0)6 27 82 40 14; Email:gite.etape.st.christophe@gmail.com; gite-etape-saint-christophe.com; Price:C,C,B; *Recently renovated. 15 places in 5 rooms on 3 floors. English spoken*

Gite l'Oustal del Camin,31, Rue François d'Estaing, 12190 Estaing, France; Tel:+33(0) 7 67 29 15 07; Email:resa.loustaldelcamin@gmail.com; tourisme-aveyron.com/fr/diffusio/hebergements-groupes/gite-d-etape-l-oustal-del-camin-estaing_TFO363100197390; Price:C,C,B; *12 places in 3 rooms kitchen available*

🏠 **Chambres d'hôtes Chez Jeannot**[Jean Dijols],Le Pont d'Estaing, 12190 Estaing, France; Tel:+33 (0)670 384 281; +33 (0) 565 447 151; Email:jean.dijols12@orange.fr; tourisme-espalion.fr/diffusio/en/hebergements/chambres-d-hotes/estaing/chez-jeannot_TFO024337370995.php; Price:-,C,-; *Across the bridge on the route leaving town. 5 bedrooms*

Hotel Aux Armes d'Estaing,1, quai du Lot, 12190 Estaing, France; Tel:+33(0)565447002; estaing.net; Price:A,A,A; *Centrally located simple hotel with 32 rooms of various sizes and restaurant operated by the owner-chef. (Avoid rooms in the annex to the hotel)*

ℹ️ **Office de Tourisme - Terres d'Aveyron**,24, rue François d'Estaing, 12190 Estaing, France; Tel:+33 (0)5 65 44 10 63; Email:accueil@terresdaveyron.fr; terresdaveyron.fr

Estaing to Espayrac

stage 9

Length:	23.1km
Ascent:	1306m
Descent:	1235m
Le-Puy:	172km
Roncevaux:	610km

Landscape leaving Estaing

Route–The route is well-marked and follows mostly asphalt roads. After a breezy walk along the Lot River, the route turns south-west and steadily but steeply climbs through pine forests and exposed pastures to Golinhac, before descending into Espeyrac.

Pointers–When leaving Estaing, pay attention to follow the GR®65 along the Lot River, as opposed to the GR®6, which uses the same red and white way markings.

Advance planning: Be certain to leave Estaing with sufficient water and provisions. While there is a watering point before Golinhac, there are no restaurants or grocers, and the climb is long and hot in summer.

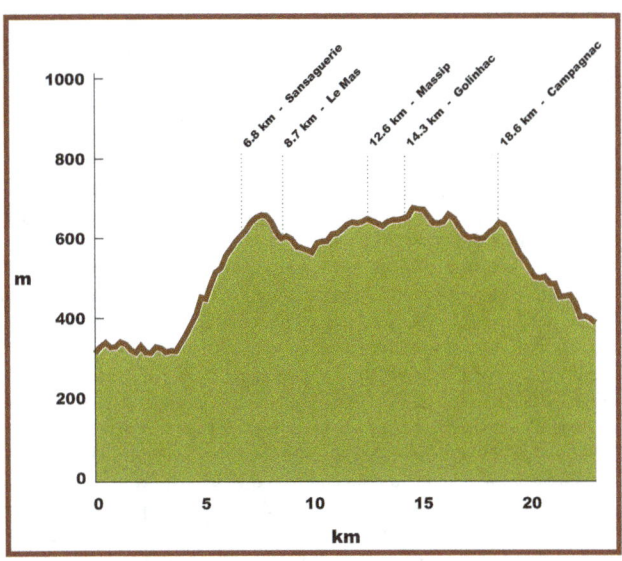

stage 9 — Estaing to Espayrac

Cultural Discoveries

Golinhac

The Church of Saint Martin (*Eglise Saint-Martin*) in Golinhac (popl. 380, alt. 500m) has some Romanesque features that date to an original 11th century Benedictine priory, which was affiliated with Conques Abbey. The present 14th century structure was modelled on the Church of the Holy Sepulchre in Jerusalem (built on the spot where Jesus was said to have been crucified).

Shaver-Crandell, A., Gerson, P. L., & Stones, A, p. 199 (1995). *The pilgrim's guide to Santiago de Compostela: A gazetteer*. London: Harvey Miller Publishers.

Espeyrac

According to the 11th century *Book of Miracles of Saint Faith*, in 960, a pilgrim in Espeyrac (popl. 240, alt. 250m) was attacked and blinded by bandits. He miraculously recovered after praying to Saint Faith, patron saint of Conques. Espeyrac was formerly the seat of a priory that was connected to the Conques Abbey. The present church of Saint Peter was built on the site of a feudal castle.

Shaver-Crandell, A., Gerson, P. L., & Stones, A, p. 186 (1995). *The pilgrim's guide to Santiago de Compostela: A gazetteer*. London: Harvey Miller Publishers.

GR®65

(3.2) Keep left on road and continue straight[Lot River to the right and La Roquette hamlet to the right] **(4.0)** Cross bridge over the stream (Ruisseau de Luzane) and continue to right on the road. Climb until Montegut[Route changes intermittently from road to forest trails as it climbs to Montegut] **(4.1)** Turn left off road. Climb **(4.2)** Turn left rejoining road. Climb **(4.6)** Turn left onto footpath. Continue switchback climb up hill **(4.8)** Turn right onto asphalt road **(4.9)** Turn left onto footpath. Continue switchback climb **(5.1)** Turn left and continue straight on road. Climb **(6.8)** At **Sansaguerie** continue on the road, climbing[Water point and toilets on the right] **(7.7)** At intersection continue straight, direction Golinhac **(8.5)** Continue straight. Direction Le Mas[Signpost] **(8.7)** Pass through farming hamlet of **Le Mas**. Continue straight **(9.4)** At end of road turn left[Wooden cross] **(9.6)** Continue straight[Castaillac to the right] **(10.0)** Turn left onto footpath and climb[Signpost] **(10.3)** Cross stream and continue on path **(10.5)** Cross road and continue descent on footpath **(11.8)** Turn left[Follow fencing] **(12.4)** Continue on track and enter village of Massip[Signpost] **(12.6)** In the centre of **Massip** turn left up footpath. Climb[Road to the right] **(12.8)** Cross road and continue straight on footpath **(12.9)** Turn left onto road **(13.0)** Turn right onto track and continue straight **(13.6)** At end of road turn left[Cross] **(13.7)** Turn right on asphalt road and continue climb **(14.0)** Turn right on main road (D519) and continue straight towards village centre[Keep stone wall and houses to the left] **(14.3)** At place du village in **Golinhac** turn left[Keep church to the right. Pass war monument to the left] **(14.4)** Turn left, then take first right. Climb[Wrought iron cross on the left] **(14.6)** At road's end, turn right onto asphalt road and continue straight **(14.9)** Cross road and continue straight on trail passing between fields **(15.4)** Keep left and continue straight[Pass farm on the right] **(15.5)** Pass through hamlet of Le Poteau and cross D904 road. Continue straight on D42 road **(16.0)** Turn right onto track heading into pine forest and continue straight[Signpost] **(16.5)** Turn right on D42 road. Enter hamlet of Albusquiès[Farm to the right] **(16.6)** Turn left following road between stone houses. Descend[Stone cross and signpost] **(16.8)** At fork, keep to the right on trail **(17.7)** Turn left onto road[Pass public toilet] **(18.6)** At road's end, turn right and continue straight on road through hamlet of **Campagnac** **(20.1)** Continue on main road and pass through hamlet of Le Soulié[La Condamine to the left] **(21.6)** After Carboniés, turn right off road onto track[Signpost] **(22.0)** Turn right to rejoin road and continue descent into Espeyrac **(22.1)** Turn left onto footpath. Continue descent **(22.5)** Cross bridge and continue straight on track **(22.9)** Turn left towards centre of Espeyrac[Signpost] **(23.1)** Arrive at Espeyrac, turn left in front of the church for the village centre [Pass fountain on left]

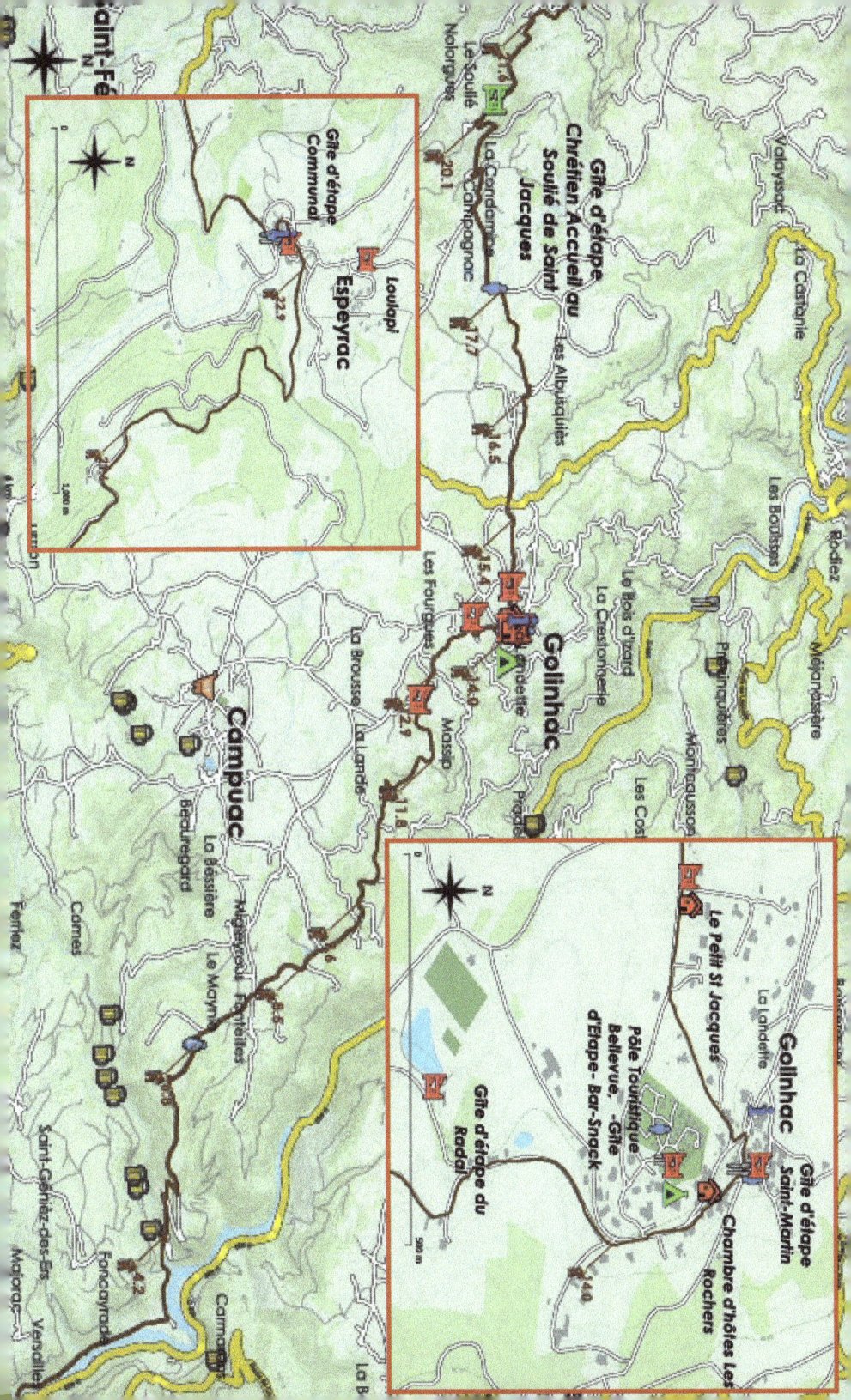

stage 9 — Estaing to Espayrac

Accommodation and Tourist Information

Espeyrac

Gîte d'étape Chrétien - Accueil au Soulié de Saint Jacques, Hameau le Soulié, 12140 Espeyrac, France; Tel:+33(0) 642 356 901; +33(0) 649 074 661; Email:donativolesoulie@gmail.com; tourisme-aveyron.com/fr/se-loger/hebergements-collectifs-en-aveyron; Price:D,D,D; *Created by former pilgrims that found faith on the Route. Run by volunteers. Simple accommodation 14 places in 2 dormitories and 2 double rooms. Accommodation for horses. Garden. Access to the Chapel of Saint Fleur.*

Gîte d'étape Communal, Le Bourg, 12140 Espeyrac, France; Tel:+33(0) 611 396 463; Email:gite.ecole@gmail.com; tourisme-aveyron.com/fr/se-loger/hebergements-collectifs-en-aveyron; Price:C,C,C; *14 places in 5 rooms. Simple hostel located in the village centre. Kitchen and Terrace. Space for donkeys.*

Loulapi, 365, route de Golinhac, 12140 Espeyrac, France; Tel:+33(0)749727351; Email:christine.deguine974@gmail.com; tourisme-aveyron.com/fr/se-loger/hebergements-collectifs-en-aveyron; Price:C,C,C; *Newly renovated barn 4places in one room equipped kitchen*

Mairie d'Espeyrac, Le Bourg, 12140 Espeyrac, France; Tel:+33(0)5 65 69 88 69; Email:mairie-espeyrac@wanadoo.fr; espeyrac-aveyron.com

Golinhac

Le Petit St Jacques [Christa Heitkamp], Les Hauts de Golinhac, 12140 Golinhac, France; Tel:+33(0)5 65 66 03 90 ; +33(0)6 37 10 24 57; Email:christa.heitkamp@orange.fr; petitsaintjacques.fr; Price:B,B,B|B,B,B; *15 places on 3 rooms English spoken*

Pôle Touristique Bellevue, Camping -Gîte d'Etape- Bar-Snack, Le Bourg, 12140 Golinhac, France; Tel:+33 (0) 565 445 073; +33(0) 689 554 632; Email:pole-bellevue12@orange.fr; pole-bellevue.fr; Price:C,-,-|C,-,-; *Holiday village with 2 gîtes d'étape chalets 31 camping pitches horses and donkeys welcome. Bar/snack bar and grocery shop*

Gîte d'étape du Radal, Le Radal, 12140 Golinhac, France; Tel:+33(0)689554632; +33(0)565445073; Email:pole-bellevue12@orange.fr; tourisme-aveyron.com/fr/se-loger/hebergements-collectifs-en-aveyron; Price:C,-,-; *Charming equestrian centre located 700 meters before the village centre offers accommodation for horses. 13 places in 1 dormitory and 1 room. Kitchen*

Gîte d'étape l'Orée du Chemin [Stephan Dissac], Massip, 12140 Golinhac, France; Tel:+33 (0)6 71 38 07 57; +33 (0)565 486 110; Email:stephan.dissac@wanadoo.fr; loreeduchemin.fr; Price:C,C,C; *In hamlet of Massip (before Golinhac) 20 places in 6 rooms in a restored barn. Run by the Dissac family a much appreciated stop on the route. English spoken. Accommodation for Horses. Kitchen.*

Gîte d'étape Saint-Martin, Le Bourg, 12140 Golinhac, France; Tel:+33(0) 633 846 433; Email:gite.golinhac@gmail.com; tourisme-aveyron.com/fr/se-loger/hebergements-collectifs-en-aveyron; Price:C,C,C; *15 places in 5 rooms in a restored presbytery meals made with local produce*

Chambre d'hôtes Les Rochers [Régine Bolis], Le Bourg, 12140 Golinhac, France; Tel:+33 565 481 885; +33 681 864 405; Email:lesrochersgolinhac12@gmail.com; hebergement-golinhac.com; Price:-,B,-; *4 places in 2 rooms in historic home in Golinhac village centre. Welcoming hosts. English spoken.*

Mairie de Golinhac, Le Bourg, 12140 Golinhac, France; Tel:+33(0)5 65 44 50 12; Email:golinhac@orange.fr; notremairiegolinhac.fr

Espayrac to Conques

stage 10

Conques Village © Alexandra Huddleston

Length:	12.4km
Ascent:	510m
Descent:	591m
Le-Puy:	195km
Roncevaux:	586km

Route–The route is well-marked and varies between paths, tracks and country roads that cross fields and forests with generally moderate climbs and descents. Nevertheless, use caution on the steep rocky descent into Conques, which can be slippery when wet. This stage is short in order to arrive early and have time to explore the historic village of Conques.

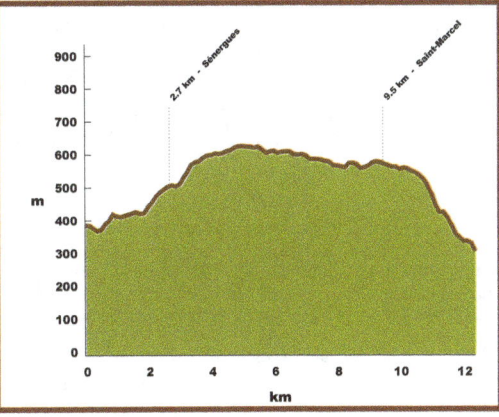

stage 10 — Espayrac to Conques

Cultural Discoveries

Conques church tympanum © Alexandra Huddleston

Conques

Conques (popl. 225, alt. 260m) is classified as one of the most beautiful villages in France and is on UNESCO's world heritage list. At the heart of the village is the abbey church of Sainte-Foy, which was once part of a monastery, though there are few remains. The church is dedicated to Saint Faith (*Sainte-Foy*), a 12 year old girl from Agen (about 220 km south-west) who was martyred by the Romans in 303 for refusing to sacrifice to pagan gods. In 866 her relics were brought to Conques.

The current church dates mostly from the 11th century, which was a time of significant prosperity for the Abbey. This prosperity stemmed in part from pilgrimage, as Saint Faith became famous for miracles, including curing blindness and releasing captives from their chains. Above the main entrance is a tympanum that dates from the mid-12th century and which depicts the Last Judgment. Christ sits in a mandorla (almond-shaped ring) with his hand raised in blessing. To his left are the damned with scenes from hell and to the right, the saved, including Saint Faith, with scenes from heaven. From 1987 to 1994, Pierre Soulages (1919-2022), a native of nearby Rodez and a major artist in the post-war abstract movement, designed the church's 100 plus modern stained-glass windows.

The **Treasury Museum** holds the abbey's *trésor*, or treasury, which includes several medieval reliquaries (containers used to hold holy objects (relics)) and the extraordinary Majesty of Saint Faith, or the Saint Faith reliquary, a gold and jewel-encrusted statue that symbolised the Saint's glory.

From April to October, each evening at 9 p.m. a priest from the abbey provides a commentary on the tympanum (in French). This is followed by an organ recital, including the opportunity to visit the church's upper ambulatory (recommended).

See Shaver-Crandell, A., Gerson, P. L., & Stones, A, pp. 179-181 (1995). The pilgrim's guide to Santiago de Compostela: A gazetteer. London: Harvey Miller Publishers.

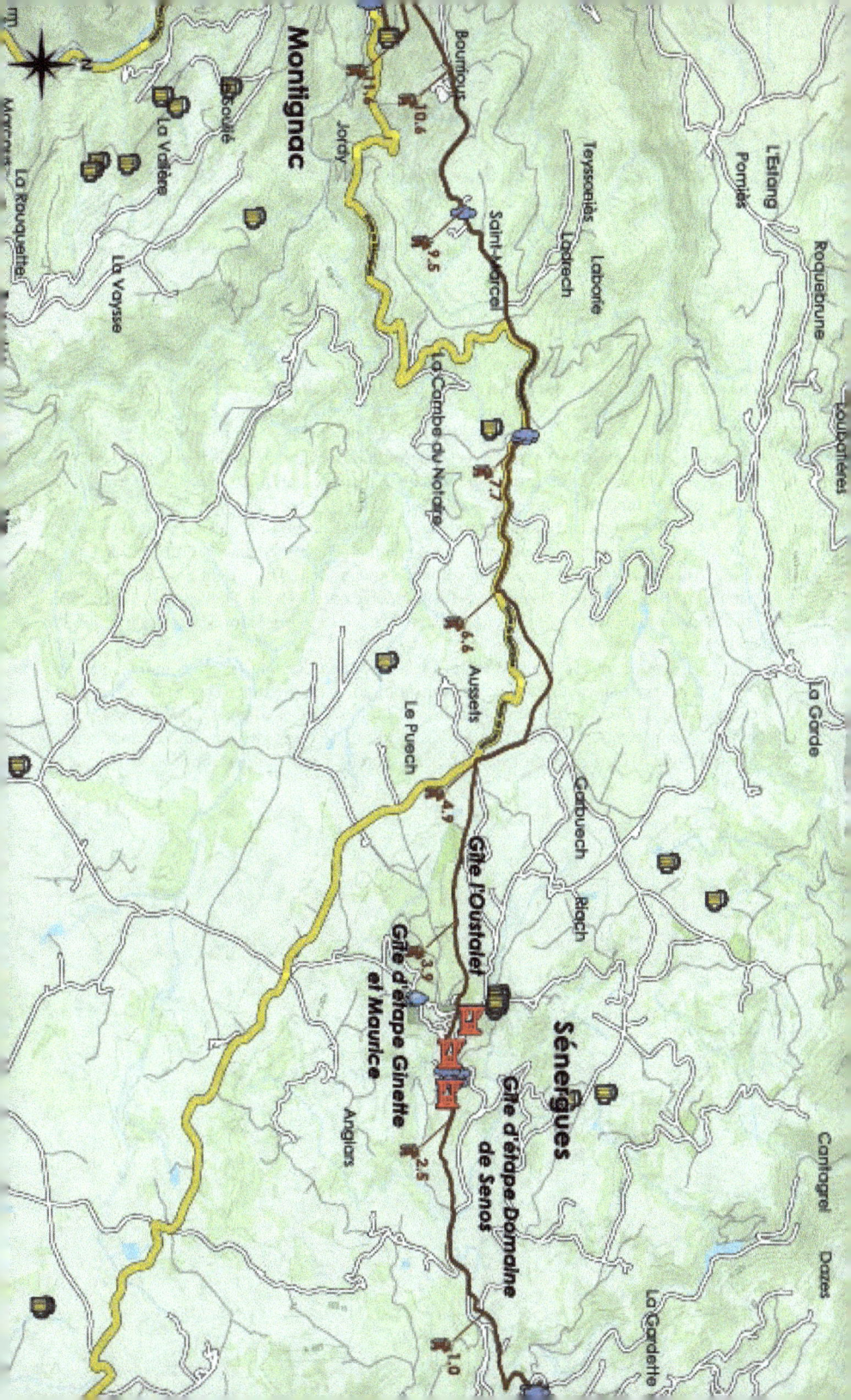

stage 10

Espayrac to Conques

GR®65

(0.0) From the church continue descent through village and take first right[Church to the left] **(0.2)** Cross the D42 road, continuing descent towards cemetery. Direction Sénergues[Pass Hôtel de la Vallée on left and cemetery on right] **(0.4)** Cross bridge over the stream (La Daze) and continue on the track **(0.7)** Keep left on road and continue straight[Farmhouse to the right] 🚶 **(1.0)** Turn left onto trail[Signpost] **(1.2)** Cross stream (Ruisseau du Tayrac) and continue straight. At the end of the track, turn right onto road (D42)[Stone house and Signpost Sénergues] **(1.8)** Cross stone bridge to enter Célis. Turn left followed by immediate right[Iron cross on left and signpost] 🚶 **(2.5)** Continue straight on trail to reach village of Sénergues[Pass cemetery on right and cross on left] **(2.7)** In **Sénergues** turn right and continue straight[Pass church on right]
(2.8) Turn left onto road (D42) to leave village[Cross] **(2.9)** Keep left at fork and continue straight on road (D242)[Keep cafe to the right] **(3.1)** Turn right off road (D242). Climb[After passing Q8 garage on left. Signpost] **(3.1)** Cross street and continue straight on footpath. Climb[Keep right of house] **(3.4)** Turn right off road onto footpath that crosses forest 🚶 **(3.9)** Continue straight on track[Forest to the left] **(4.3)** Keep left on track[Pass under power lines] **(4.9)** Turn left onto D42 road 🚶 **(4.9)** Turn right and continue straight. Direction Garbuech[Wooden cross and signpost] **(5.4)** Turn left onto track running between wooden/barbed wire fencing **(5.8)** Turn left[Signpost] 🚶 **(6.6)** Turn right onto D42 road and continue straight 🚶 **(7.7)** Turn right onto track running parallel to road D42[Road D42 to the left] **(8.6)** Merge onto D42 road and continue straight on road[Pass through hamlets of Vernhe and Saint-Marcel] 🚶 **(9.5)** In **Saint-Marcel** keep left[Toilet and watering point]
🚶 **(10.6)** In hamlet of La Croix Torte, turn left onto the track that descends into Conques 🚶 **(11.6)** At intersection, continue descent straight on footpath towards village of Conques **(11.9)** Cross road D42R and continue straight on rue Emilie Roudier to enter Conques[Pass police station (Gendarmerie Nationale) on left] **(12.2)** Keep left. Steep descent, direction church of Sainte-Foy **(12.3)** Turn right on rue Gonzagues Florens. Continue descent towards church of Sainte-Foy

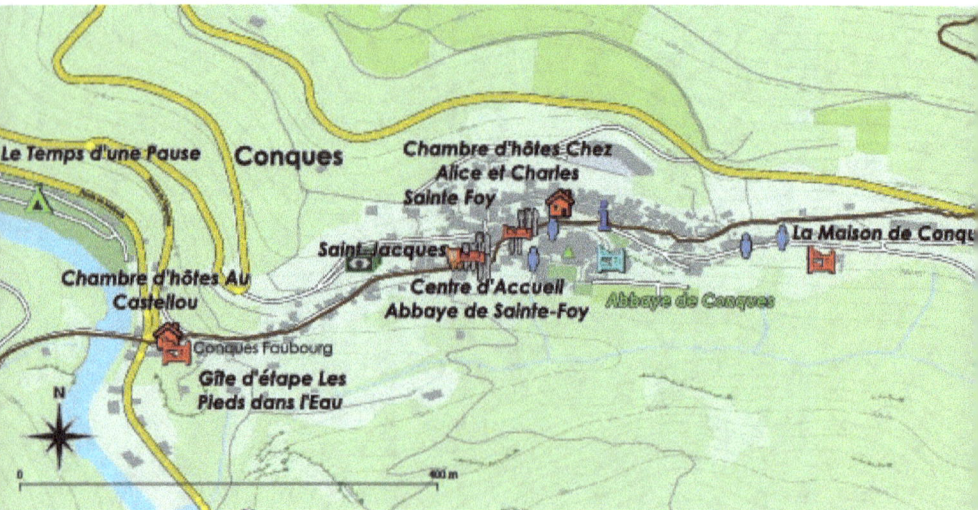

Espayrac to Conques — stage 10

Accommodation and Tourist Information

Conques-en-Rouergue

La Maison de Conques,16, rue Henri Parayre, 12320 Conques-en-Rouergue, France; Tel:+33(0)788940246; +33(0)565698618; Email:mfvconques@orange.fr; la-maison-de-conques.fr; Price:C,C,-; *Large holoiday home with 39 bedrooms for 2 to 5 people. Mainly designed for groups but welcomes pilgrims if the Saint Foy abbey is full.*

Gîte d'étape - Les Pieds dans l'Eau,77 route des Moulins, 12320 Conques-en-Rouergue, France; Tel:+33(0) 625 203 016; +33(0) 769 045 057; Email:giteconqueslespiedsdansleau@gmail.com; web.facebook.com/profile.php?id=100084551453086; Price:B,-,-; *6 places in 3 rooms*

Centre d'Accueil Abbaye de Sainte-Foy,Prieuré Sainte-Foy, 12320 Conques-en-Rouergue, France; Tel:+33(0) 565 698 943; Email:saintefoy@abbaye-conques.org; abbaye-conques.org; Price:C,-,-; *The traditional place that pilgrims stay on arriving in Conques. 96 places in 20 rooms or 4 dormitories in monastery complex. Accommodation for donkeys. English spoken. Recommended to take dinner elsewhere.*

Chambre d'hôtes Chez Alice et Charles[Alice and Charles Gaillac],Rue du Chanoine André Bénazech, 12320 Conques-en-Rouergue, France; Tel:+33(0)683183487; +33(0)787191759; Email:lecomptoirdegermain@gmail.com; tourisme-aveyron.com; Price:-,A,-; *Charming B&B in village centre with views on Abbey. 4 rooms.*

Chambre d'hôtes Au Castellou[Manu and Florence],33 rue Charlemagne, 12320 Conques-en-Rouergue, France; Tel:+33 (0)565 782 709; +33(0) 648 156 691; Email:castellou.conques@gmail.com; aucastellou.fr; Price:A,A,A; *At the exit from the village beside the river 5 bedrooms*

Hôtel Sainte Foy,Rue Gonzague Florens, 12320 Conques-en-Rouergue, France; Tel:+33 (0)5 65 69 84 03; Email:hotelsaintefoy@hotelsaintefoy.fr; hotelsaintefoy.fr; Price:A,A,A; *3 star hotel with terrace. Certain rooms have lovely views on the Abbey. English spoken.*

Auberge Saint-Jacques,8, rue Gonzague Florens, 12320 Conques-en-Rouergue, France; Tel:+33(0)5 65 72 86 36; Email:info@aubergestjacques.fr; aubergestjacques.fr; Price:A,A,A; *Hotel/restaurant located in the village centre. 13 basic rooms. English spoken. Restaurant serves traditional regional cuisine.*

Le Temps d'une Pause[Valérie and Michaël],3, route de Molinols, 12320 Conques-en-Rouergue, France; Tel:+33(0)5 65 69 82 23; +33(0)6 19 03 66 63; Email:camping.conques@gmail.com; le-temps-dune-pause.fr; Price:B,-,B; *Located in river valley after descending from village centre. Next to the GR*65 possibility to rent a modern mobile homes or pre-erected tent with half-board. Swimming pool. English spoken. Good restaurant on site.*

Office de Tourisme,Le Bourg, 12320 Conques-en-Rouergue, France; Tel:+33(0) 5 65 72 85 00; Email:contact@tourisme-conques.fr; tourisme-conques.fr

Sénergues

Gîte d'étape Ginette et Maurice,126 Route de Conques, 12320 Sénergues, France; Tel:+33(0) 5 65 72 84 47; +33(0) 682 162 239; Email:ginette.panissie@orange.fr; senergues.fr/annuaire/index.php?annuaire=&catannu=1&act1=0&act2=20&act3=0&nbreact=3; Price:-,B,-; *6 places in 3 rooms near exit from the village*

Gîte d'étape Domaine de Senos[Marie-Odile and Claude],Le Bourg, 12320 Sénergues, France; Tel:+33(0) 565 72 91 56; gites-aveyron.com; Price:C,C,C; *Hostel in a former convent hosts are welcoming. 33 places in 12 rooms. English spoken*

Gîte l'Oustalet[Fernand Costes],325 Route de Conques, 12320 Sénergues, France; Tel:+33(0) 5 65 69 83 96; +33(0) 679 690 275; Email:costes.fernand@orange.fr; tourisme-aveyron.com; Price:-,B,-; *6 places in 2 rooms 500m from village centre*

stage 11 — Conques to Livinhac-le-Haut

Length:	23.7km
Ascent:	1042m
Descent:	1130m
Le-Puy:	207km
Roncevaux:	574km

Conques Romanesque Bridge © Alexandra Huddleston

Route–The route is well-marked. The first part includes a long steep climb out of Conques through forests and fields, followed by a long descent into the post-industrial city of Decazeville. Thereafter, the route follows mostly asphalt roads to Livinhac-le-Haut.

Pointers–Be sure to keep to the GR®65 between Conques and Decazville. There are two moments of possible confusion: (1) after the Chapel of Saint Foy, the GR®6 and GR®65 have recently been interchanged for a stretch of a little over 11 km, the residents of Noailhac perhaps benefitting from the greater numbers that will follow the GR®65 and (2) where the GR®62B descends into Firmi, well before Decazeville, and which also uses the red and white way markings of the GR®.

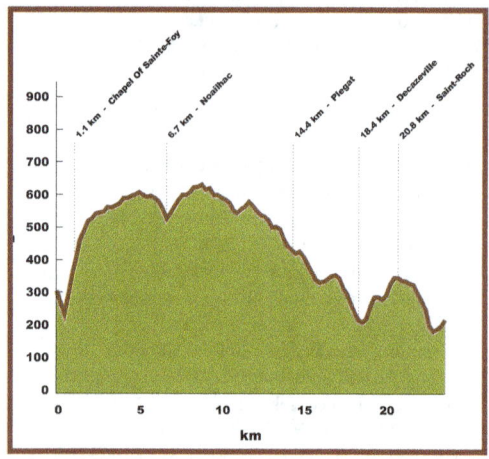

Cultural Discoveries

Romanesque Bridge
(Pont Romain)

The *Pont Romain* allowed pilgrims to Conques to cross the potentially dangerous Dourdou river. The 5 arched bridge made from red sandstone was originally medieval (14th century), though was largely rebuilt in the 16th-17th centuries.

Conques to Livinhac-le-Haut

stage 11

Decazeville

Decazeville (popl. 6000, alt. 163m) was founded in the 19th century by Duc Decazes as an industrial centre. By the mid-19th century, the city was one of the most important and productive coal and steel producers in the country. To accommodate a growing population, the **Church of Our Lady** (*Eglise Notre-Dame*) was completed in 1861. Notably, the church has 14 paintings of the Way of the Cross (1862-1863) by Gustave Moreau, an important 19th century French painter and an early leader of Symbolism (an artistic movement that used non-naturalistic or dream-like images). Moreau was particularly inspired by Italian Renaissance painting, biblical themes and mythology. His former villa and studio in Paris houses a museum dedicated to his works.

The city holds a market each Tuesday morning (Place Cabrol).

GR®65

(0.0) Arrive at Conques centre[Turn left to Place de l'Eglise] **(0.0)** From place de l'Eglise (church)/rue du Trésor turn left onto rue Charlemagne. Steep descent **(0.4)** Take staircase to the left and continue descent **(0.4)** Cross the D901 road and cross Romanesque bridge (pont Roman)[Pass Auberge du pont Romain on the right] **(0.6)** Take left onto footpath. Steep climb, switchbacking up hill[Signpost] **(0.8)** Cross road D232 and continue climb on footpath to Chapel of Sainte-Foy **(1.1)** Beside the **Chapel of Sainte-Foy**, continue climb on track which heads left
(2.4) The GR®65 formerly turned right at this point and took the more pleasant forested route. However the route has been retitled as the GR®6 while the former GR®6 has now been titled the GR®65 and continues ahead before rejoining the forest route beyond the village of Noailhac[Beware the signs may have still not been updated] **(2.7)** At the T-junction with the tarmac road, turn left **(4.0)** At the next T-junction turn left on the tarmac road[Towards the barn] **(6.1)** At the junction, turn left and follow the D580 as it turns right[Direction Noailhac] **(6.7)** At the crossroads in **Noailhac**, continue straight[Towards the restaurant]
(6.9) Fork right on the more minor road **(7.6)** At the T-junction beside chapelle Saint Roch, turn left[Follow D580] **(9.2)** At the crossroads continue straight on the D580[Direction Decazeville] **(10.4)** As the D580 bends to the right, turn left on the gravel track[Downhill] **(11.2)** Return to the D580 and turn left[Picnic area to your left] **(11.5)** Fork left on the track, GR®6 rejoins from the right **(13.0)** Cross street and follow path straight through fields[Signpost] **(13.2)** Merge right onto footpath. Continue straight through fields **(13.5)** Merge right onto track. Continue straight through fields **(13.7)** Merge left onto track[Greenhouse] **(13.8)** Turn left onto footpath[Farm to the right] **(13.9)** Turn left onto the road that descends towards Decazeville **(14.4)** Enter village of **Plegat** and keep right on main road[Signpost]
(14.8) At the farm keep left. Enter the hamlet of Le Fromental[Pass farm to the right] **(15.8)** Enter hamlet of La Combe and continue straight on road around sharp corner[Pass farm on right] **(16.2)** At fork keep right, direction Decazeville[Signpost] **(17.0)** Turn right on route de Viviole[Keep to right of wooden information sign] **(17.9)** Continue descent straight on route de Montarnal[Pass tourist information map on the left] **(18.3)** Turn left staying on route de Montarnal **(18.4)** Merge left onto the D580 road and take immediate right at fork onto D615 road towards the centre of **Decazeville**[Head away from church]
(18.7) Turn right at end of street onto avenue Laromiguière/D963. Take immediate left at picnic area onto route de Nantuech and continue straight[Rest area to the left] **(20.0)** Turn left onto chemin du Boutigou[Signpost] **(20.6)** Cross route du Puech and continue straight[Pass cemetery ahead to the left] **(20.8)** Keep left on route de **Saint-Roch**/D157[Pass church on the right]
(21.8) Turn right onto trail that leads towards forest and descends to the Lot River valley[Pass farmhouse on left] **(22.8)** Cross the D21 road and the Pont de Livinhac bridge over the Lot River[Signpost] **(23.1)** Turn left onto rue Camille Couderc towards centre of Livinhac-le-Haut[Stay left of wooden tourist information sign] **(23.4)** Cross avenue Paul Ramadier and continue straight on rue de la République. Towards village centre **(23.6)** Arrive at Livinhac-le-Haut[Place de l'Eglise]

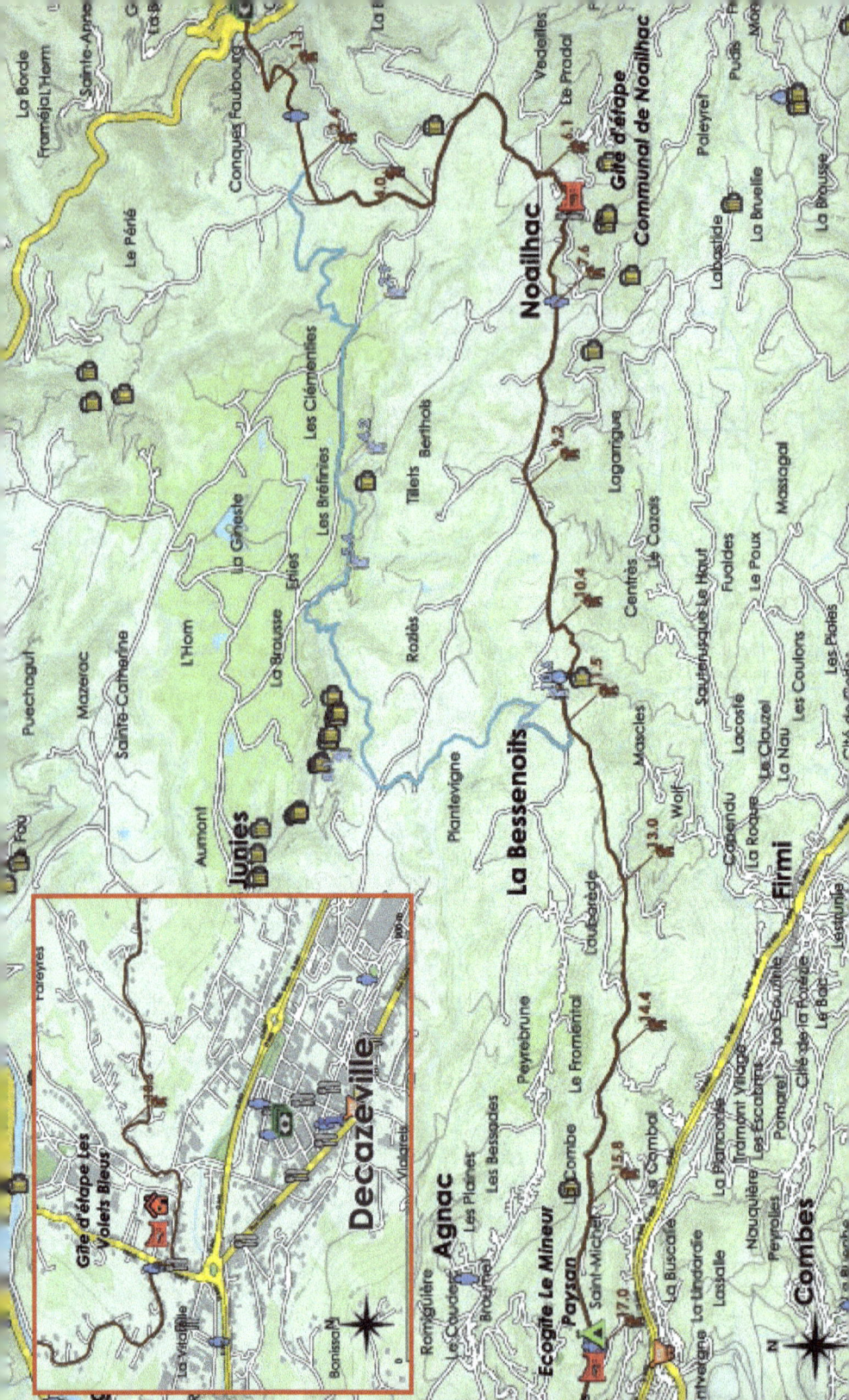

Conques to Livinhac-le-Haut   stage 11

GR®6

Route– the GR®6 alternative provides rather more shade following forested pathways and is of similar length to the revised GR®65 route through Noailhac. Beware of residual GR®65 signposts that may confuse.

Length:	11.5km
Ascent:	685m
Descent:	659m

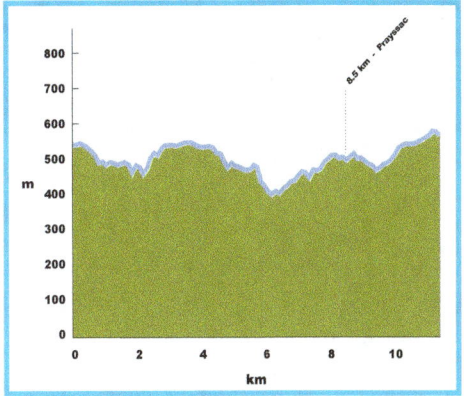

(0.0) Follow the track to the north **(0.3)** Cross road and continue straight, descending [Signpost] **(2.9)** Turn right onto road D606 **(3.2)** Turn left. Direction Les Clémenties [Signpost] **(4.2)** After passing through hamlet of Les Clémenties, turn left onto trail and pass through hamlet of Les Bréfinies [Signpost] **(5.4)** Turn left and pass through hamlet of Eyniès [Village] **(5.5)** After watering point turn left onto footpath [Watering point] **(8.1)** Cross road D183 and continue straight to village of Prayssac [Cross] **(8.5)** Cross the village of **Prayssac** and continue straight on road **(10.6)** Enter village of Roumégous and turn left [Signpost. Farm to the right] **(10.7)** Continue straight on road through village centre **(11.2)** Turn left onto D580 road [Signpost] **(11.5)** Turn right onto the track and continue straight rejoining the GR®65 [Signpost]

Accommodation and Tourist Information

Conques-en-Rouergue
Gîte d'étape Communal de Noailhac, lieu-dit Noailhac, 12320 Conques-en-Rouergue, France; Tel: +33(0)565729125; +33(0)612753009; Email: gaillacaurelien@aol.com; tourisme-aveyron.com; Price: C,-,-; *18 places in 3 rooms restaurant close by*

Decazeville
Gîte d'étape de Saint-Roch - Le Chemin, 465, route de Saint Roch, 12300 Decazeville, France; Tel: +33(0)695 306 513; Email: gitelechemin@gmail.com; web.facebook.com/profile.php?id=100049820744452; Price: C,-,C; *Located beside the church. 10 places in 3 dormitories. English spoken. Very welcoming. Horses possible.*

Gîte d'étape Les Volets Bleus [Sébastien and Jeffrey], 3, rue Camille Douls, 12300 Decazeville, France; Tel: +33(0)6 49 89 97 16; Email: voletsbleus12@gmail.com; chemindecompostelle.com; Price: C,-,-|-,-,A; *In the centre of the town close to all facilities 19 places in 3 dormitories and 3 private rooms communal dining. No dogs*

Ecogîte Le Mineur Paysan [Christian Lacombe], 765 Route de Viviole, 12300 Decazeville, France; Tel: +33(0) 623 202 997; +33(0) 565 433 344; Email: lemineurpaysan@laposte.net; lemineurpaysan.fr; Price: C,C,-|B,-,-; *14 places in 1 dormitory and 3 rooms. An eco-friendly hostel that is welcoming comfortable and well equipped. Serves organic foods (including take-away). Horses and donkeys welcome*

Office de Tourisme, Square Jean Ségalat, 12300 Decazeville, France; Tel: + 33 (0)5 65 43 18 36; Email: tourisme@decazeville-communaute.fr; tourisme-paysdecazevillois.fr

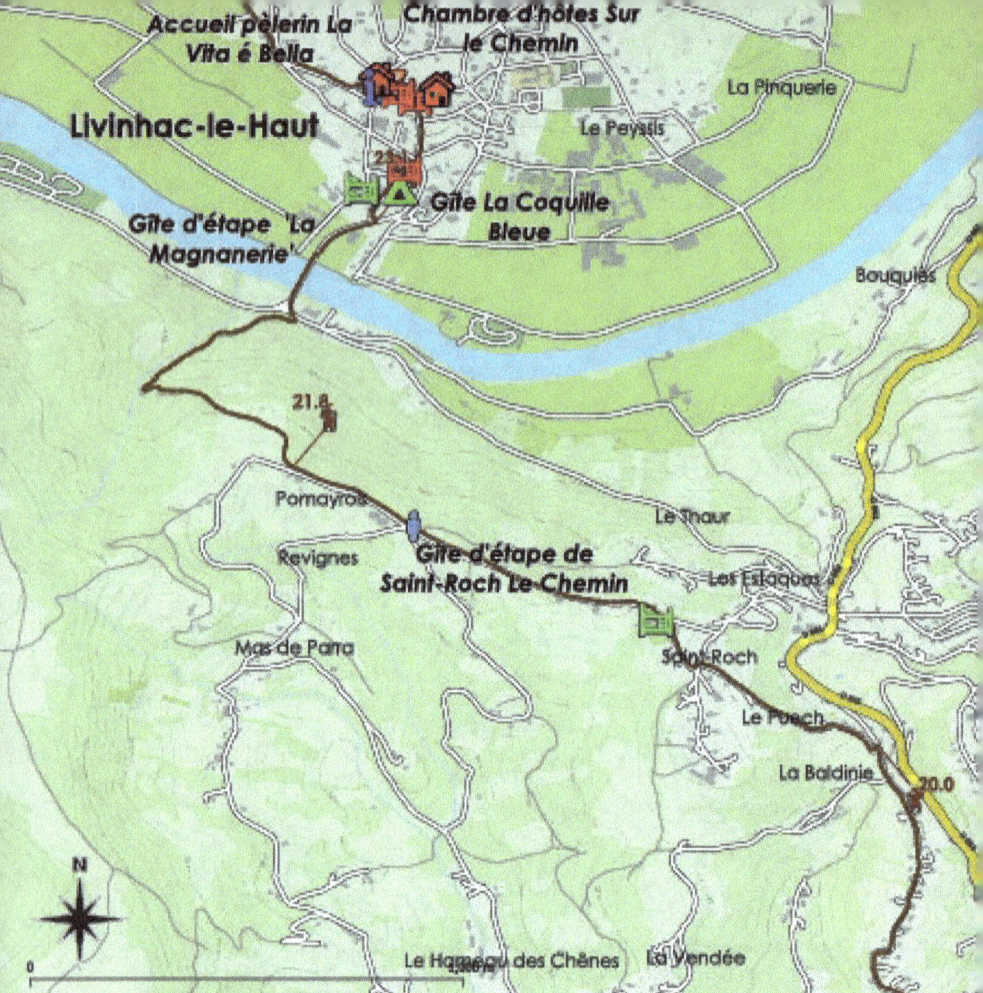

Livinhac-le-Haut

Gîte d'étape 'La Magnanerie'[Camille],170, rue du Faubourg, 12300 Livinhac-le-Haut, France; Tel:+33(0) 6 37 00 47 85; Email:Magnanerie.gite@gmail.com; gite-livinhac.com; Price:C,-,B|C,-,-; *15 places in cozy rooms and dormitory, on a charming historic property Vegetarian meals. English spoken. Animal friendly with accommodation for horses.*

Accueil pèlerin La Vita é Bella[Andrea and Jani],90, place 14 Juin, 12300 Livinhac-le-Haut, France; Tel:+33(0) 6 77 55 78 33; Email:maisonrigolo@yahoo.com; doremifamiredo.com; Price:C,-,-|B,-,-; *A bio-gîte with 16 places in 6 rooms snack bar attached*

Gîte à Chacun son Chemin[Elodie and Jean Marie],30, Impasse Panassié, 12300 Livinhac-le-Haut, France; Tel:+33(0)6 32 49 68 85; +33(0) 06 46 89 36 41; Email:elodiecarney2@gmail.co; gite-achacunsonchemin.com; Price:C,C,C; *!4 places in 5 rooms with a terrace and garden*

Gîte La Coquille Bleue[Claire],25, rue Camille Couderc, 12300 Livinhac-le-Haut, France; Tel:+33(0) 6 51 01 02 88; Email:lacoquillebleue@gmail.com; lacoquille-bleue.wordpress.com; Price:C,C,-; *14 places in 2 dormitories and 1 private room. The building includes a small art gallery.*

Chambre d'hôtes Sur le Chemin[Stéphan Gleyal],5, place du 14 Juin, 12300 Livinhac-le-Haut, France; Tel:+33(0) 616 985 477; Email:surlechemin@orange.fr; surlechemin.net; Price:-,C,-; *4 rooms recently renovated. Basic English. Free accommodation for horses with reservations. Kitchen. Accommodation for horses and donkeys possible.*

Mairie de Livinhac-Le-Haut,Place du Quatorze Juin, 12300 Livinhac-le-Haut, France; Tel:+33(0) 5 65 63 33 84; livinhac-le-haut.fr

QUERCY

Quercy gariotte © Alexandra Huddleston

Quercy, which extends from Figeac to Moissac, was the ancient home of the *Cadourques* or *Cadurci*, a Celtic people that inhabited the region before the Roman invasions of the first century. Quercy was subsequently occupied by the Visigoths (5th century) and Franks (6th century). It fell largely under English control from the 14th century until the end of the Hundred Years' War (1433) and was also a battleground in the 16th century Wars of Religion, which pitted French Roman Catholics against Huguenots (French Protestants).

Quercy is made up of a dry limestone plateau, called the *Causses,* which is covered with small oak trees. *Pigeonniers* (dovecotes or pigeon lofts) that were built in the 18th-19th centuries also dot the landscape. At the time, pigeons were raised for their droppings, or *guano*, an important fertilizer that was later replaced by chemical fertilizers. The region is also marked by *cayrous* (stone walls) and *caselles* or *gariottes*, small circular stone huts built by shepherds. Sheep farming remains an important business, and the region boasts its own race of sheep which is white with black ears and rims around the eyes.

The traditional capital of Quercy is Cahors. The region is famous for its cuisine, notably duck dishes, black truffles, and the red wines of Cahors. The Occitan language continues to be spoken by a dwindling minority (mostly the elderly).

stage 12 — Livinhac-le-Haut to Figeac

Figeac centre

Length:	23.6km
Ascent:	702m
Descent:	720m
Le-Puy:	231km
Roncevaux:	550km

Route–The route is well-marked, and consists mostly of tracks and asphalt roads through farmland, forests and villages. Proximity to the Lot and Célé Rivers makes this area agriculturally rich.

Pointers–**Culture:** The 18km section of the GR®65 from Montredon to Figeac is on UNESCO world heritage list.

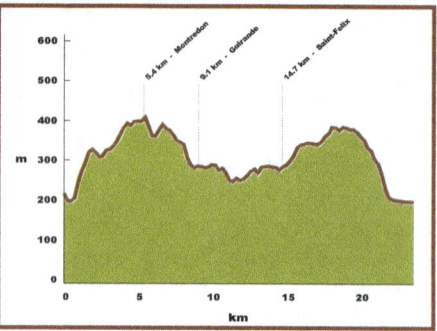

Advance planning: Ensure sufficient provisions in Livinhac-le-Haut, as there are no grocers until Figeac, and limited opportunities for meals in between.

Market: There is a lively and colourful market in Figeac on Saturday mornings, selling local produce and goods.

Cultural Discoveries

Chapel of Mary Magdalene
(*Chapelle Sainte-Marie-Madeleine*)

Built in the 12th-13th century, the chapel is remarkable for the late 15th century frescoes that decorate its vaults. These depict the tetramorph (animal representations of the four evangelists–Matthew, Mark, Luke and John), as well as a scene from the Martyrdom of Saint Namphaise (a 9th century hermit from Quercy) and Mary Magdalene.

Note, as well, the late 12th century masks that decorate the base of the arches.

Livinhac-le-Haut to Figeac

stage 12

Figeac

The vibrant city of Figeac (popl. 9,775, alt. 200m) was founded in 830 and developed around the Benedictine **Abbey of Saint Saviour** (*Abbaye Saint-Sauveur*), built in the 11th century.

Positioned on the Célé river, Figeac became a dynamic trading and religious centre. The houses and market places that make up the old town are remarkable testaments of medieval architecture.

The Hundred Years' War, however, brought an end to Figeac's prosperity. The city later became a Huguenot (French Protestant) stronghold in the Wars of Religion, when its Catholic churches were destroyed. Figeac is also famous for Jean-François Champollion (1790-1832), the historian and linguist who founded Egyptology (the study of Egyptian antiquities) and who played a major role in deciphering the Rosetta Stone and Egyptian hieroglyphs. Both Egyptology and the history of world writing are on display at the **Champollion Museum.**

The city hosts a colourful market each Saturday morning.

GR®65

(0.0) From Place de l'Eglise take rue du Couderc to leave village[Pass town hall (Mairie) and pharmacy on the left]**(0.3)**Cross avenue de Paul Ramadier/D21 and keep right on road D627[Signpost]**(0.6)**Turn right onto the small road that climbs to Pérols[Cross on the left] **(1.1)**Cross road and continue straight on Puech del Soyt in the direction of Le Thabor[Pass Gîte de Pérols on the left]**(1.9)**Turn right onto track and continue straight[Leave behind houses of Le Thabor] **(3.1)**Shortly before reaching the D21, fork left on the tree lined path**(3.4)**At the crossroads in the tracks, continue straight**(3.6)**Continue straight on trail as it passes through Feydel-Haut and Cagnac before reaching Montredon[Signpost] **(5.1)**Merge left onto the D2 road and enter the village of Montredon**(5.2)**Turn right and head towards the village centre, in the direction of the church (visible)[Chapel of Notre-Dame de Pitié behind]**(5.4)**Turn left in **Montredon** centre[Pass church on the left]**(5.7)**At road's end turn right and continue straight direction Lalaubie[Signpost]
(6.0) Continue straight through farms of Lalaubie **(6.4)**Turn left towards Tournié and pass through village[Signpost]**(7.1)**Continue straight on track[After last farm on the left] **(7.8)**Keep left into farm of Lacoste[Signpost]**(8.1)**At fork keep right**(8.4)**Turn left onto the road, followed by an immediate left leading to the Chapel of Guirande[Signpost]**(8.7)**Turn right at the Chapel of Guirande[Chapel] **(8.8)**Turn right and climb to village of Guirande[After stone house on right. Signpost]**(9.1)**After last houses in village of **Guirande**, turn right[Path lined with oaks]
(9.6) Turn left, then take the first right[Pass barn to the right] **(10.5)**At the end of the track turn left,[towards the hamlet of Terly]**(10.8)**At the crossroads in Terly, go straight and descend towards reservoir le Lac de Guironde[Metal calvaire on your left]**(10.9)**Turn right onto road D41 and continue straight towards hamlet of Terly[Signpost]**(11.3)**Cross reservoir (Ruisseau de Guiande) and continue straight past the farm of Gévaudan (on the right)[Signpost] **(12.0)**At the junction continue straight on chemin des Levades [Towards the hamlet of les Cordiers]**(12.8)**In Les Cordiers immediately after passing the grassed area on your lrfty, turn left on the gravel track[Towards the farm buildings]**(12.9)**Continue straight on Impasse de la Fontaine[Pass stone barn on your left] **(13.1)**At the T-junction, turn right[Woods to your right]**(13.7)**Cross the D2 road and continue straight on footpath **(14.5)**Turn right onto road towards village of Saint-Felix[Signpost. Pass church and picnic area on right]
(14.7) In the centre of **Saint-Felix** turn left onto street[After passing church on right]
(15.0) Turn right onto asphalt road and continue straight towards the farm Croix de Jordy**(15.1)**At crossroads turn left and then quickly right onto footpath, which leads north-west to the D206[Wooden barrier at entrance to footpath] **(16.0)**Turn left onto road D206 and then right onto footpath**(16.3)**Cross D2 and continue straight on road in the direction of the church of Saint-Jean-Mirabel[Signpost and iron cross to the right]**(16.5)**Turn left before the fork and entrance to the village (on the right). Continue straight to rejoin the D2 road[Picnic area to the left] **(17.5)**Continue straight on D2

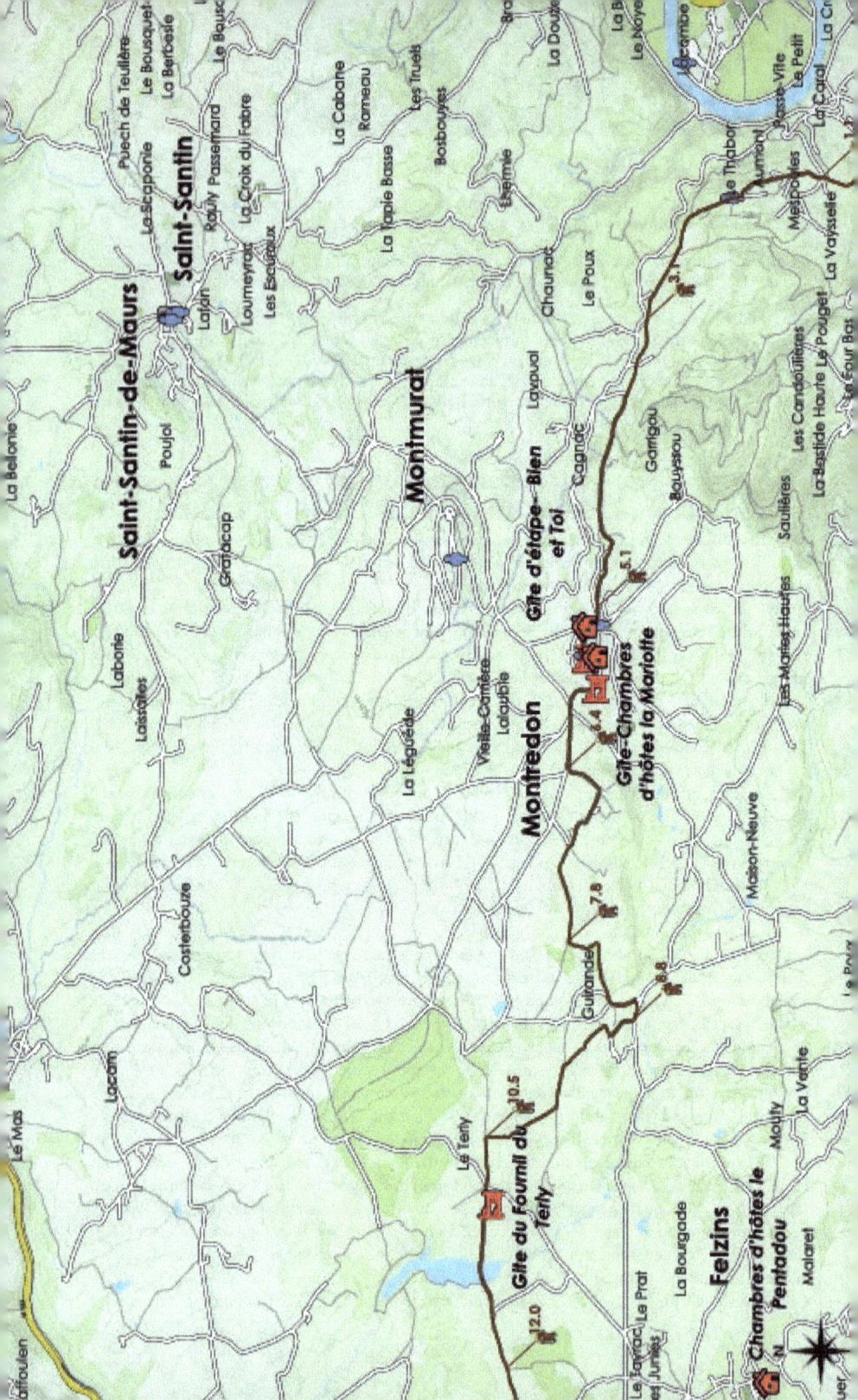

Livinhac-le-Haut to Figeac — stage 12

road[Pass stone cross on left]**(18.2)** Turn left onto narrow footpath[Immediately after stone garage on left]**(18.4)** Turn left onto road and take first right and pass through hamlet of l'Hôpital **(18.6)** Turn right onto footpath**(19.3)** Turn right onto road then turn left onto footpath (after passing cross on the left)[Pass cross on the left] **(21.2)** Continue straight on road (Roussilhe) to descend into Figeac**(21.8)** Turn left onto Le Terrie[Railway tracks to the right]**(21.9)** Pass through underpass and keep left on Le Terrie Road, which becomes Allée Victor Hugo[Le Célé River to the right] **(23.1)** Turn right onto small road - rue du Griffoul - that runs along river**(23.3)** Turn right over bridge and cross Le Célé River to enter Figeac city centre**(23.4)** Turn left onto Quai Albert Bessières**(23.6)** Arrive at Figeac city centre

Accommodation and Tourist Information

Felzins

Gîte du Fournil du Terly[Claire and Lucie],117 route du Lac - Lieu-dit le Terly, 46270 Felzins, France; Tel:+33(0) 607 748 896; Email:fournilduterly@mailo.com; web.facebook.com/lefournilduTerly; Price:C,C,C; *12 places in shared accommodation lake view from terrace*

Chambres d'hôtes le Pentadou[Nanou and Laurent Fillot],340, rue du Tour de Ronde, 46270 Felzins, France; Tel:+33(0) 5 65 40 48 12; +33(0) 7 72 06 76 48; Email:info@lepentadou.com; lepentadou.com; Price:-,A,A; *22 places 2 km from the GR*65. Located in farmhouse with pool*

Figeac

Gîte Passiflore,10, chemin du moulin de Laporte, 46100 Figeac, France; Tel:+33(0)565405693; +33(0)787466674; gitepassiflore.wordpress.com; Price:C,C,C|-,-,-; *4 places in dormitory and 1 studio. English spoken.*

Le Club Figeacois du Poney et du Cheval,Avenue de Nayrac, 46100 Figeac, France; Tel:+33(0)5 65 34 70 57; +33(0)6 46 48 47 64; Email:centre.equestre.figeac@gmail.com; cfpc.ffe.com; Price:C,-,-|-,-,-; *Accommodation for horses. Possibility to camp on grounds access to showers.*

Gîte Antoine Le Pelerin[Antoine],94, chemin de Roussilhe, 46100 Figeac, France; Tel:+33(0)670658391; Email:nativel.claudine46@gmail.com ; antoinelepelerin.fr; Price:-,-,B; *14 places in 3 rooms in a lovely home in typical Quercy style. The hosts who are both former pilgrims are famous for their hospitality. Organic food is used with vegetables from the garden.*

Gîte et chambre d'hôtes le Soleilho[Martine Garsi and Jean-Louis Royer],8, rue Prat, 46100 Figeac, France; Tel:+33(0)5 65 38 42 62; +33(0)6 75 89 96 53; +33(0)6 87 99 88 33; chambres-hotes-figeac.com; Price:C,C,C|-,-,-; *6 places in hostel and 4 bedrooms in B&B. A top-ranked hostel and B&B in Figeac with generous and welcoming hosts. Located in the old town with fully equipped kitchen. English spoken.*

Gîte et chambre d'hôtes le Chemin des Anges[Luc],30, Allée Victor Hugo, 46100 Figeac, France; Tel:+33(0)7 49 61 96 01; Email:gite.chemindesanges@gmail.com; chemindesanges.fr; Price:-,C,B|-,B,A; *Located close to historic centre run by former pilgrims welcoming with garden. 7 places in shared accommodation and 2 private rooms*

Gîte d'étape du Gua[Frédérique Latrace],14 bis, avenue du Maréchal Joffre, 46100 Figeac, France; Tel:+33(0)6 74 73 22 69; Email:gitedugua.figeac@gmail.com; figeac-gite-compostelle.fr; Price:C,C,C; *15 places in 6-pers. dormitories in old renovated house with garden and kitchen. English spoken.*

Gîte du Carmel,9, avenue Jean Jaurès, 46100 Figeac, France; Tel:+33(0) 614 320 551; Email:carmel.figeac@gmail.com; paroissede-figeac.fr/Le-Carmel-de-Figeac; Price:D,-,-; *8 places in 2 dormitories. Simple accommodations in Carmelite convent in city centre. Run by volunteers. Possibility to participate in religious ceremonies. English spoken.*

Hotel Le Quatorze,14, Place de l'Estang, 46100 Figeac, France; Tel:+33(0) 5 65 14 08 92; Email:infos@le-quatorze.fr; le-quatorze.fr; Price:A,A,-; *3 star hotel considered one of the nicest hotels in Figeac 14 stylish rooms. English spoken.*

Office de Tourisme,Place Vival, 46100 Figeac, France; Tel:+33(0) 5 65 34 06 25; Email:info@tourisme-figeac.com; tourisme-figeac.com

Lunan

Le Relais de la Bourrache - Gîte et relais Chemin Saint-Jacques de Compostelle [Alain],Lieu-dit Seyrignac, 46100 Lunan, France; Tel:+33(0)676741607; Email:delabourrache.lerelais2@orange.fr; gite-etape-figeac.fr; Price:C,C,C; *10 places in 2 rooms. 16th century property offering pilgrim accommodation for a number of years. Grocery store.*

Montredon

Gîte d'étape-Chambre d'Hôtes - Bien et Toi[Hélène and Frank],Place de l'Église, 46270 Montredon, France; Tel:+33(0) 6 09 48 56 93; +33(0)6 20 29 53 94; Email:bienettoit46@gmail.com; bien-et-toit.fr; Price:-,-,B|-,B,-; *2 dormitories each with 3 places 2 private rooms and a double bedded "cistern"*

Gîte-Chambres d'hôtes - la Mariotte[Sabrina and Damien],359, route de Lalaubie, 46270 Montredon, France; Tel:+33(0)7 68 53 96 46; +33(0)9 51 47 34 10; Email:contact@gitelamariotte.com; gitelamariotte.com; Price:-,-,B|-,B,B; *11 places in rooms of 2 to 5 places and a yourt with 4 places preferential rates for pilgrims*

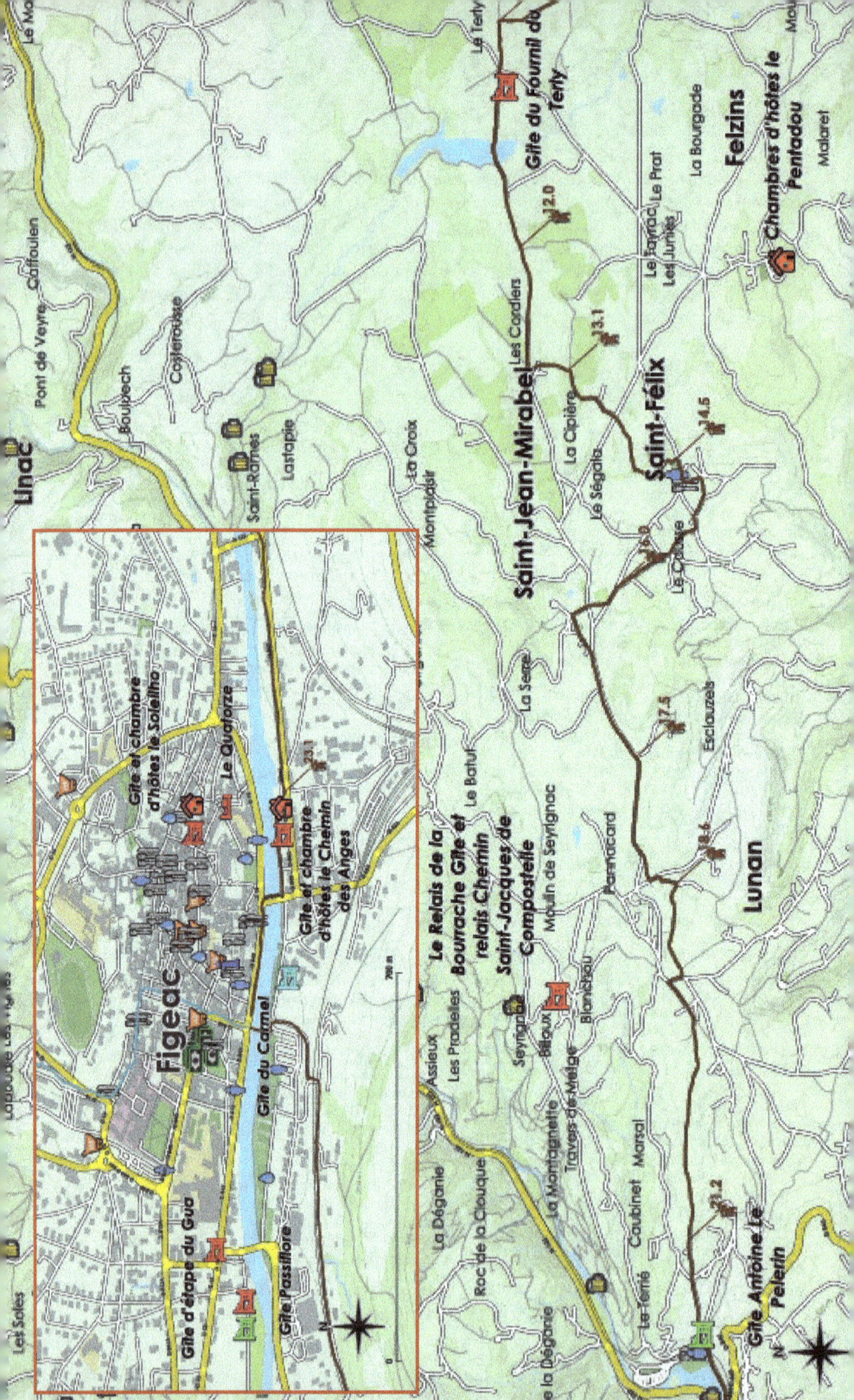

Figeac to Gréalou

stage 13

Faycelles

Length:	20.2km
Ascent:	748m
Descent:	563m
Le-Puy:	255km
Roncevaux:	527km

Route–The route is well-marked and consists mostly of asphalt roads through pastures, as one enters the sparsely populated Causses region, which is composed of several dry limestone plateaus that form part of the Massif Central. There is a long climb on small country roads out of Figeac to Mas de la Croix, followed by paths through dry oak forests towards Gréalou.

Pointers–**Culture:** The 22.5 km section of the GR°65 from Faycelles to Cajarc is on the UNESCO world heritage list. Caution: Pay attention to stay on the GR°65, particularly in Figeac, where there is an intersection with the GR°6/GR°6A, as well as in Mas de la Croix, where the variant through the Célé Valley, the GR°651, forks to the right. These GR° also use the same red and white way markings as the GR°65

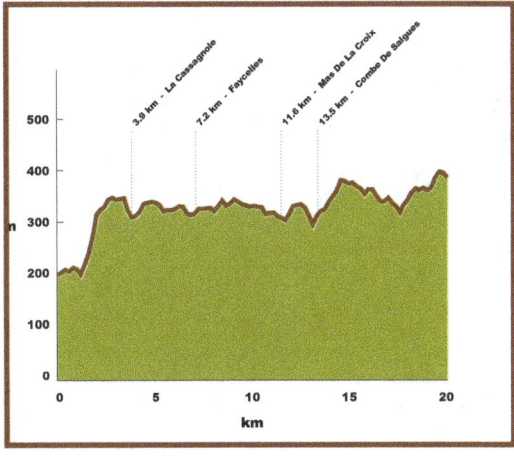

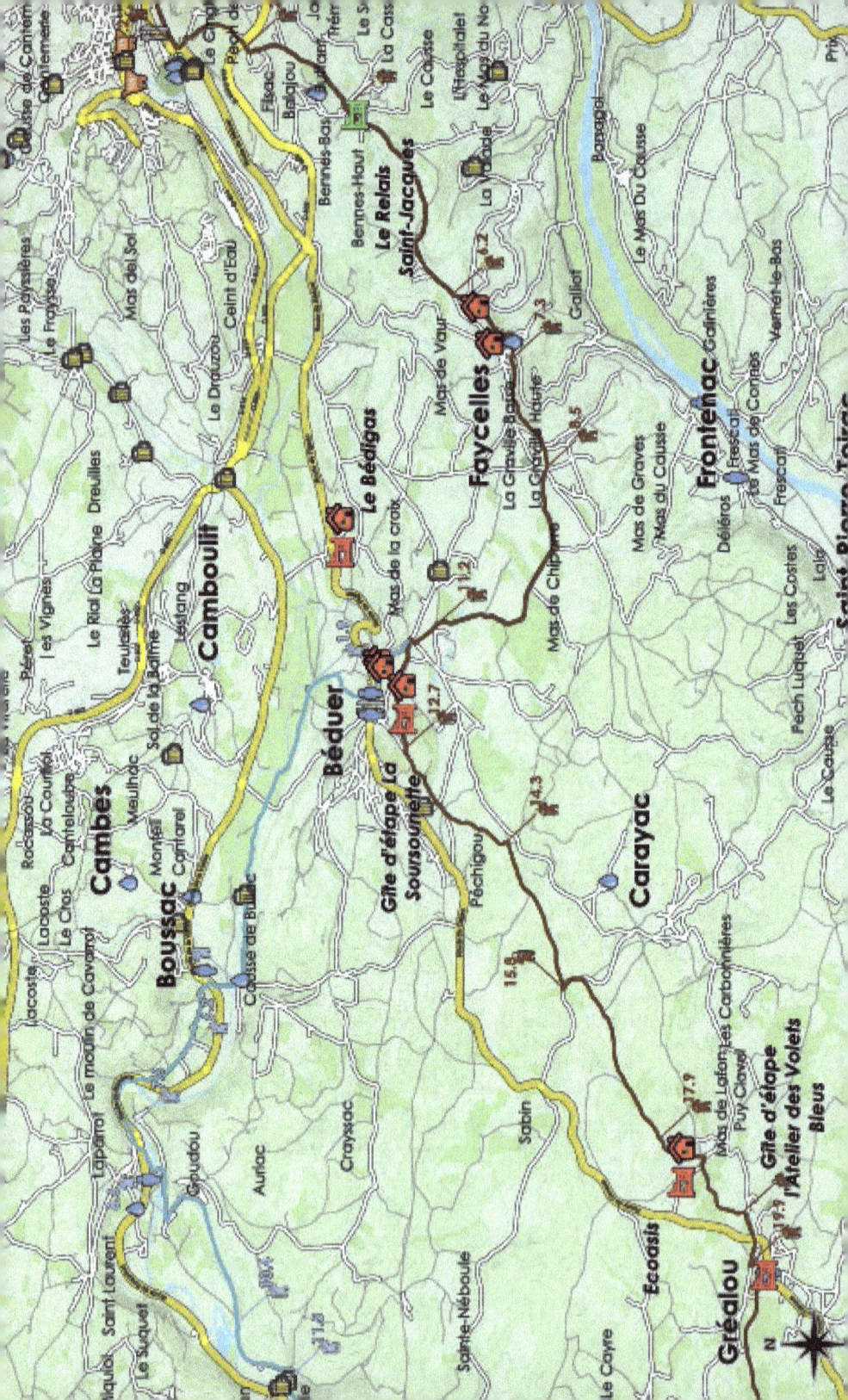

Figeac to Gréalou

stage 13

Cultural Discoveries

Faycelles

The picturesque village of Faycelles (popl. 640, alt. 170m), with its beautiful valley views, developed around a feudal castle in the Middle Ages, though excavations suggest prior Neolithic and Roman occupation nearby. During the Hundred Years' War the village was captured by the English, and in the 15th century the castle became a summer residence of the Abbot of Figeac. In an effort to centralize power, the castle was demolished under the reign of King Louis XIII (1610-1643), and a church was later built in its place (1886-1888).

Gréalou

At the centre of the tiny village of Gréalou (popl. 270, alt. 200m) is the 12th century Romanesque church of Our Lady of Assumption (*Notre-Dame-de-l'Assomption*), which was largely rebuilt in subsequent centuries, including important additions in the 15th century after the Hundred Years' War. The church has a lovely wooden sculpted pieta from the first half of the 16th century.

GR®65

(0.0) At intersection of boulevard Georges Juskiewenski and Le Célé River turn left over footbridge to cross river. The alternative route to Rocamadour - the GR®6 - also departs from this intersection, but instead heads north on the boulevard away from the river **(0.0)** After crossing foot bridge turn left into parking lot and immediately right on avenue Jean-Jaurés [Follow wall on the left] **(0.2)** At fork stay left on high road **(0.3)** Turn left though underpass and then right onto Le Cinglé Bas. Continue straight along tracks [Train tracks should be to the right] **(1.2)** Turn left onto avenue Président Georges Pompidou, then take first left [Pass through underpass] **(1.4)** Turn right onto road, direction Bois de Palhasse. Steep climb [Signpost] **(1.7)** Turn left onto footpath and continue steep climb through forest **(2.2)** Turn right onto the road and cross highway D802. Continue straight **(2.3)** Enter Balajou and continue straight on road, which continues to climb south [Signpost] **(2.8)** At road's end, turn right direction La Cassagnole [Signpost] **(3.8)** Cross road and continue straight in the direction of La Cassagnole [Signpost] **(3.9)** At **La Cassagnole** keep right at the fork and climb. Continue straight on road [Signpost]
(6.2) Keep left and fork. Direction Faycelles **(6.6)** Merge right onto road and continue straight towards Faycelles **(6.8)** Cross the D662 road and and continue straight on Voie Romaine [Beautiful valley views on the left] **(7.1)** Turn right and climb staircase on rue de la Forge **(7.1)** Continue straight on road through village [Pass church on left] **(7.2)** In **Faycelles** enter place Gallarde, pass church and turn left before cross. Then take immediate right [Church, cross and signpost]
(7.3) Take the left fork [enter the woods] **(8.1)** Turn right [follow part made farm road] **(8.3)** At the T-junction with the tarmac road, turn right then immediately left and right [pass stone garden wall on your right] **(8.5)** At the end of the track, continue straight to join the tarmac road - chemin de Cambonis [pass metal cross] **(9.3)** At the end of the road, turn right **(11.2)** As the road bends to the left bear right onto the footpath [Direction Gréalou] **(11.5)** Turn right onto road and cross stone bridge. At end of road turn left onto D21 to arrive in Mas-de-la-Croix [Signpost] **(11.6)** At **Mas de la Croix** intersection, turn left on GR®65. Direction Cajarc. The alternative route through the Célé Valley - GR®651 - continues straight on road D21 towards Béduer [Signpost]
(12.1) Leave the road and turn left onto the track [Before a bend in the road] **(12.7)** Turn onto track to the left and continue straight [Ahead pass fountain to the right] **(13.3)** Turn left onto the road. Then take first right. Direction Mas de Surgues [Signpost] **(13.5)** At fork keep left, Direction Cajarc, and pass through hamlet of **Combe de Salgues** [Signpost]
(14.3) At fork turn right and continue straight [Trail follows stone wall] **(15.8)** Turn left onto the D38 road **(16.1)** Turn right onto track and continue straight [Signpost] **(17.9)** At fork keep right on trail. Climb towards hamlet of Le Puy Clavel **(18.5)** Turn right onto the road in the hamlet of le Puy Clavel [Signpost] **(18.6)** Turn left onto track. Direction Gréalou [Signpost] **(19.4)** Turn right onto the road and continue straight and cross the D19 road **(19.9)** Turn left and then right to descend to village centre **(20.0)** Arrive at Gréalou centre [Church]

stage 13 — Figeac to Gréalou

Accommodation and Tourist Information

Béduer

Le Bédigas [Nadia Naegelen and Philippe Sandré],99, Impasse du Bédigas Haut, 46100 Béduer, France; Tel:+33(0)9 50 12 33 57; +33(0)6 74 46 17 17; Email:gite.bedigas@gmail.com; lebedigas.blogspot.fr; Price:-,B,B|-,B,A; *Located 1.5km from the GR65 with access to the GR651. 8 places in 2 dormitories and 5 B&B rooms in lovely 17th Century stone house. English spoken. Horses welcome*

Gîte d'étape - La Soursounette [Josiane Joiret],Lieu-dit Pech Rougié, 46100 Béduer, France; Tel:+33(0) 6 47 96 25 92; Email:josiane.joiret@hotmail.com; tourisme-figeac.com; Price:C,B,B|-,B,A; *Accommodation in a renovated 19th Century Quercy styled house. 5 places in a dormitory and 1 private double room*

Chambres d'hôte - La Coquille [Mme Ledoux],Le Bourg, 46100 Béduer, France; Tel:+33(0) 5 65 11 40 18; +33(0) 688 166 615; Email:lacoquille.beduer@gmail.com; tourisme-lot.com; Price:-,B,A; *Just below Chateau Béduer B&B in 12th Century home. 8 places in 3 rooms English spoken.*

Chambres d'hôtes - La Mythié [Myriam and Thierry Frugnac],60, Chemin du Château, 46100 Béduer, France; Tel:+33(0)5 65 34 22 25; +33(0)5 42 47 92 93; Email:thierry.frugnac@wanadoo.fr; en.tourisme-figeac.com/offers/la-mythie-beduer-en-3956727; Price:-,B,-; *Just below Chateau Béduer B&B with beautiful valley views 2 bedrooms*

Faycelles

Le Relais Saint-Jacques [Marie and Olivier],Lieu-dit La Cassagnole, 46100 Faycelles, France; Tel:+33 (0)5 65 34 03 08; +33(0)6 25 27 18 07; Email:olivier@fleurauchapeau.eu; fleurauchapeau.eu; Price:D,D,D; *A pilgrim aware family welcome with 14 places in 2 dormitories in a restored Quercy-style farmhouse with gardens and views. Accommodation for horses.*

La Caselle d'hôtes [Caroline and Christian Weidmann],La Croix Blanche, 46100 Faycelles, France; Tel:+33(0)565340568; +33(0)631832098; lacaselledhotes.com; Price:-,B,B; *Lovey accommodations with garden and terrace in either the studio or caselle (small shepard's house). Famous for its welcome. English spoken.*

Bleu Lumière [Anne Arbus],64, route de Béduer, 46100 Faycelles, France; Tel:+33(0) 06 86 71 13 14; Email:anne.arbus@gmail.com; chambredhotes-bleuslumiere.com; Price:-,A,A; *Before Faycelles. 1 room in artist's home. Accommodation for horses. English spoken.*

Gréalou

Ecoasis [Audrey and Emmanuel Sailly],305, route de Puy Clavel, 46160 Gréalou, France; Tel:+33(0)6 71 00 48 30; +33(0)9 50 07 74 66; Email:bonjour@ecoasis.fr; ecoasis.fr; Price:-,-,B|-,-,B; *30 places in 10 rooms of 2-5 pers. Beautiful views of Quercy. English spoken. Accommodation for horses.*

Gîte d'étape - l'Atelier des Volets Bleus [Esther Marcoux],Place de l'Eglise, 46160 Gréalou, France; Tel:+33 (0)5 65 40 69 86; +33(0)684376473; Email:gite.atelierdesvoletsbleus@gmail.com; atelierdesvoletsbleus.fr; Price:-,-,A; *Converted Swiss artist's studio located across from Romanesque church. 8 places in dormitory and 2 bedrooms. English spoken. Accommodation for horses possible.*

Figeac to Gréalou

stage 13

Alternative Route via Rocamadour

Route– The alternative route through Rocamadour takes six days (as opposed to four on the main GR®65) and uses the red and white way markings typical of the GR®.
Rocamadour, revered for its miraculous black Madonna, has been an important Christian pilgrimage destination since the middle ages. Today, this stunning village built into the cliffs is the second most visited site in France. The variant, which is less popular than the GR®65, is well marked. It departs from Figeac, following the GR®6 north through the vil-

Length:	129.7km
Ascent:	4845m
Descent:	4917m

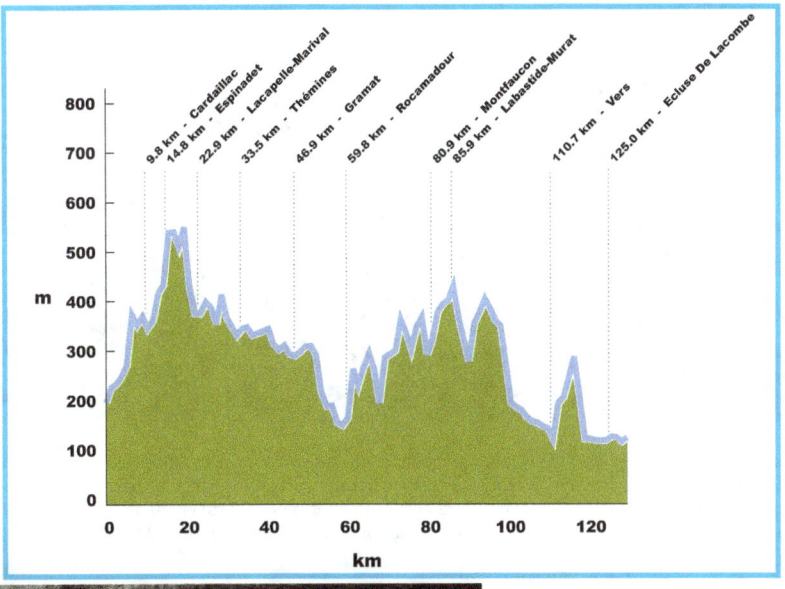

Rocamadour Sanctuary© Alexandra Huddleston

lages of Cardaillac, with its lovely medieval centre, and Gramat. The arrival at Rocamadour through the valley of Alzou is particularly beautiful. From Rocamadour, the path then descends south on the GR®46 through the Natural Park of the Causse of Quercy, before re-joining the Lot River in the village of Vers. There, the route takes the GR®36, which runs alongside the Lot to the city of Cahors, to reconnect with the main Way of Saint James (GR®65). Recommended intermediate resting places are: Lacapelle-Marival; Gramat ; Rocamadour; Labastide-Murat and Vers.

stage 13 — Figeac to Gréalou

Cultural Discoveries

Cardaillac

Cardaillac (popl. 600, alt. 375m) takes its name from the powerful family that ruled Quercy in the Middle Ages. Today, classified as one of the most beautiful villages in France, it has an impressive medieval quarter, parts of which date from the 11th century. It is possible to climb one of three medieval towers, each of which offers stunning views of the countryside. A market is held on Sunday mornings.

Lacapelle-Marival

Located at an important crossroads, the village of Lacapelle-Marival (popl. 1340, alt. 360m) developed at the end of the 13th century when Géraud de Cardillac, who was from a powerful Quercy family, built an imposing castle to defend the site. The castle was entirely renovated in the 15th century, but was abandoned during the French Revolution. Restoration of the castle began in 1992. Today, it houses the town hall (*Mairie*) and exhibitions. A market is held on Tuesday afternoons.

Fortified Church of St Martial (Rudelle)

Originally a 13th century hospital chapel, it was transformed into a defensive keep in the 14th century. An additional floor was added to provide shelter for villagers during the Hundred Years' War.

Rudelle fortified church of St Martial

Figeac to Gréalou — stage 13

Cultural Discoveries

Gramat

A picturesque town founded before the Roman period, Gramat (popl. 3,600, alt. 310m) became an important Roman town due to its position at the crossroads on the routes to Cahors and Rodez. In the Middle Ages, it was the seat of a powerful barony and an important market town. However, with the Hundred Years' War (14th-15th century), including repeated attacks by the English, and the Wars of Religion (16th century), Gramat's prosperity declined. It wasn't until the 19th century, and the arrival of the railway that the city's fortunes rebounded. It was also in the 19th century that the Congregation of Notre-Dame du Calvaire was founded by Pierre Bonhomme, the village priest who was beatified by Pope John-Paul II in 2003. The order is dedicated to teaching and helping the poor, and occupies an impressive convent (seen when entering the city) that provides accommodation for pilgrims. A market is held on Tuesday and Friday mornings.

Rocamadour

The Catholic sanctuary and village of Rocamadour (popl. 650, alt. 280m), which is built into the yellow cliffs that rise out of the Alzou river valley, is one of the most visited sites in France. A 216 step climb leads to the sanctuary with its seven Romanesque chapels. These include the Basilica of Saint Saviour (*Basilique Saint-Sauveur*) and the 12th century crypt of Saint Amadour, the hermit who according to legend founded Rocamadour. There is also the Chapel of Our Lady (*Chapelle Notre-Dame*), which houses the venerated 12th century Black Madonna whose miracles have drawn pilgrims from across Europe since the Middle Ages, including Henry II of England and several French kings. A bell that hangs in the chapel is said to ring by itself each time the Madonna performs a miracle. The lower village consists of a long street with fortified gates, tourist stores and cafes. Rocamadour is also the name of the local goat cheese made from raw milk.

Rocamadour Fortified Gate

Labastide-Murat

A former *bastide* (fortified village), Labastide-Murat (popl. 670, alt. 270m) takes its name from the famed Marshal of France and Napoleon Bonaparte's brother-in-law, Joachim Murat (1767-1815), who was born in the village. The son of an innkeeper, Murat's parents encouraged him to become a priest. However, he abandoned his studies at the seminary to enlist in a cavalry regiment and won rapid promotion. Murat was renowned for his daring cavalry charges and was one of Napoleon's most celebrated officers. He was later promoted to King of Naples and married Napoleon's youngest sister, Caroline Bonaparte. His childhood home and a former inn was made into a museum which is open from 15 July to 15 September.

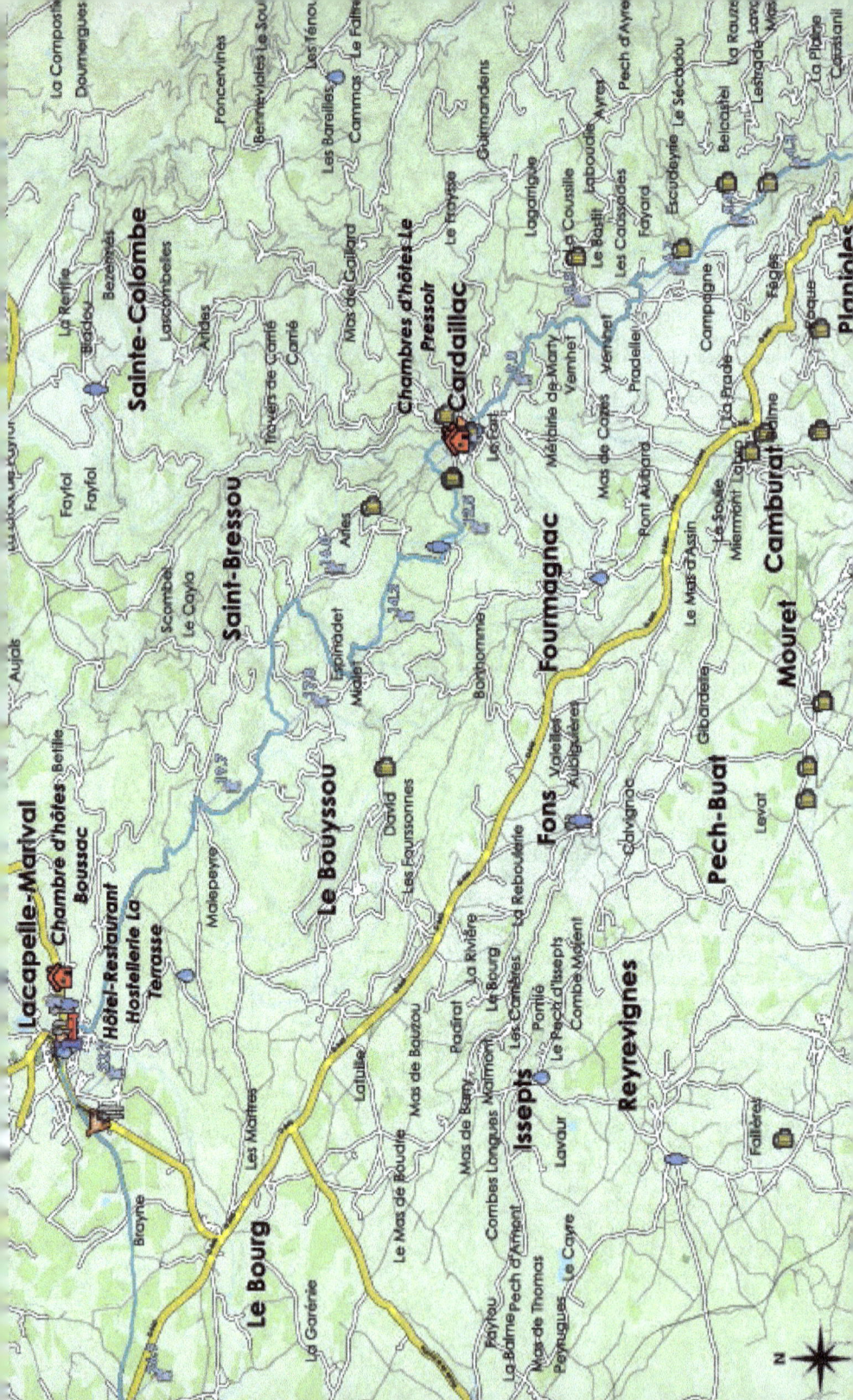

Figeac to Gréalou stage 13
Alternative Route via Rocamadour

(0.0)At intersection of boulevard Georges Juskiewenski and Le Célé River head north up boulevard away from Le Célé river on GR*6[Way markings continue to be the white and red bands of the GR*6](0.3)Turn left on rue des Maquisards(0.5)Turn right onto avenue Marcenac[Keep church of Carmes to the left](0.6)Turn left onto chemin de la Curie and continue straight[Signpost](0.9)Merge onto the road and continue straight through roundabout. Direction Cardaillac[Signpost](1.3)Leave Figeac and continue on the road[Follow stream (Ruisseau de Planioles)](3.2)Keep left on road running alongside stream(3.3)Pass picnic area on left and continue straight direction Escud[Signpost](4.3)At fork keep left, direction Escudeyrie[Signpost](4.4)Continue straight on track to the left of gate (5.4)Continue straight on trail(6.1)Continue straight and then left on asphalt road and climb hill. Direction Cardaillac[Signpost](6.7)Turn right onto road D15 and take first left. Direction Le Pech[Signpost](7.0)Turn right, direction Le Pech[Signpost](7.5)Turn right and descend hill. Continue straight[Signpost. Ahead view of Cardaillac to left across valley](8.5)Merge right onto the D15 road to Cardaillac centre[Signpost](9.3)Enter village of **Cardaillac** and continue straight on D15[Signpost](10.2)Turn left onto rue du 11 mai 1944/D18 and immediately right towards medieval village[Signpost](10.3)Turn right at the village entrance and descend behind the information sign. Continue north on the track and cross the stream (Le Drauzou)[Information panel](11.3)Turn left onto track and continue on trail through forest[Signpost. Ahead pass reservoir (Plan d'Eau des Sagnes) to the left](12.5)Keep right on road and take first left[Signpost](14.2)Turn right onto the C2 road and continue straight towards Pauly and then Espinadet(14.8)At **Espinadet**, turn right onto tree-lined path and continue straight towards Rabanel[Opposite concrete barn](15.2)Cross small street and continue straight until cross (16.0)Turn left onto road and continue straight through Saint-Bressou[Signpost](16.6)At intersection turn left onto the D92 road (direction Le Bouyssou)[Cross](16.7)Turn right onto road (direction Girou) and then take the road to the right[Signpost](17.8)Merge left onto road and continue straight (19.7)At fork keep right on trail that descends into forest[Signpost](22.6)Turn right onto street, then left onto the D15 road towards Lacapelle-Marival centre(22.9)Turn left onto the D653 road and enter the village of **Lacapelle-Marival**(23.1)Continue west on the D653 road and turn left onto the D940 road[Iron cross and pharmacy](23.7)Turn right off the D940 road onto small road D11. Cross road and continue in the same direction before turning right onto the N140 at Rudelle[Pass abandoned electricity building to the left](26.9)Cross the village of Rudelle on a road to the right and parallel to the N140. At road's end turn left and then right to rejoin the N140. Continue straight[Fortified church to the left](27.7)Turn right on small street and climb straight passing through farmland[Stone cross](29.0)At intersection turn left and continue straight[Keep farm to the right](30.1)Keep to the right[Signpost](31.1)Turn left towards water tower and keep left until reaching the D38 road[Water tower and cross](32.0)Turn right onto the D38 road (direction Rueyres), and then turn left on track. Cross the stream L'Ouysee before reaching the D40 road (33.5)Turn left onto the D40 road and cross village of **Thémines**[Signpost](33.9)After passing bakery on the left, veer right (uphill) on the road. Direction Le Cossoul[Signpost (Le Cossoul)](34.0)Keep right on road that passes to hamlet of Le Coussoul[Signpost](35.9)Continue on road through the hamlet of Gruffiel[Signpost](36.3)Turn right on the road away from Lestrade (left). Direction Soulestrein[Signpost](36.6)Turn left onto the road and continue straight through hamlet of Vernique.Keep right on track towards the D840 road and turn right[Signpost](38.0)Turn left and cross the D840 road. Continue straight direction Issendolus[Signpost](38.9)Continue straight. Then turn left to enter the village of Issendolus[Pass château to the left](39.3)At fork keep right, passing a series of houses on the right(40.0)Continue straight on track, which then turns sharply left and passes through the village of Gary[Signpost](42.6)Keep right on track and cross hamlet of Saint-Chignes[Signpost](42.9)At fork turn left onto trail. Continue straight until reaching road[Ahead pass farm on right](46.9)Turn left onto N140 road and then right onto a small road that leads to **Gramat**[Signpost. The road follows the L'Alzou stream to the right](47.5)Pass under the D807 road and keep right on rue du Barry[Underpass](47.7)To leave Gramat, turn left on rue Saint-Roch and con-

107

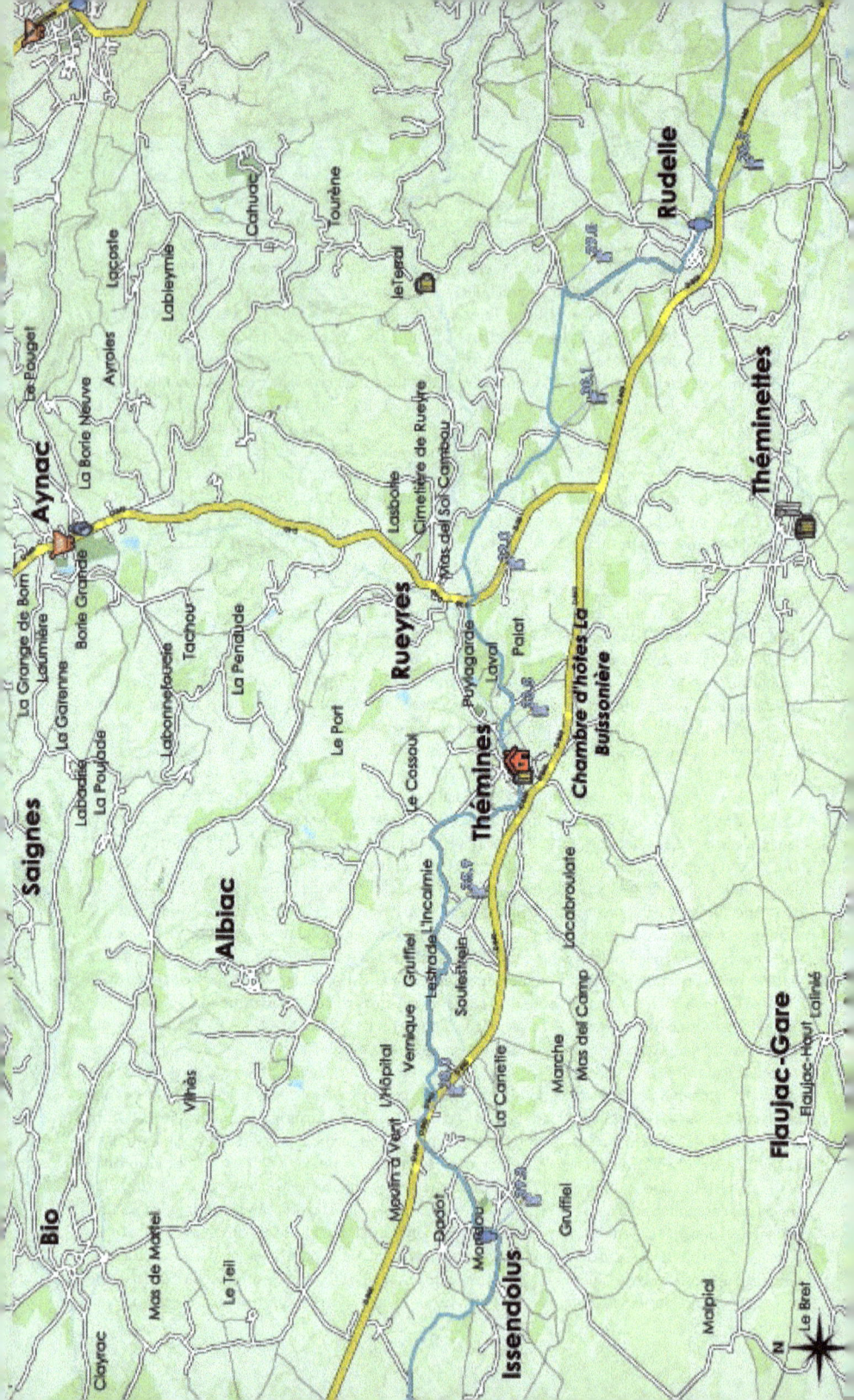

Figeac to Gréalou — stage 13

Alternative Route via Rocamadour

tinue straight[Follow cemetery wall on the left] (49.3)Turn right onto track and continue straight[Ahead pass under power lines] (51.3)Turn left onto track and then turn right onto road. Continue straight to the entrance to the Vallée de l'Ouysse[Signpost] (52.7)Turn right onto a track that descends into the stunning Vallée de l'Ouysse natural reserve and which leads to Rocamadour[Signpost. Pass the Saut mill](52.9)Keep left on rocky trail that runs alongside the L'Alzou stream and leads to Rocamadour[Signpost. Pass several abandonned mills (Tournefeuille, Mouline, Sirogne, and Boulégon)] (59.4)Turn left and rejoin road (D32) towards Rocamadour village(59.8) Turn right up staircase to enter **Rocamadour** village

(59.8)Leave Rocamadour by heading south-west on valley road (D32B). Follow the GR*46 to Vers[Signpost](60.3)Turn left off road (D32B) and continue straight[Pass mill and cross stream "Roquefraiche"](60.3)Turn right on track that climbs to the D32 road, and which offers beautiful views of Rocamadour[Pass house and Berthiol fountain on the left] (61.1)Cross road D32 and continue straight on footpath that climbs to plateau[Signpost](61.8)Take the path to the right of radio antenna and continue straight, before turning left onto the road[Signposts](62.1)Turn right and follow stone wall. Track eventually descends steeply before rejoining the the D32 road[Stone wall. Signpost] (63.1)Turn left onto the D32 road[Signpost](63.2)Turn right and then immediately left onto trail that descends and climbs[Signpost] (64.1)Turn left onto track direction Couzou[Signpost](64.7)Turn right onto the road and continue straight towards Couzou[Farm](65.0)Merge onto the D32 road and continue straight towards hamlet of Couzou[Iron cross on the left] (65.3)At fork keep right and cross hamlet of Couzou[Pass war monument, church and cemetery](66.0)At road's end, turn right[Signpost] (67.5)Turn left and continue straight in exposed valley[Signpost](68.5)Turn right through glade[Signpost] (68.6)Stay right on track direction Montfaucon[Do not pass through gate. Signpost] (70.7)Keep left[Stone cross](71.0)At fork stay right, direction Montfaucon[Signpost] (72.1)Turn right onto track[Signpost](72.5)At fork keep left. Pass through gate and continue left[Signpost] (73.7)At road's end turn right, direction Montfaucon[Signpost] (74.1)Turn left direction La Fontaine and continue straight. Take trail/short cut off road, before rejoining road and turning right[Signpost](75.7)Turn left and climb up hill[Signpost] (77.0)Keep right leaving Rassiols and cross bridge over highway A20. Continue straight to hamlet of Places du Lac[Signposts] (78.4)After traversing hamlet Places du Lac turn left[Cross on left](78.8)Cross road D801 with caution and continue straight, direction Montfaucon[Signpost] (79.0)At fork turn right onto asphalt road through fields, which ends in a steep rocky descent to road D10[Signpost] (79.8)Turn left onto road D10 and pass through hamlet of Les Vitarelles[Signpost](80.2)At fork (with cross) keep right. Then turn left onto track, direction Montfaucon[Signpost] (80.9)Turn left onto road and continue straight[Pass pond on right. Turn right to visit village of **Montfaucon**]

(81.3)Turn left and cross bridge over A20 highway. Continue straight until road's end[A20 highway] (83.0)At road's end turn right. Then take first left on rural road and continue straight[Turn away from highway A20. Further ahead pass farm](83.6)Continue south on road[Farm] (84.1)Turn right direction Labastide-Murat[Signpost](84.5)At road's end turn right in the direction of Labastide-Murat and Lake Boutanes[Signpost] (85.1)Keep right on track[Pass Lake Boutanes and picnic area to the right] (85.7)Continue straight on gravel path towards village of Labastide-Murat[Garden](85.9)Cross road D10 and keep right at fork on rue Fortunière to enter centre of **Labastide-Murat**[Keep garden with stone cross to the left]

(86.2)Continue straight on rue du Causse/D677[Pass church on the left](86.6)At the fork stay left on the D32 road. Direction Saint Sauver La Valée[Pass tennis courts on right. Signpost] (87.3)Veer right onto track, and continue straight through forest[Turn off is opposite a waste transfer station on the left] (88.0)At bottom of descent, keep left on trail (89.3)Turn right onto the road D32. Continue straight(89.5)Turn right onto tree-lined trail[Turn-off is before a sharp right curve in the road](89.8) Keep left on track[Pass field to the right] (90.5)Turn left onto road and then an immediate right onto track. Continue straight(90.8)Cross street and continue straight on the road[Pass stone shed] (91.5)

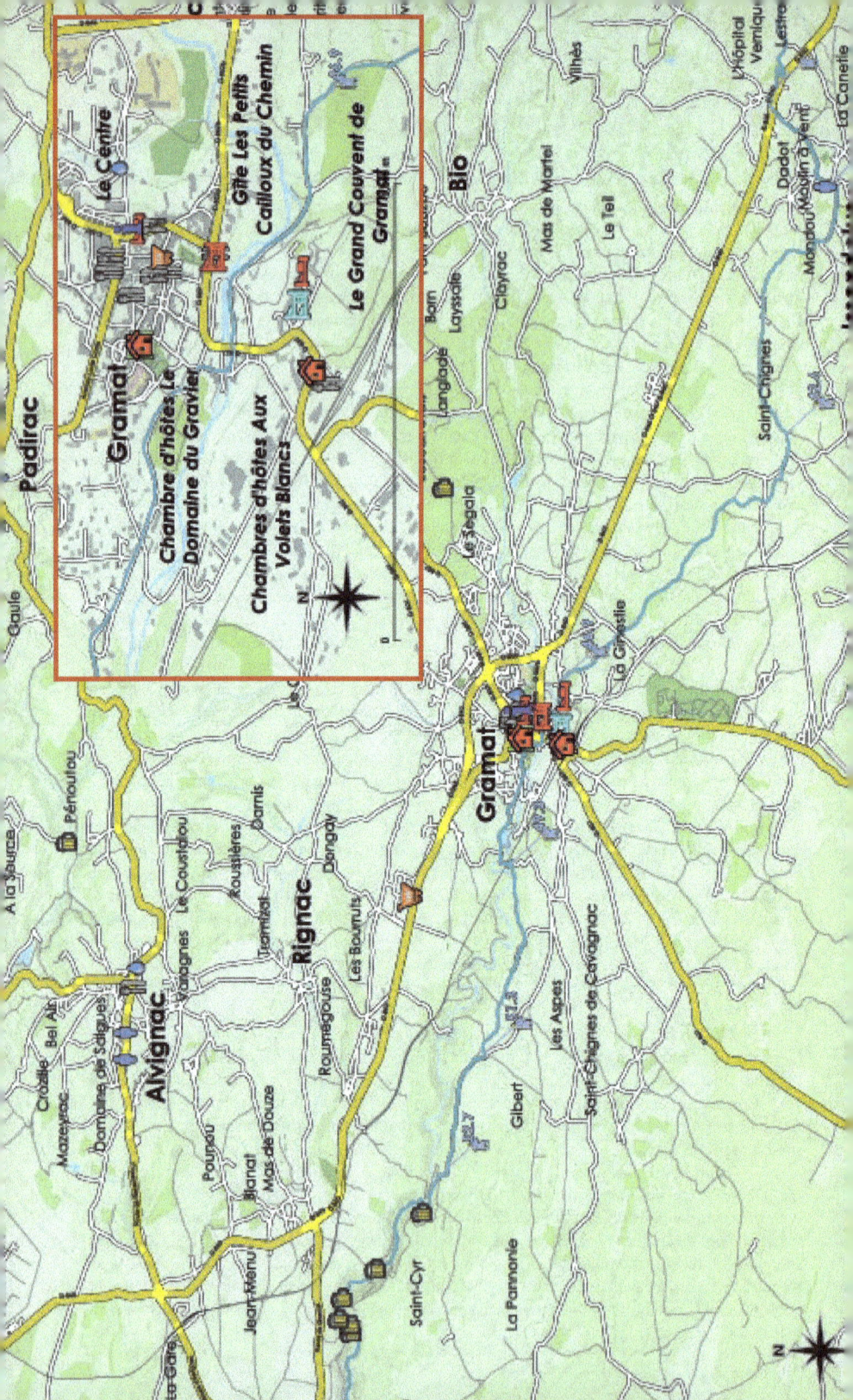

Figeac to Gréalou — stage 13

Alternative Route via Rocamadour

Pass through hamlet, and keep right on gravel road, which ascends[Pass farm buildings to the left] **(92.7)**Rejoin the road and continue straight. Climb hill ahead[Signpost] **(93.9)**At the road's end turn left and continue straight**(94.0)**Take first left onto the D13 road (around pine trees). Continue straight through hamlet of Fages[Shrine to Virgen Mary]**(94.7)**After passing goat farm on right, turn right onto track and continue straight **(95.0)**Turn right onto the road through forest. Then take first left onto the track **(96.1)**Turn right onto road D7[Electrical lines on the right]**(96.5)**Turn left before house with tower. Then turn right onto footpath towards village of Cras[Village of Cras visible ahead. Signpost (Oppidum de Mucens - archaeological site)]**(97.1)**Turn right onto the road, direction Cras. Then take first left direction Oppidum de Murcens (archaeological site)[Signposts] **(97.4)**At fork turn right, direction Le Barry[Signpost]**(97.6)**Turn left on grass road and continue straight[Cras village ahead]**(98.1)**Turn left onto the road and continue straight **(98.8)**Turn right onto track and continue descent direction Vers[Turn in opposite stone house. Signpost]**(99.0)**Turn left onto track and continue straight[Road passes between fields] **(100.5)**Keep straight on trail, direction Vers[Thick woods and signpost]**(100.6)**Turn left onto track and continue straight on trail, direction Vers[Signpost. Trail follows the La Rauze stream to the right] **(101.8)**Cross stone bridge over La Rauze stream and take immediate left. Continue on path to the hamlet of Guillot[La Rauze stream to the right] **(103.4)**At road's end, turn right onto asphalt road. Then turn right again onto road D653 and cross hamlet of Guillot[Signpost]**(104.0)**After hamlet of Guillot, turn left off road D653 onto dirt path. Climb **(104.6)**Turn left onto track. Direction Vers[Signpost] **(106.1)**Continue straight on trail towards the village of Vers[Pass house]**(106.8)**Pass through thick woods/moss and keep right. Continue on trail, which runs alongside Le Vers river[Le Vers to the right] **(108.6)**Turn left off the road and continue straight on track to village of Vers[Stone building. Le Vers river to the right] **(110.5)**Turn right onto the road and continue straight towards Vers village[Signpost]**(110.7)**Turn right onto rue de la Plaquette. Continue straight to **Vers** village centre and cross Le Vers river[Signpost]
(110.9) Continue straight on the D653 road[Pass La Truite Dorée on the left]**(111.2)**Keep left at fork

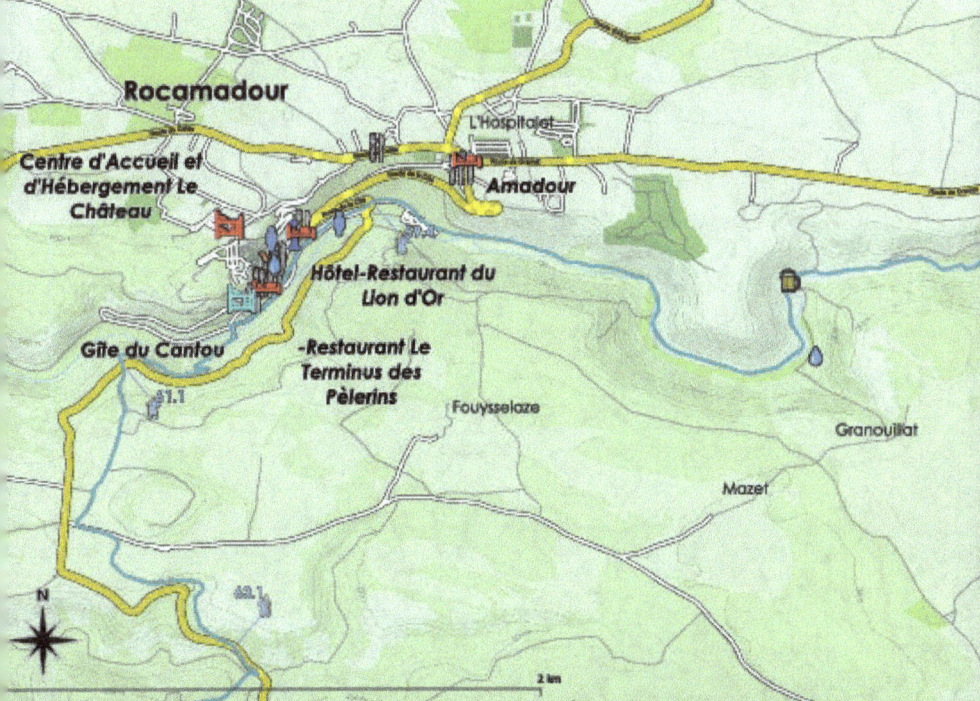

stage 13

Figeac to Gréalou

Alternative Route via Rocamadour

and cross bridge over Lot River towards Béars[Signpost, bridge] (111.6)Keep right eventually rejoining the D49/route de Arcambal to pass through the hamlet of Béars[Signpost](111.8)Keep to left[Abutting road](112.1)After passing through village of Béars, and opposite the last house, turn left onto small road[Road is between a field and barn](112.2)Pass under power lines and turn right onto trail that climbs steeply[Power lines] (112.9)At summit continue straight on GR°36. Direction Les Mazuts. Here, the alternative route through the Célé Valley and the Rocamadour Route meet and both proceed on the GR°36 to Cahors[Signpost] (114.1)Merge left onto road D49 and continue straight direction Les Mazuts[Signpost] (115.2)Turn right onto rocky footpath and climb[Signpost](115.6) Turn right, then again immediately right onto asphalt road. Direction Cahors[Signpost](116.0)Turn right onto the road and continue straight[Turn into forest] (116.8)Turn left onto rocky footpath and descend[Signpost] (118.0)Continue straight on the road[Pass residential area to the right](118.8) Turn right onto route de Mondies[Signpost](119.0)Continue straight on Impasse de la Tour, which descends steeply towards river[Signpost and stone wall] (119.1)After steep descent, turn left following the Lot River[Keep Lot River to the right](119.5)Turn right into parking lot and continue straight on trail running alongside Lot River. Direction Arcambal[Signpost. River to the right] (120.6)Pass under highway A20 and continue following Lot River[Underpass, Lot River to the right, pass locks

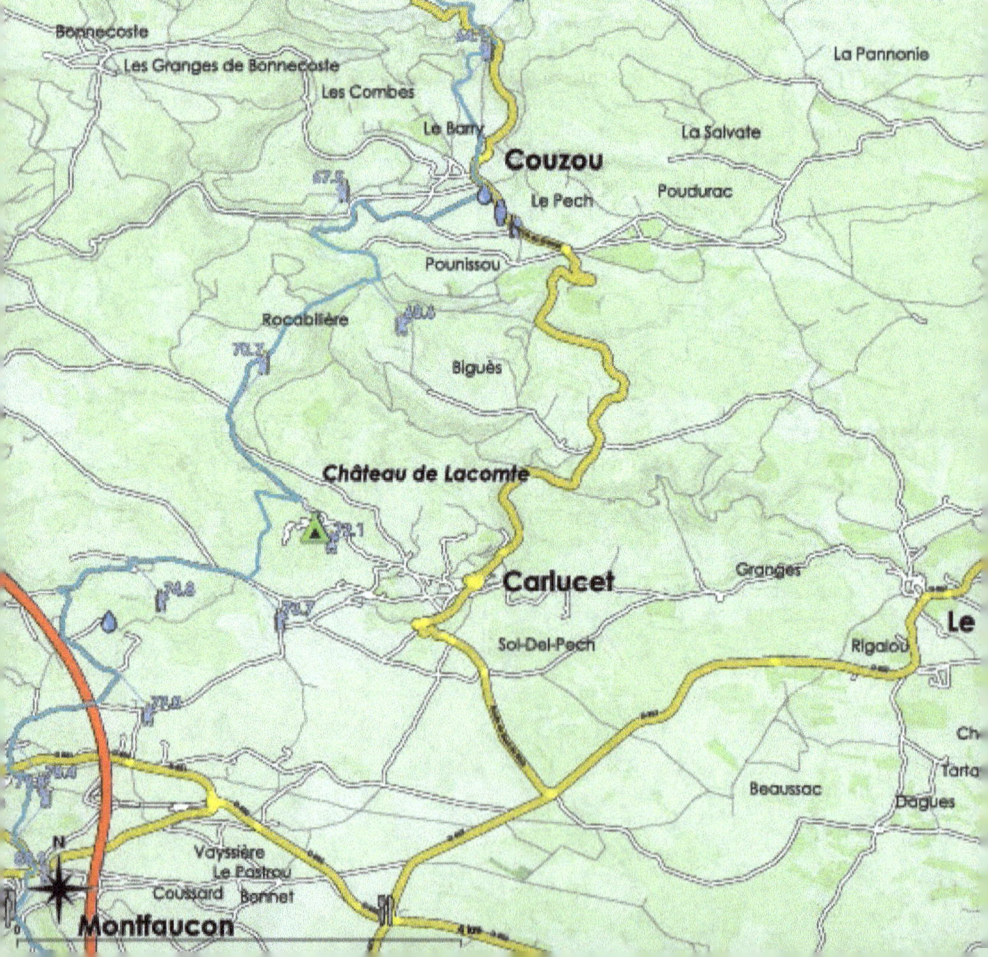

Figeac to Gréalou

stage 13

Alternative Route via Rocamadour

"Ecluse de Arcambal" ahead on right] **(122.3)** Keep to the right on GR°36, which runs alongside the Lot River[Signpost and river to the right] **(125.0)** Pass locks **Ecluse de Lacombe** on right and continue straight on track running alongside Lot River[Locks, communal gardens to the left and river to the right]

(126.3) Turn right onto chemin du Mas de Mansou[City of Cahors visible ahead] **(127.5)** Turn right onto rue de la Guinguette[Sports complex ahead] **(127.8)** At end of road turn left and continue straight towards city[Sport complex. River on the right as you approach the city] **(128.6)** Continue straight along Lot River to cross into Cahors from the south - Pont Louis Philippe bridge[Lot River should be to the right] **(129.0)** Pass Moulin de Coty on the right and turn right on Promenade de Coty. Continue straight until Pont Louis Philippe bridge[Signpost and bridge] **(129.7)** Take staircase to the left to access bridge **(129.7)** Turn right and cross Pont Louis Philippe bridge to enter Cahors

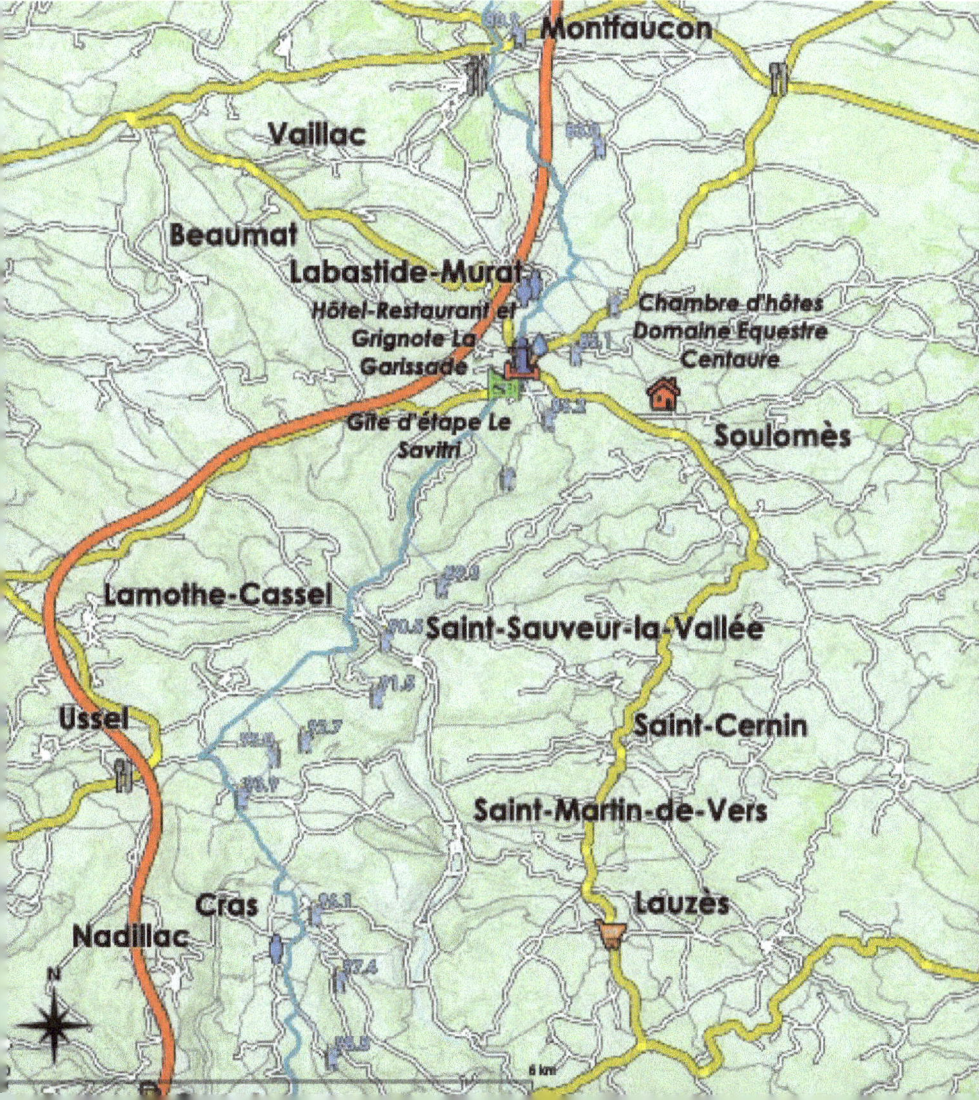

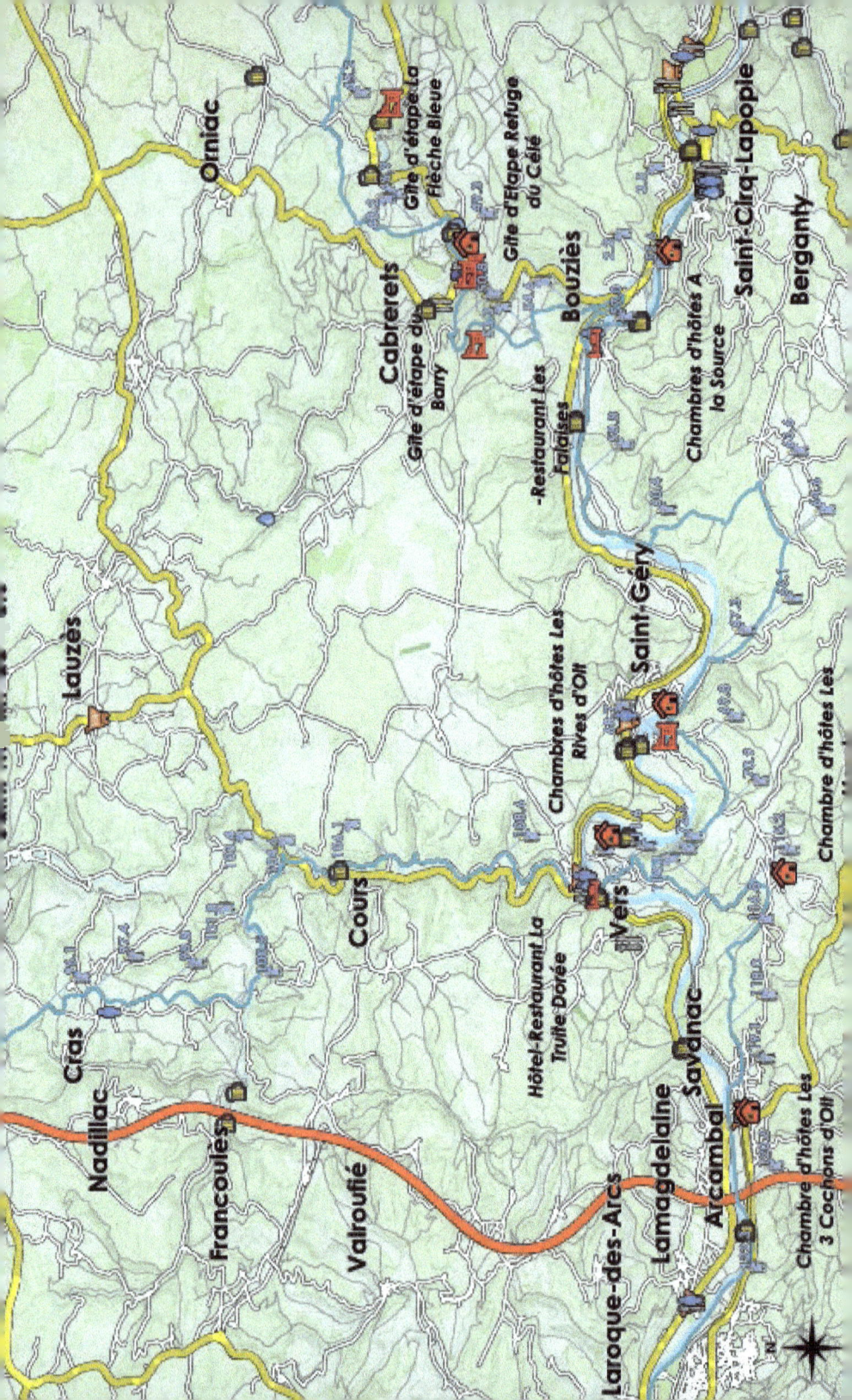

Figeac to Gréalou — stage 13

Accommodation and Tourist Information

Arcambal

🏠 **Chambre d'hôtes Les 3 Cochons d'Olt**[Ulrike Currie],135, route de St.Cirq-Lapopie, 46090 Arcambal, France; Tel:+33 (0)5 65 21 20 51; +33 (0)6 42 82 30 54; Email:ulrikecurrie46@orange.fr; chambres-et-table-dhotes-les3cochons-dolt. jimdosite.com; Price:-,B,-; *3 rooms in family house. English spoken.*

🏠 **Chambre d'hôtes Les Mazuts**[Carmen and Pierre Nouyrit],Lieu-dit - Les Mazuts, 46090 Arcambal, France; Tel:+33 (0)565239529; Email:carmenpierre@free.fr; lesmazuts.free.fr; Price:-,C,-; *In the village of Mazuts before Arcambal. 4 rooms in a restored Quercy farmhouse. Horses and donkeys welcome*

🏠 **Chambres d'hôtes - Les Rives d'Olt**[Evelyne Andlauer],13, impasse de l'Écluse, 46000 Arcambal, France; Tel:+33 (0)6 74 42 12 13; lesrivesdolt.com; Price:-,B,A; *5 lovely rooms of varying sizes. English spoken.*

Cardaillac

🏠 **Chambres d'hôtes - Le Relais des Conques**[Jacky Fabre],Rue des Conques, 46100 Cardaillac, France; Tel:+33 (0)5 65 40 17 22; +33 (0)6 42 73 96 44; Email:contact@relais-des-conques.fr; relais-des-conques.fr; Price:-,B,A; *4 rooms in B&B*

🏠 **Chambres d'hôtes - Le Pressoir**[Sylvie and Bruno],Rue Sénéchal, 46100 Cardaillac, France; Tel:+33 (0)6 22 48 09 63; Email:le pressoir46@gmail.com; lepressoir46.wixsite.com/my-site; Price:-,B,-; *Located in the village centre 2 rooms in an 18th Century home. Kitchen*

Carlucet

⛺ **Château de Lacomte**[Sheila and Stuart Coe],Château de Lacomte, 46500 Carlucet, France; Tel:+33 (0) 565 38 75 46; Email:info@chateaulacomte.com; campinglacomte.com; Price:A,-,-; *Adults only upmarket camping in the grounds of a ruined château. Possibility to rent mobile homes or cabins (call in advance). English spoken. Pool.*

Gramat

🛌 **Gîte Béthanie d'Alzou**[Jean Baptiste],5, rue Saint Félix, 46500 Gramat, France; Tel:+33(0)7 81 40 00 02; Email:bethanie.dalzou@gmail.com; giteparoissialdegramat.jimdofree.com; Price:D,D,D; *Simple accommodations including 14 places in 2 dormitories communal dinner in the evening. Possibility to take part in vespers*

🛌 **Gîte Les Petits Cailloux du Chemin**[Association Les Petits Cailloux du Chemin],1, avenue Louis Mazet, 46500 Gramat, France; Tel:+33(0)565407936; +33(0)658121183; Email:gite.gramat@gmail.com; gitelespetitscailloux.wordpress.com; Price:C,C,C; *Welcoming and clean hostel run by volunteers. 14 places in 5 rooms. English spoken.*

🛌🏠 **Le Grand Couvent de Gramat**,33, Avenue Louis Mazet, 46500 Gramat, France; Tel:+33(0)565387329; Email:reception@grandcouventgramat.fr; grandcouventgramat.fr; Price:B,B,B|B,B,B; *Several places in convent complex including in dormitories of 5 10 or 20 or in rooms as part of the hospitality service of the convent. Private rooms also available in hotel section*

🏠 **Chambres d'hôtes - Aux Volets Blancs**[Marie-Josée and Charles],34, avenue Louis Mazet, 46500 Gramat, France; Tel:+33(0)5 65 33 70 96; +33(0)0 60 32 83 19; auxvoletsblancs.fr; Price:-,B,-; *9 places in various sized rooms*

🏠 **Chambre d'hôtes Le Domaine du Gravier**[Françoise and Michel],Lieu-dit Le Gravier, 46500 Gramat, France; Tel:+33(0)6 70 05 00 74; Email:ledomainedugravier@gmail.com [undefined:ledomainedugravier@gmail.com; ledomainedugravier.com; Price:-,B,-; *Highly rated B&B on restored farm with 5 rooms. Pool. English spoken.*

🛌 **Hôtel - Le Centre**,Place de la Republique, 46500 Gramat, France; Tel:33 (0)5 65 38 73 37; Email:lecentre@lecentre.fr; lecentre.fr; Price:A,A,A; *Well run and clean hotel in village centre.*

ℹ️ **Office de Tourisme**,Place de la Republique, 46500 Gramat, France; Tel:+33 (0)5 65 33 22 00; vallee-dordogne.com

Labastide-Murat

🛌 **Gîte d'étape - Le Savitri**[Véronique Vanel],64, Grande rue du Causse, 46240 Labastide-Murat, France; Tel:+33 (0)6 74 40 14 15; Email:vero.vanel@laposte.net; tourisme-labastide-murat.fr; Price:C,-,-; *13 places in a dormitory*

🏠 **Chambre d'hôtes - Domaine Equestre Centaure**[Erica de Graaf],La Devèze, 46240 Labastide-Murat, France; Tel:+33 (0)6 31 96 50 57; +33 (0)6 61 17 01 44; Email:centaure@paardrijvakantie.com; paardrijvakantie.com; Price:-,B,-; *4 rooms. Horses welcome.*

stage 13 — Figeac to Gréalou

Hôtel-Restaurant et Grignote La Garissade,20, place de la mairie , 46240 Labastide-Murat, France; Tel:+33 (0)5 65 21 18 80; Email:hotel@garissade.com; garissade.com; Price:A,A,A; *Centrally located with 19 rooms. English spoken. Accommodation for horses possible.*

Hôtel-Restaurant et Grignote La Garissade,20, place de la mairie , 46240 Labastide-Murat, France; Tel:+33 (0)5 65 21 18 80; Email:hotel@garissade.com; garissade.com; Price:A,A,A; *Centrally located with 19 rooms. English spoken. Accommodation for horses possible.*

Office de Tourisme,9, place de la Mairie, 46240 Labastide-Murat, France; Tel:+33 (0)5 65 21 11 39; Email:tourisme@cc-labastide-murat.fr; tourisme-labastide-murat.fr

Office de Tourisme,9, place de la Mairie, 46240 Labastide-Murat, France; Tel:+33 (0)5 65 21 11 39; tourisme-labastide-murat.fr

Lacapelle-Marival

Chambre d'hôtes - Boussac[Marcel and Annie Boussac],899, route d'Aurillac, 46120 Lacapelle-Marival, France; Tel:+33(0)6 79 39 45 48; +33(0)5 65 40 84 15; tourisme-figeac.com; Price:-,B,-; *Located outside the village centre. 1 room in lovely home with garden.*

Hôtel-Restaurant Hostellerie La Terrasse,Place de Larroque près du Château, 46120 Lacapelle-Marival, France; Tel:+33(0) 5 65 40 80 07; Email:hotel-restaurant-la-terrasse@orange.fr; hostellerie-la-terrasse.com; Price:A,A,A; *Across from the chateau charming hotel with 13 rooms serving local specialities.*

Mairie de Lacapelle-Marival,Route d'Aurillac, 46120 Lacapelle-Marival, France; Tel:+33(0) 5 65 40 80 24; Email:lacapelle.mairie@wanadoo.fr; lacapelle-marival.fr

Rocamadour

Centre d'Accueil et dHhébergement Le Château,Le Château, 46500 Rocamadour, France; Tel:+33 (0)5 65 33 23 23; Email:hebergement@lerelaisdupelerin.fr; lerelaisdupelerin.fr; Price:C,C,-; *Located in Rocamadour castle above the village. 79 places in single or double rooms or dormitory*

Gîte du Cantou,rue de la Mercerie, 46500 Rocamadour, France; Tel:+33(0)565337369; Email:cantou.46@free.fr; notre-dame-du-calvaire.fr/nos-offres-evenements/accueil-et-hebergement/le-gite-du-cantou-de-rocamadour; Price:C,-,-; *Located in the old town near the sanctuary. 16 places in 6 single rooms 2 double rooms and a dormitory for 6. Priority given to pilgrims on their way to Santiago. Possibility to take part in religious ceremonies. Kitchen.*

Hôtel-Restaurant du Lion d'Or,Cité Médiévale, 46500 Rocamadour, France; Tel:+33(0)5 65 33 62 04; Email:contact@liondor-rocamadour.com; liondor-rocamadour.com; Price:B,A,A; *Low budget and friendly hotel located in old town centre. English spoken.*

Hôtel - Amadour,Place de l'Europe, 46500 Rocamadour, France; Tel:+33(0)5 65 33 73 50; Email:contact@amadour-hotel.com; amadour-hotel.com; Price:B,-,-; *Located in Hospitalet (a 10 min walk on the Sacred Way to Rocamadour) great value with beautiful views.*

Hotel-Restaurant Le Terminus des Pèlerins,85, rue de la CouronnerieLL, 46500 Rocamadour, France; Tel:+33 (0)565336214; Email:hotelterm.pelerinsroc@wanadoo.fr; terminus-des-pelerins.fr; Price:A,A,A; *2 star hotel located in the old town 12 bedrooms*

Maison du Tourisme,5066, rue Roland le Preux, 46500 Rocamadour, France; Tel:+33(0) 5 65 33 22 00; vallee-dordogne.com

St-Géry-Vers

Hôtel-Restaurant La Truite Dorée,Rue de la Barre, 46090 St-Géry-Vers, France; Tel:+33(0) 5 65 31 41 51; Email:contact@latruitedoree.fr; latruitedoree.fr; Price:A,A,A; *28 rooms in hotel with one of the best restaurants in the area. English spoken.*

Thémines

Chambre d'hôtes La Buissonière[Elisabeth de Lapérouse Coleman],Le Bout du Lieu, 46120 Thémines, France; Tel:+33(0)5 65 40 88 58; +33(0)6 07 63 82 36 ; Email:edelaperouse.coleman@wanadoo.fr; leboutdulieu.weebly.com/chambres-dhocirctes.html; Price:-,B,-; *2 rooms. English spoken.*

Figeac to Gréalou

stage 13

Alternative Route via the Célé Valley

Route–From Figeac, the alternative route through the Célé Valley, which also uses red and white way markings, takes five days (as opposed to four days on the GR®65), despite being about 10 kilometres shorter than the main route. It is generally considered more beautiful than the main route, as it crosses the limestone hills typical of the Causses region, beautiful villages built into the cliffs and follows the refreshing Célé river. The route, known as the GR®651, departs from the GR®65 in Mas-de-la-Croix, where it descends into the Célé Valley, and passes through the lovely medieval village of Espagnac. From there, it climbs and descends along the limestone cliffs, in dry and often difficult and rocky terrain, passing through several historic villages on the Célé River, before re-joining the Lot near the village of Bouziès. There, the route takes the GR®36, which runs alongside the Lot river to the city of Cahors, to reconnect with the main Way of Saint James (GR®65). In Bouziès it is also possible to make a day trip (recommended) to Saint-Cirq-Lapopie, considered one of the most beautiful villages in France, which is a lovely four kilometre walk along the Lot.

Length:	72.8km
Ascent:	4066m
Descent:	4153m

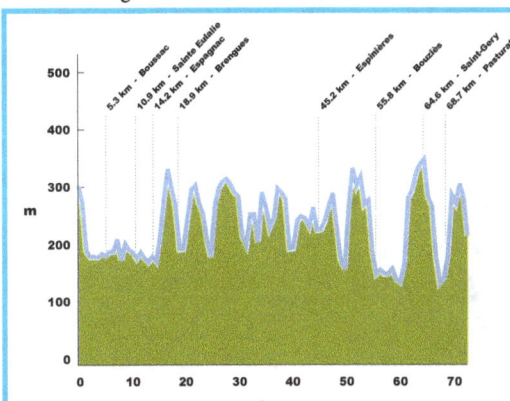

Pointers–The terrain is more challenging than the GR®65, and hikers should ensure that they have sufficient water and provisions.

Alternatives: For a fun alternative to walking, especially if it gets hot, it is possible to travel by canoe or kayak down the Célé River from various points between Saint-Sulpice and Cabrerets. Several canoe rental companies organise trips: (1) Marcilhac-sur-Célé–Passion Aventure, Pont de Marcilhac Route de Saint-Chels, 46160 Marcilhac-sur-Célé, tel.: +33 6 10 73 73 12, www.location-canoe-cele.com, (2) Nature & Loisirs, Anglanat, 46330 Orniac , tel.: +33 5 65 30 25 69, www.nature-et-loisirs.com. Recommended intermediate resting places: Espagnac; Marcilhac-sur-Célé and Cabrerets.

Walking to Saint-Cirq-Lapopie

stage 13 — Figeac to Gréalou

Cultural Discoveries

Espagnac

Espagnac (popl. 100, alt. 294m) developed in the 13th century around the convent of Val Paradis, which was founded by Aymeric Hébrard de Saint Sulpice, the son of a powerful Quercy family who became bishop of Coimbra, in Portugal. The convent suffered during the Hundred Years' War, during which time the church was set on fire and the cloisters destroyed. The church contains the tombs of local rulers, including Aymeric Hébrard.

In the 15th century, the Hébrard de Saint-Sulpice family oversaw the abbey's reconstruction; however, in 1569, during the Wars of Religion, the abbey was attacked by French Protestants and burned. The structure was later converted into a parish church which contains lovely 17th century wood work.

There is an annual jazz festival in early August.

Sauliac-sur-Célé

Only ruins remain of the medieval "old Sauliac" which was built into the cliffs around a castle–*château des Anglais*–overlooking the Célé river in the valley. the castle of Géniez dates from the 13th century and was a protestant stronghold during the Wars of Religion.

Peche Merle Grotto
(*La Grotte du Peche Merle*)

Located above Cabrerets, the museum and grotto of Peche Merle contain beautiful prehistoric cave paintings of bison, bears, horses and mammoths that are about 25 thousand years old.

Marcilhac-sur-Célé

The village of Marcilhac-sur-Célé (popl. 200, alt. 140m) developed around a 10th century Benedictine abbey, which was pillaged in 1368, during the Hundred Years' War.

Figeac to Gréalou

stage 13

Alternative Route via the Célé Valley

(0.0) At Mas de la Croix, continue straight on D21 road towards Béduer. Follow GR®651 through the Célé valley[Signpost] (0.3) Descend into Béduer on the D21 road[Château de Béduer on the left] (1.0) Turn right onto footpath steep descent into Célé River valley[Signpost] (1.9) At the end of the road, turn left onto the track through corn fields and cross the D21 road[Célé River to the right] (4.9) Turn right and cross the bridge over the Célé River. At road's end turn right onto the D41 road[Bridge] (5.3) In **Boussac**, before church, turn left, direction Manden, and continue straight[Signpost] (6.2) Continue straight on track[Pass château on left] (6.7) Merge right onto D41 road and continue straight on road (caution) to arrive in village of Corn[Pass large property on the left] (7.6) Turn right into village on narrow passage that passes church[Signpost and church] (7.7) Cross the D113 road and take the footpath along the stream. Cross the D41 road to leave Corn[Church and D41] (7.8) Cross road and continue straight on track[Pass cross on the right] (8.1) Cross bridge over Célé River and then turn right and continue straight[Célé River to the right] (8.2) Turn right and continue straight on main road (8.6) At fork in hamlet of Goudou keep left[Château] (9.0) Turn right onto track and continue straight through forest[Signpost] (10.4) Merge left onto track that runs alongside the Célé River and pass through the hamlet of Sainte-Eulalie[River] (10.9) At fork, keep left on high road to leave hamlet of **Sainte Eulalie** and continue straight
(11.5) Take left onto footpath before bridge to enter forest. Turn left, crossing over iron pipe, and continue straight on trail[Célé River to the right] (12.5) Continue straight on trail until Espagnac[Pass stone houses to the right] (14.2) Merge right onto road leading to the village and Espagnac. Then turn right at cross to enter village of **Espagnac**[Signpost]
(14.5) From church, continue straight on D211 road to leave Espagnac. Cross bridge over Célé River[Church on the left] (14.7) Turn right onto the D41 road, direction Corn[Signpost] (15.0) Turn left into hamlet of Pailhès. Keep left onto a trail that switchbacks through forest until it joins a road, and turn left[Cross] (16.4) Turn left onto a trail through the forest and then cross the D38 road. Continue straight (17.4) Turn right onto the D38 and then left onto a trail that leads to cliffs and the ruins of the Tour des Anglais[Signpost] (18.3) Continue to follow trail in its rocky descent to the D38 road, and turn left to Mas de Bessac[Signpost] (18.9) Keep right on the the D38 road as it descends towards the valley into the village of **Brengues**[Signpost]
(19.2) Turn right towards Vignes-Grandes[Road runs parallel to the D41] (19.7) Keep right on trail that climbs through forest, then turn right on a road that climbs to a fork (21.0) Keep left, and at the fork turn left on a trail that climbs towards the crests and then descends parallel to the valley floor[Signpost] (23.1) Turn left onto the D13 road and descend towards the valley[Pass iron cross] (23.6) Turn right onto a track and pass the Château of Saint-Sulpice, continue straight to leave Saint-Sulpice[Signpost] (24.5) Turn left onto trail that descends into valley, then turn right onto trail that climbs the hills and passes Pech Merlu[Iron cross] (27.4) Turn right onto the D17 road and at the fork keep left on the D17[Cross] (27.7) Turn left onto trail that climbs to Pech Peyroux, and then descends south to the D14 road (31.2) Keep right on the D14 road[Continue straight to visit village (off GR)] (31.3) Turn right in Jean-Fabret square, and continue straight away from D14 to leave village[Signpost] (31.4) Turn left on a road that climbs between houses, and then switchbacks(32.1) Turn left and continue straight, on trail until reaching the route de Combes-Basses, turn left[Pass access road to B&B Le Picarel on left] (33.6) Turn right on trail that switchbacks. Keep left[Cross] (35.1) Turn left on road direction Montagnac and then turn right (opposite farm)(36.1) At fork, turn left on trail that follows ledge of plateau before descending to a small road[Ahead pass farm] (37.6) Turn left onto road, and at the first bend continue straight on trail that descends to Sauliac-sur-Célé[Signpost] (39.6) Continue straight and pass along cliffs through old Sauliac. Road curves to right[Turn left to visit village (off GR)] (40.6) At fork keep left, and continue on trail that switchbacks uphill. Keep left and then turn left on wall lined trail, to road leading to Château de Cuzals (42.6) Turn left at castle gate, and continue straight[Pass Musée de plein-air du Quercy on right] (42.8) Continue straight (43.4) Turn right onto track through fields and pass through gate. Continue straight until the D40 road[Signpost] (45.2) Cross the D40

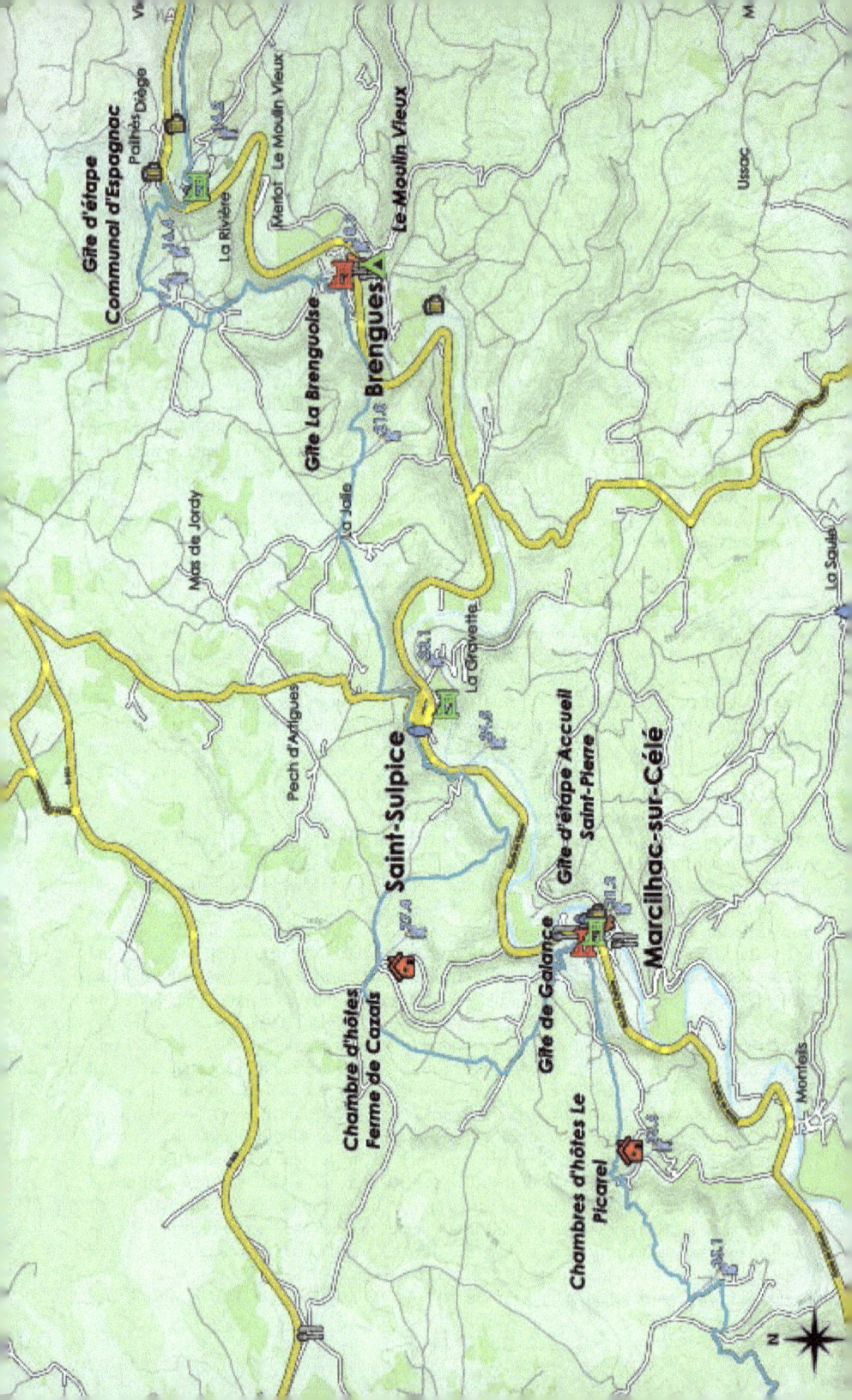

Figeac to Gréalou stage 13

Alternative Route via the Célé Valley

road and continue straight through village of **Espinières**[Signpost]
(45.5)Continue straight on the shrub-lined road, which becomes a rocky trail. Keep right until arriving at a small road before the D42 road (46.9)Turn left onto the road and continue straight. Then turn right on footpath between an oak tree and field. Cross hilltop fields with amazing views of the Causse region (48.2)After crossing field follow path along stone walls, and descend towards Cabrerets. At road's end, turn right(48.8)Continue straight on steep rocky descent into Cabrerets (49.3)Merge right onto road running alongside the Célé River. Take first right and cross through (strong>Cabrerets centre[Pass bridge and Célé river to the left](49.7)Keep left, cross main road and head towards church[Church and signposts](49.9)At top of hill, at church, turn left onto road next to cemetery and take the rocky trail to Grotte du Pech Merle[On trail pass picnic area on left] (50.8)Pass through gate and continue to Grotte du Pech Merle and museum, and then climb stairs to the right(50.9)Cross through parking lot and then turn left onto road(51.3)Turn left on rock trail, direction Bouziès[Signpost] (51.4)Turn left at fork and continue straight on trail along hill crest[Beautiful valley views to the left] (53.3)Turn left, direction Bouziès and continue straight on trail along the crest of the hill[Signpost] (54.6)Continue straight on long descent that switchbacks towards the Lot River valley (55.6)Re-join the road to the right, which descends to the D41 road[Pass château on right](55.8)Turn right onto the D41 road with care, and continue straight direction Bouziès. Turn left and cross bridge and enter **Bouziès**[Célé river to the left]
(57.0)In Bouziès, after crossing bridge, turn right to follow the GR°36 to Cahors. The alternative route to Saint-Cirq-Lapopie - GR°36 - departs from the church/bridge in Bouziès and follows the Lot River south[Signpost](57.3)Cross bridge over abandoned railway tracks, and at cross turn right onto road and continue straight[Signpost] (58.8)At fork, keep right heading towards shed in the distance. At the shed, take immediate right towards river[Cross](59.3)Cross railway tracks and continue on the road as it turns left and runs alongside river. Before reaching the bridge, turn right onto footpath running alongside a field (60.4)Keep right on trail running alongside Lot River[River to the right](60.8) Turn left and pass under bridge, followed by long climb towards the D8 road[Head away from river] (63.6)Turn right on path towards Pasturat and then merge onto the D8. Continue straight[Cross and picnic area](64.0)Turn right off D8 road onto track running parallel. Continue straight[Signpost] (64.6)Turn right onto track, heading away from the D8 and continue straight. Cross hamlet of **Saint-Gery**[Signpost]
(66.1)Pass electrical tower and cross street, before steep descent towards D10 road(67.0)Turn right towards forest. Direction Pasturat. Pass under bridge and descend towards Lot River[Signpost](67.0) Merge left onto road and take immediate left before bridge onto trail. Continue straight[Bridge] (67.3)Pass under bridge and descend towards river, keep left and continue straight on path bordering the Lot River[Lot River to the right](67.9)Continue along path that, which veers left before bridge[Bridge](68.0)Cross street and continue straight on long climb to Pasturtat (68.7)At road's end, turn left and enter **Pasturat**[Head towards church]
(68.8)Before church turn right on Route du Travers Rouge[Signpost](68.9)Turn left on small footpath[Before lovely stone house](69.0)Turn right onto the road, and continue straight on long climb out of valley(69.4)Turn right and continue straight, steep climb[Trail passes between houses] (69.8) Turn right onto track, direction Les Mazuts, and continue straight[Pass farm house on left](70.6)Turn right onto road and continue climb, direction Les Mazuts (70.9)Turn right onto track, direction Vers (on GR°36) (72.6)Beautiful view of valley, continue straight[Pass radio tower on right](72.8)At end of trail, turn left onto GR°36 towards Cahors. Direction Les Mazuts. At this point, the alternative routes from Rocamadour and Célé valley meet and proceed to Cahors[Signpost]right onto track, direction Vers (on GR°36) (72.6)Beautiful view of valley, continue straight[Pass radio tower on right](72.8)At end of trail, turn left onto GR°36 towards Cahors. Direction Les Mazuts. At this point, the alternative routes from Rocamadour and Célé valley meet and proceed to Cahors[Signpost]

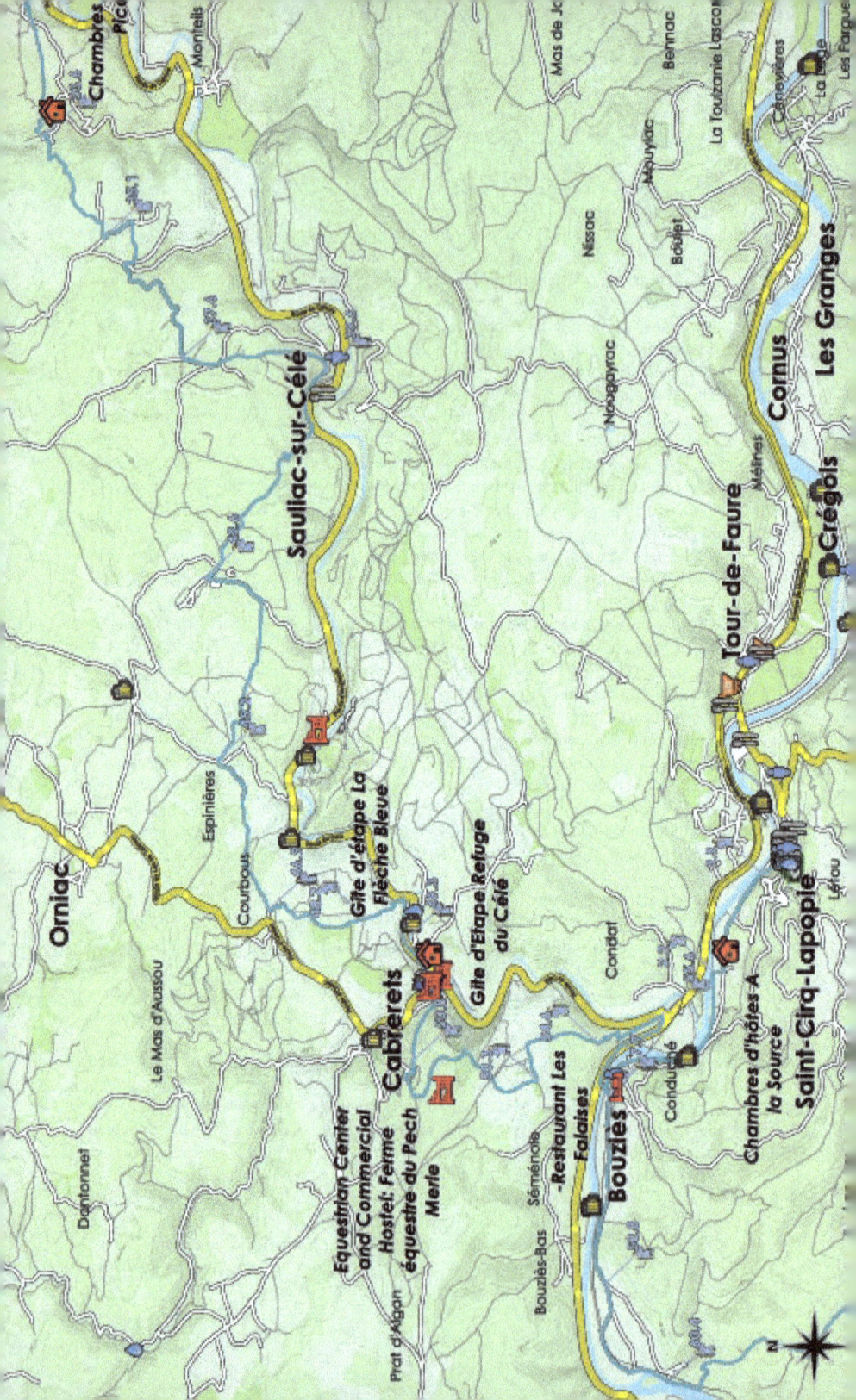

Figeac to Gréalou

stage 13

Excursion to Saint-Cirq-Lapopie

Route–The route to Saint-Cirq-Lapopie is an out and back excursion from Bouziès; it is possible to make the round trip to the village in one day. The route, which is well-marked with the white-red way markings of the GR°36, is mostly flat, as it follows the Lot river at the foot of impressive limestone cliffs, but for a short steep climb to the medieval village of Saint-Cirq-Lapopie, which is perched on a cliff overlooking the Lot river. The village boasts 13 historic monuments and has been classified as one of the most beautiful villages in France.

Length:	7.7km
Ascent:	474m
Descent:	474m

Cultural Discoveries

Saint-Cirq-Lapopie

The medieval village of Saint-Cirq-Lapopie (popl. 200, alt. 120m) is perched on a cliff overlooking the Lot river and boasts 13 historic monuments. It is classified as one of the most beautiful villages in France. In the 20th century, the site was appreciated by artists and writers, including French writer and founder of surrealism, André Breton, who lived in the village and famously said "I have ceased to wish myself elsewhere." In July and August, the village holds a market on Wednesday afternoons (4p.m. to 8p.m.).

stage 13
Figeac to Gréalou

Excursion to Saint-Cirq-Lapopie

(0.0)From Bouziès church, descend to the left of the bridge towards river and turn right.[Signpost](0.3) Take GR®36 to Saint-Cirq-Lapopie.(0.5)Cross camping grounds and join trail. Continue straight with river to the left on footpaths and roads. 🏠 (2.2)Turn right, away from river, and then take first left and continue straight on the road towards Saint-Cirq. 🏠 (3.5)Turn right onto footpath to climb out of river valley. Steep.[Signpost](3.9)Turn left out of staircase, and arrive in **Saint-Cirq**. To return to the Célé valley route, retrace your steps to Bouziès.[Place du Sombral, village centre] 🏠 (7.7)Rejoin the Célé Valley route beside the church in Bouziès.

Accommodation and Tourist Information

Arcambal

🛏️🏠 **Gîte d'étape - Chambre d'hôtes - Le Relais de Pasturat**[Jacques and Anne-Marie Charazac],54, route du Travers Rouge, 46090 Arcambal, France; Tel:+33(0) 5 65 31 44 94; +33(0)6 13 46 46 85; tourisme-lot.com; Price:C,C,C|-,B,-; *15 places in hostel and 4 B&B rooms. Horses welcome.*

Boussac

🏠 **Chambre d'hôtes - Mas de Lum Domaine Villedieu**,705, route de Reyrevignes, 46100 Boussac, France; Tel:+33(0)6 48 05 46 84; mas-del-lum.fr; Price:-,A,-; *Top-rated B&B on 18th Century estate. 4 rooms and a 4-pers. cottage. Closed in July and August. English spoken. Eco-pool.*

Bouziès

🛏️**Hotel-Restaurant Les Falaises**,245, route Touristique, 46330 Bouziès, France; Tel:+33(0)565312683; Email:hotelfalaises@gmail.com; hotel-falaises-bouzies46.fr; Price:A,A,A; *Charming hotel on the Lot with views on cliffs. Pool. English spoken. 45 simple rooms. Good restaurant.*

Brengues

🛏️**Gîte La Brenguoise**,Le Bourg, 46320 Brengues, France; Tel:+33(0)630206806; Email:contact@labrenguoise.fr; labrenguoise.fr; Price:C,C,C; *Located in the village of Brengues.11 places in 3 rooms. English spoken. Horses welcome.*

⚠️ **Camping Le Moulin Vieux**,Lieu-dit Le Moulin Vieux, 46320 Brengues, France; Tel:+33(0) 5 65 40 00 41; Email:lemoulinvieux@outlook.com; camping-lemoulinvieux.com; Price:B,-,-; *Located on the Célé river possibility to rent mobile home. Pool. English spoken. Accommodation for horses. Possibility to canoe a stage(s) down river (instead of walking).*

Cabrerets

🛏️🏠 **Gîte d'étape - du Barry**[Ms Daulny],Le Bourg, 46330 Cabrerets, France; Tel:+33(0)7 88 62 81 18; Email:gitedubarrycabrerets@gmail.com; laroue-lot.fr; Price:B,B,B|B,B,B; *Located in the village centre. 15 places in 5 rooms for 4 to 6 pers. Pool. Accommodation for horses.*

🛏️**Gîte d'Etape - Refuge du Célé**,Le Bourg, 46330 Cabrerets, France; Tel:+33(0)565312015; Email:refugeducele@gmail.com; lerefugeducele.com; Price:B,A,A; *Located near village centre and the Célé river 5 triple and double rooms. English spoken. Pool. Recently renovated*

🛏️**Equestrian Centre and Commercial Hostel: Ferme équestre du Pech Merle**[Pascal Gaudebert],Ferme équestre du Pech Merle, 46330 Cabrerets, France; Tel:+33(0)611932523; Email:randocheval@gmail.com; pechmerle.fr; Price:C,C,C; *2 double dooms and dormitory sleeping 4. English spoken. Horses welcome. Possibility to organize trail rides.*

ℹ️ **Mairie de Cabrerets**,Le Bourg, 46330 Cabrerets, France; Tel:+33(0) 5 65 31 26 61; cabrerets.fr

Corn

🏠 **Gîte d'étape - La Maison de Cécile**[Madame Chiminello Sylvie Lapparot],Lieu-dit Mendens, 46100 Corn, France; Tel:+33(0)565400124; +33(0)679427736; Email:aymonde.roques123@orange.fr; chemindecompostelle.com; Price:C,C,C; *400m from the GR®beautiful stone house with sweeping valley views. 10 places. English spoken.*

Figeac to Gréalou — stage 13

Espagnac-Sainte-Eulalie
Gîte d'étape - Communal d'Espagnac, Chemin des Dames, 46320 Espagnac-Sainte-Eulalie, France; Tel:+33(0)565114266; espagnac-ste-eulalie.fr/nos-gites/notre-gite-detape/; Price:C,-,-; *21 places in a historic tower in the heart of the medieval village. Kitchen.*

Marcilhac-sur-Célé
Gîte d'étape - Accueil Saint-Pierre[Laurence and Jean-Michel],3, route de Compostelle, 46160 Marcilhac-sur-Célé, France; Tel:+33(0)5 81 24 06 30; +33(0)6 34 36 54 60; Email:gitemarcilhac@gmail.com; accueilsaintpierre.sitew.com/; Price:C,C,C; *Located in the village centre. 11 places. Horses and donkeys welcome. No dogs. Kitchen.*

Gîte de Galance[Véronique and Jean],137, Route de Pailhès, 46160 Marcilhac-sur-Célé, France; Tel:+33(0) 5 65 34 23 97; +33(0)615949197; Email:contact@gitedegalance.fr; gitedegalance.fr; Price:C,B,B; *Recently built and fully equipped hostel with 15 places in 6 rooms. English spoken. Horses welcome.*

Chambres d'hôtes - Le Picarel[Lyn and Ian Thomas],Mas de Picarel, 46160 Marcilhac-sur-Célé, France; Tel:+33 (0)626462963; Email:lepicarelbandb@gmail.com; lepicarel-bandb.eu; Price:-,B,A; *Located after village on the GR°lovely B&B owned by British couple. 4 double rooms.*

Chambre d'hôtes Ferme de Cazals[Fabienne and Jean-Michel Bos],route de Pailhès, 46160 Marcilhac sur Célé, France; Tel:+33(0)5 65 50 07 89; Email:fabiennebos2017@gmail.com; fermedecazals.hautetfort.com; Price:-,B,A; *Organic farm with 4 rooms run by couple who moved from the city. English spoken. Horses welcome.*

Orniac
Gîte d'étape - La Flèche Bleue[Mathieu Flaujac],Les Granges, 46330 Orniac, France; Tel:+33 (0)5 65 23 36 72; +33(0)6 32 31 97 09; Email:laflechebleue46@gmail.com; la-fleche-bleue.fr/; Price:C,C,C; *Before Cabrerets and 1 km from the GR°651 (but worth the detour) 32 places in 11 various sized rooms. Kitchen. English spoken. Horses welcome. Nature and bird watching walks organized.*

Saint-Cirq-Lapopie
Chambres d'hôtes - A la Source[Claquin Bérengère],Leu-dit Castan, 46130 Saint-Cirq-Lapopie, France; Tel:+33(0)6 21 72 43 56; alasource46.fr; Price:-,B,-; *A charming B&B with 3 spacious rooms. Ideal for those wanting to make a detour to visit the beautiful village of Saint Cirq. English spoken. Horses welcome*

Saint-Sulpice
Camping du Célé,Le Bourg, 46100 Saint-Sulpice, France; Tel:+33(0) 6 29 46 48 22; +33(0)604089686; Email:campinglecele@gmail.com; camping-du-cele.fr; Price:B,-,-; *Located next to the Célé river. Possibility to rent tipi chalet or caravan*

stage 14 — Gréalou to Limogne-en-Quercy

Length:	29.9km
Ascent:	996m
Descent:	1071m
Le-Puy:	275km
Roncevaux:	507km

View of Cajarc

Route–The route continues to be well-marked as it crosses the arid Causses Region. It consists mostly of asphalt roads and paths through oak forests and dry sheep pastures. The rocky descent to the Lot River valley and the city of Cajarc is steep, as is the climb out of the valley to Saint-Jean-de-Laur.

Pointers–Advance planning: Ensure sufficient water, as the Causses region is particularly demanding due to the heat, rocky terrain and dryness.

Gréalou to Limogne-en-Quercy — stage 14

Cultural Discoveries

Pech Lagaire2 Dolmen

Dolmens were built some 3,500 years ago as monumental stone funerary tombs or sepulchres. Some 600 dolmens have been found in the department of Lot in Quercy. The Pech Laglaire2 Dolmen is one of three dolmens built on the Pech Lagaire hilltop site, and it is classified as a historical monument. It consists of a square sepulchral chamber with a large stone cover, all of which would have originally been buried under a mound of earth and stone (called a tumulus).

Cajarc

In Cajarc (popl. 1,140, alt. 160m), following a revolt against the Bishop of Cahors in 1256, the town's citizens were granted a charter recognizing their "customs and privileges." Specifically, the charter set forth a new relationship between the baron and his subjects and provided for certain fundamental rights, such as due process, which the baron was to respect. With this, Cajarc was one of the first communes in Quercy to gain rights and a degree of independence from the barony. During the Hundred Years' War, thanks to its strategic position encircled by cliffs as well as strong walls, the city was never captured by the English. In the Middle Ages, Quercy was also an important producer of saffron, a precious spice made from the saffron crocus flower. Since 1997, saffron production has been revived and an association of producers is based in Cajarc. An annual saffron fair is held on the last weekend of October.

GR®65

(0.0) From church turn right and continue straight towards cemetery[Church]**(0.2)** Continue straight[Pass cemetery on the right]**(0.7)** Turn left and continue straight on track[Cross on the right] **(1.8)** After the **Pech Laglaire Dolmen**, turn left on track that descends to the D82 road
(2.3) Cross the D82 road and continue straight on trail and pass farm Martigne on the left
 (3.8) Turn right onto asphalt road and continue straight towards the hamlet of Le Verdier**(4.0)** At fork in the hamlet of Le Verdier turn right and continue straight[Signpost]**(4.6)** At intersection, climb straight until the D82 road[Cross to the right] **(5.2)** Turn left onto the D82, and before curve in road keep left on track**(5.7)** Continue straight at intersection
(6.4) Cross D17 road and continue straight on trail**(7.0)** At road's end, turn left and continue straight and cross road[Pass cut tree trunk on left] **(8.4)** Merge left onto asphalt road and then turn left onto track**(9.3)** Turn left and descend on road. Direction Cajarc[Signpost]
(9.4) Turn right onto trail that descends sharply into village of Cajarc[Turn before tree and area with beautiful views of Cajarc] **(10.5)** In the centre of **Carjac**, cross Place du Foirail and take the narrow street straight ahead[Direction Eglise St. Etienne]

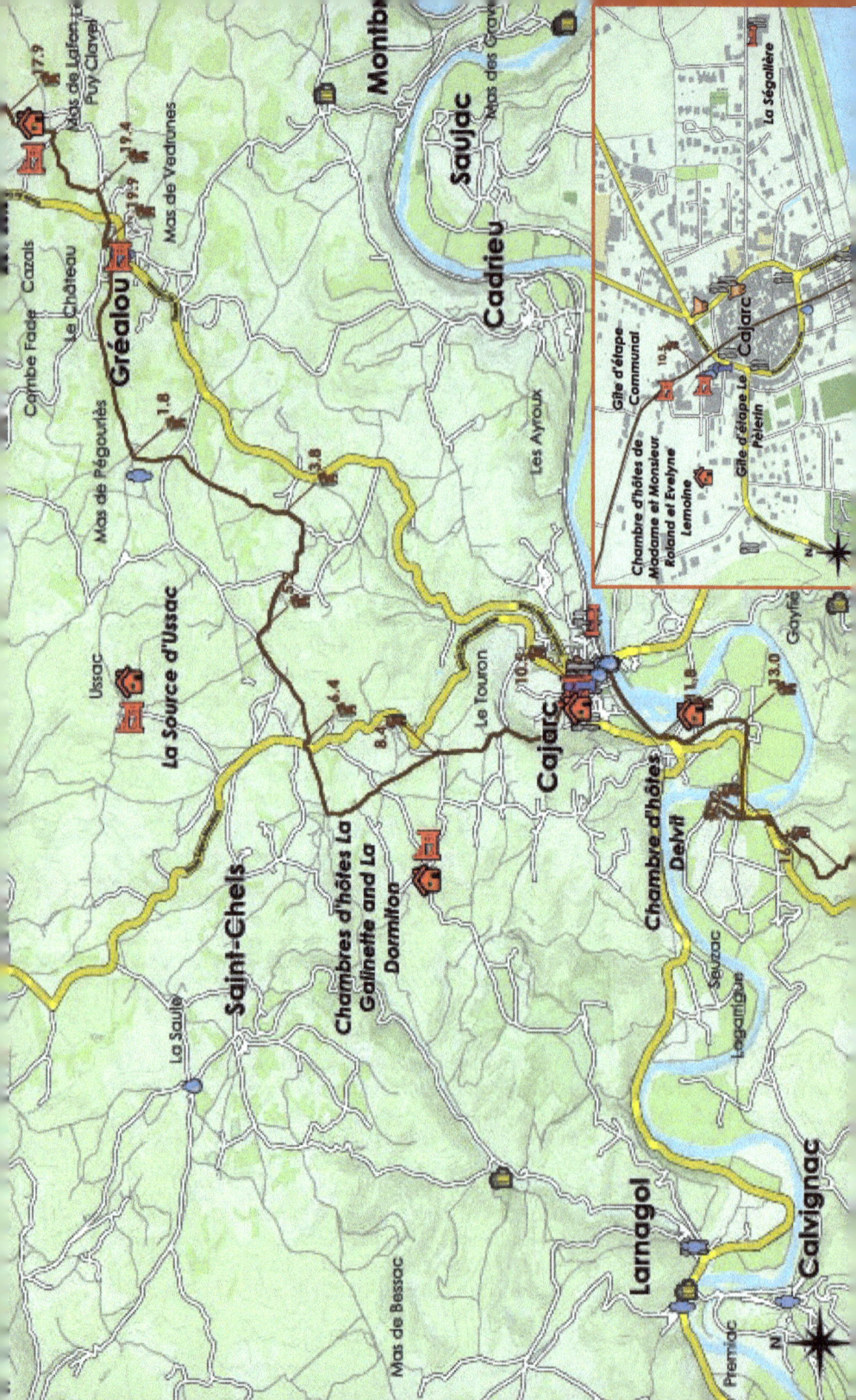

Gréalou to Limogne-en-Quercy — stage 14

(10.7) Pass the church on your left and continue straight[Towards the Mairie] **(10.8)** Cross the road and take the narrow street[pass an ancient water pump on your right] **(11.0)** At the end of the road, turn right[keep the river close on your left] **(11.8)** Take the narrow path beside the EDF building and then bear right on the track to reach the road above **(12.0)** On reaching the road, turn left and keep left at fork and continue straight on chemin de la Route Vieille[Pass Chapel Madeleine to the left and wooden cross to the right] **(13.0)** Turn right[Pass car garage to the right] **(13.3)** Merge right onto the D19 road (caution[) and continue straight to cross the Lot River] **(13.8)** At the end of the bridge, turn right on the small road and keep left[pass through **Gaillac**]

(15.2) Cross the D19 and take the smaller road to the left uphill[pass cemetery on you right] **(15.4)** Keep left on asphalt road, then turn right onto trail running along wall to climb into forest **(15.9)** Keep left on trail through woods. Climb **(16.4)** At fork keep to right[Signpost] **(17.4)** Keep right at fork **(18.2)** Turn right onto asphalt road and continue straight **(20.2)** Turn right onto trail[Stone cross] **(21.1)** On the outskirts of **Saint-Jean-de-Laur** turn right onto asphalt road[Picnic area and refuge on left]

(21.4) Cross the D79 road and continue straight on trail to leave Saint-Jean-de-Laur **(22.6)** At fork keep left **(22.7)** Turn left[Signpost] **(23.4)** Continue straight[Farm to the right] **(23.6)** Merge right onto asphalt road and continue straight through village of Mas de Bories **(23.8)** Continue straight on road and leave village[Cross on left] **(24.8)** Turn left onto trail. Direction Limogne-en-Quercy[Signpost] **(25.5)** Keep right on trail[Following fence to the left] **(25.8)** Turn right at end of path and descend[House and yard] **(26.1)** Turn right and climb into village of Mas de Dalat **(26.2)** Turn left at fork and traverse village od **Mas de Dalat**[Pass cross on the left]

(26.2) Keep right on road to leave village **(26.4)** Turn right off asphalt road and continue straight on track **(26.5)** Turn left onto footpath[Follow stone wall] **(26.8)** Turn left[Pass farm] **(27.0)** Turn left onto asphalt road D143 and continue straight through Mas de Palat **(27.2)** Turn right and again right (U-turn) and follow the wall of the farm[Farm with concrete buildings] **(27.4)** Turn right onto track[Keep left of cross] **(27.9)** Turn right **(29.2)** Merge left onto road and continue straight in the direction of Limogne-en-Quercy **(29.6)** Merge left onto road D911 to enter village of Limogne-en-Quercy[Signpost] **(29.9)** From Place d'Occitanie ascend avenue de Cahors **(29.9)** Arrive at Limogne-en-Quercy centre - Place d'Occitanie[Office of Tourism]

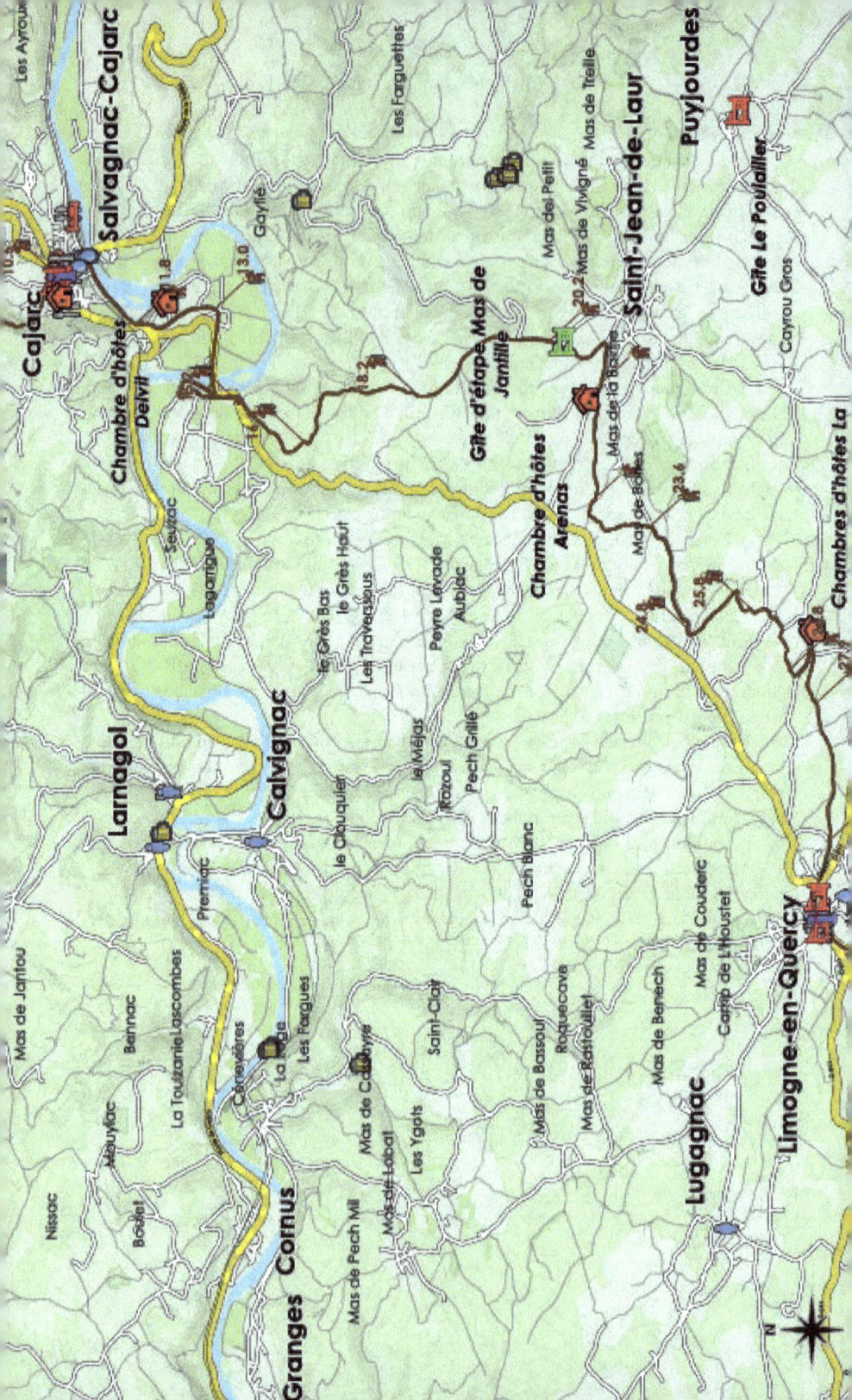

Gréalou to Limogne-en-Quercy   stage 14

Accommodation and Tourist Information

Cajarc

Gîte d'étape - Le Pèlerin,11, Rue Lacaunhe, 46160 Cajarc, France; Tel:+33(0) 674 324 440; +33 (0)565 406 531; Email:gitelepelerincajarc@orange.fr; tourisme-figeac.com; Price:C,C,-; *In a modern building close to the village centre designed for pilgrims. 20 places in rooms of 2-3 or dormitory. Kitchen. Accommodation for horses.*

Gîte d'étape - Communal,1, rue de la Cascade, 46160 Cajarc, France; Tel:+33(0)6 14 66 54 89; Email:gaston4146@gmail.com; gitecajarc.com; Price:C,C,-; *20 places in very basic conditions.*

Chambres d'hôtes - La Galinette and La Dormiton[Anne Conseil],Lieu-dit Semberot, 46160 Cajarc, France; Tel:+33(0)565110344; Email:lagalinette46@orange.fr; galinette.dormiton.free.fr; Price:-,B,B|B,C,-; *An eco-friendly recently renovated house. Private rooms or separate hostel located in a cabin with 2 4-pers. rooms. English spoken. Camping possible.*

Chambre d'hôtes de Madame et Monsieur Roland et Evelyne Lemoine[Evelyne and Roland Lemoine],Impasse du Couvent, 46160 Cajarc, France; Tel:+33(0)5 65 50 15 28; +33(0)6 09 64 32 18; Email:roland.lemoine46@orange.fr; tourisme-lot.com; Price:-,B,-; *1 room. English spoken.*

Chambre d'hôtes Delvit[Michel Delvit],Pech d'Andressac , 46160 Cajarc, France; Tel:+33(0)5 65 40 70 00; +33(0)6 24 11 11 69; Email:michel.delvit@orange.fr; Price:-,B,-; *2 rooms in welcoming home with lovely view of Cajarc.*

Hôtel - La Ségalière,380, avenue François Mitterrand, 46160 Cajarc, France; Tel:+33(0) 5 65 40 65 35; Email:contact@cajarcbluehotel.fr; hotel-lasegaliere-cajarc.com; Price:A,A,A; *Located on the banks of the Lot river. A well maintained hotel with 23 rooms. Lovely pool and garden*

Office de Tourisme,Boulevard du Tour de Ville, 46160 Cajarc, France; Tel:+33(0) 5 65 40 72 89; Email:info@tourisme-figeac.com; tourisme-figeac.com

Limogne-en-Quercy

Gîte d'étape - La Maison en Chemin[Juliette Roumegous],99, rue de Lugagnac, 46260 Limogne-en-Quercy, France; Tel:+33(0)5 65 23 24 41; +33(0)6 85 37 20 59; Email:bonjour@lamaisonencheming r65.fr; lamaisonencheming r65.f; Price:-,-,B; *One of the nicest hostel on the Chemin both for its hospitality and fine accommodations. 14 places in 6 rooms with 1-3 beds*

Gîte d'étape - Communal La Halle,36, rue de la Halle, 46260 Limogne-en-Quercy, France; Tel:+33(0)6 12 84 86 47; Email:gite-etape@limogneenquercy.fr; mairie-limogne.fr/Hébergements.html; Price:C,-,-; *9 places in 4 rooms. Basic accommodations.*

Chambres d'hôtes - La Hulotte[Claudine and Lionel Baudin],Mas des Games, 46260 Limogne-en-Quercy, France; Tel:+33(0)565315851; +33((0)617388447; Email:chambreslahulotte@orange.fr; chambreslahulotte.fr; Price:-,B,-; *A 4-room B&B housed in a lovely Quercy-style restored farmhouse with garden. Kitchen. Accommodation for horses. English spoken.*

Office de Tourisme,55, place d'Occitanie, 46260 Limogne-en-Quercy, France; Tel:+33(0) 5 65 24 34 28; Email:contact@cahorsvalleedulot.com; cahorsvalleedulot.com

Puyjourdes

Gîte Le Poulailler[Françoise Pillon],Le Poulailler, 46260 Puyjourdes, France; Tel:+33(0)6 88 10 57 34; +33(0)6 17 89 61 62; Email:lepoulailler46@orange.fr; lepoulailler46.fr; Price:B,-,C; *5 places in dormitory including in the lovely restored poulailler (hen house) with private Moroccan styled terrace. English spoken.*

St-Jean-de-Laur

Gîte d'étape - Mas de Jantille[Colette and Roger Sohn],Mas de Jantille, 46260 St-Jean-de-Laur, France; Tel:+33 (0)6 88 85 07 18; Email:masdejantille@gmail.com; masdejantille.com; Price:C,C,-; *Housed in a lovely 18th century restored farmhouse. The owners are former pilgrims that fell in love with the region. 10 places in dormitory. Kitchen. Food available for purchase.*

Chambre d'hôtes - Arenas[Jacqueline and Roland],Mas del Pech, 46260 Saint-Jean-De-Laur, France; Tel:+33(0) 565 114 695; +33(0) 621 096 061; chambrehotesinfo.com; Price:-,-,A; *2 bedrooms with dinner en famille*

Saint-Chels

La Source d'Ussac[Sylvie and Dominique Pourcel],Ussac, 46160 Saint-Chels, France; Tel:+33(0) 5 65 40 79 89; Email:dominique.pourcel@orange.fr; source-ussac.fr; Price:C,C,C|B,B,B; *12 places in 4 rooms in beautifully renovated farm near the natural spring of the Ussac. Warm welcome and use of farm and garden products. Accommodation for horses.*

stage 15 — Limogne-en-Quercy to Mas-de-Vers

Length:	22.1km
Ascent:	342m
Descent:	377m
Le-Puy:	305km
Roncevaux:	477km

Route–The route continues to be well-marked, as it crosses the Causses Region, becoming largely flat and straight from Bach, where it follows a former Roman road, le Cami Ferrat, for 15km to Mas de Vers.

Pointers–Culture: The 26 km section of the GR®65 from Bach to Cahors is on the UNESCO world heritage list.

Reservations: Advance reservations are recommended in Mas de Vers, as accommodation possibilities in this sparsely populated stretch of the route

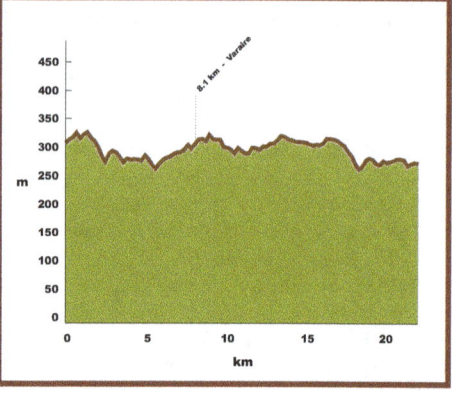

are few and sometimes several kilometres from the main route. There are also no grocers/restaurants, though meals may be reserved with accommodation.

Cultural Discoveries

Varaire–Cami Gasco

Varaire (popl. 300, alt. 240m) boasts a defensive tower from a 13th century fortress that belonged to the Cardaillac family as well as an impressive large *lavoir* (communal laundry) with butterfly-designed washing stones.

From Varaire, the GR®65 follows an ancient Roman road, known as the *Cami Gasco*, which connected the cities of Caylus and Cahors.

stage 15 — Limogne-en-Quercy to Mas-de-Vers

GR®65

(0.3) At fork keep left on the D19 road[Total gas station]**(0.5)** Turn right on chemin du Joncas and continue straight**(0.6)** Turn left onto track at fork[Oak tree] **(2.4)** Turn right onto asphalt road. Direction Ferrieres Bas and continue straight[Signpost]**(2.8)** At fork keep left direction Ferrieres le Dolmen and continue straight[Stone cross, signpost] **(3.5)** Turn right off track onto trail and continue straight[Ahead pass farm on the right]**(4.4)** At road's end, turn right onto asphalt road **(4.7)** Turn left onto track and continue straight**(5.5)** Keep straight on asphalt road and then turn left on track[Signpost] **(7.5)** Merge right onto asphalt road and continue straight towards village of Varaire**(8.1)** On the outskirts of **Varaire** turn right[Signpost. Keep left to visit Varaire village and facilties] **(8.5)** Turn right onto D52 and continue straight to leave village of Varaire**(8.7)** Turn left onto track towards the hamlet of La Plane[Signpost for Bach. Pass Farm on the left]**(9.7)** Turn left, continuing south on track **(11.4)** Turn left[Signpost] **(12.4)** Arrive in Bories-Basses and continue straight through intersection[Building to the right]**(13.1)** Turn left and enter village of Bach[Signpost]**(13.3)** At road's end turn right onto road and continue straight through village[Church] **(13.9)** Turn right onto track[Opposite beige house]**(14.9)** Turn right at road's end. Direction Vaylats and Mas de Vers[Signpost] **(16.2)** Cross the D42 road and then a smaller road. Continue straight on trail[Pass cross on right] **(20.4)** Cross asphalt road and continue straight **(21.6)** Continue straight ahead, direction of Cahors**(22.2)** Arrive at Mas-de-Vers

Accommodation and Tourist Information

Bach
La Grange Saint Jacques[Michelle and Mike Spain],Les Nougayrols , 46230 Bach, France; Tel:+33(0)565310875 ; +33(0)645383761; Email:lagrangesaintjacques@gmail.com; gitecompostellebach.weebly.com; Price:C,C,C|-,B,B; *Lovely gîte located at the entrance to Bach. Owner Mike (English) is a former pilgrim who with his wife Michelle (French) renovated the 19thCentury granary to accommodate pilgrims includes 10 places in 3 rooms (hostel) and 1 double room (B&B).*
Gîte- Le Relais Arc-en-Ciel[Sandrine and Jean],Les Moulins, 46230 Bach, France; Tel:+33 (0)6 65 09 04 82; Email:relaisarcenciel46@gmail.com; relais-arcenciel.com; Price:C,C,C; *The gîte is in a tastefully restored farm consisting of 12 places in 4 3-person rooms with garden and living room, large fire place. English spoken. Accommodation for horses. Located about 1 km before Bach.*

Lalbenque
Gîte d'étape - Poudally[Elsa and Manu],440, chemin de Poudally, 46230 Lalbenque, France; Tel:+33(0)5 65 22 08 69; Email:manu.elsa@poudally.com; poudally.com; Price:C,C,C; *A restored farm run by a young couple 300 meters from Mas de Vers on the GR°65. 27 places in 9 1-6 pers. rooms. Accommodation for horses. English spoken. Very welcoming. Dinner is recommended.*

Varaire
Gîte d'étape - Clos des Escoutilles[Louise and Patrice],Lieui-dit Escoutilles, 46260 Varaire, France; Tel:+33(0)674157723; +33(0)565245084; Email:info@clos-des-escoutilles.eu; clos-des-escoutilles.eu; Price:C,-,-; *50 meters from the GR°the hostel offers a dormitory with 6 places and 2 or 3 person rooms. Kitchen. Very welcoming.*
Gîte d'étape-Café-Restaurant des Marronniers[Marie-Claire Bousquet],Le Bourg , 46260 Varaire, France; Tel:+33(0)5 65 31 53 85; +33(0)6 11 12 12 78; Email:lesmarronniers46@sfr.fr; cahorsvalleedulot.com; Price:-,-,B; *15 places in 4 rooms Reputed for its gourmet restaurant's fixed-menu serving regional specialities rather than for its basic accommodation*

Vaylats
Couvent de Vaylats,100, rue du Couvent, 46230 Vaylats, France; Tel:+33(0)565316351; Email:accueil@couventdevaylats.fr; couventdevaylats.fr; Price:-,-,C; *An easy detour from the GR°65 the convent has a history of welcoming pilgrims. 13 places in 3 and 4 person rooms. Ability to take part in religious services*
Les Yourtes de Bascot - B&B[Pascal Pons],602, chemin de Bascot, 46230 Vaylats, France; Tel:+33(0)6 71 50 54 17; lesyourtesdebascot.com; Price:-,B,B; *A unique experience. 8 places in 2 comfortable yurts situated on the GR°in the forest of the Parc Régional des Causses du Quercy. Accommodation of horses. Host Pascal very welcoming.*

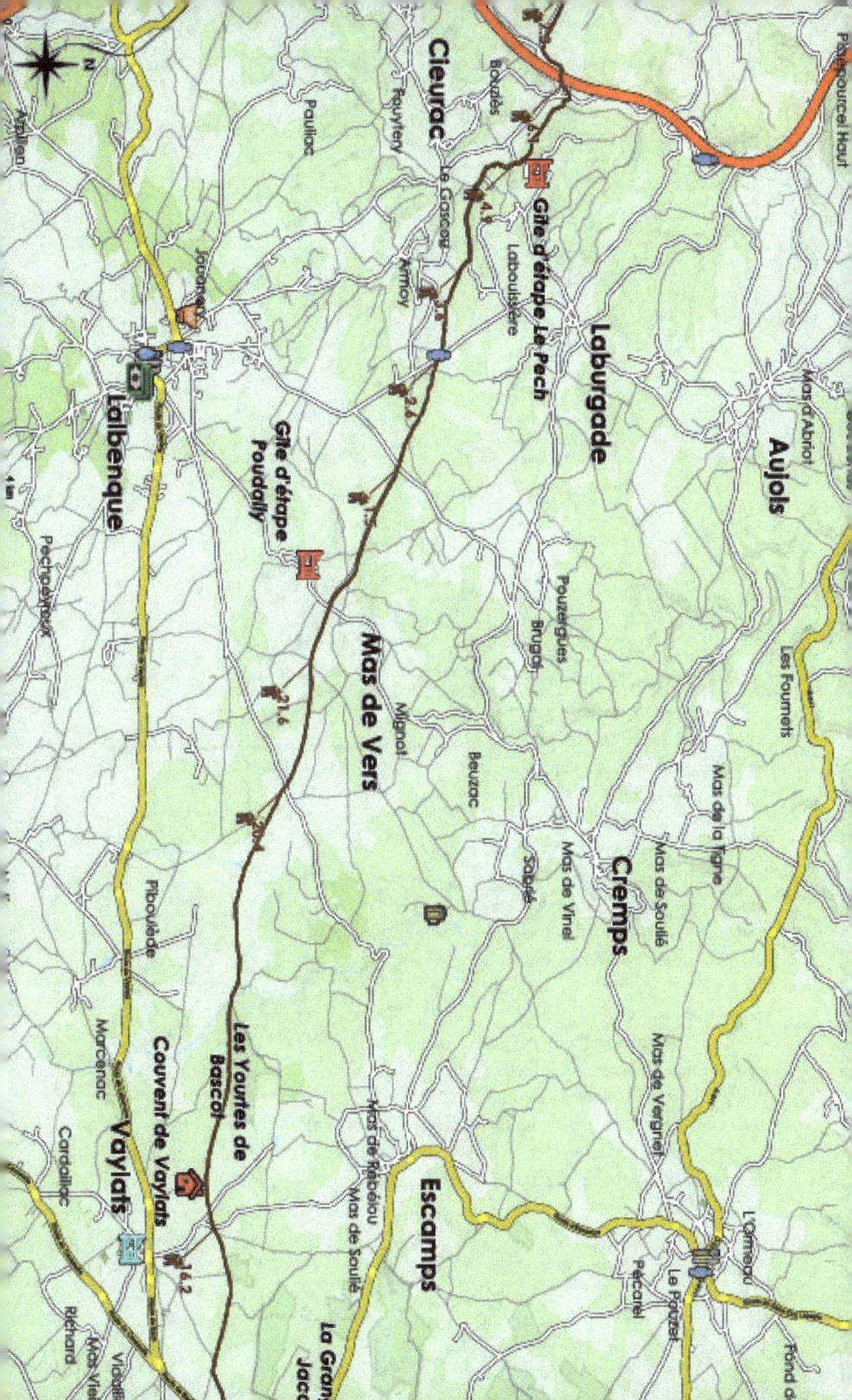

stage 16 — Mas-de-Vers to Cahors

Valentré Bridge Cahors © Alexandra Huddleston

Length:	18.3km
Ascent:	492m
Descent:	633m
Le-Puy:	327km
Roncevaux:	455km

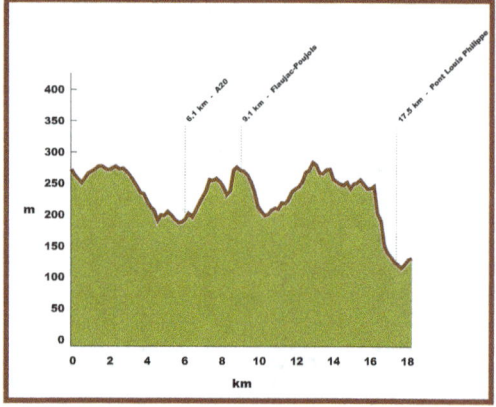

Route - The route continues to be well-marked, as it descends into Cahors and the Lot River Valley. From Mas de Vers, it follows the Roman road, the Cami Ferrat, to Pech. From Pech there is a long descent on mostly small asphalt roads, into Cahors. This stage is short in order to arrive earlier and have time to explore the historic city of Cahors.

Pointers–**Pilgrim welcome:** The GR®65 enters Cahors by the Louis-Philippe bridge. A pilgrim welcome and information centre is set up on the left hand (western) side of the bridge.

Market: Cahors' old town (Place Chapou) hosts a large and colourful market each Wednesday morning and the first and third Saturday of the month.

Mas-de-Vers to Cahors — stage 16

Cultural Discoveries

Cahors

Cahors (popl. 20,000, alt. 120m) is the largest city in the Quercy Region. It was founded by the Romans in the 1st century, in a bend in the Lot River. In addition to benefiting from navigation and protection (being surrounded on three sides) afforded by the Lot river, Cahors was also the meeting place of Roman roads leading to Toulouse, Bordeaux and Rodez. Roman ruins include a forum, Diane's arch (a remnant of the former baths), the remains of a large amphitheatre and the fountain of Chartreux.

Cahors was a rich merchant city in the 12th-14th centuries and an important intellectual and administrative centre in the 16th-18th centuries, due in part to its famous university (which no longer exists). Commerce, wine and administration formed the heart of the city.

Cahors remains famous for its wine (once called "black wine" by the English), which is made from Malbec grapes and was historically an important export, as it survived transport and could be kept over long periods. Black truffles (or "black diamonds") are another delicatessen. These grow on the roots of oak trees on the limestone plateau and are harvested in winter with the help of pigs or dogs. Other specialities include *croustilot* bread (made from local wheat), melons and *Pastis du Quercy* (a cake made with filo pastry and apple purée made with alcohol). Cahors hosts a lively market each Wednesday (Place Chapou).

Cathedral of Saint Stephen
(*Cathédrale Saint-Étienne*)

According to legend, the Cathedral of Saint Stephen and its ecclesiastical complex was built in the 7th century by Saint Didier. However, most of the structure dates from the 12th century, when Pope Calixtus II consecrated the cathedral's two main altars. The cathedral has undergone several additions and renovations over the centuries. It remains, however, one of the best examples in France of a Romanesque Dome-church, with its 17 metre cupola stretching across the central nave. The tympanum over the northern entrance is from the middle of the 12th century and depicts Christ's Ascension and the preaching and martyrdom of Saint Stephen, one of the first Christian martyrs and the cathedral's patron saint. The cathedral also contains important Romanesque frescoes depicting Old Testament scenes, including the story of Genesis.

Valentré Bridge

Built in the second half of the 14th century, the Valentré Bridge is the oldest surviving bridge across the Lot River. The bridge was extensively restored in the 19th century–its military defences were reinforced and a small devil-figure was added to the central tower as a symbol of the legend that Satan had a role in the bridge's completion. With its three imposing towers, the Valentré Bridge is one of the best examples in France of a medieval fortified bridge.

Cathedral of Saint Stephen

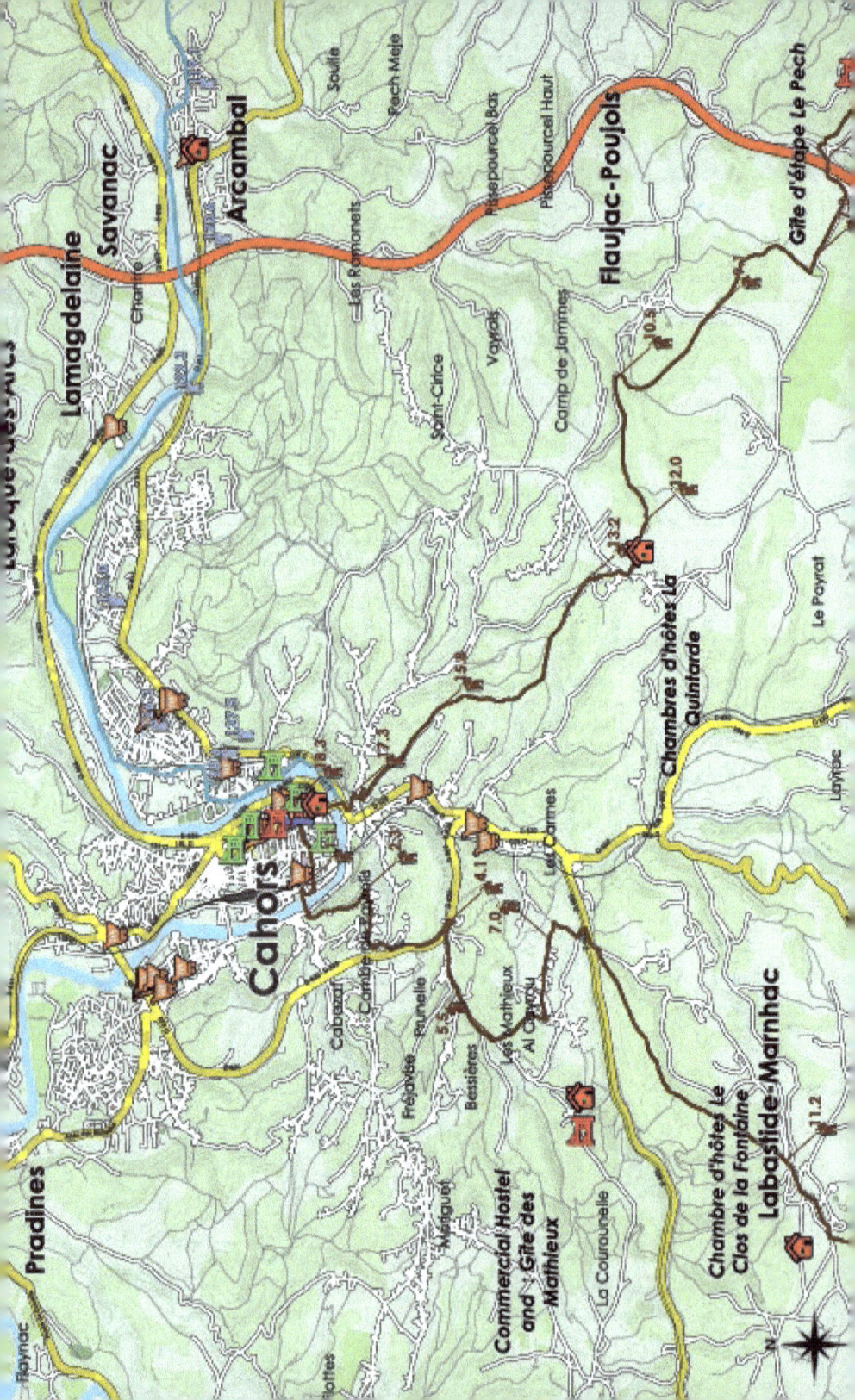

Mas-de-Vers to Cahors

stage 16

GR®65

(0.0) Continue straight on road[Pass cross on the right] **(1.5)** Cross the D10 road and continue straight on track **(2.6)** Cross asphalt road and continue straight on track **(3.6)** Turn left onto asphalt road[Pass *lavoire* on right] **(4.9)** Turn right towards Le Pech and then immediate left on asphalt road direction Cahors[Signposts] **(5.8)** Turn left and follow path running along road. Cross road and turn left onto footpath **(6.1)** Go through underpass below the **A20** highway and take trail to the right, which runs alongside road
(7.3) Turn right onto footpath and continue climb. Direction Cahors[Signpost. Farm building to the left] **(7.4)** Turn right onto asphalt road and continue straight **(7.9)** Turn left onto track and continue straight[Ahead pass sports pitch to the right] **(9.1)** Enter village of **Flaujac-Poujols** and keep left. Continue straight on chemin de Saint Jacques[Signpost]
(10.5) Turn left on trail[Before D22 road] **(12.0)** Keep to the right of stone shed and continue straight on trail **(12.6)** Turn right onto the D6 road and then take first right onto route de la Marchande[Signpost] **(12.8)** Turn left after house number 71 onto chemin de la Marchande **(13.2)** Cross D6 and continue straight on chemin de Cabridelle[Cross residential area followed by barren hilltop] **(15.8)** Merge onto chemin du Pech de Fourques and begin descent into Cahors **(17.3)** At road's end turn left, pass under train tracks and continue straight towards Lot River[Signpost] **(17.5)** Turn right onto rue St Georges and take staircase on left to cross bridge **Pont Louis Philippe**. Here, on bridge Louis Philippe, the alternative routes from the Célé Valley and Rocamadour rejoin the Way of Saint James - GR®65[Pilgrim Welcome Centre on the left-hand side of the bridge]
(17.8) At the roundabout after crossing the bridge into Cahors centre, turn right and then left[take place Hélène Metges leading to Rue Nationale] **(18.3)** Arrive at Cahors[place Jean Jacques Chapou]

stage 16 — Mas-de-Vers to Cahors

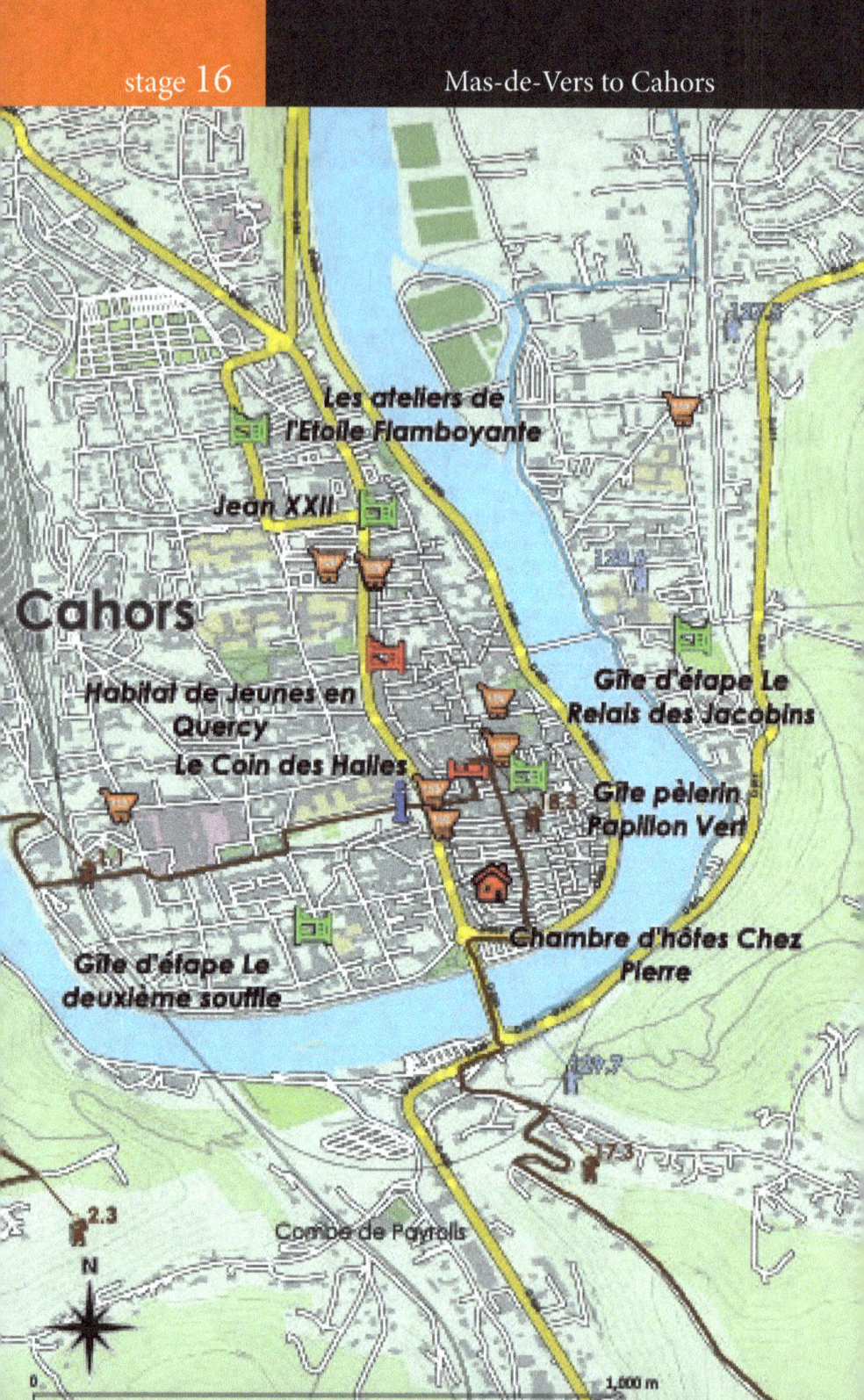

Mas-de-Vers to Cahors

stage 16

Accommodation and Tourist Information

Cahors

Hôtel Jean XXII,2, rue Edmond Albe, 46000 Cahors, France; Tel:+33(0) 9 87 75 77 48; hotel-jeanxxii.com; Price:A,-,-; *Charming two-star hotel in the old town and housed in the former 13th Century palace of Duèze with 9 rooms for 1 to 4-persons.*

Gite d'étape - Le Petit Refuge[Catherine],7, cote des Anes, 46000 Cahors, France; Tel:+33 (0)6 52 97 33 00; Email:lepetitrefugecahors@gmail.com; lepetitrefuge.webador.fr; Price:C,C,C; *A new facility with 5 beds in a single dormitory*

Gîte pèlerin - Papillon Vert[Jaqui],1, rue du Tapis Vert, 46000 Cahors, France; Tel:+33 (0)6 75 80 58 42; +33(0)581701409; Email:papillonvert@gmail.com; papillonvert.fr; Price:C,C,C; *Located in a quiet street next to the Cathedral tastefully decorated town-house with 8 places in 3 rooms. Kitchen. English spoken.*

Gîte d'étape Le Relais des Jacobins[Serge Bouquet],12, rue des Jacobins, 46000 Cahors, France; Tel:+33 (0)565 210 084; +33(0)6 29 47 85 30; Email:lerelaisdesjacobins@gmail.com; cahors-valleedulot.com; Price:C,C,C; *Down to earth hostel with 15 places in 5 rooms. A short walk to the Cathedral and famous for its welcoming and knowledgeable owner Serge. Large garden. English spoken.*

Les ateliers de l'Etoile Flamboyante,50, rue Jean de Vayrac, 46000 Cahors, France; Tel:+33 (0)619 212 986; Email:anne.karthaus@gmail.com; lesateliersdeletoile.com; Price:D,D,D; *4 places in a single dormitory*

Gîte d'étape - Le deuxième souffle[Louis-Philippe and Valentré],178, rue Hautesserre, 46000 Cahors, France; Tel:+33(0)777266424; Email:L2S.accueil@gmail.com; ledeuxiemesouffle.fr; Price:C,C,C; *6 places in 2 dormitories and 1 private room possibility to camp in the garden English spoken*

Habitat de Jeunes en Quercy,129, rue Fondue Haute, 46000 Cahors, France; Tel:+33(0)565352932; Email:afjq46@yahoo.fr; logement-cahors.fr; Price:C,-,-; *Basic budget accommodations including 18 places in 10 rooms (based on availability). English spoken. Garden. No animals*

Chambre d'hôtes - Chez Pierre[Pierre Capredon],62, rue Etienne Brives, 46000 Cahors, France; Tel:+33(0) 6 09 96 28 32; Email:noderpac@gmail.com; gitechezpierre.com; Price:-,C,-; *10 places in rooms of 1 to 3 persons. English spoken. Located in the historic centre. Pierre comes from Cahors and knows the region well.*

Hôtel - Le Coin des Halles,30, place Saint-Maurice, 46000 Cahors, France; Tel:+33(0) 5 65 30 24 27; Email:contact@lecoindeshalles-hotel.com; coin-des-halles.com; Price:B,-,-; *Centrally located 2 star hotel with 13 roooms*

Office de Tourism,Place François Mitterrand, 46000 Cahors, France; Tel:+33(0) 5 65 53 20 65; Email:contact@cahorsvalleedulot.com; cahorsvalleedulot.com

Flaujac-Poujols

Chambres d'hôtes - La Quintarde[Christine and Christophe],185, chemin de la Quintarde, 46090 Flaujac-Poujols, France; Tel:+33(0) 6 65 13 95 12; Email:contact@laquintarde.com; Price:-,A,A; *Newly renovated Quercy style home with 4 2-3 person rooms*

Laburgade

Gîte d'étape - Le Pech[Annelise Latour],Gîte d'étape le Pech, 46230 Laburgade, France; Tel:+33 (0)565247284; 33 (0)637436013; Email:haneliese@hotmail.com; gitelepechlatour.fr; Price:-,C,-; *10 places in comfortable hostel. Kitchen. Horses welcome. English spoken. No dogs. No shops in the immediate area*

stage 17 — Cahors to Lascabanes

Length:	23.3km
Ascent:	673m
Descent:	621m
Le-Puy:	345km
Roncevaux:	436km

Route–The route continues to be well-marked, and uses mostly footpaths and tracks. After crossing Cahors' beautiful Valentré bridge, there is a short but steep climb up cliffs, offering beautiful views of the city. The route becomes more moderate as it passes through villages, pine forests and sunflower and wheat fields, typical of the high plateau of Quercy Blanc, before arriving in Lascabanes.

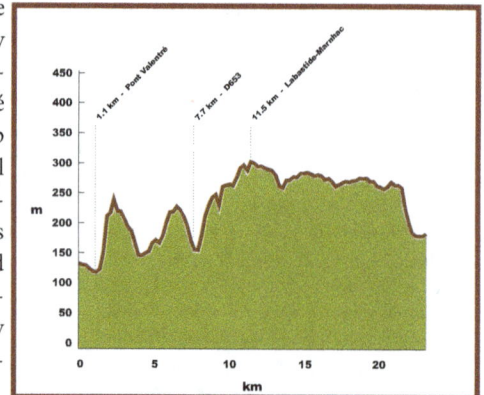

Cultural Discoveries

Labastide-Marnhac

Labastide-Marnhac (popl. 1,200, alt. 140m) is a medieval fortified village founded by baron Guillaume de Lard of Cahors. In the 13th century, a castle and hospital were built of which only the current Romanesque chapel remains.

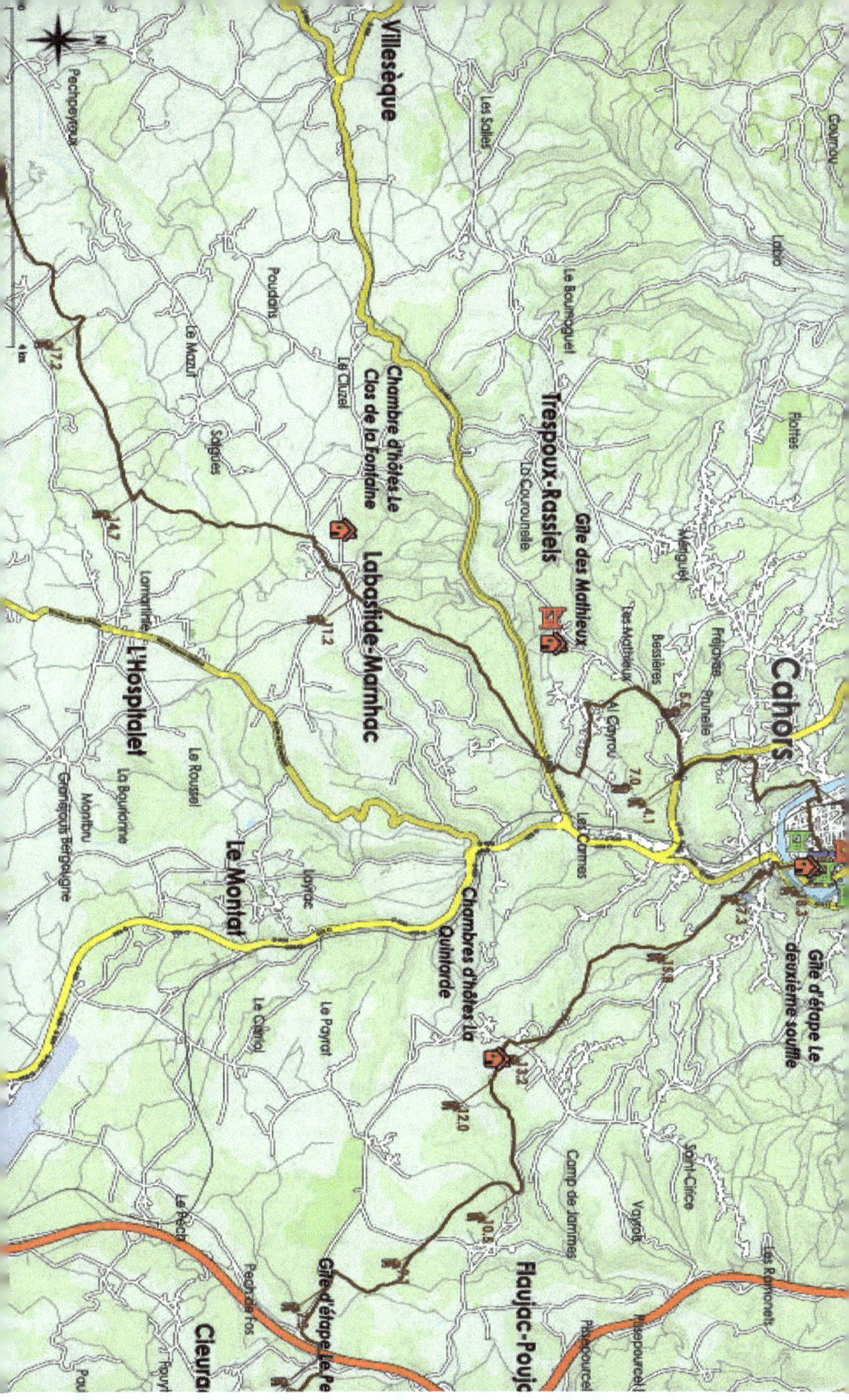

stage 17

Cahors to Lascabanes

GR®65

(0.0) From the south-west corner of place Jean Jacques Chapou take place Saint Maurice and take the first left[keep Halle de Cahors on your left]**(0.1)** At the end of the road turn left[rue Georges Clemenceau]**(0.5)** Cross the park to your left then turn right[rue Saint Géry]**(0.7)** At the end of the road, turn right and immediately left[towards the river]**(1.0)** Turn right on the riverside path **(1.1)** Cross **Pont Valentré** bridge[Bridge]
(1.4) Cross C21 road and climb steep footpath that leads to plateau. Keep left on a trail that runs alongside the cliffs[Signpost] **(2.3)** Turn right onto asphalt road, and then left to descend to the D820 road. Use underpass[Signposts] **(4.1)** Turn left onto road running next to the D820 road, and then continue straight[D820 road on the right] **(5.5)** Continue straight on chemin de la Combe Nègre towards La Rozière[Signpost]**(6.3)** Shortly before reaching the church turn sharp left[chemin des Amandiers]**(6.5)** Right fork **(7.0)** Fork right then turn right[descend the hill]**(7.5)** At the T-junction, turn left towards the garage**(7.7)** At the T-junction with the **D653**, turn right and then take the first left[D7, Labastide-Marnhac]
(8.0) Take the first track to the right, steeply uphill[follow the ridge] **(11.2)** Cross street and continue straight on path to the left of the road to enter Labastide-Marnhac**(11.5)** In **Labastide-Marnhac** continue straight on main road, direction commerce[Pass church on left]
(11.8) Continue straight on asphalt road[Pass townhall (Mairie) on left]**(12.1)** Turn right at stop sign and immediate left onto D7 road[Signpost]**(12.2)** Turn left on chemin du Roy and continue straight[Sign post] **(14.7)** Turn left and then right onto road towards Fabre **(17.2)** Turn left and continue straight towards Lascabanes **(20.5)** Turn left onto asphalt road and then keep right. Descend into the valley towards the village of Baffalie **(23.0)** Enter Lascabanes. Turn right and cross stream (Le Verdanson) towards village centre[Signpost and stream]**(23.3)** Arrive at Lascabanes

Accommodation and Tourist Information

Labastide-Marnhac

Commercial Hostel and B&B: Gîte des Mathieux, Domaine des Mathieux, 46090 Labastide-Marnhac, France; Tel:+33(0)565317513; Email:domainedesmathieux@gmail.com; domainedesmathieux.com; Price:C,C,C|-,B,A; *Owned by a former pilgrim; 28 places in dormitory rooms or B&B. English spoken. Pool.*

Chambre d'hôtes - Le Clos de la Fontaine, 444, chemin du Moulin et de la Fontaine, 46090 Labastide-Marnhac, France; Tel:+33(0) 7 81 76 76 87; Email:closdelafontaine.lot@gmail.com ; closdelafontainelabastidemarnhac.com; Price:A,A,A; *4 bedrooms in charming B&B with pool special price for pilgrims*

Lascabanes

L'étape bleue[Marie-Claude and Jean-Michel Cayon-Glayère],64, route de Durand , 46800 Lascabanes, France; Tel:+33(0)5 65 35 34 77; Email:mc.cayon-glayere@orange.fr; gite-etape-bleue.com; Price:C,C,C|-,C,-; *About 800m off the GR®65 and 1 km before Lascabanes. The B&B is a restored farmhouse owned by welcoming former pilgrims offering 1 B&B room and 4 dormitories with 2 to 4 places. Horses and donkeys welcome Camping space available.*

Yourte Le Sabatier[Jean Sébastien],Lieu-dit Sabatier, 46800 Lascabanes, France; Tel:+33 (0)565 23 98 54; Email:jslascabanes@gmail.com; Price:C,C,C; *Choose between a Mongol or Inuit yurt each accommodating between 1- 4 pers. Pool. English spoken. Horses possible.*

Gîte Le Nid des Anges[Mme. Cécile Maupoux],Gîte d'étape de Lascabanes, 46800 Lascabanes, France; Tel:+33(0) 5 65 31 86 38; Email:chiha-maupoux@wanadoo.fr; lenidesanges.com; Price:C,C,C; *17 places in rooms of 2 to 5 pers. A former presbytery. The dinner using local products is recommended.*

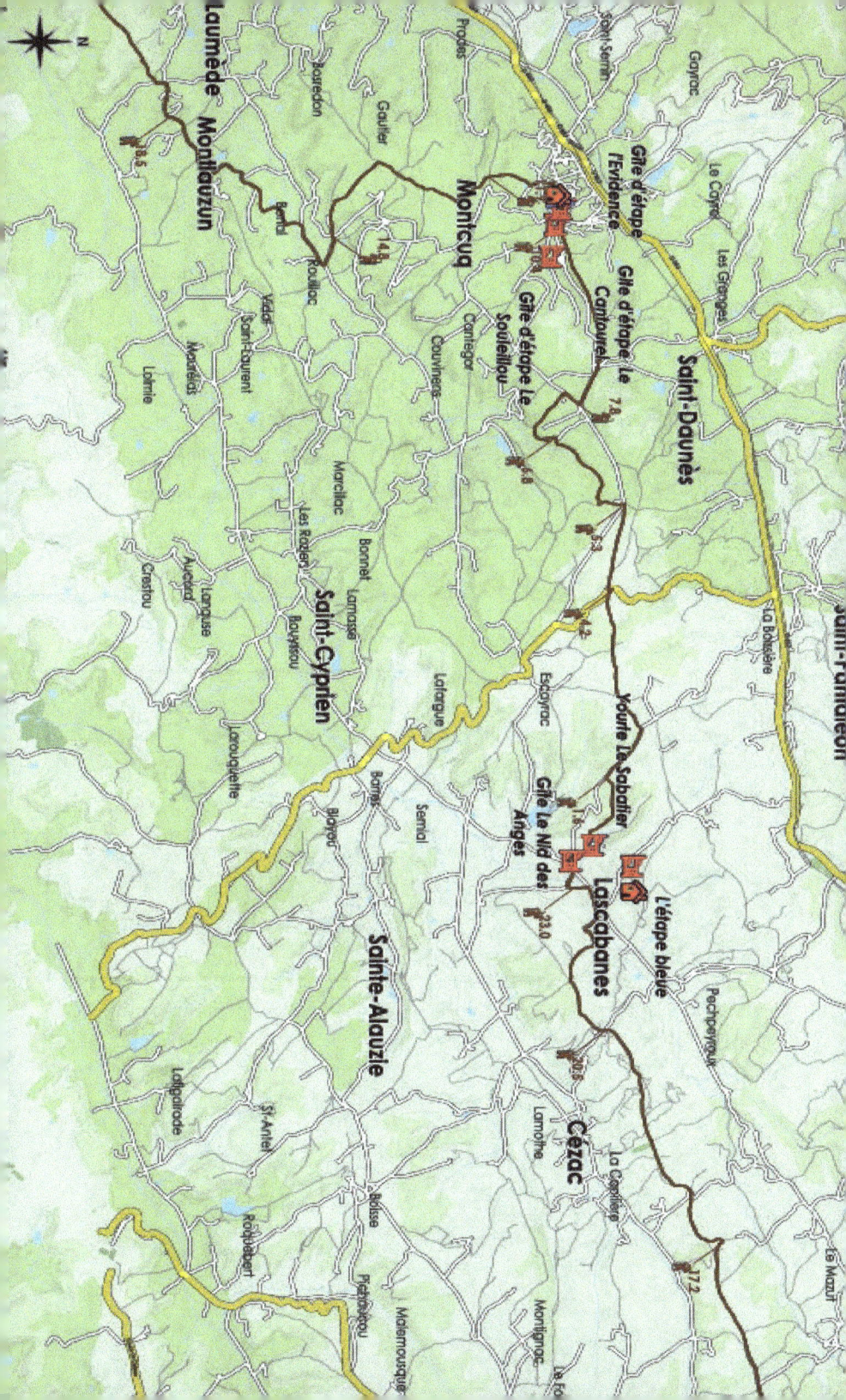

stage 18 — Lascabanes to Lauzerte

Lauzerte

Length:	25.8km
Ascent:	858m
Descent:	828m
Le-Puy:	368km
Roncevaux:	413km

Route–The route, which uses mostly asphalt roads and tracks, continues to be well-marked, as it passes through a rich agricultural zone including sunflower and wheat fields, vineyards and medieval villages perched atop hills.

Pointers–Be careful on the brief but steep descent after Montlauzan (Pech-de-la-Rode), which can be slippery when wet.

Market: Lauzerte hosts a market each Wednesday and Saturday morning (8a.m. to 1p.m.). Festival: Lauzerte also hosts an annual nocturnal contemporary arts festival the first weekend in August. www.lauzerte.fr

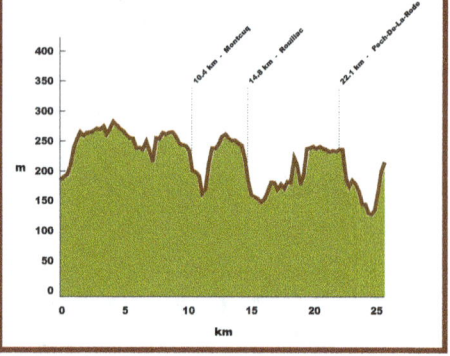

Lascabanes to Lauzerte

stage 18

Cultural Discoveries

Montcuq

The medieval walls that once surrounded Montcuq (popl. 1300, alt. 150m) were raised by order of the king in 1229. Only some vestiges remain, including a 12th century square 24 metre tower that dominates the village, and which today houses a medieval history exposition. The 14th century **Church of Saint Hilary** (*Eglise Saint-Hilaire*), with an octagonal clock tower, has impressive frescoes. More recently, the village became famous for a 1970s comic skit that poked fun at the name Montcuq. In French, Montcuq is pronounced (mon kü), or *mon cul*, meaning my backside, while in the native Occitan language the pronunciation is mon kük. A local market is held on Thursday and Sunday mornings.

Lauzerte

The village of Lauzerte (popl. 1488, alt. 200m) was designed as a *castelnau*, or settlement founded around a castle for defensive purposes. It was perched on a summit, and included a fortress, surrounding walls, towers and six gates. Despite these defences, Lauzerte fell to the English during the Hundred Years' War and passed between Protestant and Catholic control in the Wars of Religion. The main street, Grand Rue, is lined by impressive medieval houses from the 14th-16th centuries that attest to a former prosperity from the wheat trade. The village is considered one of the most beautiful in France and has a lively artistic community. A local market takes place on Saturday mornings.

GR®65

(0.0) Leave Lascabanes on main street (D7) and take immediate right on road C3[Alternatively, make your way to the church, from whence the path departs]**(0.2)** Take first right and head towards church. Stay left on road to the left of church (route de Saint-Géry) and continue straight[Signpost and bridge] **(1.6)** Turn right onto C3/Route de Saint-Pantaléon and continue straight**(2.4)** Turn left at Chapel Saint-Jean le Froid and continue straight past the turn off on the left to Escayrac[Water spring (La fontaine de Saint-Jean) near chapel was once revered as "miraculous."] **(4.2)** Turn left on the D37 road and then right onto track, direction Montcuq[Signpost] **(5.3)** Turn left to cross the D4 and take the track gently up the hill[pass the déchèterie on your right]**(5.6)** On reaching the trees turn right on the track **(6.8)** Close to the houses, turn left and left again[descend the ridge]**(7.2)** Turn right into the narrow valley **(7.8)** At the T-junction with the tarmac road, turn right[barn to your left]**(8.1)** Turn left and join the path beside the D4[barn to your left]**(8.4)** Take the right fork and then follow the pathway to the left to join the minor road and enter Montcuq **(10.4)** Turn right to visit **Montcuq** village centre (off the GR*). The main route continues to the left[Signpost]
(10.5) At the crossroads bear right on rue Faubourg StPrivat into the heart of the village[Opposite church]**(10.6)** Keep left[towards Tourist Office]**(10.9)** Take the left fork and zig-zag down the hill before turning right on the narrtow downhill road[pass school on your left]**(11.1)** At the crossroads continue straight**(11.3)** Turn right on the path[pass pond on your left] **(11.9)** Cross the farm track and continue downhill[pass pond on your left]**(12.5)** At the T-junction with the farm track turn right **(14.8)** Cross the road into **Rouillac** then take the next right at the church, direction Berty[Church and signpost]
(15.2) In Berty, turn right onto C17 road and continue straight[Pass farm on left]**(15.7)** Turn left off road and cross stream (Ruisseau du Tartuguié). Continue straight towards Montlauzun[Stream. Further south, pass farm on the right] **(18.5)** Turn right to visit hilltop village of Montlauzun (off the main route)**(18.9)** Turn left onto the D45 road and then right on track through forest towards Le Pech-de-la-Rode **(22.1)** In **Pech-de-la-Rode** cross street and continue straight (steep descent). Continue on trail until reaching the D54 road, and turn right towards Lauzerte
(24.7) At roundabout, continue straight on road (crossing the D953). Climb towards Lauzerte**(25.1)** Take trail to the right and continue steep climb towards Lauzerte centre[Pass Gîte Les Figuiers on right] **(25.5)** Turn right and continue climb towards village of Lauzerte. Then turn left to enter village centre **(25.7)** Continue straight through village[Signpost]**(25.8)** Arrive at Lauzerte[Place des Corniers]

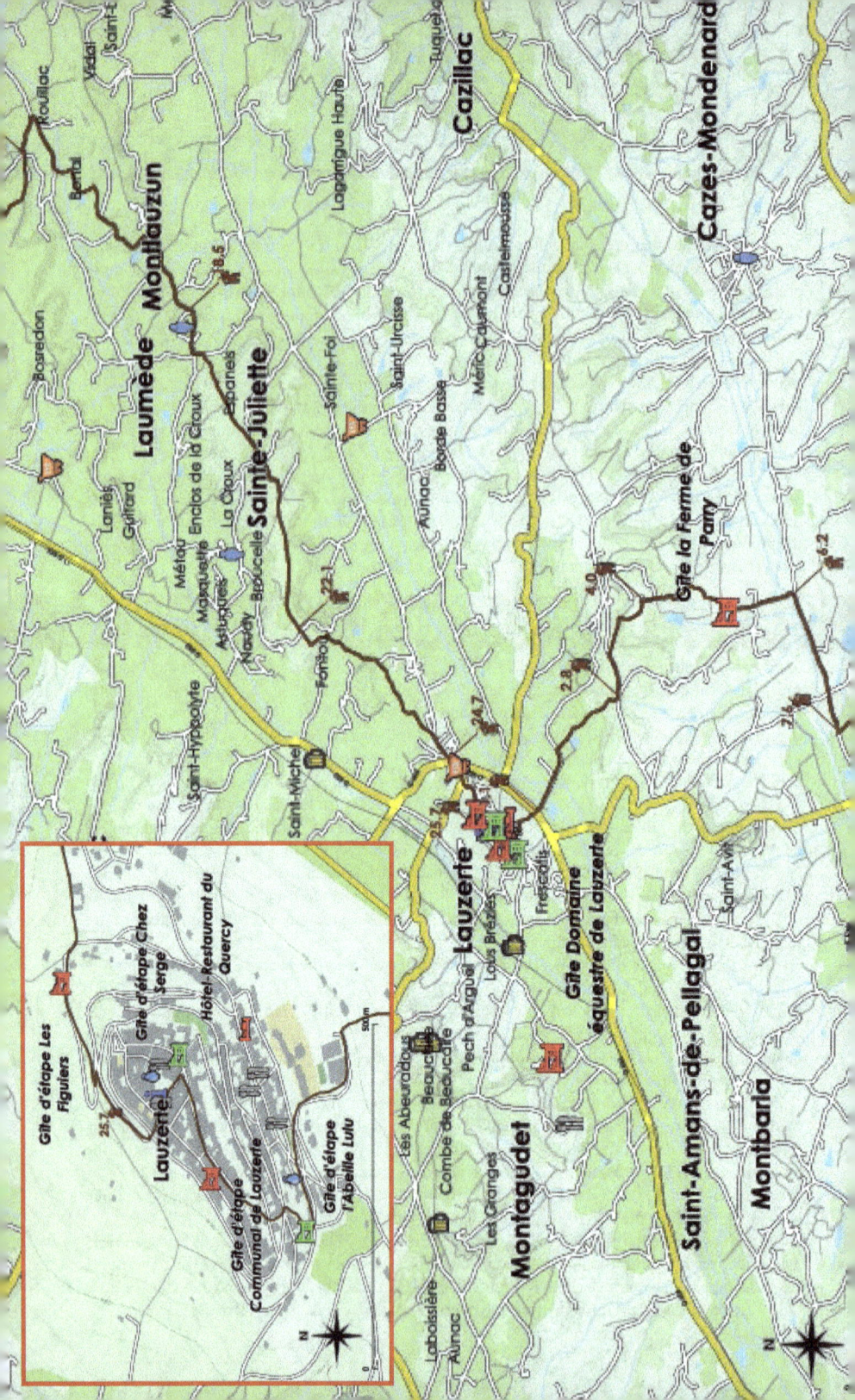

Lascabanes to Lauzerte — stage 18

Accommodation and Tourist Information

Lauzerte

Gîte d'étape - Chez Serge[Serge Pradin],32, rue de la Garrigue, 82110 Lauzerte, France; Tel:+33(0) 672 241 985; +33(0) 563 957 416; Email:serge.pradin@orange.fr; quercy-sud-ouest.com; Price:C,C,C; *4 places in a single dormitory*

Gîte d'étape - l'Abeille Lulu,1, chemin de la Fontaine, 82110 Lauzerte, France; Tel:+33(0)687055360; Email:abeillelulu82@gmail.com; gitedetapelabeillelulu.fr; Price:C,C,-; . *Close to the heart of the village but with great country views*

Gîte - Domaine équestre de Lauzerte[Isabelle and Frédéric Favrot],647, chemin de Las Boutes, 82110 Lauzerte, France; Tel:+33(0)563946346; +33(0)563946613; domaine-de-lauzerte.fr; Price:B,B,B; *Located on the hill facing Lauzerte 3 km off the GR*65 this equestrian center offers a hostel mobile homes and pool. Accommodation for horses. English spoken.*

Gîte d'étape - Les Figuiers[Florence and Alain],25, chemin du Coudounier, 82110 Lauzerte, France; Tel:+33(0)563291185; +33(0)685317131; Email:accueil@lesfiguiers-lauzerte.com; lesfiguiers-lauzerte.com; Price:C,C,C; *Located on the ascent to the village of Lauzerte 30 places in modern facility. The hosts are famous for their hospitality.*

Gîte d'étape - Communal de Lauzerte,15, rue du Millial, 82110 Lauzerte, France; Tel:+ 33(0) 6 19 70 89 49; Email:lecamino123@gmail.com; gitecommunal-lauzerte.com; Price:C,C,C; *Basic accommodation offering 15 places in the medieval village center run by former pilgrim. Kitchen. Possibility to have vegetarian or gluten free meal (but call in advance)*

Hôtel-Restaurant du Quercy,11, route de Cahors, 82110 Lauzerte, France; Tel:+33(0)5 63 94 66 36; Email:hotel.du.quercy@wanadoo.fr; hotel-du-quercy.fr; Price:A,A,A; *The restaurant is better than the hotel with nice terrace. English spoken.*

Office de Tourisme,10, place des Cornières, 82110 Lauzerte, France; Tel:+33(0) 5 63 94 61 94; Email:accueil@lauzerte-tourisme.fr; quercy-sud-ouest.com

Montcuq-en-Quercy-Blanc

Gîte d'étape - Le Cantourel [Pierre Marcastel],32, rue du Faubourg Saint-Privat, 46800 Montcuq-en-Quercy-Blanc, France; Tel:+33(0) 6 82 13 18 65; Email:gite.cantourel@gmail.com; gite-cantourel.fr; Price:C,C,C; *15 places in rooms for 23 and 4 persons.*

Gîte d'étape - l'Evidence[François and Lucy],8, rue du Couvent des Cordeliers, 46800 Montcuq-en-Quercy-Blanc, France; Tel:+33(0) 606 480 388; Email:levidence.sas@orange.fr; levidence-90.webself.net; Price:C,C,C; *9 places in 4 rooms kitchen. Close to the village centre*

Gîte d'étape - Le Souleillou[Detlev Bahler],356, rue du Souleillou, 46800 Montcuq-en-Quercy-Blanc, France; Tel:+33 (0)7 61 51 69 41; Email:lesouleillou@gmail.com; le-souleillou.fr; Price:C,C,C; *29 places in rooms of 2-6 pers. Accommodation for horses. English spoken. Camping also possible.*

<type5</type**Chambre d'hôtes - Le Coucou**[Gisèle and Jean-Pierre Couture],4, rue Droite, 46800 Montcuq-en-Quercy-Blanc, France; Tel:+33 (0)6 08 66 71 30; +44 (0) 7813 552 181; Email:info@lecoucoumontcuq.fr; lecoucoumontcuq.fr; Price:-,A,-; *3 double rooms. English spoken. Located in the village centre*

Mairie de Montcuq,1, place des Consuls, 46800 Montcuq-en-Quercy-Blanc, France; Tel:+33(0) 5 65 31 80 05; mairie-montcuq-en-quercy-blanc.fr

stage 19 — Lauzerte to Moissac

Moissac Cloister

Length:	27.9km
Ascent:	857m
Descent:	997m
Le-Puy:	394km
Roncevaux:	387km

Route–The route continues to be well-marked, and uses mostly asphalt roads as it passes through farms and orchards to makes its way to Moissac, a major stop along the Way of Saint James.

Pointers–**Treats:** Possibility to buy local produce at a farm stand before Durfort-Lacapelette (bring coins).
Advance planning: Ensure that you have enough water and provisions between Durfort-Lacapelettte and Moissac, as there are no watering points or grocers in this stretch.

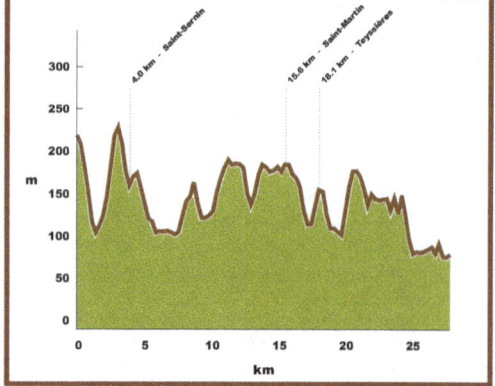

Lauzerte to Moissac

stage 19

Cultural Discoveries

Moissac

Moissac (popl. 12,570, alt. 70m) occupied a strategic position on the main land and water routes that connected Toulouse, Bordeaux, Quercy and Gascony. It is most famous, however, for the **Abbey of Saint Peter** (*Abbaye Saint-Pierre*). According to legend, the abbey was founded in the mid-7th century by Clovis, the first Christian French King. In the mid-11th century, the abbey became affiliated with the powerful Cluny order, after which important building projects began, including a new church, consecrated in 1063, and the cloister finished in 1100. With its 76 intricately sculpted capitals (topmost part of a column), depicting saints and biblical and creation scenes (such as flora and fauna), the cloister of Saint Peter is a treasure of Romanesque art. Later in the 12th century, the church's magnificent tympanum over the southern entrance was sculpted, depicting Christ in Majesty (as recounted in the Book of Revelation). A market is held each Saturday morning (Place des Récollets).

Detail of Prophet Jerome

GR®65

(0.0) Depart Lauzerte fom Place des Cordieleieres[Signpost]**(0.1)** Turn right onto Grand Rue, then turn left onto stairs at end of road[Staircase before Retirement home (Maison de retraite)]**(0.3)** Turn left and descend staircase**(0.4)** Turn right on Passage du Pèlerin[Signpost]**(0.5)** At path's end, turn left[Cemetery]**(0.7)** Turn right onto chemin de Ruppe and descend**(0.9)** Turn right onto steep trail and descend to the D953 road[Pass modern building] **(1.1)** Cross D953 road and continue straight on the D81 road crossing stream (Le Lendou)[Signpost]**(1.8)** Turn right and continue straight, climbing. Keep to right on track and pass pond to the right **(2.8)** Turn left onto asphalt road and continue straight to Charton. After passing "pigeonnier" (dovecote), turn right onto trail to Chapel of Saint-Sernin **(4.0)** Pass Chapel of **Saint-Sernin** on left and continue to the right on trail[Chapel]
(4.4) Turn right at fork and continue straight to the D57 road **(6.2)** At road's end, turn right and continue straight on the D57 road **(7.7)** Turn left off the D57 road and climb footpath. Keep left on road towards Mirabel[Signpost] **(9.4)** Turn left before asphalt road and continue on track through fields**(10.1)** Turn right and climb hill, which can be covered with sunflowers in summer **(11.2)** Turn left onto small street before D2 road. Then turn right on trail next to residential area and rejoin the D2 and enter Durfort-Lacapelette**(11.9)** At roundabout continue straight towards Durfort-Lacapelette centre[Sign post]**(12.0)** Pass through Durfort. At intersection with the D2 road, continue straight on the D16 road[Sign post] **(12.3)** Turn left (before houses) onto trail. Then keep right and walk around a small pond (to the left)[Houses and pond]**(13.0)** Turn right onto footpath and climb through orchards until reaching a small road. Turn right[Pass through orchards and farm to the left] **(14.1)** Cross the D16 road and continue straight to the hamlet of Saint-Martin **(15.6)** Turn left and pass the chapel of **Saint-Martin** on the right. Continue straight until reaching the D16 road
 (17.0) Cross the D16 road, and then the stream (Ruisseau de Laujol). Continue straight**(17.4)** Cross the road then turn sharp left into the woodland[uphill] **(18.1)** Mount the steps and turn right on the tarmac towards the hamlet of **Teyssières**
(19.0) Turn left onto the D16 road **(19.4)** Turn left onto trail and continue straight **(20.4)** At top of steep climb turn right and then keep right towards Carbonnières (farm). Continue straight **(25.2)** Turn left on the D957 road and continue straight towards Moissac[Signpost]**(25.9)** Turn right onto the chemin des Vignes, and then right onto the D927 road **(26.5)** Before bridge, turn right onto chemin de Richard, keeping train tracks to the left**(27.2)** Turn left and then right on rue du Faubourg Sainte-Blanche/D927 and continue straight towards city centre**(27.7)** At roundabout, continue straight on rue Malaveille[Signpost] **(27.9)** Arrive at Moissac centre[Place des Récollets]

stage 19 — Lauzerte to Moissac

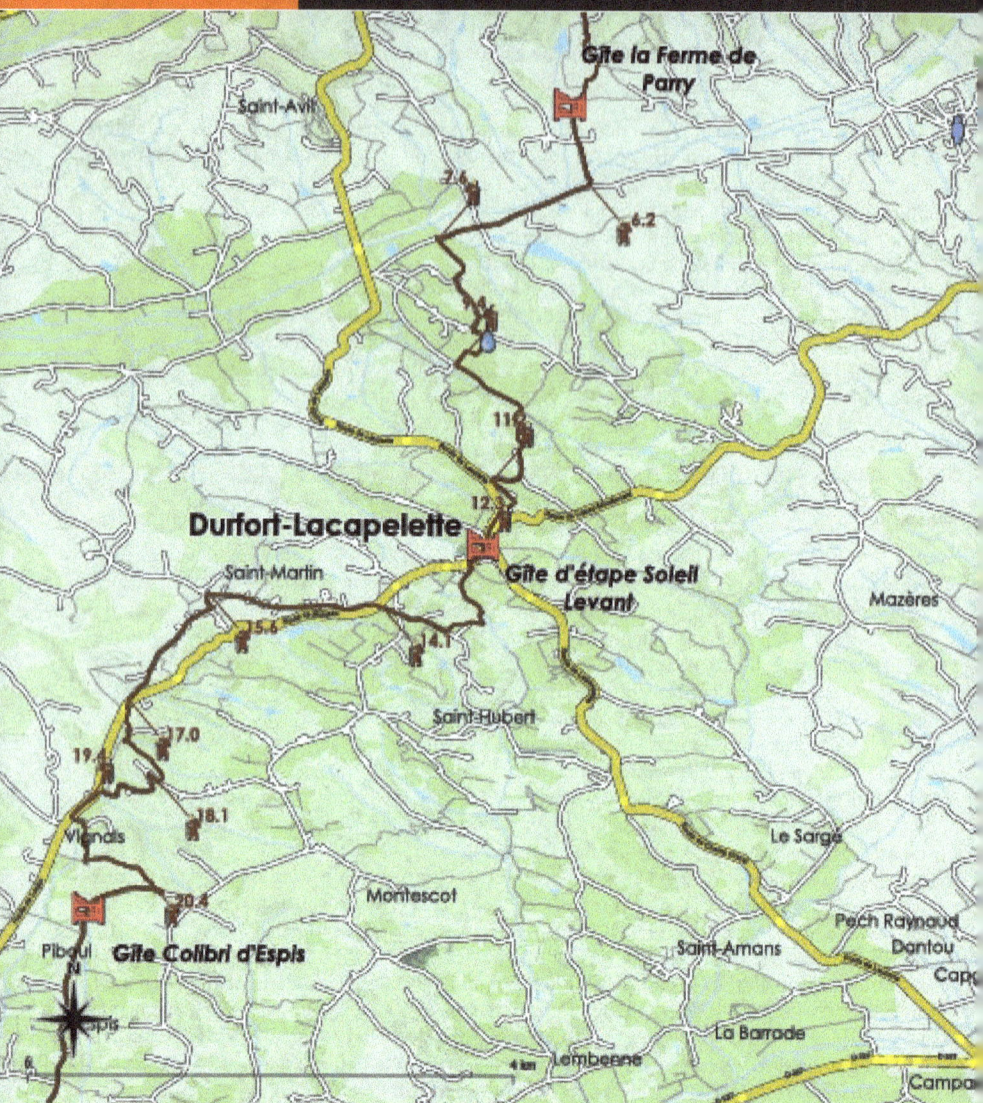

Accommodation and Tourist Information

Durfort-Lacapelette

Gîte d'étape - Soleil Levant [Christophe Delmas],20, rue des pèlerins, 82390 Durfort-Lacapelette, France; Tel:+33 (0)6 14 96 00 30; Email:gitedusoleillevant@hotmail.fr; gitedusoleillevant.fr; Price:B,-,-; *10 places in 2 rooms and a dome! Accommodation for donkeys possible. Bar-restaurant close-by.*

Lauzerte

Gîte la Ferme de Parry[Jean Yves and Marie],Lieu-dit Parry, 82110 Lauzerte, France; Tel:+33 (0)6 80 64 45 79; Email:contact@lafermedeparry.fr; lafermedeparry.fr; Price:-,-,C; *10 places in 3 bedrooms local produce*

Lauzerte to Moissac stage 19

Moissac

Gîte d'étape-Chambres d'hôtes - Ultreia [Carole and Marc],45, rue Pierre Chabrié, 82200 Moissac, France; Tel:+33(0)563051506; Email:info@ultreiamoissac.com; ultreiamoissac.com; Price:-,C,C|-,B,B; *This charming gîte with garden offers 14 places in small dormitories and 5 B&B rooms and is located on the GR°65 across from the train station.*

Gîte - Colibri d'Espis,2105, chemin d'Espis, 82200 Moissac, France; Tel:+33 (0)6 16 48 07 29; Email:colibridespis@gmail.com; colibridespis.com; Price:C,C,B; *14 places in 3 rooms horses welcome*

Gîte d'étape - La Petite Lumière,1183, chemin du Calvaire, 82200 Moissac, France; Tel:+33 (0)674 681 294; Email:lapetitelumiere@free.fr; lapetitelumiere.org; Price:D,D,D; *2 dormitories with 9 places 1 private room and a tipi. Camping possible. Panoramic views*

Gîte l'Ancien Carmel,5, Sente du Calvaire, 82200 Moissac, France; Tel:+33(0)563046221; Email:contact@lanciencarmelmoissac.com; lanciencarmelmoissac.com; Price:C,C,C; *Located in a former convent with extensive capacity basic accommodations. Run by volunteers. English spoken. Dinner is served under the arcades in the courtyard. Reduced charges for pilgrims*

Gîte d'étape - Auberge des Chemins [Agnes],17, rue du Pont, 82200 Moissac, France; Tel:+33(0)624 34 80 87; Email:aubergedeschemins@gmail.com; aubergedeschemins.com; Price:C,C,C; *Recently renovated with 14 places in 2 dormitories and 2 private rooms*

Accueil de la communauté religieuse Marie Mère de l'Eglise,20, boulevard Camille Delthil, 82200 Moissac, France; Tel:33 (0)5 63 32 28 87; Email:communaute@mariemeredeleglise.fr; mariemeredeleglise.fr; Price:D,D,D; *8 places in 2 rooms in an working convent located in the centre of town. Possibility to take part in religious ceremonies. Run by volunteers. Kitchen.*

Hôtel - l'Armateur,22, rue du pont, 82200 Moissac, France; Tel:+33 (0)5 63 32 85 10; +33(0)671740314; Email:hotelarmateur@orange.fr; hotelarmateur.fr; Price:A,A,A; *An 18th century residence that has been a long established stopping place on the chemin. Today it is a well appointed hotel with 16 bedroom restaurant and pool*

Office de Tourisme,1, boulevard de Brienne, 82200 Moissac, France; Tel:+33 (0) 5 32 09 69 36; Email:accueil@tourisme-moissacconfluences.fr; tourisme-moissac-terresdesconfluences.fr

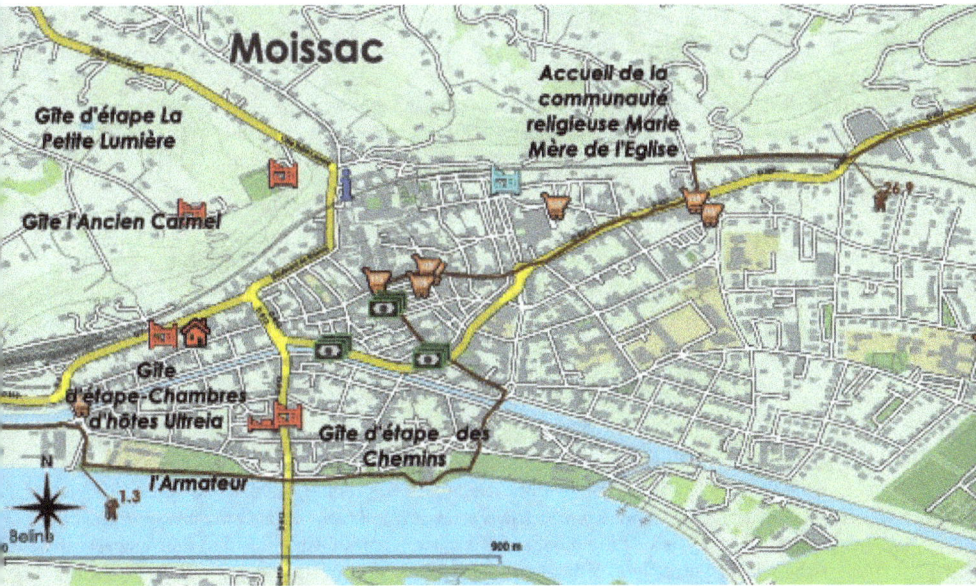

Gascony Fruit Stand © Alexandra Huddleston

Gascony's historic natural borders were the Atlantic ocean to the west, the Pyrenees mountains to the south, and the Garonne River, which originates in the Pyrenees and flows northwest through Toulouse to Bordeaux. Gascony also includes the vineyards of Armagnac that grow on the hills between the Garonne and Adour rivers.

Over the centuries, Gascony has been occupied by several different cultures — in pre-historic times it was the land of the Vascones, or Basques, who were later conquered by the Romans (1st century), Visigoths (5th century), Franks (6th century), Basques (7th century), Norsemen (9th century) and finally by the English in 1154. By the 13th century, England's last small possession in France was the duchy of Gascony. When King Philip VI of France (1328-1350) seized Gascony in 1337, King Edward II of England declared war, thus starting the devastating Hundred Years' War. The region was taken from the English in 1453 and was united with France in 1607 under the rule of Henry IV of France.

The land in Gascony is fertile. Close to the Garonne river are fruit orchards (including plums for which the region is famous), and further south, crops such as corn for animal feed and wheat. It is renowned for its natural and hearty foods, such as duck *confit* (duck legs cooked in fat), blood sausage, prunes, *foie gras* (a French delicacy made from duck liver) and *garbure* (a stew made from cabbage, vegetables and preserved meats). Gascony also produces Armagnac (a type of brandy distilled from grapes) and *floc*, a lighter aperitif made from local grapes and fortified with Armagnac. The Gascon dialect is a variant of Occitan and is different from the Basque language.

Moissac to Auvillar

stage 20

Length:	22.3km
Ascent:	735m
Descent:	698m
Le-Puy:	422km
Roncevaux:	359km

Canal Leaving Moissac © Alexandra Huddleston

Route-Except for Moissac centre, the route continues to be well-marked as it follows the Tarn river and the Canal of Garonne, before climbing into the river-side hills, which offer beautiful views of orchards, vineyards and the confluence of the Tarn and Garonne rivers. From Malause, the route is mostly flat and on asphalt roads, as it makes its way to the historic city of Auvillar.

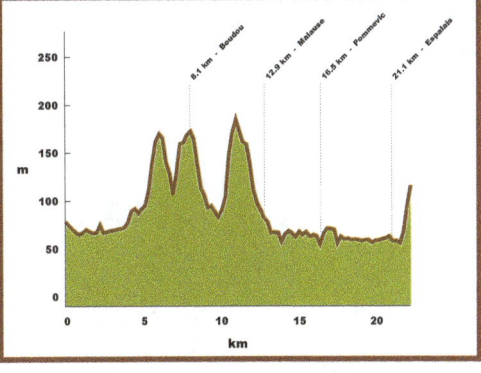

Pointers-Choice of routes: After Moissac, at the Ecluse (lock) de l'Espagnette, it is possible to take the flat alternative route that continues along the canal and re-joins the GR®65 at Malause. This avoids the main route, which has several steep climbs and descents, but equally beautiful views of the Tarn and Garonne rivers.

Market: Auvillar hosts a local produce market every Sunday morning (8a.m. to 1p.m).

Moissac to Auvillar

stage 20

Cultural Discoveries

Auvillar

The fortified village of Auvillar (popl. 942, alt. 65m) was built in the 10th century on a point overlooking the Garonne River. By the 11th century it housed a viscount, whose castle stood at Place du Château, which offers panoramic views of the river valley. The village fell to successive rulers, including the Counts of Armagnac and the Kings of Navarre, before being joined to the French crown under King Henry IV. By the 19th century, Auvillar had become a busy port and an important producer of earthenware and goose-feather quills. It was during this period, in 1830, that the *Halle*, the circular market hall, which is supported by 20 columns and designed in a Tuscan style, was built. Also of note is the elegant late 17th century clock tower, which replaced a fortified gate and drawbridge. Auvillar is classified as one of the most beautiful villages in France.

GR®65

(0.0) From Place des Récollets head south-east on the narrow rue Jean Moura **(0.0)** Arrive at Moissac centre[Place des Récollets] **(0.3)** Pass eglise Saint Jacques on your left and then turn right to cross the canal bridge **(0.5)** Continue to the riverside and then turn right and follow the riverside path[pass le Moulin de Moissac on your right] **(1.3)** At the end of the path turn right on the tarmac **(1.4)** Turn left on Promenade Saint-Martin[Canal to the right and Tarn River to the left] **(3.8)** Turn right and cross bridge over train tracks and turn right onto the D813 road[An alternative route, which avoids the steep climbs, continues straight along the canal and rejoins the main route after about 7.5 km in Maulause] **(4.0)** Turn left intothe car park, and then left onto the path between the stream and the olive grove **(5.2)** Bear left to cross the stream and climb the hill **(5.8)** At the T-junction with the road, turn left **(6.0)** At the T-junction, turn right **(6.4)** Turn left onto track to descend into valley and then merge left on asphalt road[Pass farmhouse on the left] **(7.0)** Turn right onto trail, and then take first left to climb out of valley (steep) **(7.5)** Turn left onto main road and continue straight towards Boudou[Signpost] **(8.1)** In **Boudou**, turn right at central square - Place Bertrand de Montaigut[Signpost]
(8.2) Turn right at church, and continue straight on chemin Roubiac **(8.3)** Continue straight on Impasse des Roseaux, running alongside orchard **(8.9)** Turn left at end of trail, and continue straight on track along valley bottom **(10.0)** Turn right onto track. After climb, turn left on D4 road and continue straight **(11.3)** Keep left on Route du Phare **(11.7)** Turn right onto track after passing church of Sainte-Rose to descend into Malause[Stone cross] **(12.6)** Turn left and descend Route Royale towards village centre[Signpost] **(12.9)** In **Malause** cross the roundabout (left) and continue down rue de la Marie towards the canal
(13.1) Turn right onto rue Paul Riquet and then immediately left to cross the train tracks and the Canal Latéral à la Garonne **(13.5)** Turn right and continue straight alongside canals[Canals on both sides] **(16.5)** Turn right and cross bridge. Continue straight until reaching the D813 road and turn left to pass through village of **Pommevic**
(16.8) Take the raised pathway on the right of the road and then climb the steps to the right[pass metal calvaire] **(16.9)** Pass in front of the church and then bear left to continue to follow the D813 **(17.3)** Turn left onto the D116E1 road and cross the Canal de Golfech. Continue straight **(17.9)** Keep right on road, direction Espalais. Continue on road through Espalais[Signpost] **(21.7)** After crossing **Espalais** turn left onto the D11 road and cross the Garonne River. Turn left onto Rue-Saint-Catherine which climbs to the centre of Auvillar[Bridge and Pass Chapel Saint-Catherine]
(22.3) Arrive at Auvillar[Place de la Halle]

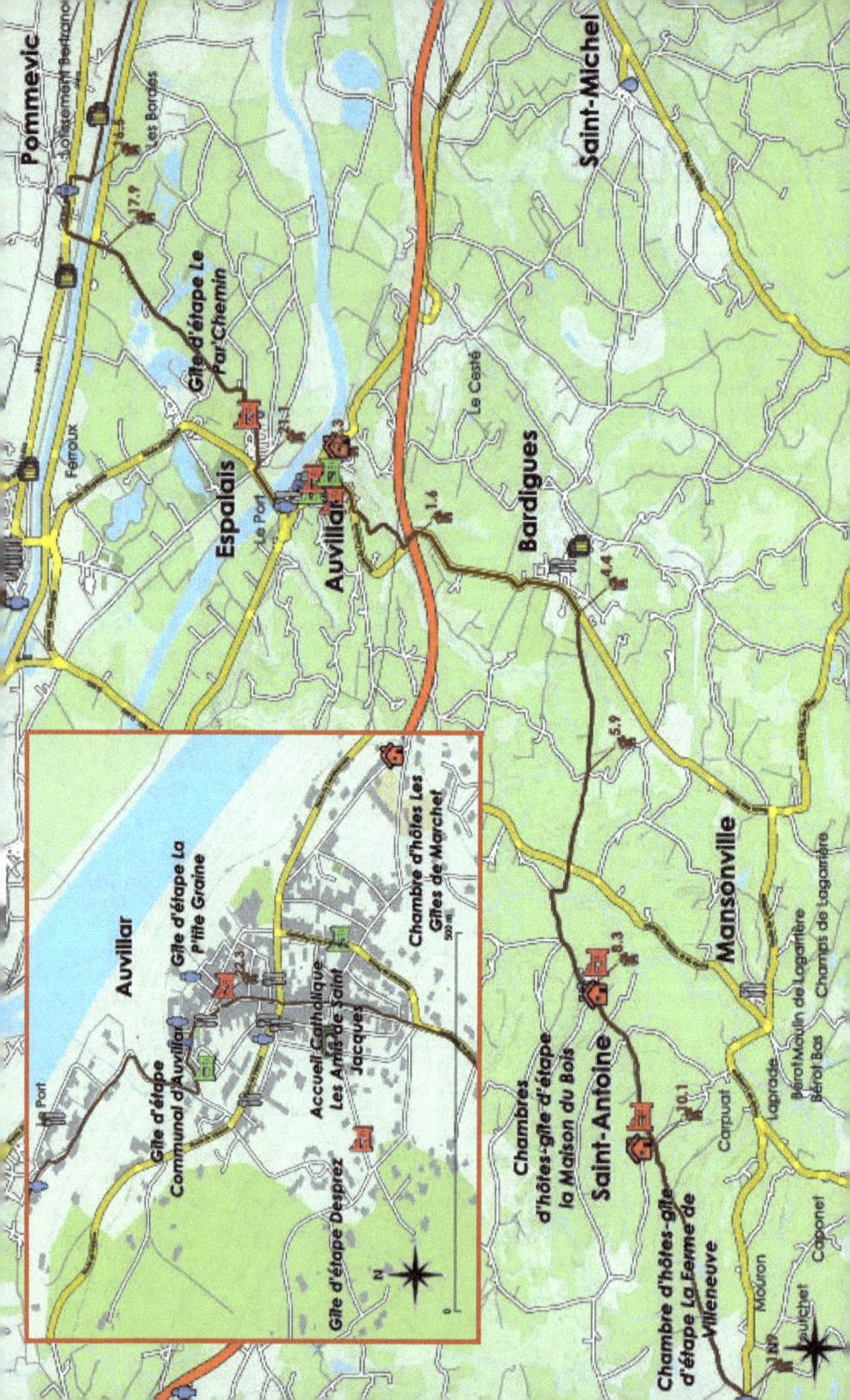

Moissac to Auvillar

stage 20

Accommodation and Tourist Information

Auvillar

Gîte d'étape - Communal d'Auvillar,11, rue Junca, 82340 Auvillar, France; Tel:+33(0) 563 39 89 82; Email:ot-auvillar@cc-deuxrives.fr; officedetourismedesdeuxrives.fr; Price:C,-,-; *Located in the old town centre renovated in 2015 a former presbytery with garden. A comfortable hostel with 18 places in 6 rooms of 2 to 4. Kitchen. English spoken.*

Accueil Catholique Les Amis de Saint Jacques[Monique Bianco],23, boulevard de la Papayette, 82340 Auvillar, France; Tel:+33 (0) 784 92 75 15; Email:monique.bianco83@gmail.com; officedetourismedesdeuxrives.fr; Price:C,C,-; *10 places in 2 dormitories kitchen. Expect a warm welcome from Monique*

Gîte d'étape - La P'tite Graine[Matthieu Ferré],14, place de la Halle, 82340 Auvillar, France; Tel:+33 (0)7 89 31 42 59; +33 (0)695 798 871; Email:gite.matthieu@gmail.com; laptite-graineauvillar.fr; Price:-,B,B; *Welcoming hostel with 14 places in 7 rooms in an old house in the village centre. English spoken*

Gîte d'étape - Desprez[Marie-Thérèse Desprez],761, chemin du Moulin, 82340 Auvillar, France; Tel:+33(0)5 63 39 01 08; podiensis.com; Price:-,A,-; *Located 1 km from the town centre 4 places in bunk beds in small pavilion. Pool and Garden. English spoken. Very welcoming.*

Chambre d'hôtes - Les Gîtes de Marchet[Nathalie and Marc],11, rue Marchet, 82340 Auvillar, France; Tel:+33 (0)615 387 661; Email:contact@gitesdemarchet.com ; gitesdemarchet.com ; Price:-,B,A; *Located 300m from the town centre considered one of the best B&Bs in Auvillar. 4 places. With pool and garden. Reduced price for pilgrims*

Office de Tourisme des Deux Rives,4-6, rue du Couvent, 82340 Auvillar, France; Tel:+33(0) 5 63 39 89 82; Email:ot-auvillar@cc-deuxrives.fr; officedetourismedesdeuxrives.fr

Espalais

Gîte d'étape - Le Par'Chemin[Vincent and Sylvie Bernard],34, avenue Montplaisir, 82400 Espalais, France; Tel:+33 (0)563 947 378; +33 (0)666 460 903; Email:parchemin82@orange.fr; tourisme-tarnetgaronne.fr; Price:C,C,C; *Mythic stop on the Chemin famous for hospitality familial atmosphere communal dinners and music room. The owners are both former pilgrims who were drawn to this special place. Worth stopping in for refreshments even if you don't spend the night. 14 places in 3 bedrooms*

Malause

Chambre d'hôtes - Chez Josiane,96, chemin de las Moles, 82200 Malause, France; Tel:+33(0) 683 573 684; Email:josiane.rosolen@gmail.com; Price:-,C,-; *2 double bedrooms in modern house close to amenities*

Chambre d'hôtes-Bar-Pizzaria - Chez Willy,7, avenue de Bordeaux, 82200 Malause, France; Tel:+33(0)563 395 590; Email:josiane.rosolen@gmail.com; Price:C,C,-; *2 double bedrooms in modern house close to amenities*

stage 20 — Moissac to Auvillar

Auvillar Market Hall © Alexandra Huddleston

Auvillar to Castet-Arrouy

stage 21

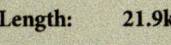

Length:	21.9km
Ascent:	857m
Descent:	997m
Le-Puy:	444km
Roncevaux:	337km

Route–The route continues to be well-marked, as it crosses the rolling and rich agricultural region of Gascony, with endless wheat and sunflower fields. The route follows principally asphalt roads and paths through fields or alongside roads.

Pointers–**Advance planning:** The route is highly exposed, be sure to have sun protection (hat, sunscreen, etc.) as well as sufficient water

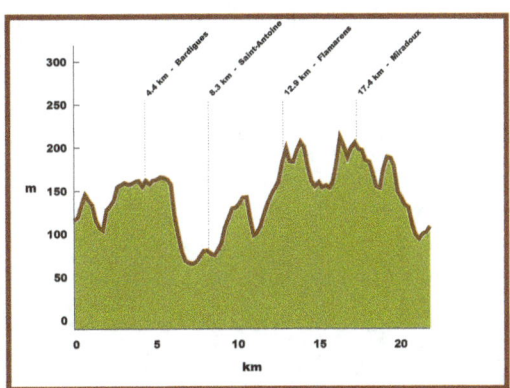

Wheat-scape © Alexandra Huddleston

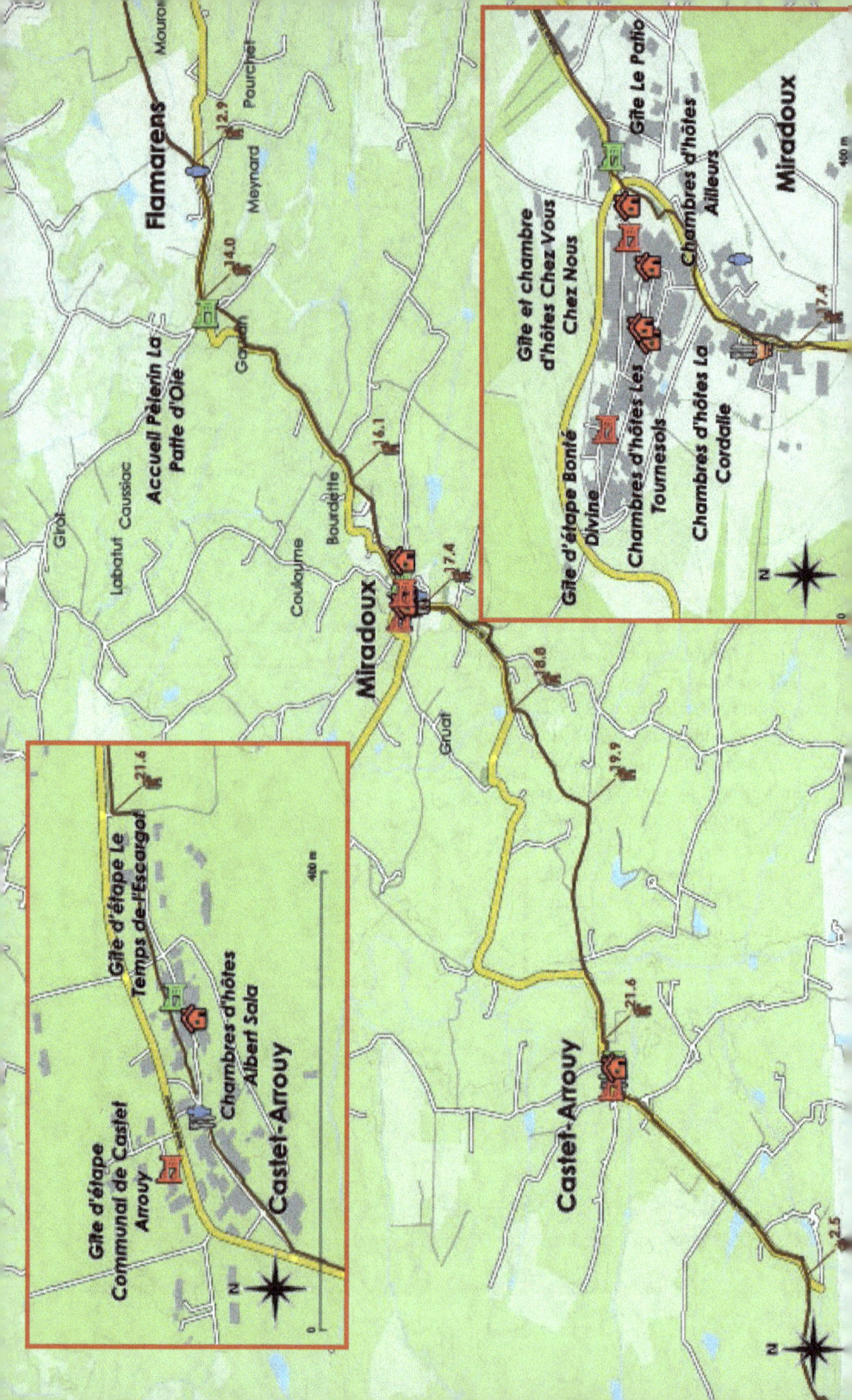

Auvillar to Castet-Arrouy

stage 21

Cultural Discoveries

Castle of Flamarens

The 13th century Castle of Flamarens (popl. 130, alt. 100m) was given as a dowry to the niece of Pope Clement V in 1289. During the 100 Years' War it was used as a fortress and in 1469 the main body of the building and an enormous keep were added. In the 17th century and at the beginning of the 18th century the castle was luxuriously furnished. However by the 20th century the place was abandoned, and its roof destroyed in a fire. Since 1983, it has been privately owned and restored.

Miradoux

The fortified village of Miradoux (popl. 530, alt. 280m) appears to have been founded in 1253, making it one of the oldest *bastides* in the region. The village became an important trading centre in the 17th century. During *La Fronde* (a series of French civil wars from 1648 to 1653 that sought to limit King Louis XIV's power), the loyalist village was captured by the Prince of Condé's troops, forcing the villagers to take refuge in the church. De Condé's troops were eventually and heroically pushed back by loyalist forces. The village continues to celebrate the battle through re-enactments. The large 16th century church, is dedicated to and houses a reliquary of Saint Orens (the 5th century Bishop of Auch (a town in south-western France)). The region is dependent on agriculture and produces wheat, garlic, melon and oil seeds. A market is held on Saturday mornings.

Castet-Arrouy

Casetet-Arrouy (popl. 200, alt. 107m) has a 16th century church dedicated to Saint Blandine (a 2nd century Christian martyr from Lyon), which is classified as a historic monument. It has lovely 19th century wall paintings by the celebrated local artist Paul Lasseran (1868-1935, a French painter and poet from Lectoure).

GR®65

(0.0) From Place de la Halle continue south on rue de l'Horloge/D11, direction Bardigues[Pass through clock tower]**(0.7)** Turn left onto small road between houses. Continue south-west on trail, which passes through Lafume and then rejoins the D11 road[Signpost] **(1.6)** Turn left onto the D11 road. Cross under A62 highway and continue on D11 road until Bardigues[Highway A62] **(4.4)** After passing **Bardigues**, turn right onto asphalt road and continue straight, direction Pessanton
(5.9) Turn right and then immediate left onto footpath, and descend to the D88 road[Trail runs parallel to large power-lines to the right]**(6.8)** Cross the D88 and continue straight. Then turn left and cross the the Arrats river. Continue straight to Saint-Antoine[Signpost] **(8.3)** On entering **Saint-Antoine** turn left and pass through village on rue de la Commanderie. Continue straight through village
(8.5) Leave Saint Antoine, and continue straight on the D953 road**(9.0)** At fork, keep right on the Voie Communal 13 and continue straight[Signpost] **(10.1)** Continue straight through intersection and then on trail through woods which descends to the stream (Ruisseau de la Teulère)**(11.1)** Cross stream and continue straight climbing to Flamarens **(12.9)** Turn left and then right to enter **Flamarens** centre**(13.0)** Turn left at war monument and pass in front of church[Monument]
(13.1) Turn left and continue straight on the D953 road to leave Flamarens[Pass château on left] **(14.0)** Turn left on small street, direction Miradoux[Signpost]**(14.1)** Turn right on the path and descend towards the D953. Then turn left onto path running alongside the D953 road and continue straight[Signpost] **(16.1)** Turn left and climb steep trail along pine grove (to the right), then turn right

stage 21 — Auvillar to Castet-Arrouy

onto asphalt road**(16.7)**Turn left onto the D953 road and continue straight on D953 through village of Miradoux[Signpost] **(17.4)**Continue straight on D953 road and leave **Miradoux**, direction Lectoure **(17.8)**Bear left to briefly leave the D23 and skirt the farm of Caillavet on your right **(18.8)**Turn left (opposite reservoir) onto small road and climb on trail through fields[Reservoir and signpost] **(19.9)**Keep right and continue straight to rejoin the D23 road and enter Catet-Arrouy[Pass Château du Gachepouy on right] **(21.3)**Turn left and immediately right to pass through centre of Castet-Arrouy[Signpost]**(21.9)**Arrive at Castet-Arrouy centre[Beside the church]

Accommodation and Tourist Information

Castet-Arrouy

Gîte d'étape - Le Temps de l'Escargot[Jean-Patrick],10, rue des Glycines, 32340 Castet-Arrouy, France; Tel:+33(0) 6 11 44 80 53; Email:letempsdelescargot@gmail.com; podiensis.com; Price:B,B,B; *7 places in 2 dormitories. English spoken*

Gîte d'étape - Communal de Castet Arrouy[Mairie de Castet-Arrouy],Place de la Mairie, 32340 Castet-Arrouy, France; Tel:+33(0) 684 927 396; +33(0) 562 292 843; Email:gitecomcastetarrouy@orange.fr; gascogne-lomagne.fr; Price:-,C,-; *18 places in rooms of 4 to 6 persons. Kitchen. Horses Welcome.*

Chambres d'hôtes - Albert Sala[Mr Albert Sala],Place de la Église, 32340 Castet-Arrouy, France; Tel:+33(0) 622 184 276; +33(0) 562 287 397; Email:aumuseedalbert@gmail.com; chemindecompostelle.com; Price:-,B,-; *12 places in 4 rooms in a restored stone house.. English spoken. Horses welcome.*

Flamarens

Accueil Pèlerin - La Patte d'Oie[Xavier and Isabelle Ballenghien], 32340 Flamarens, France; Tel:+33(0) 562 286 113; Price:D,D,D; *4-5 places in Christian home that has been welcoming pilgrims for more than 20 years. Reservations possible.*

Miradoux

Gîte Le Patio[Dominique Enjarlan],9, place du Foirail, 32340 Miradoux, France; Tel:+33(0) 6 78 20 67 01; +33 (0)953 313 723; Email:lepatio.miradoux@gmail.com; chemindecompostelle.com; Price:C,C,C; *9 places in 3 dormitories English spoken. Kitchen*

Gîte et chambre d'hôtes - Chez Vous Chez Nous[Catherine and Jean-Christophe],1, Grand Rue, 32340 Miradoux, France; Tel:+33 (0)562 293 350; +33(0) 786 053 988; Email:chezvouscheznousmiradoux@gmail.com; chezvouscheznousmiradoux.fr; Price:-,C,C|-,-,A; *6 dormitory places and 2 private bedrooms in 18th century house. Meals made with local produce.*

Gîte d'étape - Bonté Divine[Stéphane],5, rue Porte d'Uzan Nord, 32340 Miradoux, France; Tel:+33(0) 562 683 080; +33(0) 620 500 970; Email:contact@bontedivine.net; bontedivine.net; Price:C,C,C; *2 dormitories each with 4 beds and 1 double room. English spoken. Camping possible*

Chambres d'hôtes - La Cordalie[Dominique and Jean-Marie],3, place de la Mairie, 32340 Miradoux, France; Tel:+33(0) 562 288 435; +33 (0)675 574 929; Email:lacordalie@free.fr; jabbal3.wixsite.com/lacordalie; Price:B,B,B; *8 places in 3 rooms in a beautiful 18th Century home located in the old town centre.English spoken. Horses possible*

Chambres d'hôtes - Ailleurs,12, rue Major, 32340 Miradoux, France; Tel:+33 (0)672 666 287; +33 (0)954813080; Email:chrystele.pommies@sfr.fr; ailleurs64.webnode.fr; Price:-,B,B; *3 bedrooms each for 2 or 3 people, donkeys welcome*

Chambres d'hôtes Les Tournesols[Josiane Wachill],4, place de la Halle, 32340 Miradoux, France; Tel:+33(0) 5 62 28 68 53; podiensis.com; Price:C,C,C; *11 places in 4 rooms in an 18th century building opposite the market square. Garden and views. English spoken. Horses possible.*

Saint-Antoine

Chambres d'hôtes-gîte d'étape - la Maison du Bois[Karine],5, rue de la Commanderie, 32340 Saint-Antoine, France; Tel:+33(0)6 50 27 65 59; +33 (0)562 286 815; Email:maisonduboissaintantoine@gmail.com; compostellemaisondubois.com; Price:B,B,-|C,C,-; *4 bedrooms in the chambres d'hôtes and a dormitory for 2-5 people, English spoken*

Chambre d'hôtes-gîte d'étape - La Ferme de Villeneuve[Rose-Anne and Renaud des Courtis],146, Lieu-dit Villeneuve, 32340 Saint-Antoine, France; Tel:+33(0) 786 428 721; +33(0) 670 355 575; Email:fermedevilleneuve32@gmail.com; lafermedevilleneuve.fr; Price:A,A,-|-,-,-; *15 places in 5 rooms with private baths and 1 dorm in 18th Century farmhouse. Pool. English spoken. Horses welcome.*

Castet-Arrouy to Lectoure — stage 22

Length:	11.0km
Ascent:	315m
Descent:	240m
Le-Puy:	466km
Roncevaux:	315km

Lectoure Cathedral

Route–The route, which mainly follows asphalt roads, continues to be well-marked, as it crosses the rolling and rich agricultural region of Gascony to arrive at the hilltop city of Lectoure, which is popular with British tourists. This stage is short in order to arrive early and have time to explore the historic city.

Pointers–**Relaxation:** Lectoure is famous for its natural thermal springs (known as *thermes*). The spa, which is located in the town centre, offers

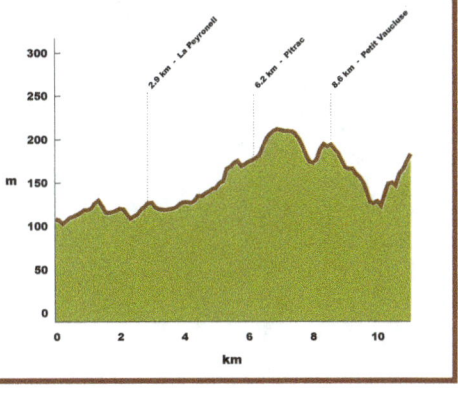

half-day pilgrim passes, including access to the spa and foot and water massages. Thermes de Lectoure, 125 rue Nationale, 32700 Lectoure, tel. : +33 5 62 68 56 00, www.valvital.fr/stations-thermales/lectoure

Recreation: (1) Lectoure has a beautiful public pool with views of the Pyrenees, entrance fee (around €4). Located next to the town hall, Place du général de Gaulle 32700 Lectoure, (2) Flea market (known as a *brocante*): more than 20 antique dealers show off their wares in the Château des Comtes d'Armagnac, located in the town centre.

Market: Lecoutre hosts a large and colourful produce market every Friday morning (8a.m. to 1p.m.)

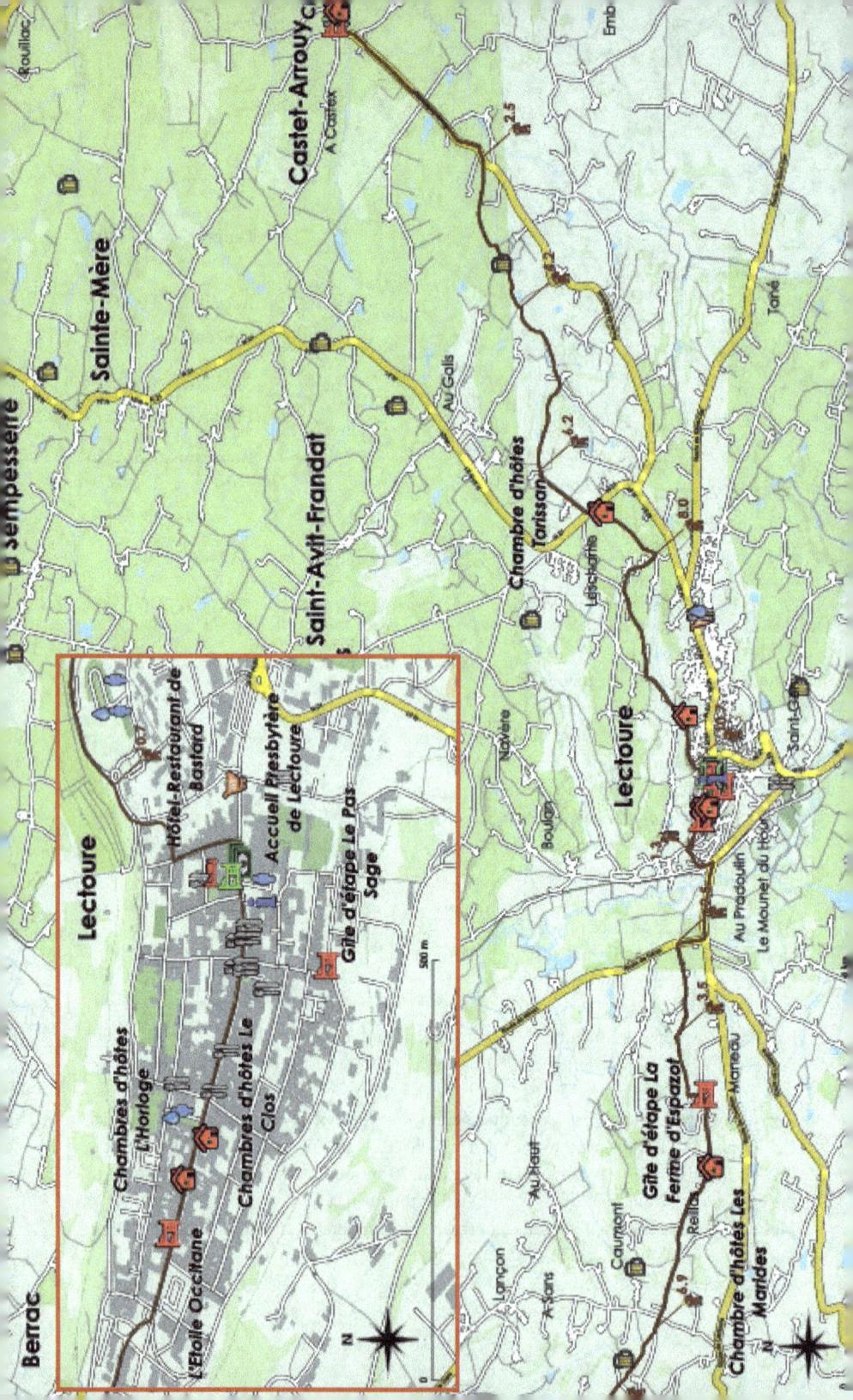

Castet-Arrouy to Lectoure
stage 22

Cultural Discoveries

Lectoure

The fortified city of Lectoure (popl. 3,700, alt. 200m) knew two periods of great prosperity: during the Middle Ages, when it was the main residence of the powerful counts of Armagnac, and in the 17th and 18th Centuries, when economic growth was driven by tanneries and agriculture. It was also during this latter period that several citizens of Lectoure gained powerful positions under Napoleon and that a number of private mansions (*hôtel-particuliers*) were built. Also of note is the former **Cathedral of Saint Gervasis and Saint Protasius** (*Cathédrale Saint-Gervais-et-Saint-Protais*), which was built on the site of a pagan sanctuary to Cybele (mother/earth goddess) and later a church dedicated to Saint Thomas (one of Jesus' 12 apostles). The church was built in 1325, and incorporated certain parts of a former 12th century monastery. A large part of the original church was destroyed in the 15th century, and was subsequently rebuilt in a Gothic style.

GR 65

(0.0) From church, continue west through village centre. Then turn left onto the D23 road, and continue straight alongside the D23 road **(2.5)** Turn right and cross the D23 road. Continue straight through agricultural fields **(2.9)** Beside **La Peyronell**, continue straight[Woods on the right]
(3.4) Turn left, and then keep right on trail running alongside stream[Stream to the left] **(4.2)** Turn right onto footpath and continue to follow trail alongside stream[Stream] **(5.1)** Merge left onto road and then turn right onto trail towards Pitrac[Pass farm on left] **(6.2)** Keep left on road (passing **Pitrac** on the right) and continue south-west until reaching the N21 road
(6.9) Turn left and then right, crossing the N21 and continue straight towards Lectoure **(8.0)** Turn right onto road (C30) and climb to Petit Vaucluse[Signpost] **(8.6)** In **Petit Vaucluse** turn left. At end of road turn left towards Lectoure[Signposts]
(10.7) Enter Lectoure. Turn left after roundabout on rue Barbacane **(10.8)** Turn right on rue de Corhuat and then take the first left. Continue straight until reaching Cathedral **(11.0)** At the T-junction, turn right on rue Nationale[alongside the cathedral] **(11.0)** Arrive at Lectoure in front of the Cathedral[Place de Gaulle]

stage 22 — Castet-Arrouy to Lectoure

Accommodation and Tourist Information

Lectoure

Accueil Presbytère de Lectoure[Véronique Delor and Marie Calmon],Rue Saint-Gervais, 32700 Lectoure, France; Tel:+33(0) 617 060 924; Email:hospitalite.lectoure@gmail.com; paroisse.lectoure.free.fr; Price:D,D,D; *Located next to the Cathedral 10 places in simple shared rooms in an imposing presbytery. Run by volunteers most of whom are former pilgrims. Space for horses and donkeys. Credentials required*

Gîte d'étape - Le Pas Sage[Bion Aurelien],29, ue des Frères Danzas, 32700 Lectoure, France; Tel:+33 (0)7 62 20 89 83; Email:aurelienduc63@live.fr; Price:C,C,C; *8 places in 2 dormitories English spoken kitchen*

L'Etoile Occitane[Isabelle Fournier],140, rue Nationale, 32700 Lectoure, France; Tel:+33(0)5 62 68 82 93; Email:isabelfournier@hotmail.fr; giteletoileoccitane.site; Price:-,C,-; *Simple but welcoming accommodations in the town centre.14 places (bunk beds) in two rooms. English spoken. Possibility to accommodate horses.*

Chambres d'hôtes - L'Horloge[Béatrice Sager],101, rue Nationale, 32700 Lectoure, France; Tel:+33 (0)5 62 28 99 62; Email:beajl.sager@free.fr; chambreshorloge-lectoure.com; Price:-,A,-; *3 rooms in tastefully decorated historic home in village centre with garden terrace. Basic English spoken.*

Chambre d'hôtes - La Mouline de Belin[Aline Salinié],Chemin de la Fontaine Saint Michel, 32700 Lectoure, France; Tel:+33 (0)562 285 731; Email:mouline-de-belin@orange.fr; lamoulinedebelin.com; Price:-,A,A; *One of the best rated B&Bs. A restored 12th Century mill and farmhouse that includes 2 rooms as well as pool stream piano and fountain on more than 15 hectares of land. English spoken.*

Chambre d'hôtes - Tarissan[Ginette and Michel Sellin],Lieu-dit Tarissan, 32700 Lectoure , France; Tel:+33(0) 6 78 38 60 60; +33 (0)5 62 68 92 73; Email:genesellin@gmail.com; gascogne-lomagne.fr; Price:-,-,B; *6 places in 4 bedrooms in a lovely and welcoming farmhouse in the heart of the countryside*

Chambres d'hôtes - Le Clos[Joëlle Pons],87, rue Nationale, 32700 Lectoure , France; Tel:+33(0)6 75 42 02 67; +33 (0)5 62 68 49 58; Email:leclos.lectoure@gmail.com; chambresdhotesleclos.jimdo.com; Price:-,B,-; *15 places in 5 rooms in a recently restored building in the historic centre and near thermal baths.*

Hôtel-Restaurant de Bastard[Mr and Mrs. Arnaud],Rue Lagrange, 32700 Lectoure, France; Tel:+33(0)5 62 68 82 44; Email:info-booking@hoteldebastard.com; hotel-de-bastard.com; Price:A,A,A; *28 rooms in this sumptuous hotel with gourmet restaurant terrace and pool. English spoken. Accommodation for horses possible through the office of tourism.*

Office de Tourisme Gascogne Lomagne,Place Gén De Gaulle, 32700 Lectoure, France; Tel:+33(0) 5 62 64 00 00; Email: contact@otgl.fr; gascogne-lomagne.fr

Lectoure to La Romieu

stage 23

Length: 18.6km

Ascent: 428m
Descent: 421m

Le-Puy: 477km
Roncevaux: 304km

Collegiate St-Pierre

Route-The route, which mainly follows tracks and asphalt roads, continues to be well-marked, as it crosses sunflower and wheat fields and some forests, to arrive in the UNESCO-listed world heritage site of La Romieu.

Pointers-Culture: The 35 km section of the GR®65 from Lectoure to Condom (including La Romieu) is on the UNESCO world heritage list.

Advance planning: The route is highly exposed, be sure to have sun protection (hat, sunscreen, etc.) as well as sufficient water.

Choice of Routes: It is possible to reach Condom and avoid La Romieu by taking a shortcut (mostly on asphalt road) at La Maurage.

Cultural Discoveries

La Romieu

According to legend, La Romieu (popl. 535, alt. 187m) was founded in the 11th century by the Benedictine monk Albert when he returned from pilgrimage to Santiago de Compostella; the word *romieu* meaning pilgrim in Gascon. The village has an impressive collegiate church that was patronized by the Avignon Papacy (the period from 1309 to 1377 when seven successive popes resided in Avignon (as opposed to Rome)). The church complex was built rapidly between 1314 and 1321, and includes a church, a sacristy with beautiful 14th century frescoes, a cloister and two towers, including a square tower with an impressive defensive staircase. Throughout the village are lovely statutes of cats by French sculptor, Maurice Serreau. These refer to the legend of Angéline's cats, which supposedly saved the village and its harvest from rats in the 14th century.

stage 23
Lectoure to La Romieu

GR®65

(0.0)From cathedral continue west on rue Nationale(0.5)Beside the water fountain, bear right and pass close to the château on your left(0.8)At the foot of the slope, turn sharp left on the road and take the first right ♦ (1.3)At the stop sign bear right then left(1.4)Turn right onto the D7 road, cross the Gers river[Signpost](2.1)Turn right on the D36[direction Ligardes] ♦ (2.5)Turn left to leave the D36 road and continue straight on small road that passes alongside corn fields[Pass farm on the left and Laslèbes on the right] ♦ (3.5)Keep left and descend trail that runs alongside stream(4.1)Turn left towards **Espazot** and then right at road's end. Continue straight through fields
♦ (6.9)Turn right onto footpath and continue straight[Stone shed and signpost] ♦ (8.2)Turn left to enter Marsolan[Pass cemetery on the left as approaching village](8.8)On entering **Marsolan** village, bear left and then turn right beside the metal cross[pass under the tiled roof]
♦ (9.3)At the T-junction after the descent, turn left and keep left ♦ (10.6)Keep left towards the hamlet of **Cauboué** and then continue straight on track to Montravail[Pass hamlet on the left]
♦ (13.5)Turn right, direction La Romieu, on trail that leads to forest[Signpost and pass reservoir on the right. Possibility to take unmarked alternative route (short cut) on asphalt road that continues straight towards Castelnau] ♦ (15.6)In forest, turn left. At asphalt road, turn right(16.3)Turn left on road. Then turn right before farm and continue straight to La Romieu[Road runs alongside forest] ♦ (17.1)At the entrance to Gîte de Beausoleil, turn right ♦ (18.2)Shortly after passing the lake on your right, turn right on the gravel path(18.4)At the T-0junction with the road, turn right and then take the next left[pass eglise Saint-Pierre on your left](18.6)Arrive at La Romieu[Place Étienne Bouet]

Accommodation and Tourist Information

La Romieu
Gîte Le Refuge du Pèlerin[Laurent],Rue du Docteur Lucante, 32480 La Romieu, France; Tel:+33 (0)43 128 101; Email:laurentfoltran@orange.fr; lerefugedelaromieu.fr; Price:C,C,C; *13 places in 3 dormitories and 1 private room*
Chambres d'hôtes - Maison d'Aux[Hervé and Martin],Place Étienne Bouet, 32480 La Romieu, France; Tel:+33 (0)682 76 66 59; +33(0) 562 28 14 89; lamaisondaux.com; Price:-,A,-; *2 double bedrooms opening onto a garden and pool*
Chambre d'hôtes - l'Etape d'Angéline[Mr. Martin],6, place Étienne Bouet, 32480 La Romieu, France; Tel:+33(0)5 62 28 10 29; Email:etapeangeline@orange.fr; chambres-hotes-restaurant-la-romieu.fr; Price:-,B,-; *5 rooms in charming B&B with fine restaurant.*
Gîte de Beausoleil[Isabelle and Oscar Coupey],Lieu-dit Moncade, 32480 La Romieu, France; Tel:+33 (0)6 71 58 50 21; Email:iocoupey@club-internet.fr; gitelaromieu.wordpress.com; Price:B,B,-; *35 places in double rooms on lovely property. Horses welcome.*
Gîte privé Domaine de Pellecahus[Francis and Marie],D166, 32480 La Romieu, France; Tel:+33(0)5 62 28 03 89; Email:contact@pellecahus.com; pellecahus.com; Price:A,-,-; *5 rooms in separate buildings on a restored farm.*

Camp de Florence,Allée du Camp, 32480 La Romieu, France; Tel:+33 (0)5 62 28 15 58; Email:info@lecampdeflorence.com; lecampdeflorence.com; Price:A,-,-; *1 night lodging not available in July or August. Campground on 15 hectares also mobile homes and cabins. Horses welcome.*
Office de Tourisme Gascogne Lomagne,1, place Etienne Boué, 32480 La Romieu, France; Tel:+33(0) 5 62 64 00 00; Email:contact@otgl.fr; gascogne-lomagne.fr

Lectoure
Gîte d'étape - La Ferme d'Espazot,Lieu-dit Espazot, 32700 Lectoure, France; Tel:+33 (0)637 648 980; Email:peregrine32@orange.fr; Price:B,B,B; *Farm in quiet agricultural area. 4 double rooms. Horses welcome. English spoken.*

Marsolan
Chambres d'hôtes - La Colline du Mieucas[Edith and Guy Tardin],Lieu-dit Mieucas, 32700 Marsolan, France; Tel:+33 (0)5 62 68 90 53; chambresdhotes-mieucas.fr; Price:-,B,A; *A comfortable B&B on a 17th Century working farm with 4 rooms, minimum booking of 2 nights*
Chambre d'hôtes - Les Marides[Laetitia Brécy],Lieu-dit Marides, 32700 Marsolan, France; Tel:+33 (0)634 274 194; +33 (0)581 681 508; santiagooo.com; Price:-,-,B; *A simple B&B with 3 rooms on a working farm with garden and terrace. English spoken. Horses welcome, camping possible*

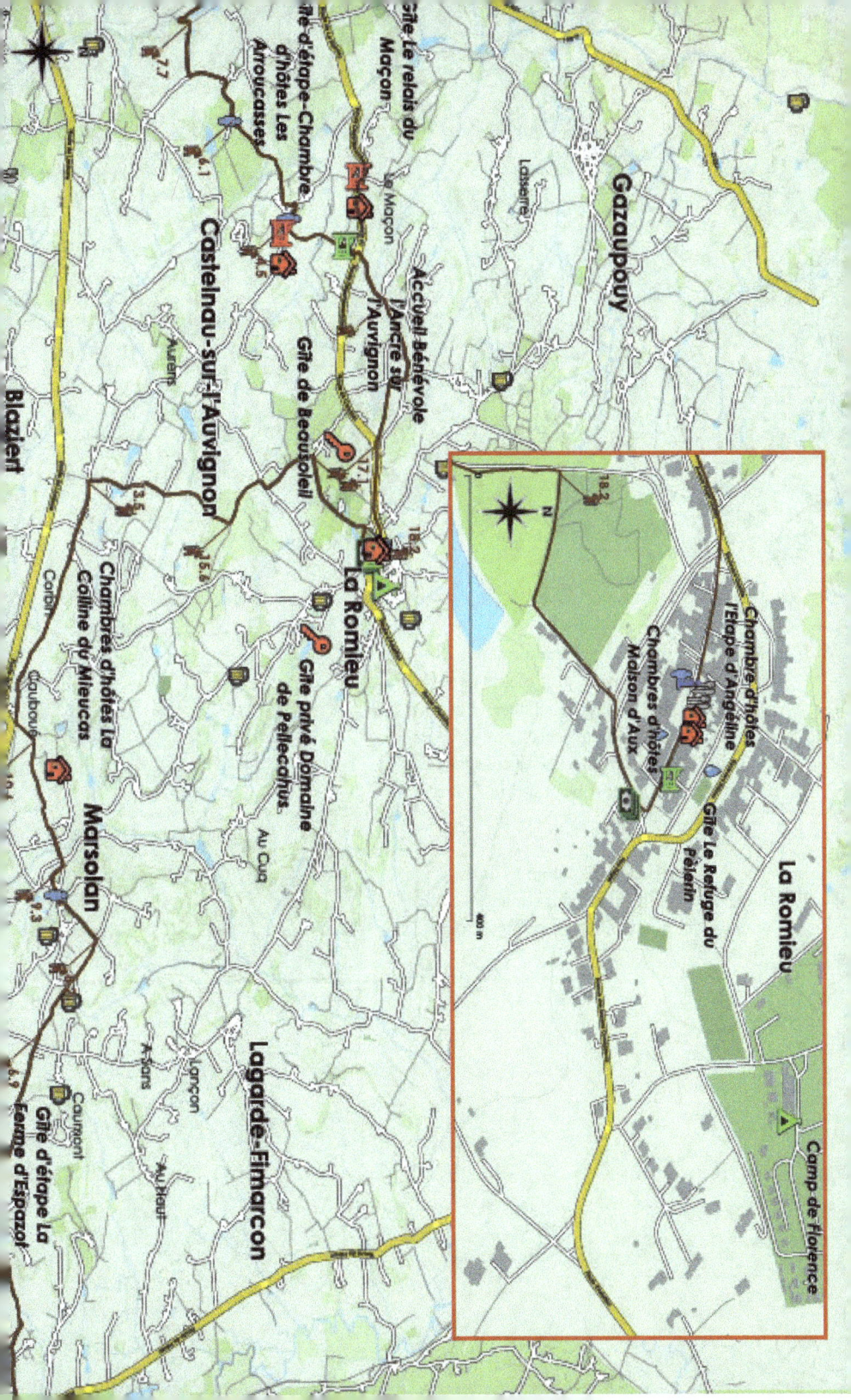

stage 24

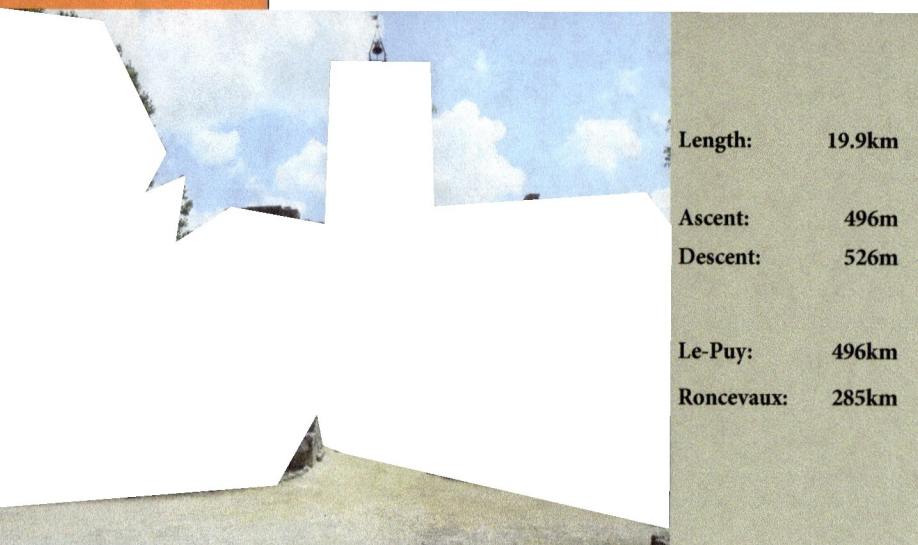

Length:	19.9km
Ascent:	496m
Descent:	526m
Le-Puy:	496km
Roncevaux:	285km

Larressingle

Route– The route is well-marked and mainly follows asphalt roads, as it makes its way to the city of Condom. The stage ends in Larressingle, one kilometre off the GR®65 in a fortified medieval village, considered to be one of the most beautiful in France. Backtrack from Larressingle to re-join the GR®65.

Pointers–**Market:** Condom hosts a large and colourful produce market each Wednesday and Sunday morning (8a.m. to 1p.m.)

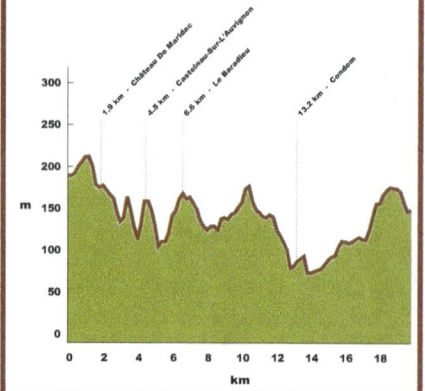

La Romieu to Larressingle — stage 24

Cultural Discoveries

Castelnau sur-l'Auvignon

Castelnau sur-l'Auvignon Tower

Castelnau sur-l'Auvignon (popl. 180, alt. 166m) was built around a 12th century fortress that was perched on a rocky outcrop overlooking the Auvignon valley. Only a watchtower remains. In 1943, the village was an important centre of French and English resistance against Nazi Germany. On 21 June 1944, Nazi forces attacked and burned the village. Before retreating, the resistance fighters destroyed a tower of the former castle which served as an arsenal, preventing the arms from falling into enemy hands. There is a monument to the Resistance in the village centre.

Condom

Condom (popl. 7,000, alt. 73m) developed around the confluence of the Baïse river and Gèle stream, from which its name is derived; *condatòmagus* is Galois for marketplace at the confluence. A Benedictine abbey dedicated to Saint Peter was built in 1011. Later, in 1317, while under English occupation during the Hundred Years' War, Condom became an important bishopric (the area for which a bishop is in charge), with 130 parish churches falling under its domain (including Larressingle). In the 16th century, the flamboyant gothic-styled former **Cathedral of Saint Peter** (*Cathédrale Saint-Pierre*) was built on the spot of the original abbey church. The city experienced a period of prosperity in the 18th century when flat-bottomed barges began to export Armagnac down the Baïse river to Bordeaux. Both the Armagnac Museum and boat rides permit visitors to discover the history of the Armagnac trade. D'Artagan, from Alexandre Dumas,' *The Three Musketeers*, was said to born in the Armagnac region; there is a statue of the trio outside the church. A market is held every Wednesday, Saturday and Sunday morning.

The Three Musketeers

Larressingle

Larressingle is an amazingly well-preserved tiny fortified medieval village. In the 13th century, during the Hundred Years' War, the village was entirely walled. At that time, there were about 40 homes, housing 250-300 people. The homes lined the defensive walls, thus buttressing them and creating a communal space in the village centre. The village also housed a castle (13th century), built for the abbots and bishops of Condom, and the Church of Saint Sigismond (12th century). Larressingle is classified as one of the most beautiful villages in France and as a historic monument.

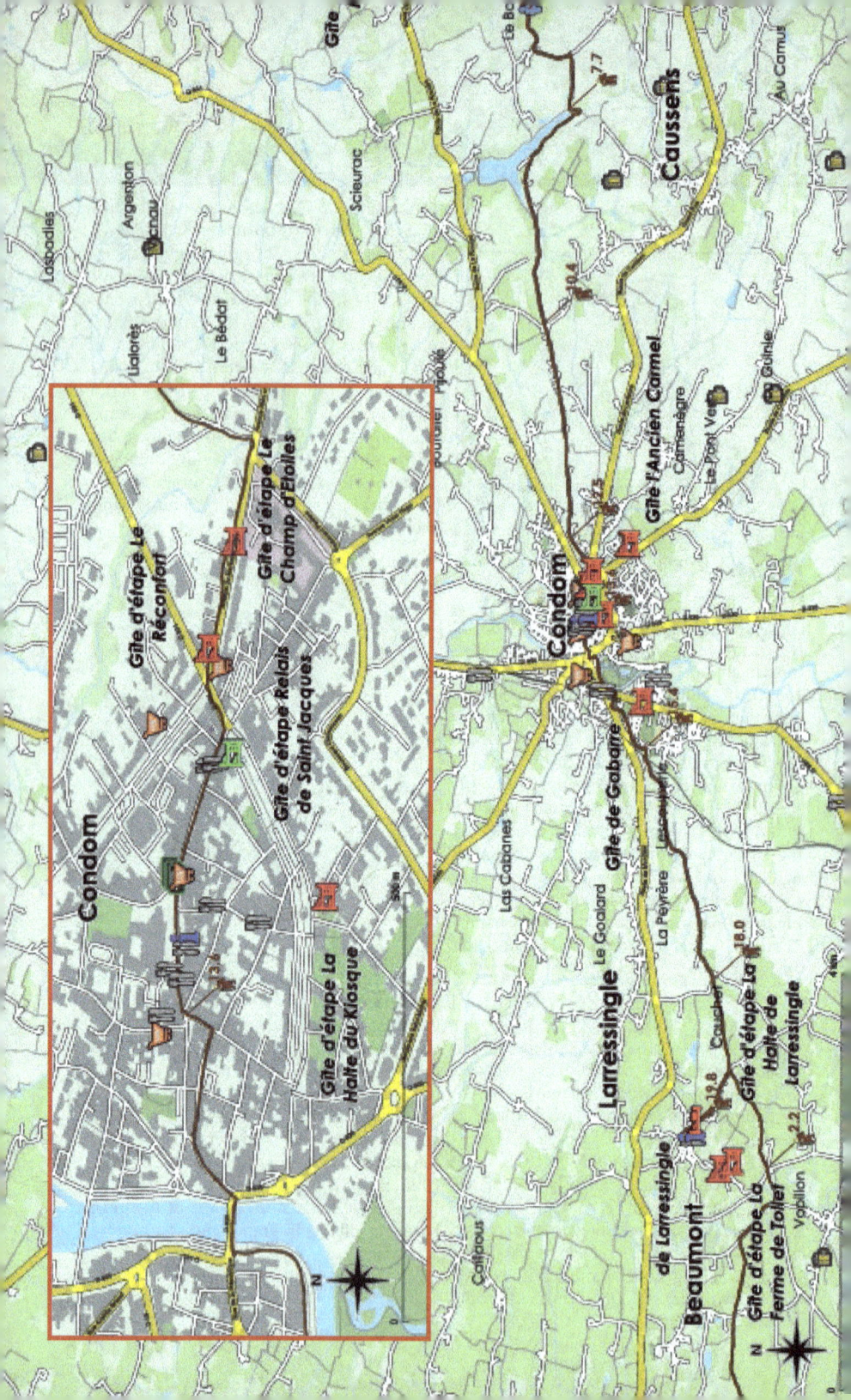

La Romieu to Larressingle — stage 24

GR®65

(0.0) Leave the place in La Romieu, heading west on rue du Dr Lucante then turn left to follow D41/ avenue Roger Lacroix direction Condom **(1.1)** At bend, turn right on trail running alongside corn field. Continue straight until road, and turn right **(1.9)** Turn left at intersection, and continue straight, direction **Château de Maridac** [Pass Château on the left]
(2.8) Turn left onto asphalt road and continue straight to the D41 road **(3.4)** Cross the D41. Turn left, followed by first right and climb towards Castelnau sur l'Avignon [Signpost]
(4.5) Arrive in **Castelnau-sur-l'Auvignon**. Bear right beside the stone cross and then turn sharp left onto the track immediately after passing the church
(5.2) Continue straight on trail and cross stream Le Grand Auvignon. Keep left and climb through fields **(6.1)** Keep right and pass Chapel of Sainte-Germaine on the left. Continue straight towards village of Le Baradieu **(6.6)** In **Le Baradieu** turn left and then take first right [Pass farm on the left]
(7.7) Keep left and then right, on trail circumscribing the Lake of Bousquètara **(8.6)** Keep left and continue straight until reaching the D204 road **(10.4)** Cross the D204 and continue straight towards Condom **(12.4)** Turn left on trail and descend towards the D7 road [Signpost] **(12.9)** Turn right onto the D7 road and continue straight towards city centre **(13.2)** In **Condom** turn left onto avenue des Anciens Combattants then turn right on rue Gambetta [Keep right of war monument]
(13.4) Take the left fork [pass cathedral on your left] **(13.6)** At the crossroads at the end of the pedestrian zone bear left [pass bank on your left] **(13.6)** Turn right on the small street [rue des Argentiers] **(13.8)** At the end of the street, bear left [rue Roques] **(13.9)** Cross bridge over the Blaise River and turn left on trail that runs along the river **(14.5)** Cross the D15 road and continue straight on road through bamboo grove. Then turn left onto chemin des Capots de Testé **(15.4)** At roundabout turn right onto "voie verte" passing through trees [Signpost and Tènaréze information panel on the right] **(15.5)** Turn left onto small road **(18.0)** Keep left on footpath that passes between fields **(18.8)** Turn right on chemin de Valence and continue straight to reach Larressingle [Signpost] **(19.8)** Turn left to enter Larressingle, historic centre [Signpost] **(19.9)** Arrive at Larressingle [Beside the gates of the medieval village]

stage 24 — La Romieu to Larressingle

Accommodation and Tourist Information

Castelnau-sur-l'Auvignon

Accueil Bénévole l'Ancre sur l'Auvignon[Jean-Pierre Knobel],Lieu-dit Le Mourelot, 32100 Castelnau-sur-l'Auvignon, France; Tel:+33 (0)6 40 05 10 48; +33 (0)6 40 05 10; tourisme-condom.com; Price:D,D,D; *5 places in 2 rooms. Kitchen. Horses welcome.*

Gîte d'étape-Chambre d'hôtes - Les Arroucasses[Jeanine and André Rodriguez],Lieu-dit Les Arroucasses, 32100 Castelnau-sur-l'Auvignon, France; Tel:+33(0) 5 62 68 12 24; Email:jeaninne32@hotmail.fr; Price:-,-,C|-,A,A; *Former pilgrims share their lovely home with garden and pool including communal dinner on the terrace. 13 places in 5 rooms. Camping possible*

Gîte Le relais du Maçon[Philippe and Nicole Pillon],D41, 32100 Castelnau-sur-l'Auvignon, France; Tel:+33(0)6 16 93 84 70; Email:n.pillon80@laposte.net; lerelaisdumacon.fr; Price:C,C,C|-,B,A; *Lovely gîte located on a renovated farm includes garden pool and billiard room. 15 places in 7 rooms.*

Condom

Gîte d'étape - Le Réconfort[Franck and Yoan],12, avenue des Anciens Combattants, 32100 Condom, France; Tel:+33(0)5 31 10 30 04; +33(0)6 71 70 15 80; Email:lereconfortcondom@gmail.com; lereconfort.jimdofree.com; Price:C,C,C; *8 places in 2 dormitories also 2 private rooms. Central location. Operated by a former pilgrim and his son*

Gîte d'étape - Le Champ d'Etoiles[Anne Charlotte],18, avenue Mal Joffre, 32100 Condom, France; Tel:+33 (0)608 052 684; +33 (0)621 712 938; Email:lechampdetoiles@gmail.com; lechampdetoiles.com; Price:C,C,C; *Located at the entrance of the city. 1 dormitory with 6 places and 3 private rooms in a house with a large garden and kitchen. English spoken. Horses welcome.*

Gîte d'étape - La Halte du Kiosque[Fabienne Rouilhes],2, square Salvandy, 32100 Condom, France; Tel:+33 (0)684 323 001; +33 (0) 562 683 776; Email:contact@lahaltedukiosque.fr; lahaltedukiosque.fr; Price:C,C,C; *Close to the city centre 10 places in 3 rooms. Cottage with garden and terrace. English spoken.*

Gîte de Gabarre[Nelly and Eric],42bis, avenue des Mousquetaires, 32100 Condom, France; Tel:+33(0)686415839; Email:contact@gitedegabarre.com; gitedegabarre.com; Price:C,C,C; *Located on a lovely property on the Blaise river, 40 places. English spoken.*

Gîte l'Ancien Carmel,35, avenue Victor Hugo, 32100 Condom, France; Tel:+33 (0)5 62 29 41 56; +33 (0)7 67 34 02 32; Email:accueil@lanciencarmel.fr; lanciencarmel.fr; Price:C,C,C; *A former convent dating back to the 13th century 37 places in rooms of 1 or 2 and dormitory for 12. Kitchen. English spoken. Horses welcome.*

Gîte d'étape - Relais de Saint Jacques[Alain Laurent and Arnaud],2, avenue du Maréchal Joffre, 32100 Condom, France; Tel:+33(0)6 13 28 52 66 ; +33(0)6 21 78 47 86; Email:laurent_crassous@orange.fr; tourisme-condom.co.uk; Price:-,C,C; *Located in an18th century former post office 15 places in rooms of 2 to 4. English spoken. Private Rooms available*

Office de Tourisme Condom - Gers - Ténarèze,5, place Saint-Pierr, 32100 Condom, France; Tel:+33(0) 5 62 28 00 80; Email:contact@tourisme-condom.com; tourisme-condom.com

Larressingle

Gîte d'étape - La Halte de Larressingle[Isabelle Ladrière and Patrice Dumas],Lieu-dit Cahuzac, 32100 Larressingle, France; Tel:+33(0)7 66 85 16 75; Email:lahaltedelarressingle@gmail.com; lahaltedelarressingle.fr; Price:C,C,C; *Lovely views. 12 places including 6 places in dormitory and 3 B&B rooms. Camping possible*

Gîte d'étape - La Ferme de Tollet[Mr and Mrs Carrère],Lieu-dit Tollet, 32100 Larressingle, France; Tel:+33 (0)687 360 434; Price:C,C,C; *Basic accommodations on a working farm which produces local specialities including Armagnac. 12 places in 6 dormitories welcoming hosts.*

Hôtel - Auberge de Larressingle,Lieu-dit Coulomet, 32100 Larressingle, France; Tel:+33 (0)5 62 28 29 67; Email:contact@auberge-de-larressingle.fr; auberge-de-larressingle.fr; Price:A,A,A; *Located next to the historic village 12 rooms which can accommodate 2 to 4 pers. Sauna and spa. Hoses welcome. English spoken.*

Office de Tourisme,Au Village, 32100 Larressingle, France; Tel:+33 (0) 5 62 28 00 80; Email:contact@tourisme-condom.com; tourisme-condom.com

Larressingle to Éauze

stage 25

Length:	29.8km
Ascent:	696m
Descent:	679m
Le-Puy:	516km
Roncevaux:	226km

Hiker before Éauze © Alexia Adamski

Route–The route is very well marked, as it makes its way to the former Roman city of Éauze, crossing fields and vineyards. From Lamothe, the route is straight and monotonous (following former railway tracks) for 6 km as it leads to Éauze.

Pointers–**Market:** Éauze hosts a local produce market every Thursday morning as well as Sunday mornings in July and August.

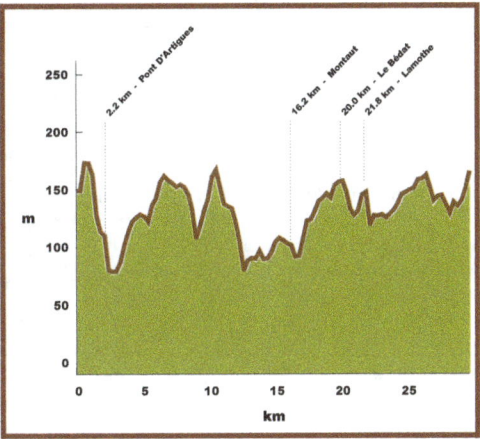

stage 25 — Larressingle to Éauze

Cultural Discoveries

Pont d'Artigues

Pont d'Artigues is a 12th century Romanesque bridge over the Osse river on the former Roman road connecting Agen to Éauze, and is considered a world heritage site. The Knights of Malta built a hospital and chapel nearby (now destroyed).

Montréal du Gers

Considered one of the most beautiful villages in France, Montréal du Gers (popl. 1,185, alt. 100m) is one of the oldest *bastides* in the region. Founded in 1255 by Alphonse de Poitiers on a summit overlooking the Auzoue river, it follows the typical design of *bastides*, with its narrow streets leading to a central square.

Éauze

Main Square Éauze

In the 1st century, Éauze (pronounced ôze, popl. 4,000, alt. 140m), which was held by the Aquitanians, fell to the Roman armies of Julius Caesar. By the 4th century, it had become the Roman capital of Novempopulana (meaning nine people–the southern part of the Roman imperial province of Aquitaine). By the 5th century, Éauze was one of the most important Catholic dioceses in France. King Henry IV (1553-1610), who played an important role during the Wars of Religion, had significant ties with Éauze and repeatedly visited the city, including with his wife, Marguerite de Valois (also known as *Reine Margot*). Most of the town's principal monuments date from this period.

In 1985, an important Roman treasure, the **Treasure of Éauze** (*Le Trésor d'Éauze*) was discovered outside the city, including 30,000 gold pieces and jewellery from the 3rd century. The treasure is on display at the archaeological museum, which also describes Roman occupation of the region.

Of note is the former **Cathedral of Saint Luperc** (*Cathédrale Saint-Luperc*), constructed from the remains of the Roman city, as well as the old timber buildings and the home of Jeanne d'Albret (Queen Regent of Navarre from 1555 to 1572, mother of King Henry IV and leader of the French Protestants).

Today, Éauze is also famous for its Armagnac, as it is surrounded by some of the most prestigious Armagnac vineyards.

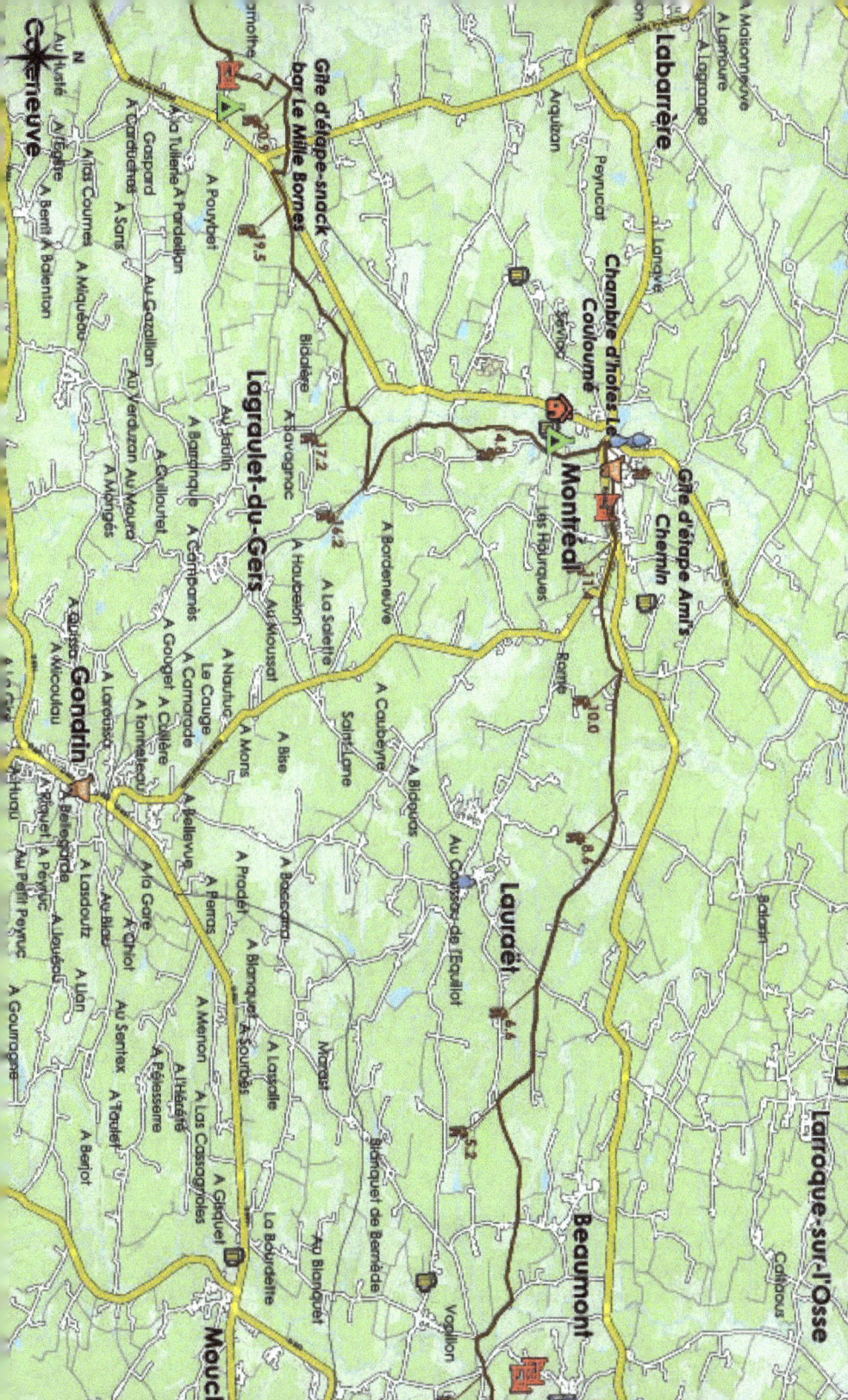

stage 25

Larressingle to Éauze

GR®65

(0.0) Retrace the route to rejoin the GR®65 from Larressingle turn right onto the chemin de Valence and then right onto the GR®65 trail**(1.0)** Descend charming trail through forest to the D278 road 🚶 **(2.2)** Cross the D278 road and cross the bridge (**Pont d'Artigues**) over the L'Osse river. Continue straight[Romanesque bridge dating from the 12-13th Century] **(2.6)** Turn right on asphalt road and continue straight**(3.2)** Turn left onto track that passes through fields. Continue straight[Signpost] 🚶 **(5.2)** Turn right onto asphalt road and descend left until junction with D254 road[Pass church of Routgès on the right] 🚶 **(6.6)** Cross the D254 road and continue straight 🚶 **(8.6)** Turn left onto trail. Continue straight crossing the stream 🚶 **(10.0)** Keep left on trail that converges with the D113 road. Turn right onto D113 and cross to Montréal-du-Gers 🚶 **(11.3)** At fork, keep right, and continue straight on rue Auresan towards village centre[Pass gas station to the left]**(12.1)** Turn left into central square of Montréal-du-Gers**(12.1)** From central square take road next to church, passing through historic gates**(12,1)** Turn right onto boulevard des Pyrenees and descend village ramparts to route de Condom/D15 🚶 **(12.5)** Turn right on D15 road and immediately left on small road that runs alongside stream Ruisseau de Lazoue. Continue straight[Stream on right]**(13.4)** Continue straight on trail[Pass Lac de la Tènarèze on the left] 🚶 **(14.8)** Continue straight on asphalt road[Pass Ribère de Bas on the left]**(15.3)** Turn right onto trail towards Montaut 🚶 **(16.2)** In **Montaut** pass under metal bridge, use ramp and turn left onto tree-lined trail that goes to D230 road. Turn left 🚶 **(17.2)** Turn right onto track through vineyards. Attention, poorly way-marked**(17.7)** Turn right onto road and then left onto trail between vineyards. Continue straight until reaching the D29 road[Pass through La Maisonnette] 🚶 **(19.7)** At the junction with the D29 turn right and then take the track to the right at the end of the field of vines[sign Bédat]**(20.0)** Beside **Le Bédat** turn left and cross the D31 road[Le Bédat on right] 🚶 **(20.9)** Immediately before the house with the metal garaghe, turn left on the track**(21.1)** At the end of the vines turn left**(21.3)** At the end of the field of vines on your left, turn right**(21.8)** Turn right onto road and descend from **Lamothe**, passing church and picnic area on the left 🚶 **(23.5)** Cross the D264 road and continue straight on former railroad track leading to Éauze until reaching the D931 road[Signpost] 🚶 **(29.1)** Turn right onto the D931 road and continue straight to Éauze historic centre[Pass Leclerc supermarket on left]**(29.8)** Arrive at Éauze[Place d'Armagnac, beside Cathedral]

Landscape before Eauze,

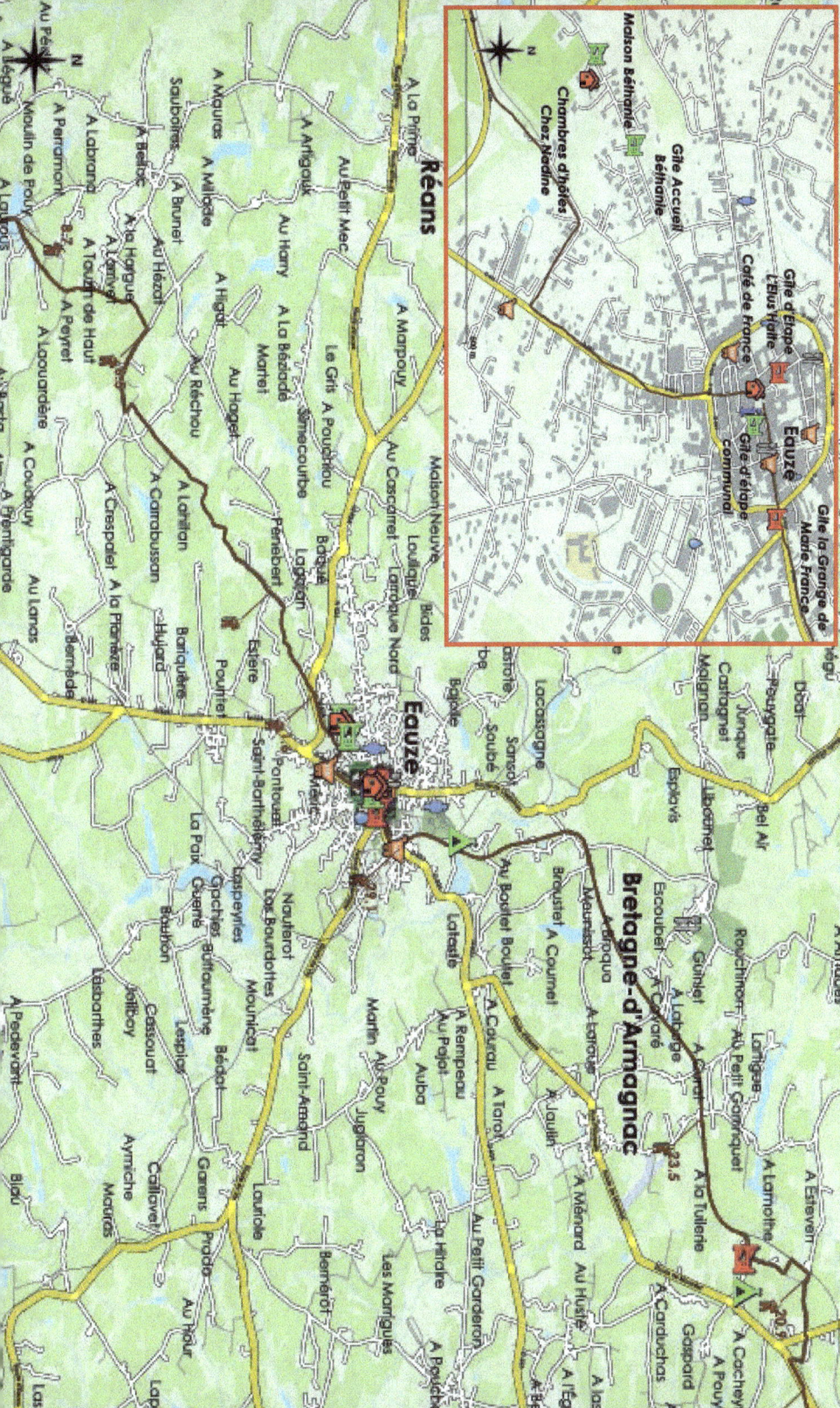

stage 25   Larressingle to Éauze

Accommodation and Tourist Information

Cazeneuve

Gîte d'étape-snack bar - Le Mille Bornes[Florence and Bernard],Lieu-dit Lamothe, 32800 Cazeneuve, France; Tel:+33 (0)650 621 346; Email:gitemillebornes@gmail.com; gitemillebornes.com; Price:C,C,C|C,-,-; *12 places in 3 dormitories. Horses and donkeys welcome. Outside kitchen for campers. Formerly the well known Casa d'Elena*

Eauze

Gîte d'étape communal,2, rue Félix Soules, 32800 Eauze, France; Tel:+33(0) 562 09 85 62; +33 (0) 756 250 346; Email:gitecommunal@armagnac-dartagnan.com; armagnac-dartagnan.com; Price:C,C,-; *15 places in 3 dormitories located in the village centre beside cathedral and tourist office. Kitchen.*

Maison Béthanie[Pauline and Marcel],34, avenue de Sauboires, 32800 Eauze, France; Tel:+33(0)+33 7 87 72 07 82; accueilbethanie.wixsite.com; Price:D,D,D; *Located 600m from the church operated by former pilgrims. 8 places in home with garden. Shared meal. English spoken. Horses welcome. Reservations taken only one day in advance.*

Gîte - Accueil Béthanie [Pauline and Marcel],34, avenue de Sauboires, 32800 Eauze, France; Tel:+33(0)787720782; bethanie-eauze.blogspot.com; Price:D,D,D; *8 places in 2 rooms communal meals - except Sunday garden and chapel available*

Gite - la Grange de Marie France[Marie France], 4, avenue de la Ténarèze, 32800 Eauze, France; Tel:+33 (0)6 61 24 48 04; +33(0)562099909; Email:lagrangedemariefrance@gmail.com ; lagrangedemariefrance.com; Price:-,-,B; *14 places in 3 buildings*

Gîte d'Etape - L'Elus'Halte,19, rue Carbonas, 32800 Eauze, France; Tel:+33 562 09 92 95; +33 683 40 19 64; Email:lelushalte@orange.fr; Price:C,-,-; *8 places in 3 rooms kitchen*

Chambres d'hôtes - Chez Nadine[Francis and Nadine Corlaiti],43, avenue de Sauboires, 32800 Eauze, France; Tel:+33(0)6 68 94 82 46; +33(0)6 50 09 60 42; Email:francis.corlaiti@wanadoo.fr; gitecheznadine.com; Price:-,-,C; *11 places in 4 rooms. 500m from the village centre. Very welcoming.*

Café de France,2, place d'Armagnac, 32800 Eauze, France; Tel:+33 (0)6 61 94 47 22; armagnac-dartagnan.com; Price:-,B,-; *Located in main square facing the cathedral B&B has 4 rooms. English spoken.*

Camping Municipal de Pouy,Allée Jean Desque, 32800 Eauze, France; Tel:+33(0)562034502; armagnac-dartagnan.com; Price:C,-,-; *70 shaded camping places pool restaurant*

Office de Tourisme,2, rue Félix Soules, 32800 Eauze, France; Tel:+33(0) 5 62 09 85 62; Email:info@armagnac-dartagnan.com; armagnac-dartagnan.com

Montréal-du-Gers

Gîte d'étape - Ami's Chemin [Domi],29, rue du 11 novembre, 32250 Montréal-du-Gers, France; Tel:+33(0)6 82 22 71 52; Email:dom.poulard@orange.fr; amischemin.com; Price:C,C,C; *8 places in 2 dormitories in a family home great views of the countryside*

Chambre d'hotes - Le Couloumé[Famille Lussagnet],Route d'Eauze, 32250 Montréal-du-Gers, France; Tel:+33(0)5 62 29 47 05; +33(0)6 85 35 51 26; +33(0)5 62 29 44 78; Email:lecouloume@orange.fr; lecouloume.com; Price:-,B,-|B,-,-; *4 private rooms and 3 independent buildings. 6 camping places with access to kitchen washing machine and showers*

Éauze to Lanne-Soubiran

stage 26

Nogaro Cloister

Length:	29.3km
Ascent:	560m
Descent:	593m
Le-Puy:	546km
Roncevaux:	236km

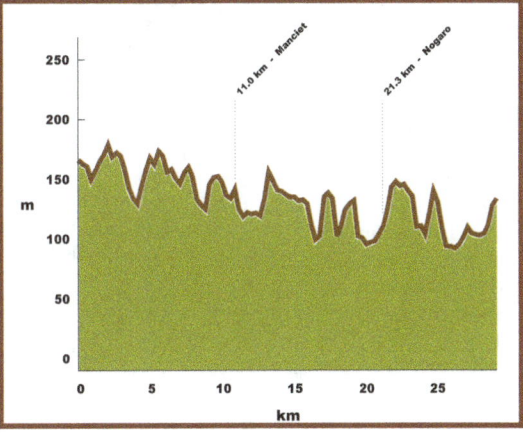

Route–The route is well-marked and uses tracks and asphalt roads, as it crosses gentle vineyards in the heart of the Armagnac region, until reaching the industrial agricultural city of Nogaro. Thereafter, it follows tracks through corn fields and forests to the village of Lanne-Soubiran.

Pointers–**Advance planning:** The route is highly exposed, be sure to have sun protection (hat, sunscreen, etc.).

stage 26

Éauze to Lanne-Soubiran

Cultural Discoveries

Chapel of the Command Post Saint Christie Hospital
(*Chapelle de la commanderie de l'Hôpital-Sainte-Christie*)

The chapel is the only remaining building of the former Saint Christie command post and hospital, which was probably built in the 12th century by the Knights of Malta. The post was destroyed in 1538 by Protestant troops during the Wars of Religion. Fifty metres west of the chapel, on the right side of the route, is a stone marker with the Cross of Malta. This was one of about 20 markers that fixed the perimeter of the command post, which in 1750 covered 280 hectares.

Nogaro

The economy of Nogaro (popl. 2,000, alt. 100m), a city located between Bordeaux, Toulouse and Bayonne, is based on the wine industry. However, the town's historical centre is the fortified mid-11th century **Church of Saint Nicholas** (*Eglise Saint-Nicolas*), which was organized as a collegiate church, where daily worship was overseen by a college of non-monastic clergy. In 1995, eight 11th century frescoes depicting the martyrdom of Saint Lawrence (a deacon of the early Christian church who was martyred in Rome during Emperor Valerian's persecutions of 258) were discovered in the north apse. In the south apse is a fresco of Christ in Majesty surrounded by the symbols of the four Evangelists and angels. These frescoes were made with a number of important blue-green pigments, including lapis-lazuli (from Afghanistan), azurite (from Germany) and aerinite (local). A Romanesque stone relief above the baptismal font represents a lion woman (*signum leonis*) with crossed legs, a Romanesque symbol that also appears on the southern portal of the Cathedral of Santiago de Compostela. Outside, to the south, are the remains of the cloister, including five delicately carved arches.

The town arena (*arènes*) is also renowned for showcasing the Gascon sport, **Course Landaise**, a traditional form of bullfighting that involves leaping or dodging charging cows. Competitions are held throughout the summer, with a major event held each 14 July.

Éauze to Lanne-Soubiran

stage 26

GR®65

(0.0) From Place d'Armagnac, turn away from Cathedral left and continue straight on rue Daury **(0.2)** Cross road and continue straight on avenue des Pyrenées[Signpost] **(0.4)** Pass the Imperial water tower (1870), which supplied drinking water to the city foutains, on the left **(0.7)** Turn right on chemin du Soumcide[Opposite Allianz Insurance office] **(1.6)** Cross road N524 and continue straight on trail through vineyards **(2.5)** Turn left onto asphalt road, route de Bonnefin[After passing house on the left] **(2.8)** Continue straight on asphalt road, direction Pennebert[Signpost] **(3.1)** Turn left onto track and continue straight[After passing farm and tower] **(6.5)** Turn left and continue straight through vineyards until reaching the D122 road[Cross stream ahead] **(8.7)** Turn left onto the D122 road and continue straight to the village of Manciet[Signpost] **(10.8)** Turn right before the D931 road, and then use the footbridge to cross left over road. Continue straight towards church **(11.0)** Turn right on rue Central (opposite church) and continue straight to leave **Manciet**

(11.3) Merge onto the D931 road and continue straight[Cross river La Douze] **(11.9)** Turn left onto the D152 road, direction Aignan[Signpost. Pass agricultural facility] **(13.0)** Opposite the entrance to the Hausse Came Refuge, turn right on the track[Continue with tress on your right] **(13.5)** Turn right onto asphalt road and then turn left on the track as it zigzags between fields **(14.3)** Turn right on the track[Pass equestrian centre on your left] **(15.5)** Turn left on the track between the vines and the D522 road **(15.6)** Take the left fork on the road[direction Pehour] **(16.5)** Turn right on trail that follows stream to the right, then continue straight until reaching road **(17.3)** Turn left onto asphalt road and then right onto trail. Continue straight **(19.1)** Turn left and then right, continuing on trail until joining the D522 road **(19.8)** Turn left onto the D522 road and continue straight through industrial city of Nogaro[Signpost] **(21.3)** At fork keep right and continue straight/climb on D143 road to leave **Nogaro**[Church directly behind]

(22.1) Keep left at fork and then turn immediately right onto track and continue straight[Pass water tower on right] **(23.9)** Turn left and continue straight towards the farm of Claverie **(24.9)** Turn right and then left on a trail (descent towards valley)[Signpost. Cross stream] **(26.4)** Turn right onto D931 road and continue straight through roundabout **(27.2)** Turn left onto small road and continue straight to reach Lanne-Soubiran[Signpost. Opposite white house] **(29.3)** Arrive at Lanne-Soubiran[Beside church]

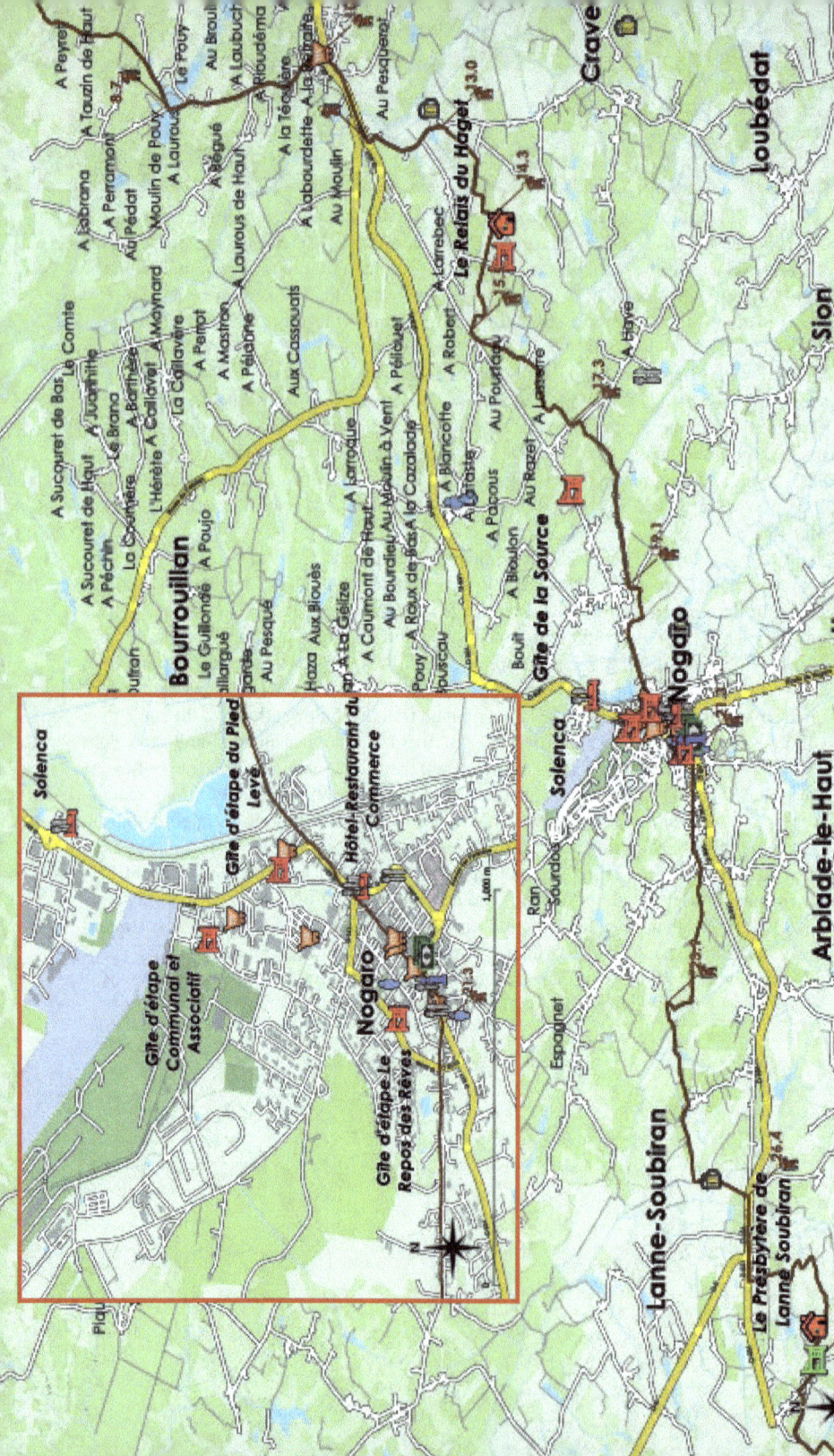

Éauze to Lanne-Soubiran

stage 26

Accommodation and Tourist Information

Cravenceres

Le Relais du Haget[Stéphanie and Jean-Bernard Ducos],Lieu-dit Le Haget, 32110 Cravenceres, France; Tel:+33(0)5 62 08 54 02; Email:stephanie.brud@wanadoo.fr; relaishaget.com; Price:C,C,C|B,B,B; *Equestrian center/farm located about 16 km after Éauze near the GR®65 (Church of l'Hopital) 10 places in 2 dormitories and 2 rooms for 2-3. Horses welcome. Camping possible*

Lanne-Soubiran

Le Presbytère de Lanne Soubiran[Pierre and Claudia],Place de l'Église, 32110 Lanne-Soubiran, France; Tel:+33(0)6 43 34 99 45; +33(0)5 62 09 70 24; Email:info@lepresbytere.org; lepresbytere.org; Price:C,C,C|-,-,A; *12 places in 3 dormitories and 2 double B&B rooms in a restored and tastefully decorated presbytery with garden. Horses welcome. English spoken.*

Nogaro

Gîte d'étape Communal et Associatif,11, avenue des Sports, 32110 Nogaro, France; Tel:+33(0)562690615; +33(0)631593472; Email:contact@gite-nogaro.fr; gite-nogaro.fr; Price:C,C,-; *12 places in double rooms 10 places in dormitory. Basic but welcoming accommodations near airport on outskirts of town in commercial area. Kitchen. Camping possible*

Gîte d'étape du Pied Levé[Sylvie],7, avenue de Daniate, 32110 Nogaro, France; Tel:+33(0) 671 237 326; Email:gitedupiedleve@gmail.com; gitedupiedlevecom.wordpress.com; Price:-,C,-; *3 rooms each for 2 people and 2 rooms for 3 or 4 kitchen. Shops close-by*

Gîte d'étape - Le Repos des Rêves[Vincent],9, rue des Fossés, 32110 Nogaro, France; Tel:+33 (0)628 902 057; Email:lereposdesreves@gmail.com; lereposdesreves.fr; Price:-,C,-; *10 places in 2 dormitories also 2 private rooms English spoken. Dinner possible with reservation*

Hôtel-Restaurant du Commerce,2, place des Cordeliers, 32110 Nogaro, France; Tel:+33(0) 5 62 09 00 95; Email:info@hotelrestaurantnogaro.com; hotelrestaurantnogaro.com; Price:A,A,-; *A family run 2 star hotel with 14 rooms and a restaurant*

Hôtel - Solenca,984, avenue de Daniate, 32110 Nogaro, France; Tel:+33(0) 5 62 09 09 08; Email:info@solenca.com; solenca.com; Price:A,A,-; *49 rooms in modern 3 star hotel with restaurant in the industrial zone*

<type>9</type>**Office de Tourisme**,77, rue de la République, 32110 Nogaro, France; Tel:+33(0) 5 62 09 13 30; Email:info@armagnac-dartagnan.com; armagnac-dartagnan.com

Saint-Griède

Domaine de la Maraude,Lieu-dit Lamarque, 32110 Saint-Griède, France; Tel:+33 (0)6 50 81 65 62; Email:contact@domainedelamaraude.fr; domainedelamaraude.fr; Price:A,-,-; *Unique 2 and 4 person cabins in wooded surroundings*

Sainte-Christie-d'Armagnac

Gîte de la Source,Lieu-dit Monneton, 32370 Sainte-Christie-d'Armagnac, France; Tel:+33 (0)6 10 78 35 22; Email:domainedelasourcegers@gmail.com; domainedelasourcegers.fr; Price:-,-,C; *Located 2.5 km before Nogaro and 500m from the GR®65 a large estate with 17 places in dormitories for 4 and 2 rooms for 2-3 people Pool.*

stage 27 — Lanne-Soubiran to Aire-sur-l'Adour

Length:	19.5km
Ascent:	270m
Descent:	322m
Le-Puy:	575km
Roncevaux:	206km

Way marking in the Landes Department

Route–The route is well-marked, with no significant climbs, and consists mostly of asphalt roads and some paths, that cross corn fields and forests. Upon approaching the Adour river, corn fields begin to dominate the landscape. The route passes through the industrial city and zone of Barcelonne-du-Gers to arrive at the historic city of Aire-sur-l'Adour, on the Adour river.

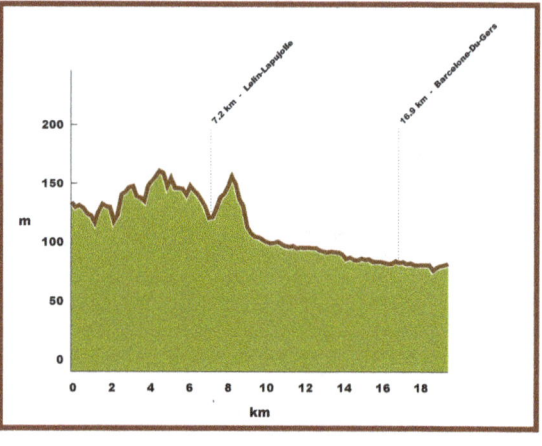

Lanne-Soubiran to Aire-sur-l'Adour stage 27

Cultural Discoveries

Aire-sur-l'Adour

The town of Aire-sur-l'Adour (popl. 8,280, alt. 70m), with its strategic position on the Ardour river, was an important Roman city, and later a royal city of the Visgoths (5th century). In 506, the Visigoth King Alaric II (484-507) promulgated his *Breviary*, a compilation of Roman laws and texts that applied to certain populations living under his rule. It was during this period that Saint Quitterie is said to have lived. According to legend, Quitterie's father, a Galician prince, wanted her to marry and renounce Christianity. Instead, the princess fled to Aire-sur-l'Adour where she was beheaded by the Visigoths. A spring emerged on the spot where she was killed, and its waters were believed to have healing powers (Saint Quitterie's Fountain). At the end of the 11th century, the cathedral was built and Benedictine monks founded the Church of Saint Quitterie and an abbey on the heights of the town. A market is held on Saturday mornings.

Church of Saint Quitterie
(Eglise Sainte-Quitterie)

The church is dedicated to Saint Quitterie. On the west wall, is the Saint's white marble tomb which has been associated with several miracles. At the far end of the church, are two semi-circular cells, where mentally disturbed people were held before being taken for cure to the Saint's tomb. The foundation of the church, however, predates Saint Quitterie. It was built on the site of a Roman temple of Mars. The laurel-leaf decorated stones in the church's crypt are from the pagan temple. Later, in the 11th century, Benedictine monks became caretakers of Saint Quitterie's tomb, and built the neighbouring abbey to accommodate a growing following.

Shaver-Crandell, A., Gerson, P. L., & Stones, A, p. 105 (1995). *The pilgrim's guide to Santiago de Compostela: A gazetteer*. London: Harvey Miller Publishers.

GR®65

(0.0) Turn right onto D152 road[Pass chuch on the right]**(0.3)** Turn left onto small road before white and brown mansard house and continue straight[House]**(0.9)** At road's end, turn left and continue straight on road/trail that leads through fields and forest called "Lande des Bois"[Pay attention to waymarking, as sometimes poorly marked] **(3.8)** Turn left onto asphalt road (away from farmhouse) and then take first right and continue straight**(4.5)** Turn left onto small road and continue straight **(4.9)** Turn left and continue straight, direction Lelin-Lapujolle[Signpost and pass farms of Bidet and La Grange on left] **(7.2)** Enter village of **Lelin-Lapujolle**. Keep right, passing church on the left to leave village[Signpost and church]

(7.6) Turn right onto D169 road and continue straight**(7.9)** Turn left onto asphalt road and continue straight passing through vineyards and fields[Passing on the left last house (beige) of the village] **(9.0)** Turn right (houses) and then left onto small road passing through fields, until reaching road **(11.2)** Turn right before railway tracks and continue straight[Railway tracks to the left] **(13.6)** Turn left. Cross railway tracks and the D935 road, and continue straight through fields[Railway tracks and D935]**(14.2)** Turn right at oak tree, direction Barcelonne-du-Gers, and continue straight [Signpost] **(16.3)** Turn right on road towards Barcelone-du-Gers, then keep left on boulevard du Midi[Signpost and pass lavoir on left]**(16.9)** In **Barcelone-du-Gers** turn right on rue de Casamont and then left on D512/Rue de l'Hôpital at Place de la Garlande. Continue straight to leave village[Pass church on the right]

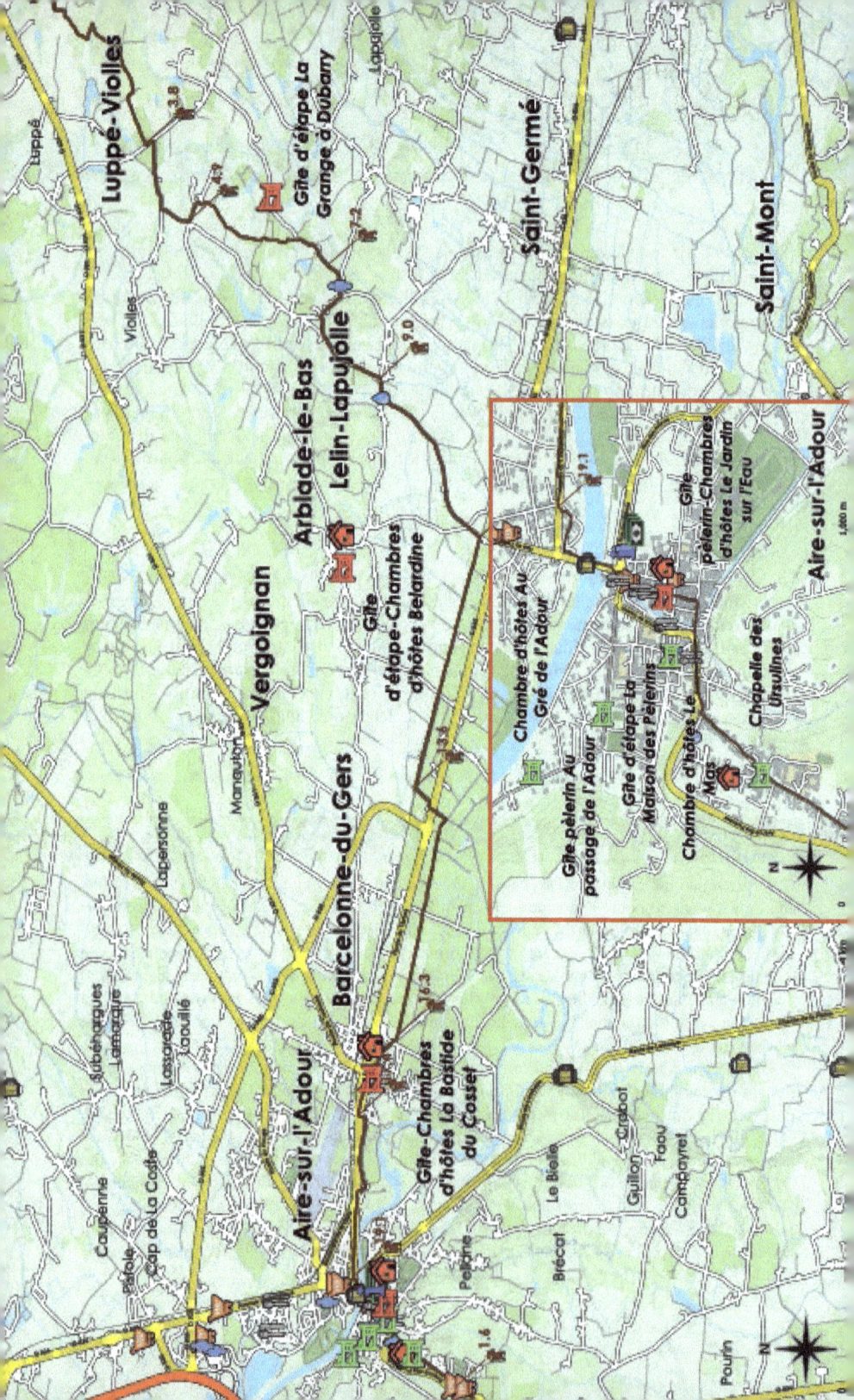

Lanne-Soubiran to Aire-sur-l'Adour stage 27

🥾 **(17.4)** Turn left onto rue du Beret and then right onto chemin des Moncaux **(18.2)** Turn right onto rue des Saligats, and then left onto avenue du 4 Septembre. Continue straight 🥾 **(19.1)** Turn left at Place de la Liberté, and then right on Impasse Frédéric Lévrier [Turn before Hôtel-Restaurant Les Platanes] **(19.3)** Turn left and cross bridge to enter Aire-sur-l'Adour centre [Bridge] **(19.5)** Arrive at Aire-sur-l'Adour [Place Général de Gaulle]

Accommodation and Tourist Information

Aire-sur-l'Adour

Chapelle des Ursulines,40, rue Félix Despagnet, 40800 Aire-sur-l'Adour, France; Tel:+33 (0)9 79 27 09 01; +33(0)6 70 49 65 26; Email:chapelle-ursulines@outlook.com; chapelledesursulines.com; Price:-,-,C; *Located in a converted chapel on the GR®65 when exiting the city 22 places in 2 dormitories and private rooms. Donkeys can be attached in nearby pasture.*

Gîte d'étape - La Maison des Pèlerins [Isabelle and Alejandro],4, rue du Général Labat, 40800 Aire-sur-l'Adour, France; Tel:+33(0)780 041 140; +33(0)6 558 716 807; +33 780 393 658; +33(0) 780 393 658; Email: lamaisondespelerins@gmail.com; lamaisondespelerins.com; Price:C,C,C; *Located in the city centre and run by former pilgrims who know the Chemin well includes 15 places in 5 rooms. English spoken.*

Chambre d'hôtes - Au Gré de l'Adour [Christine Lavie],24, route de Duhort, 40800 Aire-sur-l'Adour, France; Tel:+33(0)632965896; +33(0)5 58 52 39 79; Email:duhort40@orange.fr; tourismelandes.com; Price:-,C,C; *Pilgrim accommodation located on the banks of the Ardour river 6 minutes from the city centre calm environment with 5 places in 2 shared rooms. English spoken. Horses welcome.*

Gîte pèlerin - Au passage de l'Adour [Nanou and Etienne],30, rue Césaire Dauge, 40800 Aire-sur-l'Adour, France; Tel:+33 (0)6 51 43 68 18; +33 (0)5 58 45 34 51; Email:aupassagedeladour@gmail.com; aupassagedeladour.com; Price:-,-,C; *A private house withe a dormitiry with 5 beds and 1 private bedroom pool and garden with space for 2 tents English spoken*

Gîte pèlerin-Chambres d'hôtes - Le Jardin sur l'Eau [Juliette and Vincent],25, rue Carnot, 40800 Aire-sur-l'Adour, France; Tel:+33(0) 7 49 65 04 27; Email:lejardinsurleau@gmail.com; lejardinsurleau.com; Price:C,C,C|-,B,-; *2 dormitories for upto 5 people and 3 B&B rooms in 19th century house in a central location*

Chambre d'hôtes - Le Mas [Pascale Bertho],17, rue du château, 40800 Aire-sur-l'Adour, France; Tel:+33(0)615443682; Email:pascale.bertho757@orange.fr; le-mas.net; Price:-,A,A; *5 luxury rooms in a lovely home 50m from the GR®65 and the Church of Sainte Quitterie with garden pool and yard. Horses welcome. English spoken special pilgrim prices*

Office de Tourisme,Place du 19 mars 1962, 40800 Aire-sur-l'Adour, France; Tel:+33(0) 5 58 71 64 70; Email:accueil@tourisme-aire-eugenie.fr ; tourisme-aire-eugenie.fr

Arblade-le-Bas

Gîte d'étape-Chambres d'hôtes Belardine [Véronique Mariotti],Lieu-dit Belardine, 32720 Arblade-le-Bas, France; Tel:+33 (0)789 57 33 30; +33 (0)562 69 06 14; web. facebook.com/Gite.surleChemind.St.Jacques. deCompostelle; Price:-,C,-|-,B,-; *On a lovely restored farm 3 rooms of 2-4 pers. Kitchen. English spoken. Horses welcome. Located 2.5 km after Lelin-Lapujolle on a short cut to the GR®65.*

Barcelonne-du-Gers

Gîte-Chambres d'hôtes - La Bastide du Cosset [Florence and Freddy Fior],11, place de la Garlande, 32720 Barcelonne-du-Gers, France; Tel:+33(0)6 33 80 50 95; Email:info@bastideducosset.com; bastideducosset.fr; Price:C,C,C|-,-,-; *Located in the city centre agreeable hostel includes 14 places in shared rooms and B&B with 6 rooms. English spoken. Kitchen.*

Lelin-Lapujolle

Gîte d'étape - La Grange à Dubarry [Véronique and Philippe Biérent],La Grange à Dubarry, 32400 Lelin-Lapujolle, France; Tel:+33(0)6 41 31 73 79; +33(0)6 27 35 84 13; Email:lagrangeadubarry@gmail.com; la-grange-a-dubarry.fr; Price:C,C,V; *300m off the GR®65 restored farmhouse with 12 places in 1 room and 2 dormitories. English spoken. Horses welcome.*

stage 28 — Aire-sur-l'Adour to Arzacq-Arraziguet

Length:	34.2km
Ascent:	796m
Descent:	643m
Le-Puy:	594km
Roncevaux:	187km

Pimbo Collegiate Church

Route–Leaving Aire-sur-l'Adour, the way markings are different, and include a white/yellow/blue arrow. The route is, however, well-marked and follows mainly asphalt roads, as it crosses endless corn fields in this highly agricultural area.

Pointers–**Advance planning:** The route is exposed, be sure to have sun protection (hat, sunscreen, etc.). Stage length: This and the next two stages in the Béarn and Basque region tend to be longer due to the scarcity of accommodation and distance between villages.

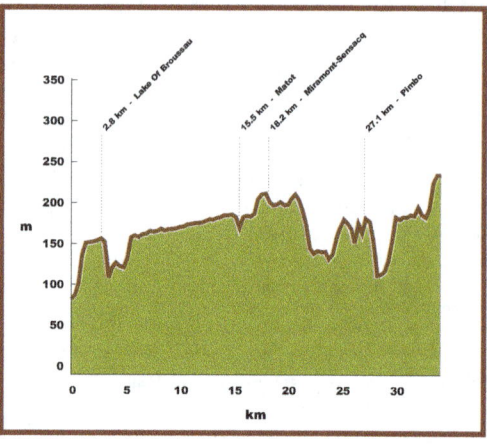

Aire-sur-l'Adour to Arzacq-Arraziguet stage 28

Cultural Discoveries

Pimbo

A document from the 13th century sets out the *paréage,* or terms, for the creation of the *bastide* of Pimbo (popl. 200, alt. 150m). Specifically, an agreement was reached between the abbot and canons of the collegiate church, on the one hand, and King Henry III of England, on the other. The *bastide,* which developed along the narrow ridge of Pimbo, linked the church and the castle and granted inhabitants religious and military protection. The Collegiate Church of Saint-Barthélemy, founded in the 12th century, is Romanesque.

Arzacq-Arraziguet

While there is not a great deal to visit in Arzacq-Arraziguet (popl. 1,000, alt. 120m), the village is welcoming. In the 13th-14th century, probably due to its strategic position near the border of the Béarn region and its important market, a *bastide* was built, of which only a tower (known as the *tour de peich*) remains. A market is held each Saturday morning.

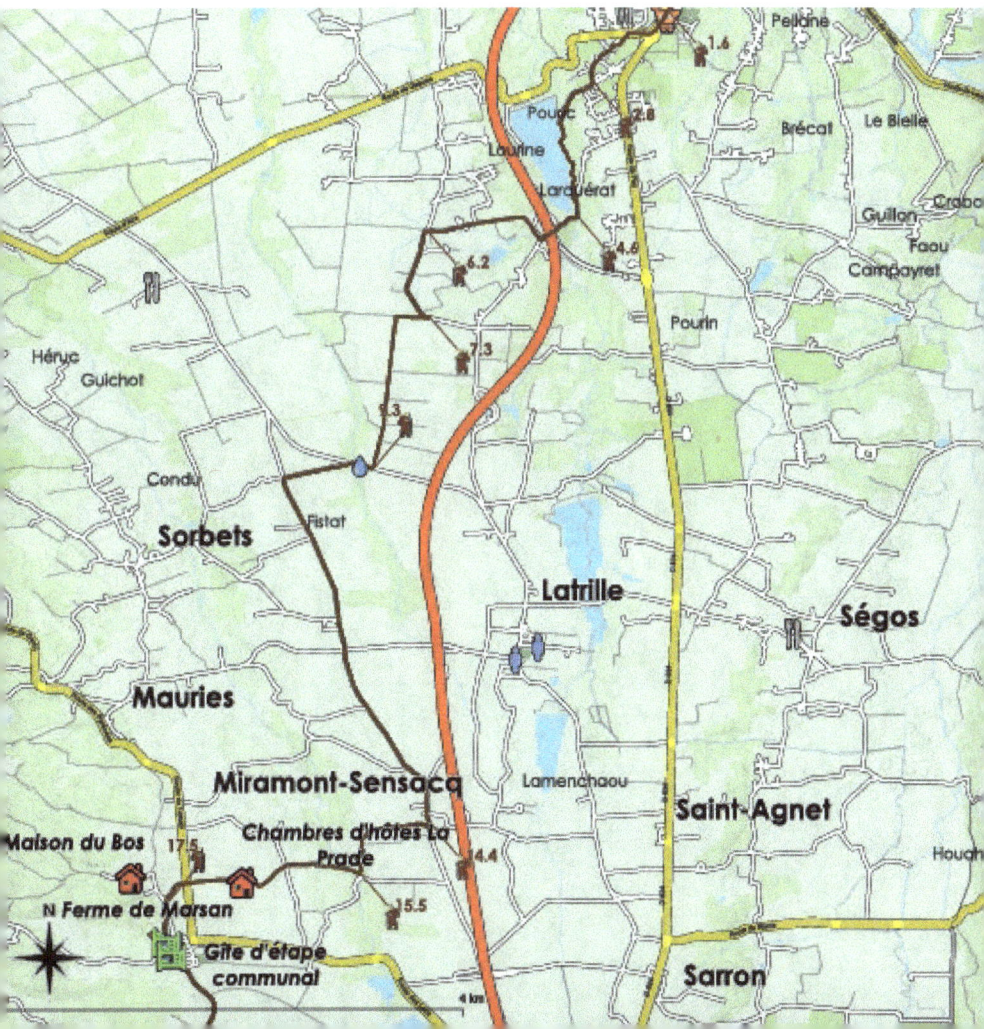

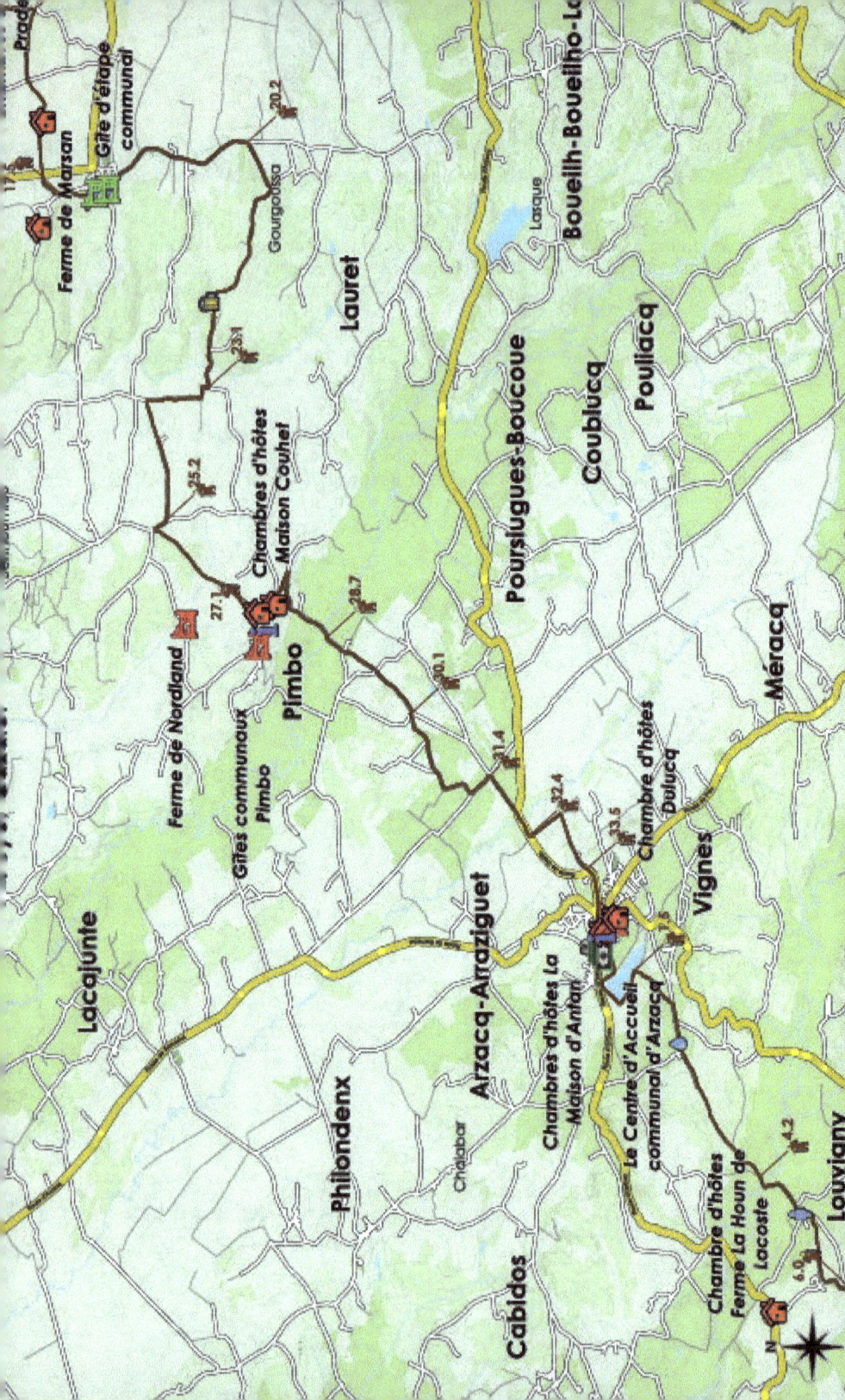

Aire-sur-l'Adour to Arzacq-Arraziguet

stage 28

GR®65

(0.0) From Place du Général de Gaulle continue (away from river) on rue Carnot**(0.3)**Turn right on rue Henri Labeyrie, and then left on avenue des Pyrénées/D834 to begin climb out of city**(0.6)**Turn left on rue Félix Despagnet and climb hill to leave city**(0.9)**Pass church of Saint Quitterie on left and continue straight on rue du Mas 🚶 **(1.6)**Turn left onto avenue des Pyrénées. Then turn right at roundabout on the D2/rue Nelson Mandela**(2.1)**Turn left on rue Georges Fraisse and then left on rue du Jardinet. Continue straight 🚶 **(2.8)**Turn right onto chemin du Brousseau, which leads to the **lake of Brousseau**
(3.4) Turn left onto trail that goes around the perimeter of the lake 🚶 **(4.6)**Turn left onto the D456 road. Go through underpasses of the A65 highway**(5.0)**Turn right onto a small road (running parallel to power line), which then veers left 🚶 **(6.2)**Turn left on small local road (Voie Communale de Lourine) 🚶 **(7.3)**Turn right and then immediately left on road 🚶 **(9.3)**Turn right on the D62 road, cross stream, and then left on route de Pitocq[Pass agricultural facility to the right] 🚶 **(14.4)**Turn right and pass the farm buildings on your right**(15.0)**Bear left and keep the trees to your right. Continue straight until reaching Matot 🚶 **(15.5)**In **Matot** turn right onto road and continue straight. Cross the Bahus stream as well as the D11 road
🚶 **(17.5)**Turn left, keep to the right and head towards Miramont-Sensacq centre[Signpost]**(18.2)**After passing through **Miramont-Sensacq** turn left onto the D314 road and continue straight
🚶 **(20.2)**Turn right. At road's end turn right again. Continue straight (climbs and descents) until the village of Sensacq 🚶 **(23.1)**Turn right towards church, then take first right and continue straight**(24.0)**Turn left and continue straight to the D111 road 🚶 **(25.2)**Turn right onto the D111 road and then left on trail through woods. Continue straight until reaching village of Pimbo 🚶 **(27.1)**Turn left and continue straight through village of **Pimbo**[Pass church on the left]
(27.5) Turn right direction Espenaturel[Signpost]**(27.7)**Turn right onto chemin du Pèlerin and descend towards valley 🚶 **(28.7)**Cross Le Gabas stream and continue straight 🚶 **(30.1)**Turn right and immediately left onto chemin de Lassalle[Signpost] 🚶 **(31.4)**Turn left and then right onto the D32 road and continue straight towards Arzacq-Arraziguet 🚶 **(32.4)**At the crossroads beside the farm turn left, then turn right at the T-junction 🚶 **(33.5)**Bear left to join the D946**(34.0)**At roundabout, keep straight on the D946 road, to reach the town centre[Pass Carrefour supermarket on the right]**(34.2)**Arrive at Arzacq-Arraziguet town centre

stage 28 — Aire-sur-l'Adour to Arzacq-Arraziguet

Accommodation and Tourist Information

Arzacq-Arraziguet

Le Centre d'Accueil communal d'Arzacq, Place du Marcadieu, 64410 Arzacq-Arraziguet, France; Tel:+33(0)5 59 04 41 41; Email:centreaccueil@arzacq.com; centredaccueil. arzacq-arraziguet.fr; Price:C,C,C; *Located in village centre largerenovated hostel with at total of 90 places in shared rooms of 2-6 and dormitorries. Kitchen. English spoken camping possible*

Chambre d'hôtes - Dulucq[Huguette Dulucq],25, place du Marcadieu, 64410 Arzacq-Arraziguet, France; Tel:+33(0) 559 044 612; Email:dulucqhuguette@gmail.com; arzacq-arraziguet.fr; Price:-,B,-; *Located in village 4 places in 2 double rooms in home with terrace and garden. Horses welcome.*

Chambres d'hôtes - La Maison d'Antan[Jean-Pierre Guerin-Recoussine],1, place de la République, 64410 Arzacq-Arraziguet, France; Tel:+33(0)559045301; Email:lamaison. dantan@orange.fr; lamaison-dantan.com; Price:-,-,A; *Located in the village centre 4 rooms in an elegant 15th Century restored country home with terrace and garden. English spoken. Special half-board price for pilgrims with credentials*

Office de Tourisme,47, place de la République, 64410 Arzacq-Arraziguet, France; Tel:+33(0) 5 59 04 59 24; Email:contact@ bearnmadiran-tourisme.fr; bearnmadiran-tourisme.fr

Miramont Sensacq

Ferme de Marsan[Bernard and Dominique Darnaudery],Lieu-dit Marsan, 40320 Miramont Sensacq, France; Tel:+33(0)558799493; Email:contact@lafermedemarsan.com; lafermedemarsan.com; Price:C,-,-; *300m from the GR®65 on a working farm with pool 10 places in dormitory and 6 double rooms in separate building. Local and farm products sold on site. Kitchen. Horses welcome.*

Gîte d'étape communal[Mairie de Miramont Sensacq],Centre Bourg, 40320 Miramont Sensacq, France; Tel:+33(0)5 58 79 94 06; Email:gite@miramont-sensacq.fr; miramont-sensacq.fr/accueil-des-pelerins; Price:C,-,-; *Adjacent to the Mairie 20 places in 4 dormitories. Kitchen. dinner and breakfast by donation*

Chambres d'hôtes - La Prade[Mme Clothilde Goubin-Peras],1294, route du Tursan, 40320 Miramont Sensacq, France; Tel:+33(0)7 82 82 13 71; chambre-table-hote-laprade.fr; Price:-,B,-; *3 large bedrooms in 18th century house with large garden. Evening meal possible for pilgrims*

La Maison du Bos[Corinne Favre],378, chemin Dubos, 40320 Miramont Sensacq, France; Tel:+33(0)5 58 79 93 18; +33(0)6 42 79 84 26; maisondubos.com; Price:-,-,B; *Refined B&B with 5 rooms in a restored 18th Century stone house with terrace an pool on 9 hectare property. Horses welcome.*

Pimbo

Gîtes communaux - Pimbo[Chez Roxette],325, rue de la Bastide, 40320 Pimbo, France; Tel:+33(0)558444657; Email:gitedepimbo@hotmail.fr; pimbo.fr; Price:C,C,C|-,C,C; *The village offers 14 places in a dormitory and 3 further gîtes with private rooms. Booking and acces is arranged by the cafe Chez Roxette*

Ferme de Nordland[Family Passicos],Lieu-dit Maouhourat, 40320 Pimbo, France; Tel:+33(0)558444980; +33(0)6 75 97 34 23; ferme-de-nordland.com; Price:B,-,B; *Located less than 2 km from the GR®before Pimbo. Two modern and fully equipped cottages for 2 and 5 pers. on working farm that sells local produce particularly fois gras.*

Chambres d'hôtes - Maison Couhet[Irène Theux],475, rue de La Bastide, 40320 Pimbo, France; Tel:33(0) 6 84 98 21 64; Email:contact@ ferme-de-nordland.com; chambres-hotes-pimbo.e-monsite.com; Price:-,-,C; *Located in village below the church 2 rooms on first floor of large house with garden and terrace.*

Mairie de Pimbo,195, rue de la BastideL, 40320 Pimbo, France; Tel:+33 (0)5 58 44 49 18; pimbo.fr

Arzacq-Arraziguet to Arthez-de-Béarn — stage 29

Caubin Chapel

Length:	30.3km
Ascent:	706m
Descent:	735m
Le-Puy:	629km
Roncevaux:	153km

Route–This stage is relatively flat, and the route continues to follow tracks and asphalt roads through corn fields and pastures as it enters the Béarn region and approaches the Pyrenees mountains.

Pointers–**Advance planning:** The route is highly exposed, be sure to have sun protection (hat, sunscreen, etc.).

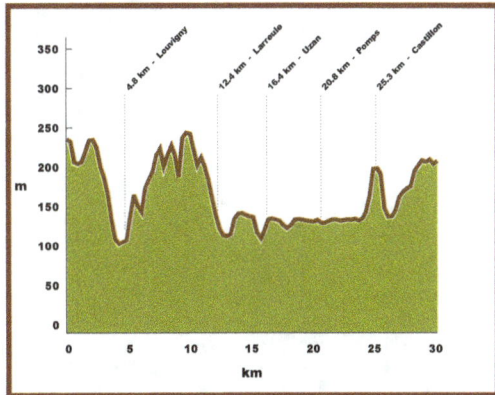

Cultural Discoveries

Larreule

In the 10th century, an important and wealthy Benedictine abbey was founded in Larreule (popl. 420, alt. 200m), which in Gascon means "the rule," and refers to the Benedictine rule (the rules promulgated by Saint Benedict in the 6th century to govern monastic life and which integrated prayer, manual labour and study into a daily routine). However, by the end of the 18th century, the last monks left the abbey, the monastery and hospital buildings were demolished and their stone sold. The parish church is the sole vestige of this once important abbey.

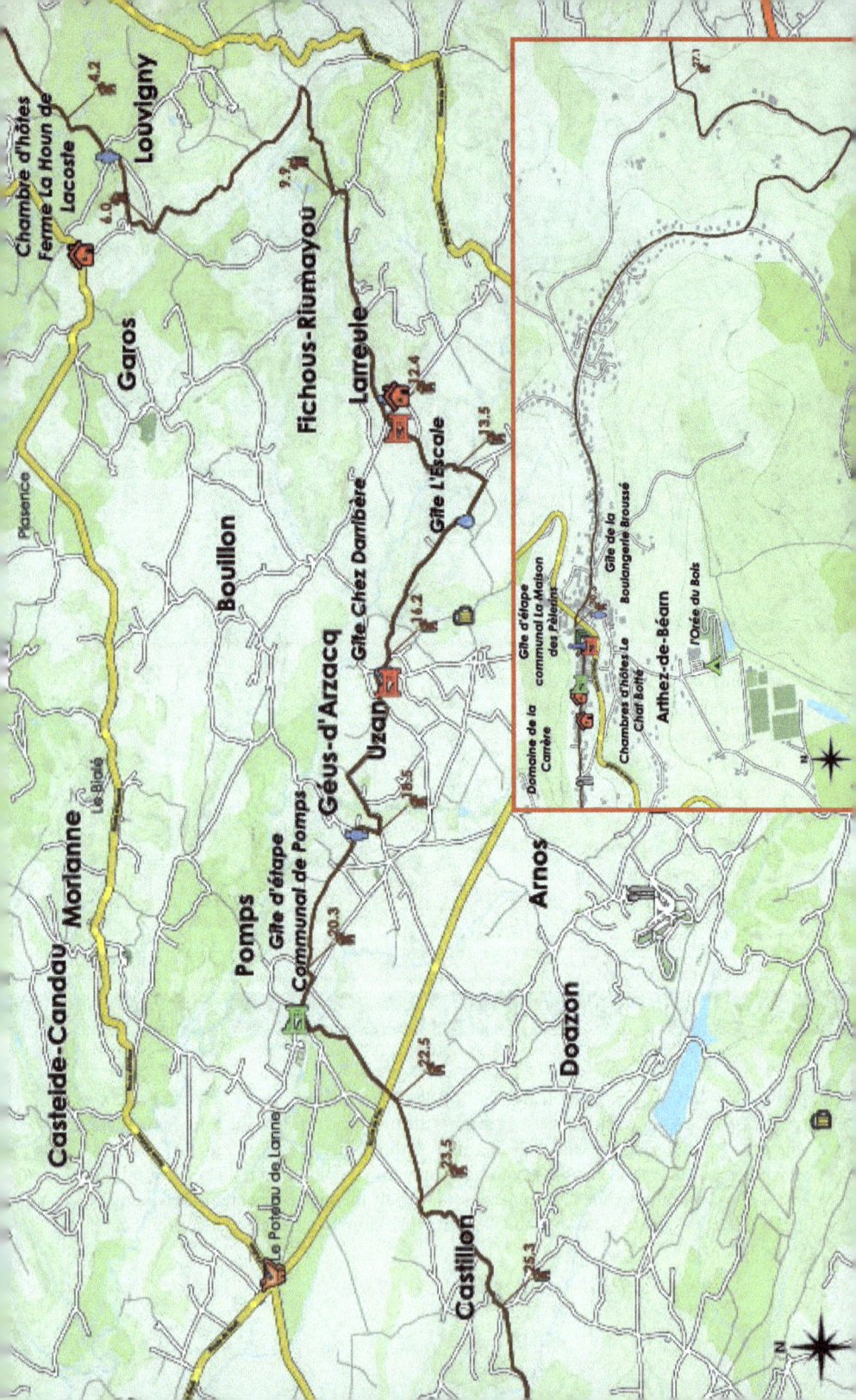

Arzacq-Arraziguet to Arthez-de-Béarn

stage 29

Arthez-de-Béarn

Before the village of Arthez-de-Béarn, on the left is the **Caubin Chapel** (*Chapelle de Caubin*), which is all that remains of an important 12th century Knights of Malta command post. The chapel, which is Romanesque, was likely built upon the orders of Gaston IV, Viscount of Béarn upon his safe return from the first crusade. Of note are the capitals and the 14th century tomb of Baron Guilhem Arnaud d'Andoins, a local ruler. A market is held in Arthez on Saturday mornings.

GR®65

(0.0) Take the D946, direction Orthez[pass the Office du Tourisme on your left]**(0.2)**At the end of the line of trees in the centre of the road, turn left on the small road[chemin de Larrouzé]**(0.6)**Turn rightt on chemin du Barada, and continue around the permimeter of the lake - Lac d'Arzacq **(1.5)**Turn rightt passing through woods and continue straight on trail[Walking away from lake]**(2.1)**Turn right onto small road (chemin de Cabirou) and continue straight. Pass Vignes, and the farms of Cabalette and Cabirou[Ahead, pass stone cross on the left] **(4.2)**Cross the Le Luy de France river and continue straight to Louvigny**(4.8)**Turn left and pass through **Louvigny**
(6.0) Turn left onto chemin de Pedebignes and climb[Pass red shed and bench on the right] **(8.6)**Turn right onto chemin de l'Eglise and continue straight to Fichous-Riumayou[Cross the La Rance river] **(9.4)**Pass church and cemetery on the right, and turn left onto D79/Route de Fichous**(10.0)**Turn right onto D278/Route de Larreule and continue straight until Larreule[Turn before Basketball court. Signpost "Larreule"] **(12.4)** In **Larreule** pass stone cross on left, and continue straight on route de Mazerolles[Ahead, cross the Le Luy de Béarn river]
(13.5) Turn left and continue straight. At fork keep right (head towards farm)**(13.9)**Turn right on Route d'Uzan and continue straight through corn fields until reaching village of Uzan[Signpost] **(16.2)**Turn right at church/cemetery, and then turn right onto the D49 road**(16.4)**In **Uzan** turn left onto La Carrère, direction Géus d'Arzacq and keep left at intersection (cross)[Signpost]
(16.8) Turn right onto Cami de la Lebe, passing through corn fields, until reaching Géus-d'ArzacqSignpost and oak tree **(18.5)**Turn right (passing church on right) and then keep left at fork on Cami de Compostelle **(20.3)**Turn left onto road and then right to enter Pomps**(20.8)**In **Pomps**, turn left at stone cross
(21.1) Turn left after bridge onto Route dou Pebe and continue straight[Bridge] **(22.5)** Turn right on track after dilapidated barn and continue straight **(23.5)**Turn left onto D269 road, cross Le Lech river and keep left on principal road until reaching Castillon **(25.3)**Cross road (D269) in **Castillon** and continue straight[Pass brown cross on the left] **(26.1)**Turn left onto the D269 road and continue straight towards Arthez-de-Béarn **(27.1)**Turn left onto chemin de Benicet and then right onto the D233 road to enter Arthez-de-Béarn **(30.3)**Arrive at Arthez-de-Béarn centre[Place du Palais]

stage 29 Arzacq-Arraziguet to Arthez-de-Béarn

Accommodation and Tourist Information

Arthez-de-Béarn

🛏 **Gîte d'étape communal La Maison des Pèlerins**[Mairie d'Arthez-de-Béarn],52, la Carrère, 64370 Arthez-de-Béarn, France; Tel:+33 (0)5 59 67 70 52; Email:mairie.arthezdebearn@wanadoo.fr; arthez-de-bearn.fr; Price:C,-,-; *Located on the GR*65 renovated hostel with 24 places in rooms of 2 to 5 near village centre and commerce. View on the Pyrenees mountains. English spoken. Horses welcome. Kitchen.*

🛏 **Gîte de la Boulangerie Broussé**[Bertrand Broussé],52, rue de Bergoue, 64370 Arthez-de-Béarn, France; Tel:+33 (0)559 677 446; Email:bertrand.brousse@wanadoo.fr; haltesvers-compostelle.eu; Price:C,C,C; *Located close to village centre on the GR*65 4 rooms for 4-6 pers. in 18th century building. English spoken. Accommodation for horses possible. Check-in at the bakery*

🛏 **Gîte d'étape - Domi** [Dominique],14, chemin Diserane, 64370 Arthez-de-Béarn, France; Tel:+33 (0)7 70 09 32 65; gitedetapedomi.com; Price:C,C,-; *2 bedrooms each for 4 people in the host's home. Kitchen. Space for donkeys possible but no dogs.*

🏠 **Chambres d'hôtes - Le Chat Botté**[Aïcha Reix],35, rue la Carrère, 64370 Arthez-de-Béarn, France; Tel:+33 (0)6 43 15 73 29; chambres-hotes.fr; Price:-,B,-; *3# bedrooms in historic building in the village centre dinner possible with reservation*

🏠 **Domaine de la Carrère**[Fritz Kisby and Mike Ridout],24, rue la Carrère, 64370 Arthez-de-Béarn, France; Tel:+33 (0)5 59 67 78 07; +33(0)660518291; Email:domainedelacarrere64@gmail.com; domaine-de-la-carrere.com; Price:-,A,-; *Luxury B&B located on the GR*65 in village centre in a beautifully restored and decorated 17th Century historic residence with gardens and pool. English spoken.*

⛺ 🔑 **Camping l'Orée du Bois**,2 allée des Sports, 64370 Arthez-de-Béarn, France; Tel:+33 (0)5 59 67 76 56; +33 (0) 608 639 961; nori.camp; Price:B,-,-|B,-,-; *Pitches chalets cabins and fully equipped tents in shaded surroundings restaurant and grocery*

ℹ **Mairie de Arthez-de-Béarn**,18, rue la Carrère, 64370 Arthez-de-Béarn, France; Tel:+33 (0)5 59 67 70 52; Email:mairie.arthezdebearn@wanadoo.fr; arthez-de-bearn.fr

Larreule

🛏 🏠 **Gîte L'Escale**[Patricia and Alain Bourda],1, route de Mazerolles, 64410 Larreule, France; Tel:+33(0)632022548; Email:lain.patricia64@orange.fr; gites-du-chemin-de-compostelle.fr; Price:C,C,C|-,B,-; *Located on a restored farm on the GR*65. Includes 3 double rooms (B&B) and 1 dormitory sleeping 9. Horses welcome.*

Louvigny

🏠 **Chambre d'hôtes - Ferme La Houn de Lacoste**[Jean-Michel Lacadée],1, route d'Orthez, 64410 Louvigny, France; Tel:+33 (0)6 80 42 68 94; +33(0) 5 59 04 42 73; Email:jeanmichel.lacadee@hotmail.fr; Price:-,B,B; *Located on a beautiful working farm. 500m from the village of Louvigny and run by a family of musicians. 4 rooms. Dinner prepared with local products. English spoken. Horses welcome. 15 places in 5 rooms*

Pomps

🛏 **Gîte d'étape - Communal de Pomps**,140, route de Billère, 64370 Pomps, France; Tel:+33(0) 6 84 91 94 00; Email:reservationlahaltepompsoise@gmail.com; mairie-de-pomps.jimdofree.com; Price:C,C,C; *12 places in shared rudimentary accommodation. Horses welcome. Camping possible*

Uzan

🛏 **Gîte - Chez Darribère**[Cecile Darribere],90, impasse de la Mairie, 64370 Uzan, France; Tel:+33(0) 671 598 468; Email:darribere_cecile@hotmail.fr; Price:C,C,C; *4 places in 2 bedrooms*

Arthez-de-Béarn to Navarrenx

stage 30

Navarrenx

Length:	32.0km
Ascent:	832m
Descent:	912m
Le-Puy:	659km
Roncevaux:	122km

Route–The route is well-marked and follows small country roads and paths through fields and small forests. It passes over a chain of hills that is regularly cut by rivers, so that the route includes several climbs, descents and bridges, before arriving at the beautiful fortified city of Navarrenx.

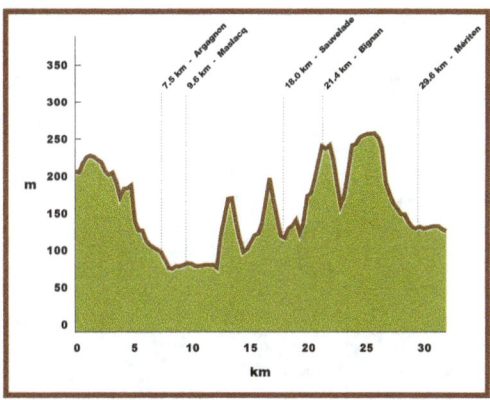

Cultural Discoveries

Oratory of Notre-Dame-de-Muret

A short walk off the GR®65 is the Byzantine-styled oratory of Notre-Dame-de-Muret (1936). It commemorates one of the oldest sanctuaries in Béarn, which was built in the 11th century by Raymond Le Vieux, bishop of Gascony.

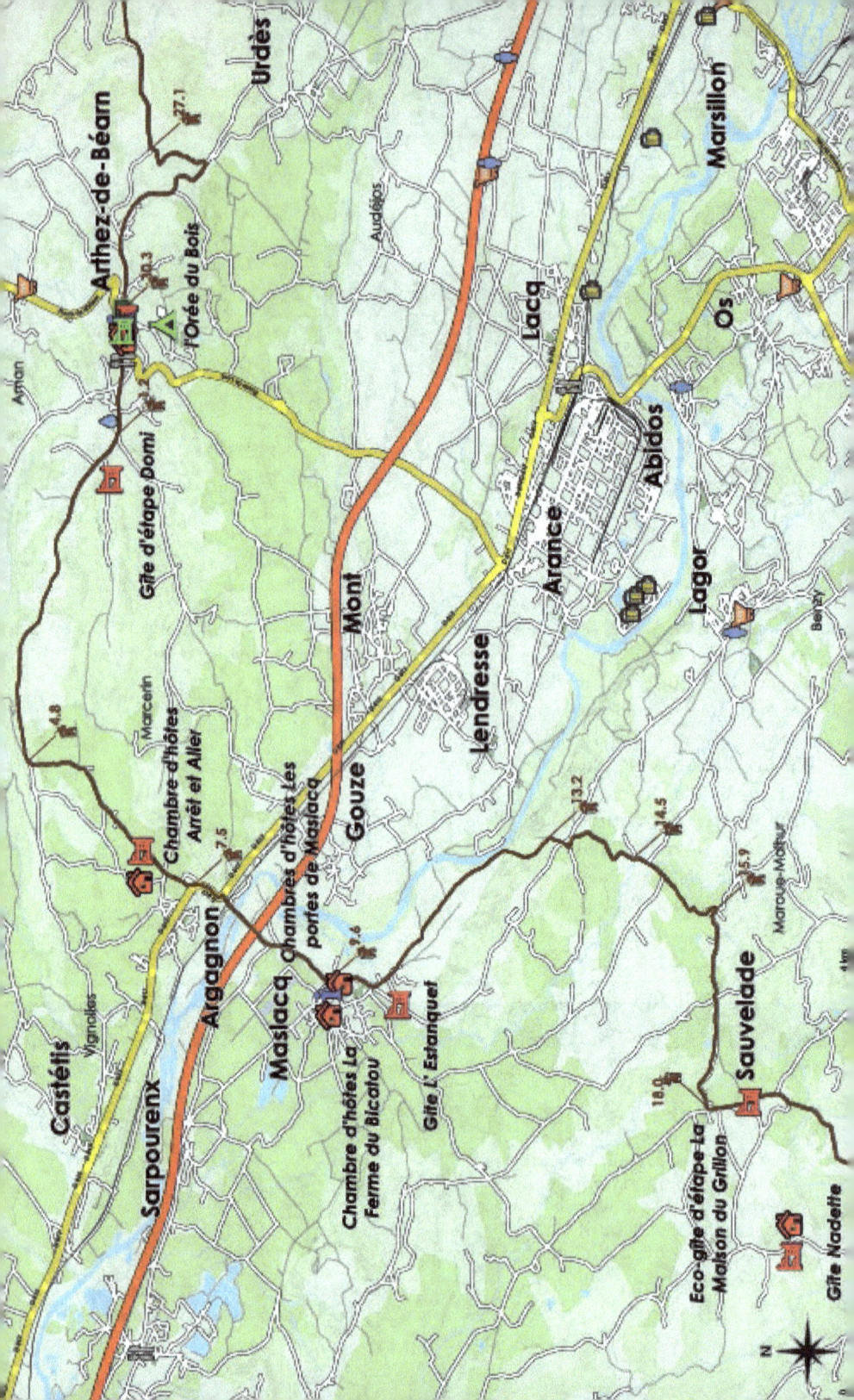

Arthez-de-Béarn to Navarrenx

stage 30

Sauvelade

Sauvelade (popl. 265, alt. 115m) once housed an important monastery. In 1127, in thanks for having survived the wars against the Moors in Spain, Gaston IV, Viscount of Béarn, made a donation to the Benedictine monks that were living in a nearby forest (called *silva lata*) so that they might build a monastery dedicated to Mary. In the 13th century, the Benedictine monastery was taken over by Cistercian monks and later sold during the French Revolution. All that remains of the monastery is the Church of Saint James the Greater (*Eglise Saint-Jacques-le-Majeure*), which was built from local sandstone in the unusual shape of a Greek cross (as opposed to a Latin cross). Today the church is owned by the State and is used for local functions.

Navarrenx

The city of Navarrenx (popl. 1,060, alt. 120m), which sits on the Gave d'Oloron river, is classified as one of the most beautiful villages in France and is also one of the region's oldest *bastides* or fortified cities. The current ramparts, however, were designed and built in the first half of the 16th century by Italian military engineer, Fabrizio Siciliano, on orders of the King of Navarre who sought to refortify the original 14th century walls. The conversion of Jeanne d'Albret (Queen Regent of Navarre, mother of King Henry IV and leader of the French Protestants) to Calvinism plunged the region into the religious wars that pitted Catholics against Protestants. But Navarrenx's fortifications withstood a three month siege by Catholic armies in 1569. The city was never conquered.

Next to the Tourist Office is La Maison du Cigare, the only company to make cigars using 100% French tobacco (visits on weekdays). A market is held every Wednesday morning.

GR 65

(0.0)Continue straight on rue la Carrère through village[Pass church on the left] (1.2)At fork keep right on chemin du Bosc[Stone cross] (4.8)Turn left on route de l'Eglise and continue straight until reaching Argagon[Signpost] (7.5)Beside **Argagnon** turn left onto the D817 road. Then ahead cross the D817 (caution), the bridge over the river (Gave de Pau) and the A64 highway. Stay on the D275 road, direction Maslacq

(9.6)In **Maslacq**, turn left onto rue du Fronton and then left onto the D9 road

(10.2)Cross the Le Geu river and turn left on the road that runs parallel to the Cave de Pau river (13.2)At top of steep climb turn right and continue straight[Sanctuary de Muret to the left](13.3)Cross the D9/Route de Maslacq and continue straight on track(13.5)Turn left and then right on chemin Saubade. Continue straight (14.5)Cross stream (Le Geu) and continue straight (15.9)Turn right on route de Sauvelade, direction Sauvelade (18.0) Turn left onto the C110 road and continue straight through **Sauvelade**

(18.9)Turn right onto Camino de Compostela and continue straight (21.4)Enter hamlet of **Bignan** and keep right[Signpost]

(21.9)At fork keep left on the Camino de Berduqueu[Signpost](22.3)Turn left on Matheu Bacot road (24.1)Turn left onto Camino de Sentier Jouan, and continue straight (25.7) Turn right on road and continue straight (27.3)Keep to right on road that runs parallel to the Le Lucq stream, and leads to Méritein[Stream to the left] (28.6)At fork, keep left and continue straight towards Méritein(29.1)Turn left and continue straight[Pass church on right] (29.6)In **Mériten** turn left on the D947 road, then (at cross) turn left onto chemin de la Biasse[Pass through residential area and underpass]

(31.1)Turn right onto avenue de Mourenx(31.6)Turn right onto avenue de France and proceed through town on main road, rue Saint-Germain(32.0)Arrive at Navarrenx Centre[Place des Casernes]

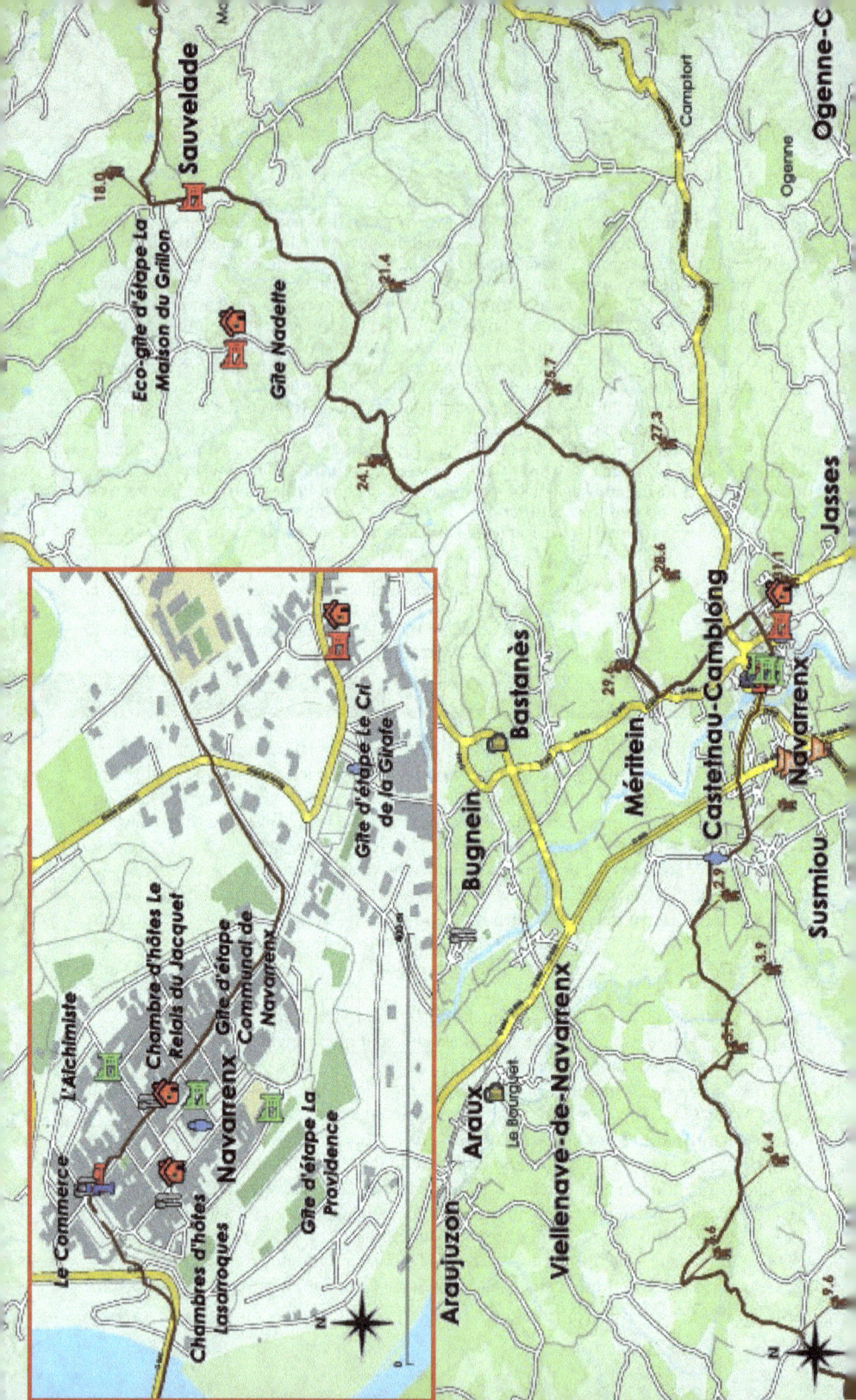

Arthez-de-Béarn to Navarrenx — stage 30

Accommodation and Tourist Information

Argagnon

Chambre d'hôtes - Arrêt et Aller[Linda and Andrew],190, route de Pedaouque, 64300 Argagnon, France; Tel:+33 (0)559 093 735; +33 (0)679 569 837; tourisme64.com; Price:-,A,-|C,C,C; *B&B with 2 rooms and 1 dormitory for 4 people on a lovely 18th Century Bearnise styled farmhouse with large property. Owned by an English couple. Horses welcome.*

Maslacq

Gite - L' Estanquet[Elisabeth and Dominique],12, route de Lagor, 64300 Maslacq, France; Tel:+33 (0)672 720 779; +33(0)559 676 895; Email:babeth.malherbe@orange.fr; Price:-,C,C; *7 p;laces in 3 dormitories*

Chambre d'hôtes - La Ferme du Bicatou[Evelyne and Philippe Gantet],8, rue de l'École, 64300 Maslacq, France; Tel:+33(0) 6 24 20 09 97; +33(0) 6 29 86 96 51; afermedebicatou.jimdofree.com; Price:-,B,A; *5 comfortable rooms in a warm family home and 1 mobile home.*

Chambres d'hôtes - Les portes de Maslacq[Béatrix],34, rue la Carrère, 64300 Maslacq, France; Tel:+33(0)6 73 12 82 06; Email:beatrixlacasse@gmail.com; les-portes-de-maslacq.fr; Price:B,B,B; *2 triple rooms and 1 double in the heart of the village*

Mairie de Maslacq,16, rue la Carrère, 64300 Maslacq, France; Tel:+33 5 59 67 60 79; Email:mairie.maslacq@wanadoo.fr; maslacq.fr

Navarrenx

Gîte d'étape - Communal de Navarrenx[Mairie],41, rue Saint-Germain, 64190 Navarrenx, France; Tel:+33 748 906 080; Email:gites.navarrenx@outlook.com; ville-navarrenx.fr; Price:C,C,C; *35 places in basic accommodation located in the village centre on the GR®65*

Gîte d'étape - La Providence,Rue Jeanne d'Albert(D847), 64190 Navarrenx, France; Tel:+33 (0)637 413 752; Email:julie.saintelivrade@gmail.com; Price:D,D,D; *11 places in 3 dormitories. Newly opened parish gîte*

L'Alchimiste[Jean-Gaétan Pélisse],10, rue de l'Abreuvoir, 64190 Navarrenx, France; Tel:+33 (0)632 781 376; Email:alchimistesurlechemin@hotmail.fr; web.facebook.com/alchimisteanavarrenx; Price:D,D,-; *9 places in 4 rooms. English spoken. Very welcoming.*

Gîte d'étape - Le Cri de la Girafe[Maria Laullon and Fabian Tumpling],12, rue du Faubourg, 64190 Navarrenx, France; Tel:+33 (0)5 59 66 24 22; +33 (0)760 75 19 14; Email:contact@lecridelagirafe.fr; lecridelagirafe.fr; Price:-,C,C|-,B,B; *8 places in dormitory and 6 places in 3 double rooms. Courtyard and garden. Horses welcome. English spoken.*

Chambre d'hôtes - Le Relais du Jacquet[Régis Gabastou],42, rue Saint Germain, 64190 Navarrenx, France; Tel:+33 (0)5 59 66 57 25; +33 (0)6 75 72 89 33; Email:regis.gabastou@orange.fr; chambres-hotes-navarrenx.com; Price:-,B,B; *5 rooms in historic building welcoming host and former pilgrim. English spoken.*

Chambres d'hôtes - Lasarroques[Monique and Jean Lasarroques],4, place d'Armes, 64190 Navarrenx, France; Tel:+33(0)5 59 66 27 59; +33(0)7 80 00 37 77; Email:lasarroques.monique@orange.fr; chambres-hotes-lasarroques.com; Price:-,B,-; *3 tastefully decorated rooms in a welcoming home and 4 places in a studio apartment with kitchen.*

Hôtel - Le Commerce,1, place des Casernes, 64190 Navarrenx, France; Tel:+33 (0)559 662 254; Email:contact@hotellecommerce.fr; hotellecommerce.fr; Price:A,-,-; *Centrally located agreeable hotel with 10 spacious rooms. English spoken.*

Office de Tourisme,2, place des Casernes, 64190 Navarrenx, France; Tel:+33(0) 5 59 38 00 33; Email:contact@bearndesgaves.com; tourisme-bearn-gaves.com

Sauvelade

Gîte Nadette[Bernadette Godfroy],998, camin Capdelas, 64150 Sauvelade, France; Tel:+33(0) 0559384879 ; +33(0)687291370; Email:gitenadette@laposte.net; gitenadette.com; Price:-,B,B|-,A,A; *A lovely 18th Century stone house with pool and terrace. 8 places in 2 dormitories and 2 double rooms. English spoken. Accommodation for horses and donkeys with advance notice.*

Eco-gîte d'étape - La Maison du Grillon[Jef Blanchard and Lili],1559, route deu Lavarth, 64150 Sauvelade, France; Tel:+33(0)684381421; +33(0)676273638; Email:oustau.grigt@gmail.com; lamaisondugrillon.fr; Price:-,B,-; *10 places in renovated home with dormitory and 4-pers. rooms. Garden. English spoken. Next to a bistrot serving regional specialities.*

Basque Landscape © Alexia Adamski

BASQUE COUNTRY

The French Basque region (French: *Pays basque français,* Basque: *Iparralde* (the northern side)) is centred around the Western Pyrenees mountains and makes up the northeastern part of the Basque country, which totals seven provinces in Spain and France.

The climate is wet and the region sparsely populated (less than 300,000 inhabitants compared with about two million in Basque Spain). Most people live in the coastal cities of Bayonne (the capital of French Basque country) and glamorous Biarritz (a major surfing destination). Inland, on the foothills of the Pyrenees, sheep are extensively grazed for cheese production.

The region boasts a history that dates to pre-Roman times, a distinct architectural style (like the white red-shuttered farm houses), musical traditions (namely choral singing), sports (*pelote*) and foods (like sheep cheese (*Ossaulraty*), red chilies (*piment rouges*), paprika-flavoured sausages and Bayonne ham). *Euskara*, the ancient Basque language that survived Roman conquest, is spoken by a minority of the population and remains at risk of disappearing. Descending deeper into the region, red, white and green Basque flags become more common.

Navarrenx to Aroue

stage 31

Length:	19.2km
Ascent:	410m
Descent:	428m
Le-Puy:	691km
Roncevaux:	90km

Basque Landscape © Alexandra Huddleston

Route–The route is well-marked, with limited climbs and follows mostly small country roads and some paths through fields (corn), small forests, and over gentle hills and streams. Enter the French Basque country by crossing the Saison river after the village of Charre.

Pointers-**Backtracking:** The village of Aroue is located approximately 300 metres off the GR®65. Backtrack from there to rejoin the main route.

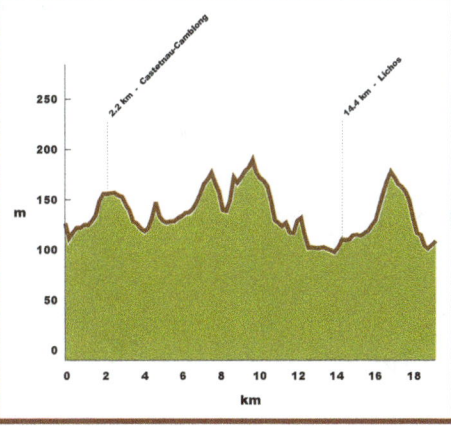

Navarrenx to Aroue

stage 31

Cultural Discoveries

Church of Saint Stephen
(*Eglise Saint-Etienne*)

While the Church in Aroue has been rebuilt, certain Romanesque features were reused in the sacristy. Notably, there is a relief sculpture above the sacristy door that has been interpreted as a hunting scene or as an early depiction of Saint James the Moor-slayer. Other figures include a woman and serpent (interpreted as Eve) and a man carrying a large stone (which could be a depiction of a traditional Basque stone lifting competition).

See Shaver-Crandell, A., Gerson, P. L., & Stones, A., p. 119 (1995). The pilgrim's guide to Santiago de Compostela: A gazetteer. London: Harvey Miller Publishers.

GR®65

(0.0) From Place des Casernes head (left) south-west and pass through historic gate Saint-Antoine **(0.1)** Turn left onto the D947 road and cross the Gave d'Oloron river **(0.3)** Turn right and continue straight on D115/Impasse des Lambrits. Continue straight through roundabout[Signpost] **(1.6)** Turn right onto the D815 road. Then turn left onto trail and finally keep right onto the D815 road and head to Castetnau-Camblong[Signpost. Ahead pass town hall (Mairie) on left] **(2.2)** In **Castetnau-Camblong** turn left onto rue des Debantets and continue straight
(2.9) Turn left onto small road and continue straight[Stone cross. Ahead Cross stream "Le Lausset"] **(3.9)** Turn right and continue straight through woods **(4.5)** Turn right and continue straight until reaching small road **(5.1)** Turn left onto road and continue straight **(6.4)** Turn right onto trail **(7.6)** At fork turn left **(9.6)** Cross the D115 road and continue straight on route de Saint-Jacques towards Lichos **(12.7)** Turn right on route du Saison/D244 and then turn left and go through underpass. Turn left on path running parallel to the D23 road[Cross Le Saison River, enter Basque country] **(13.9)** Turn right onto track (after river), and proceed to Lichos centre **(14.4)** In **Lichos**, turn left and then right[Church] **(14.7)** Turn right onto Lou Brousta and continue straight[Cross the Le Borlaas stream and the D2023 road] **(16.8)** At intersection, turn left[Farm Bouhaben] **(17.5)** Turn right and then take stairs left to rejoin the D11 **(18.1)** Turn right onto the D11 road and continue straight towards Ferme Bohoteguia (on left) **(19.2)** Continue straight to arrive at Aroue (off the GR®65)[Village visible at top of hill]

stage 31 — Navarrenx to Aroue

Accommodation and Tourist Information

Aroue-Ithorots-Olhaïby

Gîte d'étape - Maison Bohoteguia[Simone and Manu],Bohoteguia, 64120 Aroue-Ithorots-Olhaïby, France; Tel:+33 (0)6 75 83 82 61; Email:bohoteguia@aol.com; ferme-bohoteguia.com; Price:C,C,C; *27 places in 8 rooms of 1-6 pers. in a welcoming renovated farmhouse*

Gîte d'étape - Communal d'Aroue[Mairie],Route de Mauleon, 64120 Aroue-Ithorots-Olhaïby, France; Tel:+33 (0)788 899 257; Email:gite.aroue@orange.fr; tourisme64.com; Price:C,C,C; *15 places in former school house. Basic accommodations. Groceries available for purchase. Horses welcome. Camping possible*

Gîte d'étape - Bellevue[Marie-Paule and Marcel Gégu],Heguilloret, 64120 Aroue-Ithorots-Olhaïby, France; Tel:+33(0)559 657 019; +33(0) 616 486 365; Email:gegubellevue@yahoo.fr; podiensis.com; Price:C,C,-; *1.5 km before Aroue. 14 places in double rooms. Kitchen. Welcoming. English spoken. Pool*

Chambres d'hôtes - Mourénia[Sandrine and Yann],20, chemin Ekhi Zabalian, 64120 Aroue-Ithorots-Olhaïby, France; Tel:+33(0)633514348; mourenia.fr; Price:-,B,A; *5 places in 2 bedrooms in prominent house close to the church dinner available if booked in advance*

Lichos

Chambres d'hôtes - Cléromilo[Mickaël Mottier and Laurence Lorine],3, le Village Ouest, 64130 Lichos, France; Tel:+33(0) 7 82 97 65 44; +33 (0) 559 282 912; Email:laurence.pouthier@orange.fr; chemindecompostelle.com; Price:-,B,A; *A warm welcome is offered with 3 bedrooms and 1 independent building*

Chambres d'hôtes - Haïtzpean[Marie-Reine and Emile Hontaas],23, route Départementale, 64130 Lichos, France; Tel:+33(0) 5 59 28 29 45; +33 (0)667 667 309; Email:emile.ontaas@sfr.fr; cirkwi.com; Price:-,-,A; *5 double rooms. Horses welcome.*

Chambres d'hôtes - Angèle Loumpré[Angèle Loumpré],Le Village Ouest, 64130 Lichos, France; Tel:+33(0)5 59 28 81 39; +33(0)6 31 90 92 41; Email:jeanmarie.loumpre@sfr.fr; icompostelle.com; Price:-,C,C; *2 bedrooms kitchen at the exit from the village*

Aroue to Ostabat — stage 32

Length:	23.9km
Ascent:	935m
Descent:	887m
Le-Puy:	710km
Roncevaux:	71km

Basque Landscape

Route- The route is well-marked, with gentle climbs over the green hills, forests and sheep pastures, typical of the Basque country. The Pyrenees mountains are clearly in view, especially from the beautiful viewpoint at the Chapel of Soyarce.

Pointers-Culture: The section of the GR®65 from Aroue to Ostabat is on the UNESCO world heritage list.

Shortcut: Possibility to bypass Larribar-Sorhapuru by taking a short cut through Uharte-Mixe, which reconnects to the GR®65 north of Harambletz.

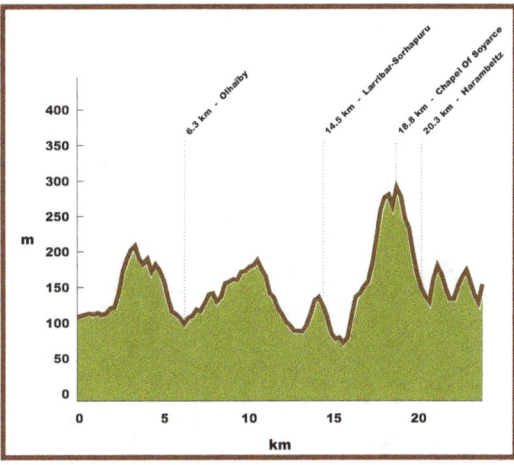

Cultural Discoveries

Chapel of Saint Nicholas
(*Chapelle Saint-Nicolas*)

The Chapel of Saint Nicholas in Harambeltz (Basque: *haram* valley and *belzt* dark), is a recently restored Romanesque chapel dating from the 12th century. It is all that remains of a former priory and hospital.

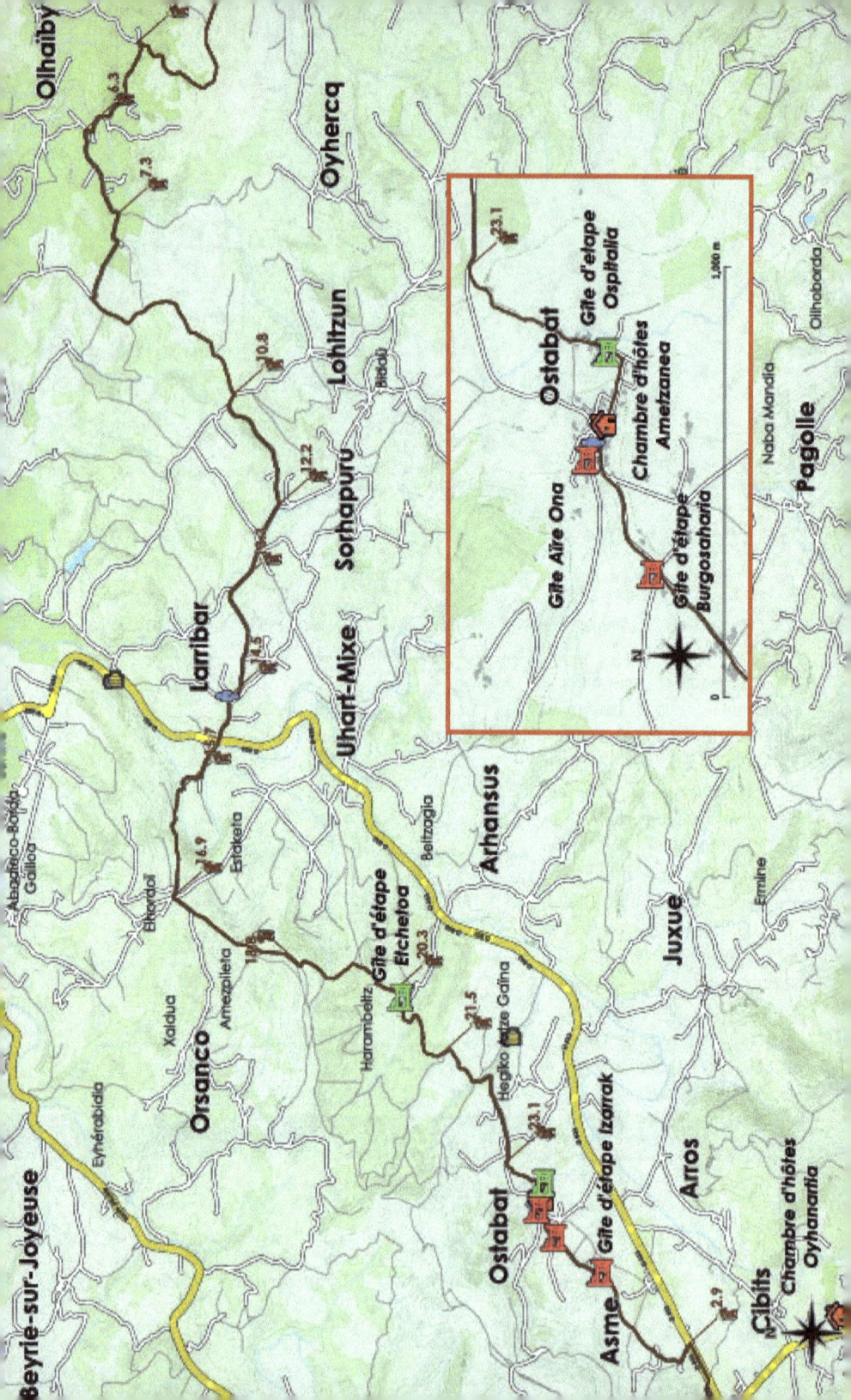

Aroue to Ostabat

stage 32

GR®65

(**0.0**)Turn left onto the D11 road, direction St Palais and continue straight[Château de Joantho (brown and red) and iron cross on left] (**2.2**)Turn right on serpentine trail that climbs (**5.0**)Turn sharply left and continue on trail(**5.9**)Turn right onto a small road, direction Olhaïby (**6.3**)In **Olhaïby**, turn left and continue on road[Turning away from village] (**7.3**)Turn right and head towards Casabonne(**7.6**)Turn right and head towards Jaurriberria(**8.3**)Turn left and continue straight (**10.8**)Turn right direction Benta(**10.9**)Turn left and continue descent until reaching the D242 road[Pass farm Benta] (**12.2**)Turn right onto the D242 road and continue straight(**12.7**)Continue straight on the D242 road[Turn left for short-cut through Uhart Mixe] (**13.3**)At fork keep left, direction Larribar-Sorhapuru (**14.5**)Keep left and cross **Larribar-Sorhapuru**[Pass town-hall (Mairie) and church on the right]
(**15.0**)Cross the D933 road and continue straight (**15.7**)Cross bridge over the Bidouze river and continue straight on trail that climbs west to Hiriburia (**16.9**)Turn left and continue straight on road that climbs to plateau, direction Chapel of Soyarce[Signpost] (**18.8**)Turn left towards **Chapel of Soyarce**
(**18.8**)Turn right on trail that descend towards Harambeltz. Attention poorly marked[Near information board](**19.6**)Keep right and descend towards village of Harambeltz (**20.3**)Turn right and descend through village of **Harambeltz**[Pass chapel on the right]
(**20.5**)Keep right on road that cuts through forest, and crosses the Harambeltzko Erreka stream. Continue straight (**21.5**)Turn left and continue straight on trail(**22.1**)Keep right and cross the Ibidiak Erreka stream(**22.3**)Turn right and continue straight (**23.1**)Turn left onto track and continue straight to village of Ostabat-Asme[Signpost and stone marker](**23.7**)Turn right (after the Ospitalia Hostel) to enter village centre(**23.9**)Continue straight on main street in Ostabat[Pass town-hall (Mairie) on the right](**23.9**)Arrive at Ostabat[Village centre]

stage 32 — Aroue to Ostabat

Accommodation and Tourist Information

Ostabat-Asme

Gîte d'étape - Etchetoa[Marie],1274, quartier Harambeltz, 64120 Ostabat-Asme, France; Tel:+33(0)7 66 02 40 10; Email:marie.etchetoa@laposte.net; etchetoa.com; Price:C,C,C; *Beautiful and spacious gîte on authentic Basque farm in a hamlet that has welcomed pilgrims for centuiries with welcoming hosts serving traditional Basque cuisine. Located 4 km before Ostabat next to the Chapel Saint Nicolas. 15 places in 4 rooms*

Gîte d'étape - Ospitalia[Mr Etcheparreborde],Village, 64120 Ostabat-Asme, France; Tel:+33(0) 559 378 317; +33(0) 610 046 575; Price:C,-,-; *A former pilgrim hospital converted into a hostel with 10 places in 3 rooms. Located at entrance to village. Basic accommodations. Kitchen.*

Gîte d'étape - Izarrak[Amélia and Alain],1020, Azmeko Bidéa, 64120 Ostabat-Asme, France; Tel:+33(0) 6 72 73 78 56; Email:contact@giteizarrak.com; giteizarrak.com; Price:-,-,B; *Located 1km from Ostabat on the way 19 places in rooms or dormitories on a restored farm terrace swimming pool and spa. English spoken. Horses welcome.*

Gîte Aïre - Ona[Françoise Irigoin],Le Bourg, 64120 Ostabat-Asme, France; Tel:+33(0)559378875; +33(0)633657715; Email:gite.aire-ona@live.fr; aireona-gite-ostabat.fr; Price:C,C,-; *Modern high quality fully renovated gîte with 4 rooms in village centre. English spoken. Kitchen.*

Gite d'étape - Burgosaharia[Valérie Harismendy],Le Bourg, 64120 Ostabat-Asme, France; Tel:+33 (0)6 72 68 13 24; Email:pilival@free.fr; tourisme64.com; Price:-,C,-; *6 places in 3 rooms no horses*

Chambre d'hôtes - Auberge Ametzanea,Le Bourg, 64120 Ostabat-Asme, France; Tel:+33(0) 559 378 156; +33(0) 623 903 260; Price:-,-,B; *3 rooms in auberge located in village centre. Accommodation for horses possible.*

Ostabat to Saint-Jean-Pied-de-Port — stage 33

Length:	22.7km
Ascent:	785m
Descent:	777m
Le-Puy:	734km
Roncevaux:	47km

Hiker on path to St-Jean-Le-Vieux © Alexia Adamski

Route–The route is well-marked, generally flat, and uses primarily asphalt roads and tracks as it makes its way deeper into the Basque country to the foot of the Pyrenees and Saint-Jean-Pied-de-Port. The route passes through typical Basque villages and green pastures.

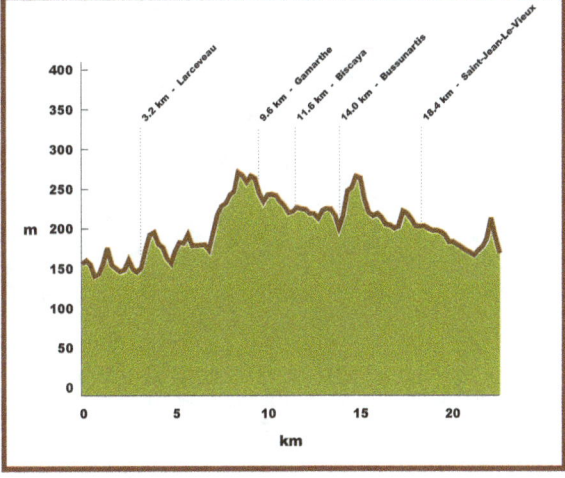

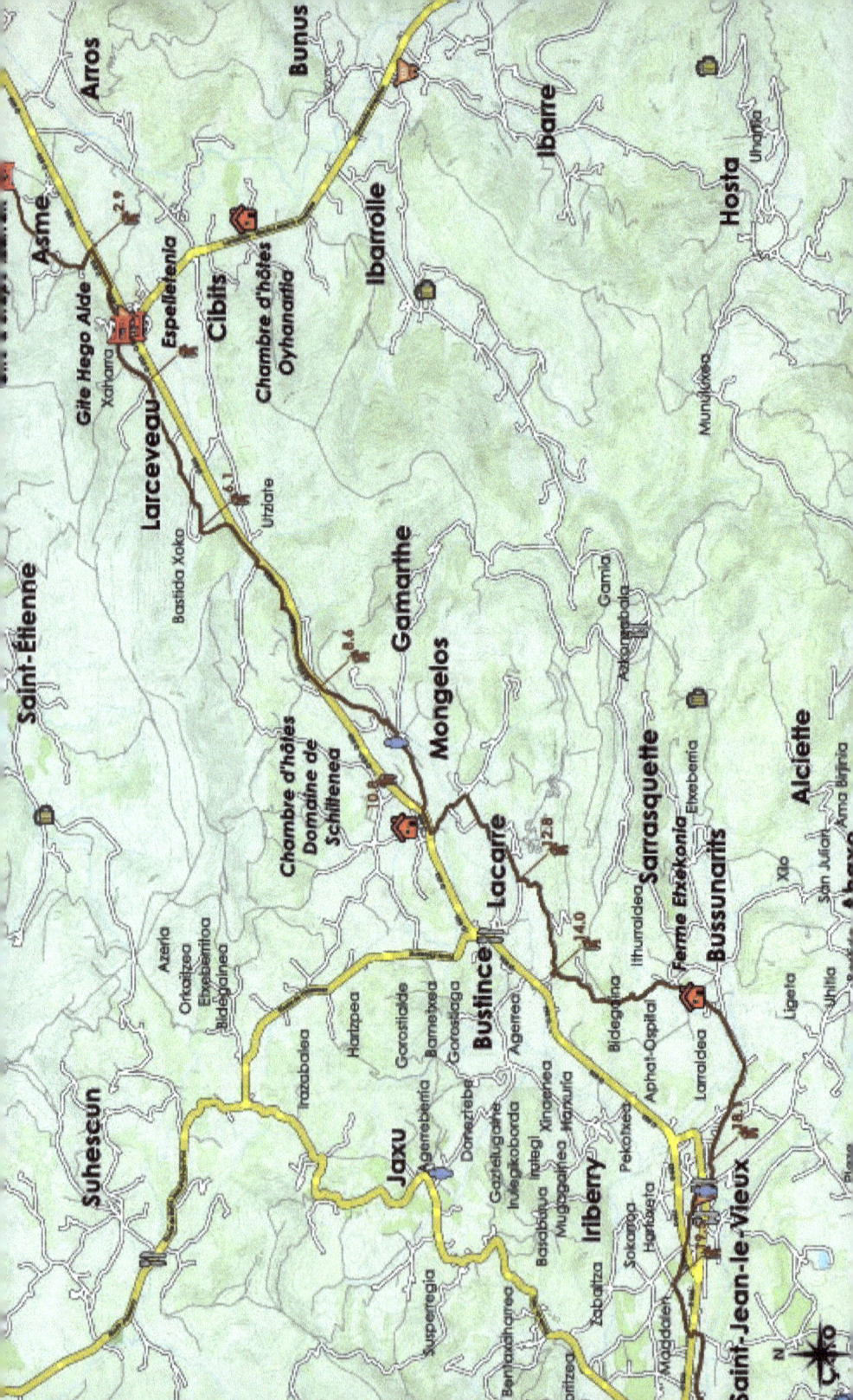

Ostabat to Saint-Jean-Pied-de-Port

stage 33

Cultural Discoveries

Saint-Jean-le-Vieux

Saint Jean-le-Vieux (popl. 870, alt. 200m) occupies a strategic position at the entrance of the Cize plain. Around 15 BC, Romans built a camp here, at the foot of the Pyrenees on the road between Bordeaux and Astorga (Spain). Archaeological excavations have unearthed Roman baths and other objects that can be seen at the local museum.

The **Chapel of Saint Peter of Usakoa** (*Chapelle Saint-Pierre d'Usakoa*)

has a beautiful Romanesque tympanum from the 12th century, which predates the destruction of the city by Richard the Lionheart in 1177. Thereafter, the city was rebuilt nearby on more easily defended site of Saint-Jean-Pied-de-Port.

Saint-Jean-Pied-de-Port

Located at the foot of the pass over the Pyrenees mountains, St-Jean-Pied-de-Port (Basque: *Donibane Garazi*, popl. 1500, alt. 160m) has served as a commercial, military and religious crossroads. It is also the last stop in France on the Way of Saint James.

Dominating the village from atop the Mendiguren hill is the 17th century **Citadel** (*Citadelle*), which was built on the site of the former fortress of the Kings of Navarre. From there, the cobblestone street, rue de la Citadelle, descends to the **Church of Our Lady at the End of the Bridge** (*Eglise Notre-Dame-du-Bout-du-Pont*), a 14th century Gothic church on the banks of the Nive river. According to legend, King Sancho VII of Navarre founded the church to commemorate his victory over the Moors in the battle of Las Navas de Tolosa (1212), a turning point in the Christian reconquest of Spain.

St-Jean-Pied-de-Port © Alexandra Huddleston

There is a pilgrim welcome centre at 39, rue de la Citadelle. The village holds a lively farmers market on Monday mornings.

Ostabat to Saint-Jean-Pied-de-Port

stage 33

GR®65

(0.2)At fork turn right onto smaller road and continue straight towards Burgosaharia[Road passes between stone walls] (2.5)Turn right onto the D933 road and continue straight(3.2) Enter **Larceveau** (signpost) and turn right onto route de Saint-Palais[Signpost]
(3.7)Keep right on road and continue straight through fields and typical white and red houses (4.5)Continue straight on road towards Bastida Choko[White house with red shutters and stone wall on right] (6.1)Cross stream (Arlako Erréka) and turn left towards the D933 road. Continue on the track that runs parallel to the D933 (8.6)Cross the D933 road and head south on the D522 towards Gamarthe(9.6)At **Gamarthe**, turn left and then right to rejoin the D522 road. Continue straight until reaching the D933 road
 (10.8)Turn left onto the D933 road. Then take first left towards Biscaya[Signpost](11.6) In **Biscaya**, turn right and continue straight[Stream to the left]
 (12.8)Turn left and climb hill[Signpost] (14.0)Turn left into the hamlet of **Bussunartis**
 (18.1)Turn left and then right to Saint-Jean-le-Vieux[Signpost](18.4)In **Saint-Jean-le-Vieux**, cross the D2933 road and continue straight through square. Turn left after Bar Sotua and continue straight to the D933 road
(19.0)Cross the D933 road and keep left[Signpost] (19.5)Turn left towards the D933 road(20.0)Pass the farm buildings on your right, then turn left to take the underpass and then turn left(20.1)At the end of the path turn right and right again. Then keep right, passing church on the left and cross the Le Laurhibar river (22.0)Cross the D401 road and veer right[Citadelle to the left](22.4)Pass through historic gates of Saint Jean Pied de Port. Continue straight on rue de la Citadelle(22.7)Arrive at Saint-Jean-Pied-de-Port[Beside church of Notre-Dame-du-Bout-du-Pont]

Accommodation and Tourist Information

Saint-Jean-Pied-de-Port

Maison Donamaria,1, chemin d'Olhonce, 64220 Saint-Jean-Pied-de-Port, France; Tel:+33 (0) 622 488 800; +33 (0) 5 59 37 75 11; Email:resa.auberge.pelerin@gmail.com; maisondonamaria.fr; Price:-,A,-; *Top ranked B&B near village centre. Pool. English spoken.12 places in rooms of 2 or 4*
Refuge Municipal des Pèlerins,55 rue de la Citadelle, 64220 Saint-Jean-Pied-de-Port, France; Tel:+33 (0)617 103 189; Email:refugemunicipal@gmail.com; terresdenavarre.fr; Price:C,C,-; *32 places in 17th century buil;ding. Reservations not accepted.*
Refuge Accueil Paroissial - Maison Kaserna[Maison Kaserna],43, rue d'Espagne, 64220 Saint-Jean-Pied-de-Port, France; Tel:+33(0) 559 37 65 17; en-pays-basque.fr; Price:-,-,C; *Located in the village centre near the citadel. 14 places in 2 dormitories. Very welcoming. Do not accept reservations.*

Gite d'étape - Beilari,40, rue de la Citadelle, 64220 Saint-Jean-Pied-de-Port, France; Tel:+33(0)5 59 37 24 68; Email:info@beilari.info; beilari.info; Price:-,-,B; *Located in the village centre on the GR®65 with garden and terrace. 14 places in various sized rooms. Communal dinner. English spoken.*
L'Auberge du Pèlerin[Danièle Ménargues],25, rue de la Citadelle, 64220 Saint-Jean-Pied-de-Port, France; Tel:+33(0) 6 59 60 73 77; Email:resa.auberge.pelerin@gmail.com; aubergedupelerin.net; Price:B,-,B|A,-,A; *Located in the village centre on the GR®65 in an 18th Century building. 28 places in rooms of 2 oto 12*
Chambre d'hôtes - Maison Errecaldia[Tim and Louisa Proctor],5, chemin de la Porte Saint-Jacques, 64220 Saint-Jean-Pied-de-Port, France; Tel:+33 (0)5 59 49 17 02; errecaldia.com; Price:-,B,-; *Located before entering the village old town centre on the GR®65 3 rooms. English spoken.*

stage 33 — Ostabat to Saint-Jean-Pied-de-Port

🏠 **Chambre d'hôtes - TaRTaSeNia**[Arnaud Youakim],1, route du Maréchal Harispe, 64220 Saint-Jean-Pied-de-Port, France; Tel:+33(0)6 84 27 24 27; Email:tartasenia@protonmail.com; tartasenia.com; Price:-,B,-; *Lovely eco-B&B near village centre with garden located at the foot of the GR*65. 4 rooms of various size. English spoken.*

🏠 **Gîte Zazpiak-Bat**[Guillaume Lopépé],13b, rue du Maréchal Harispe, 64220 Saint-Jean-Pied-de-Port, France; Tel:+33(0)6 31 01 19 63; gite-zazpiak-bat.com; Price:-,A,-; *Located 1 km from the village centre on the GR*65. 20 places in rooms of 1 to 3. Terrace. Kitchen. English spoken.*

🏠 **Chambres d'Hôtes - La Villa Esponda**,9, place du Trinquet, 64220 Saint-Jean-Pied-de-Port, France; Tel:+33(0)+33 6 10 46 54 79; Email:contact@villaesponda.com; villaesponda.com; Price:B,-,-; *Located near village centre facing the ramparts. 15 places in 5 rooms*

ℹ️ **Pilgrim Information Office**,39, rue de la Citadelle, 64220 Saint-Jean-Pied-de-Port, France; Tel:+33(0) 5 59 37 05 09; Email:caminopa@hotmail.com; compostelle.fr

ℹ️ **Office de Tourisme**,14, place Charles de Gaulle, 64220 Saint-Jean-Pied-de-Port, France; Tel:+33 (0)5 59 37 03 57; Email:saintjeanpieddeport@otpaysbasque.com; tourismefrance.info

Aïnhice-Mongelos

🏠 **Chambre d'hôtes - Domaine de Schiltenea**[Schiltenea],Chemin de l'Eglise, 64220 Aïnhice-Mongelos, France; Tel:+33 (0)559 372 256; grdodo.fr; Price:-,B,A; *B&B with 2 rooms in a 18th Century home with garden. English spoken. Accommodation for horses.*

Bussunarits-Sarrasquette

🏠 **Chambres d'Hôtes - Ferme Etxekonia**[Mrs. Marie Eliçagaray],103, Karrika Arte, 64220 Bussunarits-Sarrasquette, France; Tel:+33 5 59 37 00 40; +33 6 95 26 89 95; ferme-etxekonia-pays-basque.fr; Price:-,B,A; *B&B on farm located on GR*65 1.5 km before Saint-Jean-le-Vieux. 4 rooms. Horses welcome.*

Larceveau-Arros-Cibits

🛏️**Gite Hego Alde**[Guillaume],Quartier Xaharra, 64120 Larceveau-Arros-Cibits, France; Tel:+33 (0)6 88 76 22 01; Email:hegoalde.gt@gmail.com; gitehegoalde.wordpress.com; Price:C,C,C; *10 places in 5 rooms in typical Basque home with great views*

🏠 **Chambre d'hôtes - Oyhanartia**[Chantal and Christian Isaac],Oyhanartia, 64120 Larceveau-Arros-Cibits, France; Tel:+33(0)559378816; +33(0)6 80 85 61 73; chambre-d-hote-pays-basque.com; Price:-,A,A; *Lovely B&B with 5 rooms 2 km from the GR65. Horses welcome.*

🛏️**Espelletenia Hotel**[Maialen and Jeremi],15, route de Garazi, 64120 Larceveau-Arros-Cibits, France; Tel:+33 (0) 5 59 37 81 91; espelletenia.eus; Price:A,A,A; *20 rooms in a friendly 2 star hotel closed Mondays*

Uhart-Cize

🛏️🏠 **La Coquille Napoléon**[Lorna and Bixente Eguiazabal],Route Napoléon, 64220 Uhart-Cize, France; Tel:+33(0) 662 259 940; Email:bixente.eguiazabal@gmail.com; alberguescaminosantiago.com/albergues/albergue-la-coquille-napoleon-uhart-cize-francia; Price:C,C,-|B,B,-; *10 places in dormitory private room available 1 km from Saint-Jean-Pied-de-Port on the GR65. Horses welcome. English spoken.*

Saint-Jean-Pied-de-Port to Roncevaux — stage 34

Length: 24.7km

Ascent: 2235m
Descent: 1446m

Le-Puy: 757km
Roncevaux: 25km

Hiker in St-Jean-Pied-de-Port © Alexia Adamski

Route–The crossing of the Pyrenees, is one of the most beautiful stages of the French Way of Saint James. The route climbs rapidly from Saint Jean to its peak of 1420 metres. It is extremely well-marked, and generally follows the Route Napoleon/D 428 for about 15km until turning off onto a path to cross into Spain and then descends by a track into Roncevaux.

Pointers–While the weather in the Pyrenees is highly variable, avoid undertaking this stage in rain or foggy conditions, as visibility can be an issue. It is also worthwhile to await nice weather, in order to take advantage of the spectacular views.

Choice of Routes: If the weather has turned, from Col de Lepoeder consider taking the tarmacked road into Roncevaux, as opposed to the track, which can be slippery. This alternative route is the GR®12, which switchbacks to Puerto de Ibañeta before reaching Roncevaux.

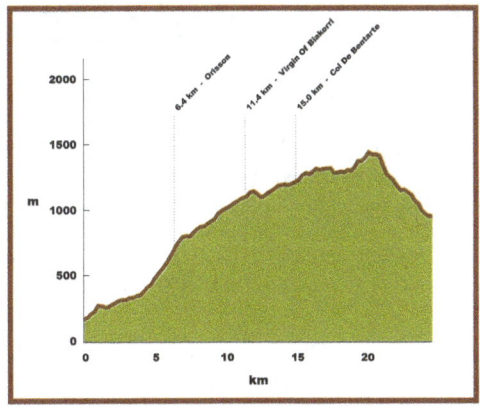

Advance planning: If you don't plan on stopping for lunch in Orisson, you should shop for lunch the evening before in Saint-Jean as there are no groceries on the route.

stage 34 — Saint-Jean-Pied-de-Port to Roncevaux

Cultural Discoveries

Virgin of Biakorri

The lovely small Virgin of Biakorria (Basque: blowing winds, alt. 1055m) was placed on this outcrop of rock near the Route de Napoléon by shepherds from Lourdes.

Virgin of Biakorri © Alexia Adamski

Roncevaux

Roncevaux (Basque: *Orreaga,* Spanish: *Roncevalles,* alt. 1,057m) became famous for Charlemagne's stunning defeat at the **Battle of Roncevaux Pass** in the evening of 15 August 778, which was evoked in the 11th century French literary work, the *Song of Roland.* While retreating from Moor-controlled Spain and passing through the narrow and wooded Roncevaux Pass, Charlemagne's rear guard was ambushed by attacking Basque forces. A number of high ranking officers were killed, including Roland, the governor of the French area known as Breton March. A monument and chapel in Roncevaux Pass commemorate the battle.

Below Roncevaux Pass, is the former monastery and hospital complex **Collégiale de Roncevaux.** As the first stop after crossing the Pyrenees, since the Middle Ages it has played an important role in receiving pilgrims. The complex, which has been modified many times since its founding in the 12th century, was historically managed by Augustinian monks, and includes the *Real Colegiata de Santa María*, one of the earliest examples of Spanish gothic church architecture. The church altar has a medieval statue of *Nuestra Señora de Roncevalles*, which commemorates Mary's apparition in the Middle Ages. The cloister (14th century) contains the enormous tomb of King Sancho VII of Navarre, who was more than seven feet tall and a hero of the decisive battle of *Las Navas de Tolosa* (*1212*).

stage 34 — Saint-Jean-Pied-de-Port to Roncevaux

GR®65

(0.0) From church, cross the bridge over the Nive River and continue straight on rue de l'Espagne **(0.2)** Leave Saint-Jean by passing through Spanish Gate and continuing straight on route de Saint-Michel/ D301 **(0.4)** Turn left onto D428/Route Napoleon, which climbs for about 16 km to the Spanish border **(0.9)** Continue on route Napolean[Signpost] **(5.5)** Turn left onto dirt path that is a shortcut and switchbacks before rejoining the D428 road **(6.4)** Rejoin the D428 road, turning left and continue climb through **Orisson**
(11.4) Bear right beside **Virgin of Biakorri** [Parking area on the left]
(15.0) Turn right (cross) off the D428 road and climb on rocky trail. Pass the **Col de Bentarte** and the Fountain of Roland and continue following the French/Spain border, until turning right on forest road **(19.0)** Keep left on track. Then descend right on rocky trail before emergency point **(20.9)** Turn left on trail that descends steeply through forest. At fork turn right onto forest road and cross the stream. The alternative route through Puerto de Ibañeta (Roncevaux Pass) departs to the right on asphalt road, after the emergency point[Signpost] **(24.7)** Arrive at Roncevaux. The alternative route through Puerto de Ibañeta (Roncevaux Pass) rejoins the main route at the foot of the monastery of Roncevaux[Beside the monastery]

Hiker at rest, Pyrenees

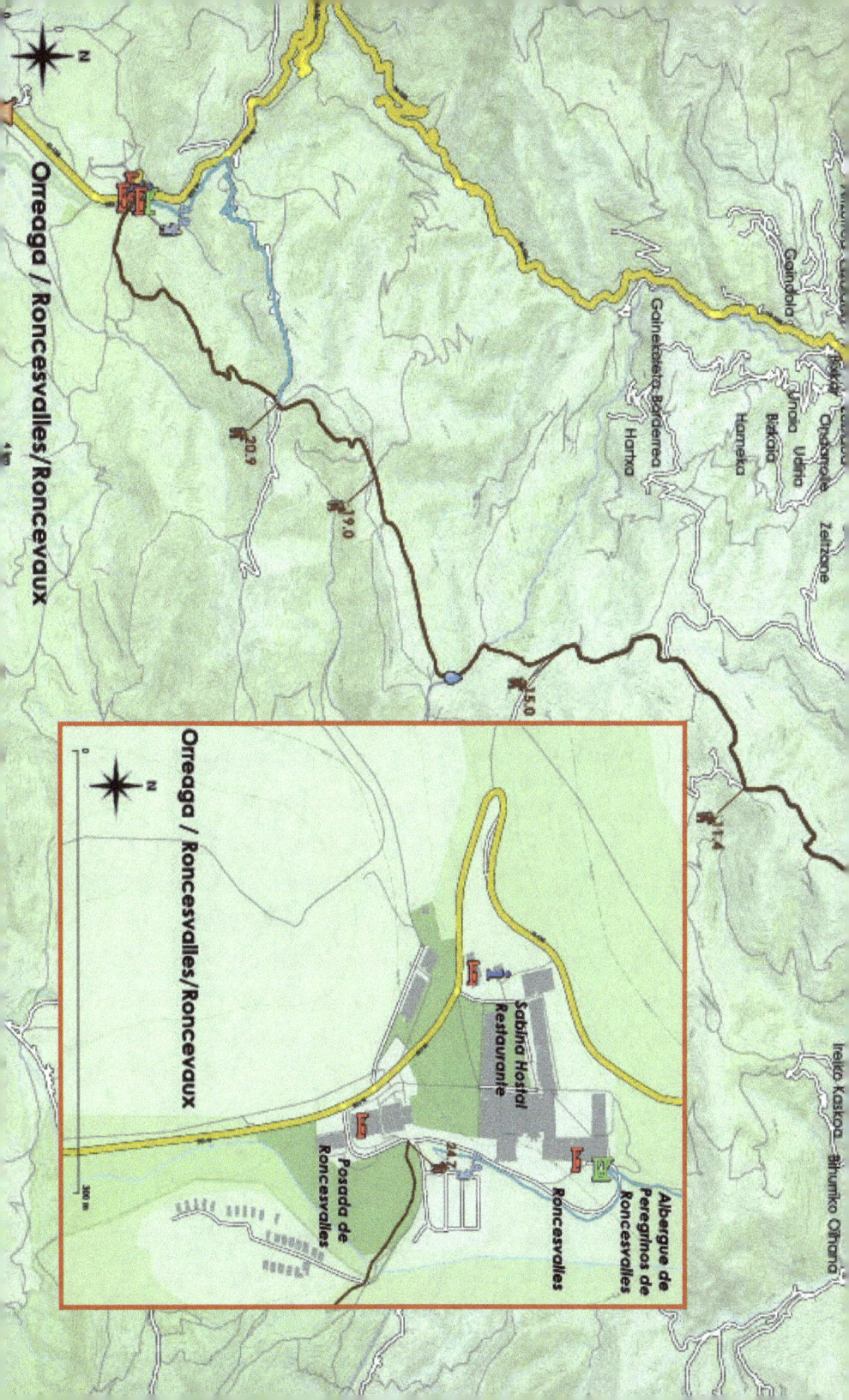

stage 34 Saint-Jean-Pied-de-Port to Roncevaux

Wet Weather Descent

Route– The alternative route from Col de Lepoeder to Roncevaux should be taken if rain or fog make the main track difficult to navigate or slippery. The route is well-marked with the white-red way markings of the GR®12. From Col de Lepoeder, it follows mostly an asphalt road that switchbacks descending to Puerto de Ibañeta (or Roncevaux Pass), where in 778 a battle took place between Charlemagne and Basque forces, which was later recounted in the Song of Roland. (Note the Charlemagne monument (1934)). From the chapel at Roncevaux Pass, the route crosses through a fenced garden and descends by footpath to the monastery of Roncevaux.

Length:	4.8km
Ascent:	93m
Descent:	567m

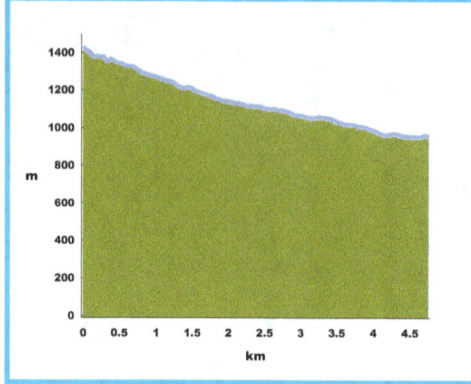

(0.0) Turn right to take the GR®12 variant on road [Signpost] (4.8) End of the route [Beside the monastery]

Saint-Jean-Pied-de-Port to Roncevaux — stage 34

Accommodation and Tourist Information

Roncesvalles

Albergue de Peregrinos de Roncesvalles, Real Colegiata, 31650 Roncesvalles, España; Tel:+34(0)948 760 000; Email:info@albergeuderoncesvalles.com; alberguederoncesvalles.com; Price:C,C,C; *Renovated and modernized in 2011 massive hostel with more than 183 places in 3 dormitories. Possibility to celebrate mass at 8 p.m. English spoken.*

Hotel - Posada de Roncesvalles,N-135, 31650 Roncesvalles, España; Tel:+34(0) 948 790 322; Email:laposada@roncesvalles.es; laposada.roncesvalles.es; Price:A,-,-; *13 double rooms and 6 duplexes for 4. English spoken*

Casa Sabina - Hostal Restaurante,Carretera de Francia, 31650 Roncesvalles, España; Tel:+34 (0)948 76 00 12 ; Email:casasabina@roncesvalles.es; casasabina.roncesvalles.es; Price:B,-,-; *4 double rooms. English spoken. Congenial place to make friends*

Hotel - Roncesvalles ,14, Calle Nuestra Señora de Roncesvalles, 31650 Roncesvalles, España; Tel:+34(0)948 76 01 05; Email:hotel@roncesvalles.es; hotelroncesvalles.roncesvalles.es; Price:A,-,-; *Beautiful and welcoming hotel in fully renovated monastery (part of main complex). English spoken. 16 rooms*

Oficina de Turismo,Calle Nuestra Señora, 31650 Roncesvalles, España; Tel:+34(0)948760301; +34(0)690 090 483; Email:oit.roncesvalles@navarra.es; visitnavarra.es

Saint-Michel

El Albergue Ferme Ithurburia[Mrs. Ourtiague],Huntto, 64220 Saint-Michel, España; Tel:+33(0) 559 371 117; +33(0) 680 530 046; Email:jeanne.ourtiague@orange.fr; albergues-caminosantiago.com/albergues/albergue-ferme-ithurburia-honto-francia; Price:C,C,C|-,B,A; *Located 5 km from Saint-Jean. B&B includes 5 private rooms and hostel has 17 places in 4 rooms. Kitchen.*

Auberge - Borda[Laurent Elicagaray],D428, 64220 Saint-Michel, España; Tel:+33 (0) 661 929 743; Email:aubergeborda@gmail.com; aubergeborda.com; Price:-,-,B; *12 places in 3 dormitories but also a private room for 2 with mountain view*

Uhart-Cize

Refuge Auberge Orisson[Jean-Jacques Etchandy], 64220 Uhart-Cize, España; Tel:+33(0)559491303; +33(0)638269738; Email:refuge.orisson@wanadoo.fr; refuge-orisson.com; Price:-,-,B; *Located in the Basque mountains 9 kilometres from Saint-Jean-Pied-de-Port 28 places in rooms or dormitories with restaurant and bar. English spoken.*

Real Colegiata de Santa María, Roncevaux

www.ingramcontent.com/pod-product-compliance
Lightning Source LLC
LaVergne TN
LVHW020137080526
838202LV00048B/3960